1001
Community
Recipes

Easy Everyday Favorites

★ ★ ★

Cookbook Resources, LLC
Highland Village, Texas

1001 Community Recipes
Easy Everyday Favorites

1st Printing - March 2008
2nd Printing - December 2008

International Standard Book Number: 978-1-59769-034-8

Library of Congress Control Number: 2008937227

Cover by Nancy Bohanan

Edited, Designed, Published and Manufactured in the United States of America
Cookbook Resources, LLC
541 Doubletree Drive
Highland Village, Texas 75077
Toll Free 866-229-2665

www.cookbookresources.com

cookbook
resources® LLC
Bringing Family and Friends to the Table

Introduction

There is nothing that tastes better than favorite dishes you have enjoyed at friends' homes in communities across the United States and Canada. And this book contains a delicious variety of easy-to-prepare recipes.

Quick, simple recipes give you many choices for your menus. Fix a main dish, a special salad or a delectable dessert; and fill out the meal with easy convenience foods.

The most important thing is to bring your family and friends to your table for meals. They'll love the special times together sharing good food and good conversation.

Contents

Appetizers 7

Choose dips, salsas, spreads and specialty appetizers from 111 recipes for tasty teasers that everyone enjoys!

Beverages 51

You'll love making these flavorful smoothies, party punches and special coffees and you have 65 selections!

Breakfast & Brunch 73

Nothing whets the appetite like aromas from breakfasts and tempting brunch entrees and 49 recipes make variety easy!

Breads 97

Hot breads and biscuits add a special attraction to any meal. Decide on 32 easy recipes from breadsticks to corn bread!

Soups & Stews 113

"Comfort" comes immediately to mind when we think of warm and hearty soups and stews from 31 delicious recipes!

Salads 129

Many easy to assemble salads (there are 124 plus 30 dressings) with fruit, pasta, veggies or meat can be a main dish!

Sandwiches 181

A delicious sandwich can be the center of a simple meal or a yummy after-school snack; select from 26 different ones!

Side Dishes 193

Side dishes can make an everyday dinner into something special and 156 choices allow plenty of variety!

Beef 263

Beef is a dinner-time favorite with almost everyone. Decide from 50 variations of roasts, steaks, briskets and more!

Contents

Family Meals

Maybe the little things in life, such as having meals around the table with family and friends, are more important than we realize. Maybe these little things are really big things we never forget. And, maybe these little things become traditions that make family bonds stronger and memories more treasured.

There is a time every day when phones don't have to be answered, when the TV is off, and e-mails and text messages can wait. For a few moments, you are not an executive, a worker, a salesperson or a student. For this special time, you are family gathered for dinner together.

This cookbook is dedicated with gratitude and respect to all who bring family and friends to the table.

Note: Recipes from Canada are indicated by a maple leaf ( ).

★ ★ ★

Appetizers

Choose dips, salsas, spreads and
specialty appetizers from 111 recipes
for tasty teasers that everyone enjoys!

1001
Community
Recipes

Appetizers Contents

Appetizers Contents

Artichoke-Bacon Dip

1 (14 ounce) jar marinated artichoke hearts, drained, chopped
1 cup mayonnaise
2 teaspoons Worcestershire sauce
5 slices bacon, cooked crisp, crumbled
Crackers

- Preheat oven to 350°.

- Combine all ingredients in large bowl. Pour into sprayed 8-inch baking dish and bake for 12 minutes.

- Serve hot with crackers. Yields 1 pint. *Marshfield, Missouri*

Avocado-Onion Dip

1 (1 ounce) packet dry golden onion soup mix
1 (8 ounce) carton sour cream
½ cup mayonnaise
2 ripe avocados, mashed
1 tablespoon lemon juice
Wheat crackers

- Mix all ingredients in bowl. Work quickly so avocados do not turn dark.

- Serve with wheat crackers. Yields 1 pint. *El Dorado, Kansas*

Avocado Olé

3 large ripe avocados, mashed
1 tablespoon fresh lemon juice
1 (1 ounce) packet dry onion soup mix
1 (8 ounce) carton sour cream
Chips or crackers

- Mix avocados with lemon juice in bowl and blend in soup mix and sour cream. You may want to add a little salt.

- Serve with chips or crackers. Yields 1 pint. *Palmdale, California*

Beer and Cheese Dip

1 large onion, finely chopped
2 tablespoons butter
1 cup beer
1 (32 ounce) box Mexican Velveeta® cheese
Tortilla chips

- Cook onion in butter in large saucepan, but do not brown; add beer. Cut cheese into large chunks and add to onion and cook on medium-low heat, stirring constantly until all cheese melts.

- Serve with tortilla chips. Yields 1 quart. *Brookhaven, Mississippi*

Black Bean Dip

2 (15 ounce) cans black beans, rinsed, drained
1 sweet onion, finely chopped
1 green bell pepper, finely chopped
1 (4 ounce) can chopped pimentos
3 tablespoons olive oil
2 tablespoons red wine vinegar
2 teaspoons minced garlic
2 teaspoons sugar
Tortilla chips

- Place 1 can of beans in bowl and mash. Add second can of whole beans, onion, bell pepper and pimentos.

- In separate bowl, combine olive oil, vinegar, garlic, sugar and a little salt and pepper, mixing well. Stir into bean mixture.

- Serve at room temperature with tortilla chips. Store leftover dip in refrigerator. Yields 1 quart. *Casa Grande, Arizona*

The Big Dipper

2 (15 ounce) cans chili
1 (10 ounce) can tomatoes and green chilies
1 (16 ounce) package cubed Velveeta® cheese
1 bunch fresh green onions, chopped

- Place all ingredients in slow cooker and cook on LOW for 1 hour to 1 hour 30 minutes.

- Serve right from slow cooker. Stir before serving. Yields 1 quart. *Silver City, New Mexico*

Easy Cheesy Bean Dip

1 (15 ounce) can refried beans
1 teaspoon minced garlic
1 cup milk
1 (16 ounce) package cubed Mexican Velveeta® cheese
Chips

- Combine beans, garlic and milk in large saucepan and stir on low heat until smooth.

- Add cheese to bean mixture. On low heat, stir until cheese melts. Serve warm with chips. Yields 1½ pints. *Kerrville, Texas*

TIP: Use this dip for soft, bean tacos or burritos. Spread bean dip on flour tortillas, add chopped tomatoes, chopped jalapenos and shredded cheese, roll and pig out.

Hot Broccoli Dip

2 (16 ounce) packages cubed Mexican Velveeta® cheese
1 (10 ounce) can golden mushroom soup
1 (10 ounce) box frozen chopped broccoli, thawed, drained
Chips

- Melt cheese with soup in saucepan and stir in broccoli. Heat thoroughly.

- Serve hot with chips. Yields 3 pints. *Sparks, Nevada*

Broccoli Dip

1 (10 ounce) package frozen, chopped broccoli, thawed
Butter
1 (10 ounce) can cream of chicken soup
3 cups shredded cheddar cheese
1 (7 ounce) can chopped green chilies
Tortilla chips

- Cook broccoli with butter and ½ teaspoon salt in saucepan for 5 minutes.

- Add soup, cheese and green chilies.

- Heat until cheese melts. (If chilies are not hot enough in dip, add several dashes of hot sauce.)

- Serve with tortilla chips. Yields 1 quart. *Los Alamos, New Mexico*

Zippy Broccoli-Cheese Dip

1 (10 ounce) package frozen chopped broccoli, thawed, drained
2 tablespoons butter
2 ribs celery, chopped
1 small onion, finely chopped
1 (16 ounce) package cubed mild Mexican Velveeta® cheese
Chips

• Make sure broccoli is thoroughly thawed and drained.

• Place butter in large saucepan and saute broccoli, celery and onion on medium heat for about 5 minutes. Stir several times.

• Add cheese. Heat just until cheese melts and stir constantly.

• Serve hot with chips. Yields 1 quart. *Norman, Oklahoma*

TIP: *If you want the "zip" to be zippier, use hot Mexican Velveeta® cheese instead of mild.*

Confetti Dip

1 (15 ounce) can whole kernel corn, drained
1 (15 ounce) can black beans, drained
⅓ cup Italian salad dressing
1 (16 ounce) jar salsa
Chips

• Combine all ingredients in bowl. Store in refrigerator for several hours before serving.

• Serve with chips. Yields 2½ pints. *Watsonville, California*

Cottage Dip

1 (16 ounce) carton small curd cottage cheese
1 (1 ounce) packet dry onion soup mix
½ cup mayonnaise
½ teaspoon garlic powder
Chips, crackers or veggies

• Combine all ingredients in bowl.

• Refrigerate and serve with chips, crackers or veggies. Yields 1 pint. *Newton, Kansas*

Creamy Ham Dip

2 (8 ounce) packages cream cheese, softened
2 (6 ounce) cans deviled ham
2 heaping tablespoons horseradish
¼ cup minced onion
¼ cup finely chopped celery
Crackers

• Beat cream cheese in bowl until creamy. Stir in ham, horseradish, onion and celery.

• Refrigerate and serve with crackers. Yields 1½ pints.
  Jacksonville, Illinois

TIP: *This will also make great little sandwiches on party rye bread.*

Cottage Cheese-Ham Dip

1 (16 ounce) carton small curd cottage cheese, drained
2 (6 ounce) cans deviled ham
1 (1 ounce) packet dry onion soup mix
½ cup sour cream
Crackers

• Blend cottage cheese in blender or with mixer until smooth.

• Add ham, soup mix and sour cream and mix well. Serve with crackers. Yields 1½ pints. *Jeannette, Pennsylvania*

Creamy Bacon Dip

1 (1 pint) carton sour cream
1 cup mayonnaise
1 (1 ounce) packet onion soup dip and mix
1 (4.3 ounce) package real crumbled bacon
Crackers or chips

• Combine sour cream, mayonnaise and onion soup mix in bowl, mixing well. Fold in real crumbled bacon and mix well.

• Serve with crackers or chips. Yields 1½ pints. *Hillsboro, Ohio*

Creamy Dilly Dip

1 (8 ounce) carton sour cream
1 cup mayonnaise
2 tablespoons lemon juice
4 green onions with tops, chopped
1 tablespoon dill weed
2 teaspoons marinade for chicken (Lea & Perrins)
Raw vegetables

• Combine all ingredients in bowl until they blend well. Sprinkle lightly with paprika for color, if you like. Cover and refrigerate.

• Serve with carrot sticks, broccoli florets or jicama sticks. Yields 1 pint. *Ames, Iowa*

Creamy Sausage Dip

1 (16 ounce) package sausage
1 teaspoon minced garlic
2 (8 ounce) packages cream cheese
1 (10 ounce) can tomatoes and green chilies
Chips

• Cook sausage in skillet over medium heat, slightly brown. Drain well.

• Stir in garlic, cream cheese, and tomatoes and green chilies. On medium heat, stir until cream cheese melts and dip is thoroughly hot.

• Serve with chips. Yields 1 quart. *Montrose, Colorado*

Cucumber Dip

2 seedless cucumbers, shredded, well drained
1 (8 ounce) carton sour cream
2 teaspoons white vinegar
2 teaspoons olive oil
1 teaspoon minced garlic
Wheat crackers or pita wedges

• Combine all ingredients with 1 teaspoon salt in bowl and mix well.

• Refrigerate and serve with wheat crackers or pita wedges. Yields 1½ pints. *Aiken, South Carolina*

Curry Lover's Veggie Dip

1 cup mayonnaise
½ cup sour cream
1 teaspoon curry powder
¼ teaspoon hot sauce
1 teaspoon lemon juice
Paprika
Raw vegetables

- Combine all ingredients mayonnaise, sour cream, curry powder, hot sauce and lemon juice in bowl and mix until they blend well.

- Sprinkle a little paprika for color, if you like. Cover and refrigerate. Serve with raw vegetables. Yields 1½ cups. *Salem, Indiana*

Egg and Cheese Dip

5 eggs, hard-boiled, mashed
1 cup mayonnaise
4 ounces shredded Monterey Jack cheese
½ teaspoon mustard
Wheat crackers

- Combine eggs, mayonnaise, cheese and mustard in bowl and mix well. Add a little salt and store in refrigerator.

- Serve with wheat crackers. Yields 1 pint. *Garden City, Kansas*

Fiesta Dip

1 (15 ounce) can tamales
1 (16 ounce) can chili without beans
1 cup salsa
1 (8 ounce) package shredded sharp cheddar cheese
1 cup finely chopped onion
Crackers or chips

- Mash tamales with fork and combine with remaining dip ingredients in saucepan. Heat and mix.

- Serve hot with crackers or chips. Yields 1 quart. *Gallup, New Mexico*

Five-Minute Dip

1 (8 ounce) package cream cheese, softened
1 cup mayonnaise
1 (1 ounce) packet ranch-style salad dressing mix
½ onion, finely minced
Fresh vegetables

- Combine cream cheese and mayonnaise in bowl and beat until creamy.

- Stir in dressing mix and onion.

- Refrigerate and serve with fresh vegetables. Yields 1 pint.
  Gooding, Idaho

Great Balls of Fire

1 pound lean hot sausage
3 green onions, chopped
1 (4 ounce) can chopped tomatoes and green chilies
2 (16 ounce) packages cubed Velveeta® cheese
Chips

- Brown sausage in large skillet. Drain fat.

- Add onions, tomatoes and green chilies and mix.

- Add cheese to sausage mixture and cook on low heat until cheese
  melts. Serve with chips. Yields 3 pints. *McCook, Nebraska*

Quick Onion Guacamole

1 (8 ounce) carton sour cream
1 (1 ounce) packet dry onion soup mix
2 (8 ounce) packages avocado dip
2 green onions with tops, chopped
½ teaspoon crushed dill weed
Chips

- Mix sour cream, onion soup mix, avocado dip, green onions and dill
  weed in bowl and refrigerate.

- Serve with chips. Yields 1½ pints. *Oakdale, Louisiana*

Holy Guacamole

4 avocados, peeled
½ cup salsa
¼ cup sour cream
Tortilla chips

- Split avocados and remove seeds. Mash avocados in bowl with fork.

- Add salsa, sour cream and 1 teaspoon salt. Serve with tortilla chips.
  Yields 1½ cups. *Merced, California*

Hot Corn Dip

1 (15 ounce) can whole kernel corn, drained
1 (7 ounce) can chopped green chilies, drained
½ cup chopped red bell pepper
1½ cups shredded colby and Monterey Jack cheese
¼ cup mayonnaise
Tortilla chips

- Preheat oven to 325°.

- Combine corn, green chilies, bell pepper and cheese in bowl. Stir in
  mayonnaise. (Adding ½ cup chopped walnuts makes this dip even
  better.) Transfer to 2-quart baking dish.

- Cover and bake for 35 minutes. Serve hot with tortilla chips. Yields
  1 quart. *Duncan, Oklahoma*

*TIP: Sometimes green chilies are not very hot, so I like to add a pinch or
    two of cayenne pepper.*

Hot Sombrero Dip

2 (15 ounce) cans bean dip
1 pound lean ground beef, cooked
1 (4 ounce) can green chilies
1 cup hot salsa
1½ cups shredded Mexican Velveeta® cheese
Tortilla chips

- Preheat oven to 350°.

- Layer bean dip, ground beef, green chilies and salsa in 3-quart baking
  dish and top with cheese.

- Bake just until cheese melts, about 10 or 15 minutes. Serve with
  tortilla chips. Yields 3 pints. *Tombstone, Arizona*

Monterey Jack's Dip

1 (8 ounce) package cream cheese, softened, whipped
1 (16 ounce) can chili without beans
1 (4 ounce) can diced green chilies
1 (8 ounce) package shredded Monterey Jack cheese
1 (4 ounce) can chopped black olives
Chips

- Preheat oven to 325°,

- Layer cream cheese, chili, green chilies, cheese and black olives in 7 x 11-inch glass baking dish.

- Bake for 30 minutes.

- Serve with chips. Yields 2½ pints. *Robstown, Texas*

Sassy Onion Dip

1 (8 ounce) package cream cheese, softened
1 (8 ounce) carton sour cream
½ cup chili sauce
1 (1 ounce) packet dry onion soup mix
Raw vegetables

- Beat cream cheese in bowl until fluffy. Add sour cream, chili sauce and onion soup mix and mix well.

- Cover and refrigerate. Serve with strips of raw zucchini, celery, carrots and turnips. Yields 1½ pints. *Carson City, Nevada*

Onion-Ham Dip

1 (5 ounce) jar pimento cheese spread
1 (4 ounce) can deviled ham
1 cup mayonnaise
1 bunch fresh green onions, chopped
Crackers

- Combine cheese spread, ham and mayonnaise in medium bowl and mix until it blends well.

- Fold in chopped green onions. Serve with crackers. Yields 2 cups. *Cookeville, Tennessee*

Pep-Pep-Pepperoni Dip

2 (8 ounce) packages cream cheese
1 (3.5 ounce) package pepperoni slices
1 (12 ounce) bottle chili sauce
1 bunch fresh green onions with tops, chopped
Chips

- Beat cream cheese in bowl until creamy.

- Cut pepperoni slices into smaller pieces.

- Add pepperoni, chili sauce and green onions to cream cheese and mix well.

- Refrigerate and serve with chips. Yields 1 quart. *Rock Springs, Wyoming*

Poor Man's Pate

1 (16 ounce) package braunschweiger, room temperature
1 (1 ounce) packet onion soup mix
1 (8 ounce) carton sour cream
1 (8 ounce) package cream cheese, softened
Several dashes hot sauce
Chips

- Mash braunschweiger (pork liver sausage) in bowl with fork.

- In separate bowl, beat onion soup mix, sour cream, cream cheese and hot sauce until fairly creamy.

- Add braunschweiger and mix well. Refrigerate. Serve with chips. Yields 1 quart. *Lansing, Michigan*

Summer Sombrero Dip

1 (15 ounce) can chili with no beans
½ teaspoon chili powder
¾ cup green chili sauce
1 (2.5 ounce) can sliced black olives, drained
Chips

- Combine chili and chili powder in saucepan. Warm over low heat.

- Stir in chili sauce and olives. Serve with chips. Yields 1 pint. *Milford, Utah*

Roquefort Dip

1 (8 ounce) package cream cheese, softened
2 cups mayonnaise
1 small onion, finely grated
1 (3 ounce) package roquefort cheese, crumbled
⅛ teaspoon garlic powder
Raw vegetables

- Combine cream cheese and mayonnaise in bowl and beat until creamy.

- Add onion, roquefort (blue cheese) and garlic powder and mix well. Refrigerate.

- Serve with zucchini sticks, turnip sticks or cauliflower florets. Yields 1½ pints. *Watertown, Wisconsin*

Roasted Garlic Dip

4 - 5 whole garlic cloves with peel
Oil
2 (8 ounce) packages cream cheese, softened
¾ cup mayonnaise
1 (7 or 9 ounce) jar roasted sweet red peppers, drained,
    coarsely chopped
1 bunch fresh green onions with tops, chopped
Cayenne pepper or paprika
Chips

- Preheat oven to 325°.

- Lightly brush outside of garlic cloves with a little oil and place in shallow baking pan. Bake for about 10 minutes and cool. Press roasted garlic out of cloves and set aside.

- Beat cream cheese and mayonnaise in bowl until creamy. Add garlic, red peppers and onions and mix well.

- Sprinkle with cayenne pepper or paprika and serve with chips. Yields 1 quart. *Corning, California*

TIP: *Roasted peppers are great in this recipe, but if you want it a little spicy, add several drops of hot sauce.*

Spinach-Artichoke Dip

2 (10 ounce) boxes frozen spinach, thawed, drained
1 (14 ounce) jar marinated artichoke hearts, drained,
    finely chopped
1 cup mayonnaise
1 (8 ounce) package shredded mozzarella cheese
Chips

- Squeeze spinach between paper towels to completely remove
  excess moisture. Combine spinach, artichoke hearts, mayonnaise
  and cheese in bowl and mix well.

- Cover and refrigerate. Serve with chips. Yields 3 pints.
  Stockton, California

Green Wonder Dip

1 (10 ounce) package frozen chopped spinach, thawed
1 (1 ounce) packet dry vegetable soup mix
½ cup minced onion
1 cup mayonnaise
1 (8 ounce) carton sour cream

- Squeeze spinach between paper towels to completely remove excess
  moisture. Combine all ingredients in bowl and mix well. Cover and
  refrigerate overnight.

- Serve with crackers, chips or raw vegetable sticks. Yields 1 quart.
  Findlay, Ohio

Veggie Dive Dip

1 cup mayonnaise
1 (8 ounce) carton sour cream
1½ teaspoons seasoned salt
1 teaspoon dill weed
2 tablespoons parsley
1 bunch green onions with tops, chopped
Raw vegetables

- Combine mayonnaise, sour cream, seasoned salt, dill weed, parsley
  and green onions in bowl and refrigerate. This is better if made a
  day ahead.

- Serve with celery sticks, broccoli florets, jicama sticks or carrot sticks.
  Yields 1 pint. *Cullman, Alabama*

Vegetable Dip

You will have the family saying, "You mean this is spinach!"

1 (10 ounce) package frozen chopped spinach, thawed,
    well drained
1 bunch fresh green onions with tops, chopped
1 (1 ounce) packet dry vegetable soup mix
1 tablespoon lemon juice
2 (8 ounce) cartons sour cream
Chips

- Squeeze spinach between paper towels to completely remove excess moisture.

- Combine spinach, green onions, soup mix, lemon juice and sour cream in medium bowl and add a little salt. (Adding several drops of hot sauce is also good.) Cover and refrigerate.

- Serve with chips. Yields 1 quart. *Mankato, Minnesota*

Velvet Dip

2 (16 ounce) packages cubed Mexican Velveeta® cheese
2 cups mayonnaise
1 (4 ounce) jar chopped pimentos, drained
1 (7 ounce) can chopped green chilies
Chips

- Place cheese in saucepan and melt over low heat.

- Add mayonnaise, pimentos and green chilies and mix well. Serve with chips. Yields 3 pints. *Camden, Arkansas*

Watercress "To Do" Dip

3 ripe avocados
1¼ cups snipped watercress
¾ cup mayonnaise
¼ teaspoon ground cumin
Chips

- Peel and mash softened avocados and place in medium bowl.

- Add watercress, mayonnaise and cumin seeds and mix well.

- Add salt. Cover and refrigerate. Serve with chips. Yields 1 pint. *Yuba City, California*

California Clam Dip

1 (1 ounce) packet dry onion soup mix
2 (8 ounce) cartons sour cream
1 (7 ounce) can minced clams, drained
2 tablespoons chili sauce

- Combine onion soup mix and sour cream in bowl and mix well.

- Add clams and chili sauce and refrigerate. Yields 1½ pints.
  Vista, California

Zesty Clam Dip

1 (15 ounce) can New England clam chowder
1 (8 ounce) and 1 (3 ounce) package cream cheese, softened
2 tablespoons minced onion
2 tablespoons horseradish
2 tablespoons marinade for chicken (Lea & Perrins)
Raw vegetables or chips

- Combine clam chowder, cream cheese, onion, horseradish and Worcestershire in food processor and blend until smooth.

- Serve with raw vegetables or chips. Yields 1½ pints. *Slatersville, Rhode Island*

Unbelievable Crab Dip

1 (6 ounce) can white crabmeat, drained, flaked
1 (8 ounce) package cream cheese
½ cup (1 stick) butter
Chips or crackers

- Combine crabmeat, cream cheese and butter in saucepan. Heat and mix thoroughly.

- Serve with chips or crackers. Yields 1½ pints. *Union, South Carolina*

Hot, Rich Crab Dip

1 (10 ounce) can cheddar cheese soup
1 (16 ounce) package cubed Mexican Velveeta® cheese
2 (6 ounce) can crabmeat, flaked, drained
1 (16 ounce) jar salsa
Chips

- Combine soup and cheese in microwave-safe bowl.

- Microwave at 1-minute intervals until cheese melts.

- Add crabmeat and salsa and mix well. Serve hot with chips. Yields 3 pints. *Asheboro, North Carolina*

Elegant Crab Dip

This is really delicious and easy too!

1 (6.5 ounce) can white crabmeat, drained, flaked
1 (8 ounce) package cream cheese
½ cup (1 stick) butter
Chips

- Combine crabmeat, cream cheese and butter in saucepan. Heat and mix thoroughly.

- Serve with chips. Yields 1½ pints. *Waynesboro, Virginia*

Company Special Crab Dip

Don't count on your guests leaving the table until this dip is gone!

1 (16 ounce) package cubed Velveeta® cheese
2 (6 ounce) cans crabmeat, drained, flaked
1 bunch fresh green onions with tops, chopped
2 cups mayonnaise
½ teaspoon seasoned salt
Assorted crackers

- Melt cheese in double boiler. Add crabmeat, onions, mayonnaise and seasoned salt.

- Serve hot or at room temperature with assorted crackers. Yields 3 pints. *Harrington, Delaware*

Cheesy-Crab Dip

1 (6 ounce) roll processed garlic cheese, diced
1 (10 ounce) can cream of mushroom soup
1 (6 ounce) can crabmeat, drained, flaked
2 tablespoons sherry
Assorted crackers

- Mix all ingredients in medium pan and heat and stir until cheese melts.

- Serve with assorted crackers. Yields 1½ pints. *Hardwick, Georgia*

Quickie Shrimp Dunk

1 (8 ounce) package cream cheese, softened
1 (8 ounce) bottle of cocktail sauce
1 teaspoon Italian herb seasoning
1 (6 ounce) can tiny shrimp, drained
Crackers

- Place cream cheese in bowl and beat until smooth.

- Add cocktail sauce, seasoning and shrimp and refrigerate.

- Serve with crackers. Yields 1½ cups. *Beckley, West Virginia*

Hurrah for Shrimp

1 (8 ounce) package cream cheese, softened
½ cup mayonnaise
1 (6 ounce) can tiny, cooked shrimp, drained
1¼ teaspoons Creole (or Cajun) seasoning
1 tablespoon lemon juice
Chips

- Blend cream cheese and mayonnaise in bowl until creamy. Add shrimp, seasoning and lemon juice and whip only until they mix well.

- Serve with chips. Yields 1 pint. *Sulphur, Louisiana*

TIP: The Creole (or Cajun) seasoning is the key to this great dip!

Favorite Stand-By Shrimp Dip

2 cups tiny, cooked shrimp, finely chopped
2 tablespoons horseradish
½ cup chili sauce
¾ cup mayonnaise
1 tablespoon lemon juice
Cucumber or zucchini slices

- Combine shrimp, horseradish, chili sauce, mayonnaise, lemon juice
  and a few dashes of salt in bowl and refrigerate. (If shrimp has been
  frozen, be sure to drain well.)

- Serve with cucumber or zucchini slices. Yields 1½ pints.
  Kingsport, Tennessee

Chunky Shrimp Dip

2 (6 ounce) cans shrimp, drained
2 cups mayonnaise
6 green onions, finely chopped
¾ cup chunky salsa
Crackers

- Crumble shrimp in bowl and stir in mayonnaise, green onions and
  salsa.

- Refrigerate for 1 to 2 hours. Serve with crackers. Yields 1 quart.
  Cullman, Alabama

Tasty Tuna Dip

1 (6 ounce) can tuna in spring water, drained
1 (1 ounce) packet Italian salad dressing mix
1 (8 ounce) carton sour cream
¼ cup chopped black olives, drained
Melba rounds

- Combine tuna, dressing mix, sour cream and olives in bowl and stir
  until all blends well.

- Refrigerate for 8 hours. Serve with melba rounds. Yields 1½ cups.
  Huron, South Dakota

Easy Tuna Dip

1 (6 ounce) can tuna, drained
1 (1 ounce) packet Italian salad dressing mix
1 (8 ounce) carton sour cream
2 green onions with tops, chopped

- Combine tuna, salad dressing, sour cream and green onions in bowl and mix well.

- Refrigerate for several hours before serving. Yields 1 pint.
  Fulton, Missouri

Tuna Melt Appetizer

1 (10 ounce) package frozen spinach, drained
2 (6 ounce) cans white tuna in water, drained, flaked
¾ cup mayonnaise
1½ cups shredded mozzarella cheese, divided
Crackers

- Preheat oven to 350°.

- Squeeze spinach between paper towels to completely remove excess moisture.

- Combine spinach, tuna, mayonnaise and 1 cup cheese in large bowl and mix well.

- Spoon into sprayed pie pan and bake for 15 minutes.

- Remove from oven and sprinkle remaining cheese over top. Bake for an additional 5 minutes. Serve with crackers. Yields 1 quart.
  Morgantown, West Virginia

Nutty Apple Dip

1 (8 ounce) package cream cheese, softened
1 cup packed brown sugar
1 teaspoon vanilla
1 cup finely chopped pecans
Apple slices

- Combine cream cheese, brown sugar and vanilla in small mixing bowl. Beat until smooth. Stir in pecans.

- Serve with sliced apples for dipping. Yields 1 pint. *Chippewa Falls, Wisconsin*

Caramel-Apple Dip

1 (8 ounce) package cream cheese, softened
1 cup packed brown sugar
1 teaspoon vanilla
½ cup chopped dry roasted peanuts

- Combine cream cheese, brown sugar and vanilla in bowl. Beat until creamy. Stir in peanuts. Store in refrigerator.

- Serve with crisp apple slices. Yields 1 pint. *Hudson, New York*

Fruit Dip for Nectarines

1 (8 ounce) package cream cheese, softened
2 (7 ounce) cartons marshmallow creme
¼ teaspoon ground cinnamon
⅛ teaspoon ground ginger
Nectarines

- Beat cream cheese, marshmallow cream, cinnamon and ginger in bowl. Mix well and refrigerate.

- Serve with slices of nectarines with peel or any other fruit. Yields 1½ pints. *Leesburg, Florida*

Delicious Dip for Fruit

1 (8 ounce) package cream cheese, softened
½ cup sour cream
½ cup packed brown sugar
2 tablespoons maple syrup
Fruit

- Beat cream cheese and sour cream in bowl until smooth and stir in brown sugar and maple syrup.

- Serve with strawberries, apple slices or fresh pineapple chunks. Yields 1 pint. *Lakeland, Florida*

Black Olive Spread

1 (8 ounce) package cream cheese, softened
½ cup mayonnaise
1 (4 ounce) can chopped black olives
3 fresh green onions, chopped very fine
Rye bread

- Beat cream cheese and mayonnaise in bowl until smooth.

- Add olives and onions and refrigerate. Spread on slices of party rye bread. Yields 1 pint. *Grants Pass, Oregon*

Beef or Ham Spread

1 pound leftover roast beef or ham
¾ cup sweet pickle relish
½ onion, finely diced
2 celery ribs, chopped
2 hard-boiled eggs, chopped
Mayonnaise

- Chop meat in food processor and add relish, onion, celery and eggs. Add a little salt and pepper.

- Fold in enough mayonnaise to make mixture spread easily and refrigerate.

- Spread on crackers or bread for sandwiches. Yields 1½ pints. *Devils Lake, North Dakota*

Walnut-Cheese Spread

¾ cup chopped walnuts
1 (16 ounce) package shredded cheddar cheese
3 fresh green onions with tops, chopped
½ - ¾ cup mayonnaise
½ teaspoon liquid smoke
Assorted crackers

- Preheat oven to 250°.

- Roast walnuts on baking sheet for 10 minutes.

- Combine walnuts, cheese, green onions, mayonnaise and liquid smoke in bowl and refrigerate overnight.

- Spread on assorted crackers. Yields 1½ pints. *Columbus, Indiana*

Sweet Cheese-Garlic Spread

2 (8 ounce) packages cream cheese, softened
¼ cup apricot preserves
1 teaspoon minced garlic
¼ cup finely chopped walnuts
3 fresh green onions tops only, finely chopped
Assorted crackers

- Beat cream cheese and preserves in bowl until they blend well.

- Stir in garlic, walnuts and onions and refrigerate.

- Serve with assorted crackers. Yields 1½ pints. *Athens, Tennessee*

Orange-Cheese Spread

2 (8 ounce) packages cream cheese, softened
⅔ cup powdered sugar
1 tablespoon grated orange peel
2 tablespoons triple sec liqueur
2 tablespoons frozen orange juice concentrate, undiluted

- Blend all ingredients in bowl until smooth and refrigerate.

- Spread on dessert breads to make sandwiches or use as dip for fruit. Yields 1½ pints. *Yakima, Washington*

Jiffy Tuna Spread

1 (7 ounce) can white tuna, drained
½ cup chopped ripe olives
1 (1 ounce) packet Italian salad dressing mix
1 (8 ounce) carton sour cream
Paprika
Crackers

- Combine tuna, olives, salad dressing and sour cream in bowl and mix well.

- Sprinkle with a little paprika for color and serve with crackers. Yields 1 pint. *Rutland, Vermont*

Hot Artichoke Spread

1 (14 ounce) can artichoke hearts, drained, finely chopped
1 cup mayonnaise
1 cup grated parmesan cheese
1 (1 ounce) packet Italian salad dressing mix
Assorted crackers

- Preheat oven to 350°.

- Remove tough outer leaves and chop artichoke hearts.

- Combine artichoke hears, mayonnaise, parmesan cheese and salad dressing in bowl and mix thoroughly. Pour into 8-inch square baking pan.

- Bake for 20 minutes. Serve hot with assorted crackers. Yields 1½ pints. *Torrington, Connecticut*

Curried Cheese Spread

2 (8 ounce) packages cream cheese, softened
1 (10 ounce) jar mango chutney
1 (5 ounce) package slivered almonds, toasted
2 teaspoons curry powder
Assorted crackers or apple slices

- Combine cream cheese, chutney, almonds and curry powder in blender until creamy. Cover and refrigerate for at least 2 hours.

- Shape into round ball shape. Serve with assorted crackers or as a dip for apple slices. Yields 1 quart. *Oil City, Pennsylvania*

TIP: Toasting brings out the flavors of nuts and seeds. Place nuts or seeds on baking sheet and bake at 225° for 10 minutes. Be careful not to burn them.

Devil's Spread

1 (4 ounce) can deviled ham
¾ cup mayonnaise
1 tablespoon grated onion
1 (4 ounce) can chopped green chilies, drained
Wheat crackers

• Mix deviled ham, mayonnaise, onion and green chilies in bowl.

• Spread on wheat crackers. Yields 1 pint. *Auburn, Alabama*

Black Bean Salsa

1 (15 ounce) can black beans, drained
4 - 6 green onions with tops, diced
½ - ¾ cup snipped fresh cilantro leaves
1 - 2 cloves garlic, minced
1 tablespoon oil
1 teaspoon fresh lime juice

• Mix all ingredients and refrigerate before serving. Yields 1 pint.
El Cajon, California

Sausage Balls

1 pound hot pork sausage
1 (16 ounce) package shredded cheddar cheese
3 cups biscuit mix
⅓ cup milk

• Preheat oven to 375°.

• Combine all ingredients in bowl and form into small balls. If dough is
a little too sticky, add 1 teaspoon more biscuit mix.

• Bake for 13 to 15 minutes. Yields 36 to 48 balls. *Athens, Texas*

Sweet-and-Sour Sausage Balls

1 pound hot pork sausage
1 pound mild pork sausage
2 eggs
2 cups soft breadcrumbs

- Mix sausages, eggs, ½ teaspoon salt and breadcrumbs and from into small balls.

- Brown sausage balls in skillet and drain.

Sauce:

1 (12 ounce) bottle cocktail sauce
¾ cup packed brown sugar
½ cup wine vinegar
½ cup soy sauce

- Combine all sauce ingredients in bowl and pour over sausage balls.

- Simmer for about 1 hour. Serves 10 to 14. *Forest City, Arkansas*

TIP: *You could also use a slow cooker to simmer the sausage balls and serve in the slow cooker if it is an informal occasion.*

Ranch Cheese Ball

1 (1 ounce) packet dry ranch-style salad dressing mix
2 (8 ounce) packages cream cheese, softened
¼ cup finely chopped pecans
1 (3 ounce) jar real bacon bits

- Beat dressing mix and cream cheese in bowl.

- Roll into ball. Roll cheese ball in pecans and bacon bits.

- Refrigerate for several hours before serving. Yields 1½ pints. *Killeen, Texas*

Chili-Cheese Balls

1 (8 ounce) package shredded sharp cheddar cheese, softened
½ cup (1 stick) butter, softened
1 cup flour
1 (4 ounce) can chopped green chilies

- Preheat oven to 375°.

- Mix cheese and butter in bowl.

- Add flour, green chilies and ½ teaspoon salt.

- Form dough into 2-inch balls and place on baking sheet. Bake for 14 to 15 minutes. Yields 12 to 16 balls. *Lawton, Oklahoma*

Beefy Cheese Ball

2 (8 ounce) packages cream cheese, softened
2 (2 ounce) jars dried beef
1 bunch fresh green onions with tops, chopped
1 teaspoon cayenne pepper
Crackers

- Beat cream cheese in bowl until smooth and creamy.

- Chop dried beef in food processor or blender.

- Combine beef, cream cheese, onions and cayenne pepper. Form into ball and refrigerate overnight.

- Serve with crackers. Serves 12 to 16. *Alban, Oregon*

Cucumber Squares

1 (8 ounce) package cream cheese, softened
½ teaspoon dill weed
3 medium cucumbers, peeled, grated
1 (1 ounce) packet dry ranch salad dressing mix
Pumpernickel or rye bread

- Combine cream cheese and dill weed in bowl and beat until creamy. Fold in grated cucumbers and ranch dressing.

- Spread on pumpernickel or rye bread slices. Yields 1 pint. *Logan, Utah*

Stuffed Jalapenos

12 - 15 medium jalapeno peppers with stems
1 (8 ounce) package cream cheese, softened
¾ cup finely shredded Monterey Jack cheese
3 slices cooked ham, finely chopped
1 tablespoon lime juice
1 tablespoon garlic powder

- Preheat oven to 325°.

- Cut each jalapeno lengthwise through stem and remove ribs and seeds.

- Combine remaining ingredients in bowl and mix well.

- Fill each jalapeno half with cheese mixture.

- Place on sprayed baking sheet and bake for 15 minutes. Cool slightly before serving. Yields 24 to 30 stuffed jalapeno halves. *Paris, Texas*

TIP: Wear rubber gloves when removing seeds from jalapenos.

Holiday Mix Snacks

2 cups pistachio nuts
2 cups honey-roasted peanuts
1 (6 ounce) package dried, sweetened pineapple
1 (12 ounce) package white chocolate chips
1 (6 ounce) package Craisins®

- Combine all ingredients and store in airtight containers. Serves 10 to 14. *Kennewick, Washington*

Zorro's Nutty Snacks

2 cups jalapeno pretzel pieces
1 (12 ounce) can whole cashews
1 (8 ounce) package vanilla-yogurt raisins
2 cups chocolate pretzel dips
1 (7 ounce) package maple-nut goodies
1 (16 ounce) jar honey-roasted peanuts

- Combine all ingredients in bowl. Yields 2 quarts. *Shawnee, Oklahoma*

Salty-Sweet Skittle Diddles

1 (8 ounce) package cheddar cheese pretzel sandwiches
1 (16 ounce) package fruit-flavored Skittles®
2 cups sour dough pretzel nibblers
4 (1 ounce) cubes white chocolate, broken up
1 (12 ounce) can mixed nuts
1 (6 ounce) package dried, sweetened pineapple

• Combine all ingredients in bowl. Yields 2 to 3 quarts.
  Glasgow, Kentucky

Christmas Caramel Corn

8 cups popped popcorn
1½ cups whole almonds, cashews or pecans
1 (16 ounce) package dried fruit bits
1 cup packed brown sugar
½ cup sugar
⅔ cup (1⅓ sticks) butter
⅓ cup light corn syrup
½ teaspoon baking soda
½ teaspoon vanilla

• Preheat oven to 300°.

• Place popcorn, nuts and dried fruit on baking sheet.

• Combine brown sugar, sugar, butter and syrup in heavy saucepan,
  bring to a boil and stir often.

• Continue to cook and stir for about 15 minutes until mixture is golden
  brown. Remove from heat, stir in baking soda and vanilla and pour
  over popcorn mixture. Stir gently to cover popcorn, nuts and fruit.

• Bake for 15 minutes, stir and continue baking an additional 5 minutes.
  Transfer to foil and cool thoroughly. Break up and store in airtight
  container. Yields 1 gallon. *Randolph, Vermont*

Saturday Night Nibblers

1 (12 ounce) package chocolate-covered peanuts
1 (8 ounce) package vanilla-yogurt raisins
1 (12 ounce) package M&M's®
1 cup slivered almonds, toasted
1 (12 ounce) can whole cashews

• Combine all ingredients in bowl and store in airtight containers.
  Yields 2 quarts. *Brainerd, Minnesota*

Oat Munchies

This is great for munching!

1 (16 ounce) package oat squares cereal
2 cups whole pecans
½ cup corn syrup
½ cup packed brown sugar
¼ cup (½ stick) butter
1 teaspoon vanilla
½ teaspoon baking soda

• Preheat oven to 250°.

• Combine cereal and pecans in 9 x 13-inch baking pan and set aside.

• Combine corn syrup, brown sugar and butter in 2-cup bowl.
  Microwave on HIGH for 1½ minutes, stir and turn bowl. Microwave
  on HIGH for about 1 minute or until boiling.

• Stir in vanilla and baking soda. Pour over cereal mixture and stir well
  to coat evenly.

• Bake for 1 hour and stir every 20 minutes. Spread on baking sheet to
  cool. Yields 2 quarts. *Canton, Illinois*

Roasted Mixed Nuts

1 pound mixed nuts
¼ cup maple syrup
2 tablespoons brown sugar
1 (1 ounce) packet dry ranch-style salad dressing mix

- Preheat oven to 300°.

- Combine nuts and maple syrup in bowl and mix well.

- Sprinkle with brown sugar and salad dressing mix and stir gently to coat.

- Spread in sprayed 10 x 15-inch baking pan.

- Bake for 25 minutes or until light brown. Cool. Yields 1 pint.
  Beloit, Wisconsin

Spiced Pecans

You can't eat just one!

2 cups sugar
2 teaspoons ground cinnamon
1 teaspoon ground nutmeg
½ teaspoon ground cloves
4 cups pecan halves

- Combine sugar, cinnamon, nutmeg, cloves, ½ cup water and ¼ teaspoon salt.

- Mix well, cover with wax paper and microwave on HIGH for 4 minutes. Stir and microwave for an additional 4 minutes.

- Add pecans, quickly mix well and spread on wax paper to cool.

- Break apart and store in covered container. Yields 1 quart.
  Waycross, Georgia

Cinnamon Pecans

1 pound pecan halves
1 egg white, slightly beaten
2 tablespoons ground cinnamon
¾ cup sugar

- Preheat oven to 325°.

- Combine pecan halves with egg white in bowl and mix well.

- In separate bowl, combine cinnamon and sugar; sprinkle over pecans. Stir until all pecans coat well.

- Spread on baking sheet and bake for about 20 minutes. Cool and store in covered container. Yields 1 quart. *Troy, Alabama*

TIP: Use fork to beat egg white slightly.

Chili-Honey Wings

1½ cups flour
18 - 20 chicken wings
¼ cup (½ stick) butter
¾ cup honey
⅔ cup chili sauce

- Preheat oven to 325°.

- Combine flour and a little salt in shallow bowl and dredge each wing in flour.

- Melt butter in large skillet and brown 5 to 6 wings at one time on medium-high heat. When brown, place in sprayed 9 x 13-inch baking pan.

- Combine honey and chili sauce in small bowl and mix well. Spoon honey mixture over each wing. Cover and bake for 45 minutes. Serves 6 to 10. *Jackson, Tennessee*

Raspberry-Glazed Chicken Wings

¾ cup seedless raspberry jam
¼ cup cider vinegar
¼ cup soy sauce
1 teaspoon garlic powder
16 whole chicken wings

• Combine jam, vinegar, soy sauce, garlic powder and 1 teaspoon pepper in saucepan. Bring to a boil and boil for 1 minute.

• Cut chicken wings into 3 sections and discard wing tips. Place wings in large bowl, add raspberry mixture and toss to coat. Cover and refrigerate for 4 hours.

• When ready to bake, preheat oven to 350°.

• Line 10 x 15-inch baking pan with foil and spray. Use slotted spoon to place wings in pan and set aside marinade.

• Bake for 30 minutes and turn once. Cook reserved marinade for 10 minutes, brush over wings and bake for 25 minutes longer. Yields 16 wings. *Tiffin, Ohio*

Orange-Glazed Chicken Wings

3 pounds chicken wings
1¼ cups soy sauce
1¼ cups orange juice
1 cup packed brown sugar
1 teaspoon minced garlic

• Dry wings with paper towels. Combine soy sauce, orange juice, brown sugar and garlic in large resealable plastic bag. Place wings in bag and seal. Refrigerate overnight.

• When ready to bake, preheat oven to 325°.

• Drain wings and discard marinade. Place wings in sprayed, foil-lined 10 x 15-inch baking pan.

• Bake for 45 minutes or until wings are light brown and glazed. Turn once while baking. Serves 8 to 10. *Lock Haven, Pennsylvania*

Bacon-Wrapped Water Chestnuts

1 (8 ounce) can whole water chestnuts, drained
¼ cup soy sauce
¼ teaspoon cayenne pepper
About ½ pound bacon, cut in thirds

- Preheat oven to 375°.

- Marinate water chestnuts for 1 hour in soy sauce and cayenne pepper.

- Wrap one-third slice bacon around water chestnuts and fasten with toothpick.

- Bake for 20 minutes or until bacon is done. Drain and serve hot. Yields 1 cup. *Haynesville, Louisiana*

Crab Crackers

1 (6 ounce) can crabmeat, drained, flaked
1 (8 ounce) package cream cheese, softened
2 (10 ounce) cans cream of celery soup
1 (4 ounce) can chopped black olives
Crackers

- Combine all ingredients in saucepan until cheese melts.

- Serve hot with crackers. Yields 1 quart. *Nampa, Idaho*

TIP: For an extra kick, add several drops of hot sauce.

Mini-Reubens

½ cup thousand island dressing
24 slices party rye bread
1⅓ cups well drained, chopped sauerkraut
½ pound thinly sliced, corned beef
¼ pound sliced Swiss cheese

- Preheat oven to 375°.

- Spread dressing on slices of bread. Place 1 slice corned beef on bread and top with sauerkraut.

- Cut cheese same size as bread and place over sauerkraut.

- Place open-face sandwiches on baking sheet. Bake for 10 minutes or until cheese melts. Yields 24 open-face sandwiches. *Hanover, Pennsylvania*

No-Fuss Meatballs

1 (14 ounce) package frozen cooked meatballs, thawed
1 tablespoon soy sauce
½ cup chili sauce
⅔ cup grape or plum jelly
¼ cup dijon-style mustard

• Cook meatballs in soy sauce in skillet until heated through.

• Combine chili sauce, jelly and mustard in bowl and pour over meatballs. Cook and stir until jelly dissolves and mixture comes to a boil.

• Reduce heat, cover and simmer for about 5 minutes. Serves 8 to 12.
Franklin, New Hampshire

Deviled Ham Roll-Ups

1 (8 ounce) package crescent dinner rolls
1 (2 ounce) can deviled ham
½ cup sour cream
1 teaspoon dijon-style mustard

• Preheat oven to 350°.

• Unroll crescent rolls on sheet of wax paper and form triangles.

• Combine deviled ham, sour cream and mustard in bowl and place heaping teaspoon ham mixture on each roll.

• Spread filling, leaving ½ inch at edge. Roll each crescent, beginning at wide end and rolling toward point.

• Place point-side down on sprayed baking pan and bake for 15 minutes or until light brown. Serve warm. Yields 18 roll-ups.
Amherst, Massachusetts

Cocktail Ham Roll-Ups

1 (3 ounce) package cream cheese, softened
1 teaspoon finely grated onion
Mayonnaise
1 (3 ounce) package sliced ham
1 (15 ounce) can asparagus spears

- Combine cream cheese, grated onion and enough mayonnaise in bowl to make spreading consistency.

- Separate sliced ham, spread mixture on slices and place 1 or 2 asparagus spears on ham and roll. Cut each roll into 4 pieces.

- Spear each piece with toothpick for serving and refrigerate. Serves 6 to 12. *Knoxville, Iowa*

Cheesy Vegetable Squares

1 (8 ounce) package refrigerated crescent rolls
1 (8 ounce) package cream cheese, softened
½ cup mayonnaise
1 (1.4 ounce) packet ranch salad dressing mix
1 cup broccoli slaw
1½ cups shredded cheddar cheese

- Preheat oven to 325°.

- Press crescent roll dough into 9 x 13-inch baking dish and press perforations to seal. Bake for 12 minutes or until dough is golden brown; cool.

- Beat cream cheese, mayonnaise and ranch dressing mix in bowl; spread over crust. Sprinkle with broccoli slaw and top with cheese; gently press into cream cheese mixture.

- Cover and refrigerate for at least 3 hours. Cut into squares to serve. Serves 6. *Midland, Michigan*

Cheese Strips

1 loaf thin-sliced bread
1 (8 ounce) package shredded cheddar cheese
6 slices bacon, fried, drained, coarsely broken
½ cup chopped onion
1 cup mayonnaise

- Preheat oven to 400°.

- Remove crust from bread.

- Combine cheese, bacon, onion and mayonnaise in bowl and spread filling over slices.

- Cut slices into 3 strips and place on cookie sheet. Bake for 10 minutes. Serves 8 to 12. *Winchester, Kentucky*

TIP: *For a special touch, add ⅓ cup slivered toasted almonds.*

Cheddar Toppers

1 cup chopped black olives
1 cup shredded cheddar cheese
½ cup mayonnaise
½ cup finely minced green olives
3 - 4 English muffins

- Preheat oven to 350°.

- Combine all ingredients in bowl and mix well.

- Spread mixture on English muffin halves. Bake for 30 minutes.

- After baking, quarter muffins and serve as hors d'oeuvres. Serves 6 to 8. *La Crosse, Wisconsin*

Caviar-Artichoke Delights

2 (8 ounce) packages cream cheese, softened
1 (14 ounce) can artichoke hearts, drained, chopped
½ cup finely grated onion
1 (3 ounce) jar caviar, drained
3 eggs, hard-boiled, grated
Crackers

- Beat cream cheese in bowl until smooth and add artichoke hearts and onion. Spread in 8 or 9-inch glass pie pan and refrigerate.

- Before serving, spread caviar on top of cream cheese mixture and place grated eggs on top. Serve with crackers. Serves 8 to 12.
  Magnolia, Arkansas

Festive Smokies

2 finely chopped jalapeno peppers
Oil
1 (12 ounce) jar peach preserves
1 (12 ounce) bottle chili sauce
2 (16 ounce) packages Lit'l Smokies®

- Saute jalapenos in skillet with a little oil for about 3 minutes. Stir in peach preserves and chili sauce and mix well.

- Add Lit'l Smokies®, bring to a boil, reduce heat and simmer for about 10 minutes. Serves 10 to 14. *Lafayette, Louisiana*

Frankfurter Bits

1 (8 count) package frankfurters
1 (8 ounce) package corn muffin mix
½ teaspoon chili powder
⅔ cup milk
Oil
Chili sauce

- Cut franks into 1-inch pieces.

- Combine corn muffin mix, chili powder and milk in bowl. Add frankfurter pieces to corn muffin mix and stir well to coat each piece.

- Drop one at a time into hot oil in deep fryer. Fry for 2 minutes or until brown, then drain.

- Serve warm with chili sauce for dunking. Serves 10 to 14. *Yazoo City, Mississippi*

Blue Cheese Crisps

2 (4 ounce) packages crumbled blue cheese
½ cup (1 stick) butter, softened
1⅓ cups flour
⅓ cup poppy seeds
¼ teaspoon cayenne pepper

- Beat blue cheese and butter in bowl at medium speed until fluffy.

- Add flour, poppy seeds and cayenne pepper and beat until they blend well.

- Divide dough in half and shape each portion into 9-inch log. Cover and refrigerate for 2 hours.

- When ready to bake, preheat oven to 350°.

- Cut each log into ¼-inch slices and place on baking sheet.

- Bake for 13 to 15 minutes or until golden brown and cool. Serves 8 to 12. *Van Wert, Ohio*

Pizza in a Bowl

1 pound lean ground beef
1 (26 ounce) jar marinara or spaghetti sauce
2 teaspoons dried oregano
1 (16 ounce) package shredded mozzarella cheese
¾ teaspoon garlic powder
Italian toast

- Cook beef in saucepan over medium heat until no longer pink and drain.

- Stir in marinara sauce and oregano and simmer for about 15 minutes. Gradually stir in cheese until it melts.

- Pour into fondue pot or small slow cooker to keep warm. Serve with Italian toast (panetini – found in the deli). Serves 10 to 14. *Vineland, New Jersey*

Tex-Mex Pizzas

8 flour tortillas
1 (8 ounce) jar marinara sauce
1 (15 ounce) can bean dip
1 (8 ounce) can whole kernel corn, drained
1 (8 ounce) package shredded Mexican 4-cheese blend

- Preheat oven to 425°.

- Place tortillas on 2 sprayed foil-lined baking sheets. Bake for about 4 minutes on each side or until crisp and light brown.

- Combine marinara sauce and bean dip in bowl and mix well. Spread mixture on each tortilla and sprinkle with corn and cheese. Bake for an additional 3 minutes or until cheese melts. Cut each tortilla in half to serve. Serves 12 to 16. *Vernon, Texas*

Spinach Pinwheels

1 (8 ounce) can crescent dinner rolls
1 (8 ounce) package garlic-herb spreadable cheese, softened
6 thin slices cooked deli ham
30 fresh spinach leaves, stems removed

- Separate crescent dough into 4 rectangles and press perforations to seal. Generously spread rectangles with cheese, leaving ¼-inch around edge without cheese. Top with ham slices and spinach leaves.

- Starting at short side of dough, roll each rectangle and press edges to seal. Refrigerate rolls for 30 minutes to 1 hour and slice each roll into 6 slices.

- When ready to bake, preheat oven to 350°.

- Place slices on baking sheet and bake for about 15 minutes or until light brown. Serves 8 to 12. *Rochester, New Hampshire*

Shrimp-Stuffed Eggs

8 eggs, hard-boiled
¼ cup mayonnaise
1 (6 ounce) can tiny shrimp, drained
2 tablespoons sweet pickle relish, drained

- Cut eggs in half lengthwise and set aside egg whites. Mash egg yolks with mayonnaise in small bowl. Add shrimp and pickle relish and mix well. Refill egg whites and refrigerate. Yields 16 stuffed eggs. *Lumberton, North Carolina*

Artichoke Bites

1 (14 ounce) jar artichoke hearts, drained, chopped
1½ cups mayonnaise
¾ cup freshly grated parmesan cheese
1 (4 ounce) can chopped green chilies
Toasted rounds (bite-size)

- Remove any spikes or tough leaves from artichokes. Mix mayonnaise, parmesan cheese, green chilies and artichoke hearts in bowl.

- Place 1 teaspoon mixture on bite-size toast rounds. Broil until light brown. Serves 8 to 12. *Carthage, Missouri*

Spicy Cheese Bites

1 cup flour
½ teaspoon cayenne pepper
1 (8 ounce) package finely shredded sharp cheddar cheese
½ cup (1 stick) butter, softened

- Combine all ingredients with a little salt in bowl. Mixture will be hard to combine, so the easiest way is to work with your hands until dough forms a ball.

- Place dough on large piece of wax paper and form into log. Roll tightly in plastic wrap and refrigerate for at least 2 to 3 hours.

- When ready to bake, preheat oven to 375°.

- Slice dough into ¼-inch rounds and place on baking sheet 1 inch apart. Bake for about 17 to 18 minutes or until edges are golden. Cool before serving. Serves 8 to 12. *Texarkana, Arkansas*

Party Sausages

1 cup ketchup
1 cup plum jelly
1 tablespoon lemon juice
2 tablespoons mustard
2 (5 ounce) packages tiny smoked sausages

- Combine all ingredients except sausages in saucepan, heat and mix well until jelly melts.

- Add sausages and simmer for 10 minutes. Serve with cocktail toothpicks. Serves 8 to 12. *Lander, Wyoming*

Sausage Rounds

1 (8 ounce) package crescent dinner rolls
½ teaspoon garlic powder
½ cup shredded cheddar cheese
1 pound sausage

- Open package of rolls, smooth out dough with rolling pin and seal seams. Sprinkle dough with garlic powder and cheese.

- Break up sausage with hands and spread thin layer sausage over rolls. Roll into a log, wrap in wax paper and freeze for several hours.

- When ready to bake, preheat oven to 350°.

- Slice into ¼-inch rounds. Place on baking sheet and bake for 20 minutes or until light brown. Serves 8 to 12. *Alexandria, Louisiana*

Sweet Onions

5 Texas 1015 or Vidalia® onions, chopped
1 cup sugar
½ cup white vinegar
⅔ cup mayonnaise
1 teaspoon celery salt
Crackers

- Soak onions in sugar, vinegar and 2 cups water in bowl for about 3 hours. Drain.

- Toss with mayonnaise and celery salt. Serve on crackers. Serves 10 to 12. *Cordele, Georgia*

Sausage-Pineapple Bits

1 pound link sausage, cooked, skinned
1 pound hot bulk sausage
1 (15 ounce) can crushed pineapple with juice
2 cups packed brown sugar
1 tablespoon marinade for chicken (Lea & Perrins)

- Slice link sausage into ⅓-inch pieces. Shape bulk sausage into 1-inch balls. Brown sausage balls in skillet.

- Combine pineapple, brown sugar and marinade for chicken in large saucepan. Heat, add both sausages and simmer for 30 minutes.

- Serve from chafing dish or small slow cooker with cocktail toothpicks. Serves 10 to 14. *Parkersburg, West Virginia*

★ ★ ★

Beverages

You'll love making these flavorful
smoothies, party punches and special
coffees and you have 65 selections!

1001
Community
Recipes

Beverages Contents

Very Special Coffee Punch

This will be a hit! It is great!

1 (2 ounce) jar instant coffee
2¼ cups sugar
2 quarts half-and-half cream
1 quart ginger ale, chilled
1 pint whipping cream, whipped
½ gallon French vanilla ice cream

- Dissolve instant coffee in 2 quarts hot water in bowl and cool. Add sugar and half-and-half cream, mix well and refrigerate.

- When ready to serve, pour coffee-sugar mixture in punch bowl, add chilled ginger ale, whipped cream and ice cream. Let some chunks of ice cream remain.

- Serves 60 (4 ounce). *Gainesville, Florida*

Mocha Punch

4 cups brewed coffee
¼ cup sugar
4 cups milk
4 cups chocolate ice cream, softened

- Combine coffee and sugar in container and stir until sugar dissolves. Refrigerate for 2 hours.

- Just before serving, pour into small punch bowl.

- Add milk and mix well. Top with scoops of ice cream and stir well. Serves 36 to 48. *Santa Rosa, California*

Apricot Punch

1 (12 ounce) can apricot nectar
1 (6 ounce) can frozen orange juice concentrate, thawed
2 tablespoons lemon juice
1 (2 liter) bottle ginger ale, chilled

- Combine apricot nectar, orange juice concentrate, lemon juice and 1 cup water in bowl. Refrigerate.

- When ready to serve, stir in ginger ale. Serves 36 to 48. *Ocala, Florida*

Best Tropical Punch

1 (46 ounce) can pineapple juice
1 (46 ounce) can apricot nectar
3 (6 ounce) cans frozen limeade concentrate, thawed
3 quarts ginger ale, chilled

- Combine pineapple juice, apricot nectar and limeade concentrate in bowl and refrigerate.

- When ready to serve, add ginger ale. Serves 48 to 60.
  Ft. Pierce, Florida

Cranberry Punch

2 (28 ounce) bottles ginger ale, chilled
1 (48 ounce) can pineapple juice, chilled
1 quart cranberry juice, chilled
1 quart pineapple sherbet, broken up

- Combine all ingredients in punch bowl. Serves 48.
  Durham, New Hampshire

Cranberry-Lemon Punch

2 quarts cranberry juice
1 (6 ounce) can lemonade concentrate, thawed
⅔ cup maraschino cherry juice
1 (2 liter) lemon-lime soda, chilled

- Combine all ingredients in punch bowl and mix well. Serves 24 to 28.
  Bowling Green, Kentucky

TIP: It would be very nice to make an ice ring out of cranberry juice, lemon slices and maraschino cherries for the punch bowl.

Cranberry-Pineapple Punch

1 (48 ounce) bottle cranberry juice
1 (46 ounce) can pineapple juice
½ cup sugar
2 teaspoons almond extract
1 (2 liter) bottle ginger ale, chilled

- Combine cranberry juice, pineapple juice, sugar and almond extract in bowl and stir until sugar dissolves. Cover and refrigerate for 8 hours.

- When ready to serve, add ginger ale and stir. Serves 48.
  Oak Ridge, Tennessee

Creamy Strawberry Punch

1 (10 ounce) package frozen strawberries, thawed
½ gallon strawberry ice cream, softened
2 (2 liter) bottles ginger ale, chilled
Fresh strawberries

* Process frozen strawberries through blender. Combine strawberries, chunks of ice cream and ginger ale in punch bowl.

* Stir and serve immediately with fresh strawberries. Serves 24 to 28.
  Stillwater, Oklahoma

Green Party Punch

This punch is good for St. Patrick's Day or any day.

1 (3 ounce) package lime gelatin
1 (6 ounce) can frozen limeade, thawed
1 (6 ounce) can frozen lemonade, thawed
1 quart orange juice
1 quart pineapple juice
1 tablespoon almond extract
2 - 3 drops green food coloring
1 liter ginger ale, chilled

* Dissolve lime gelatin in 1 cup boiling water in bowl and stir well.

* Combine dissolved gelatin, limeade, lemonade, orange juice, pineapple juice, almond extract and food coloring in 1-gallon bottle and refrigerate.

* When ready to serve, add ginger ale. Serves 32. *Freeport, Illinois*

Party Hardy Punch

1 (46 ounce) can pineapple juice
1 (46 ounce) can apple juice
3 quarts ginger ale, chilled
Pineapple chunks

* Combine pineapple and apple juices in very large plastic container or any container large enough to hold both juices or use 2 plastic pitchers. Freeze both juices.

* When ready to serve, place pineapple and apple juice in punch bowl and add chilled ginger ale and pineapple chunks. Stir to mix. Serves 48 to 54. *Meridian, Mississippi*

Holiday Party Punch

The almond extract really gives this punch a special taste!

3 cups sugar
1 (6 ounce) package lemon gelatin
1 (3 ounce) can frozen orange juice concentrate, thawed
⅓ cup lemon juice
1 (46 ounce) can pineapple juice
3 tablespoons almond extract
2 quarts ginger ale, chilled

• Combine sugar and 1 quart water in saucepan. Heat until sugar dissolves.

• Add gelatin and stir until it dissolves. Add fruit juices, 1½ quarts water and almond extract and refrigerate.

• When ready to serve, place in punch bowl and add chilled ginger ale. Serves 50. *Seaford, Delaware*

Perfect Party Punch

1 (12 ounce) can frozen limeade concentrate
1 (46 ounce) can pineapple juice, chilled
1 (46 ounce) apricot nectar, chilled
1 quart ginger ale, chilled

• Mix limeade concentrate with water according to can directions.

• Add pineapple juice and apricot nectar and stir well. Refrigerate

• When ready to serve, add ginger ale. Serves 40 to 48. *Winter Haven, Florida*

Pineapple-Citrus Punch

1 (46 ounce) can pineapple juice, chilled
1 quart apple juice, chilled
1 (2 liter) bottle lemon-lime carbonated beverage, chilled
1 (6 ounce) can frozen lemonade concentrate, thawed
1 orange, sliced

• Combine pineapple juice, apple juice, lemon-lime beverage and lemonade in punch bowl.

• Add orange slices for decoration. Serves 36 to 46. *Albany, Georgia*

Reception Punch

1 (6 ounce) can frozen concentrated lemonade
1 (46 ounce) can orange juice, chilled
1 (46 ounce) can apricot nectar, chilled
2 (28 ounce) bottles ginger ale, chilled

- Combine all ingredients in large punch bowl. Serves 60.
  Frankfort, Kentucky

*TIP: If you want to make this a creamy punch, at the last minute spoon in
2 quarts orange sherbet.*

Ruby Holiday Punch

The cranapple juice in this punch really makes it a "holiday" special!

2 (6 ounce) cans frozen orange juice concentrate, thawed
2 (46 ounce) cans red Hawaiian punch
1 (46 ounce) can pineapple juice
1 (48 ounce) bottle cranapple juice
2 liters ginger ale, chilled

- Combine orange juice, 4 cups water, Hawaiian punch, pineapple juice
  and cranapple juice in 2-gallon bottles and stir well. Refrigerate

- Just before serving, place in punch bowl and add ginger ale. Serves
  60. *Lancaster, California*

Sparkling Cranberry Punch

Red food coloring
2 quarts cranberry juice cocktail
1 (6 ounce) can frozen lemonade, thawed
1 quart ginger ale, chilled

- Pour water in ice mold for ice ring and a little add red food coloring for
  a brighter look.

- Mix cranberry juice and lemonade in pitcher. Refrigerate until ready
  to serve.

- When ready to serve, pour cranberry mixture into punch bowl, add
  ginger ale and stir well.

- Add decorative ice mold to punch bowl. Serves 24. *Lewiston, Maine*

Pina Colada Punch

1 (46 ounce) can pineapple juice, chilled
1 (20 ounce) can crushed pineapple with juice
1 (15 ounce) can cream of coconut
1 (32 ounce) bottle lemon-lime carbonated drink, chilled

- Combine all ingredients in bowl. Serve over ice cubes. Serves 48.
  Naples, Florida

Apple-Party Punch

3 cups sparkling apple cider
2 cups apple juice
1 cup pineapple juice
½ cup brandy

- Combine all ingredients in bowl and freeze for 8 hours.

- Remove punch from freezer 30 minutes before serving.

- Place in small punch bowl and break into chunks. Stir until slushy.
  Serves 24 to 28. *Eau Claire, Wisconsin*

Sparkling Pink Punch

3 (6 ounce) cans frozen pink lemonade concentrate
1 (750 ml) bottle pink sparkling wine
3 (2 liter) bottles lemon-lime carbonated beverage, divided
Lime slices

- Stir all ingredients, except 1 bottle carbonated beverage, in airtight
  container, cover and freeze for 8 hours or until firm.

- Let stand at room temperature for 10 minutes and place in punch bowl.

- Add remaining bottle carbonated beverage and stir until slushy. Serve
  with lime slices. Serves 36 to 44. *Gallatin, Tennessee*

Sparkling Wine Punch

6 oranges, with peels, thinly sliced
1 cup sugar
2 (750 ml) bottles dry white wine
3 (750 ml) bottles sparkling wine, chilled

- Place orange slices in large plastic or glass container and sprinkle with
  sugar. Add white wine, cover and refrigerate for at least 8 hours.

- Stir in sparkling wine. Serves 30. *Kokomo, Indiana*

Wine Punch

2 quarts ginger ale, chilled
2 (12 ounce) cans frozen limeade concentrate
2 (750 ml) bottles white wine, chilled
Lime slices

• Make ice ring with as much ginger ale as necessary.

• Combine limeade, white wine and remaining ginger ale in
  punch bowl.

• Serve with ice ring and lime slices. Serves 36 to 42.
  Marshfield, Missouri

Champagne Punch

1 (750 ml) bottle champagne, chilled
1 (32 ounce) bottle ginger ale, chilled
1 (6 ounce) can frozen orange juice concentrate
Orange slices

• Mix all ingredients in punch bowl.

• Refrigerate and serve. Serves 18. *Newburgh, New York*

Champagne-White Wine Punch

1 (750 ml) bottle dry white wine, chilled
1 cup apricot brandy
1 cup triple sec liqueur
2 (750 ml) bottles dry champagne, chilled
2 quarts club soda

• Combine white wine, apricot brandy and triple sec in large pitcher.
  Cover and refrigerate until ready to use.

• At serving time, add champagne and club soda, stir to blend and pour
  in punch bowl.

• Add ice ring to punch bowl and serve. Serves 40. *McCook, Nebraska*

Banana-Peach Smoothie

3 ripe bananas, sliced
2 cups peaches
1 cup buttermilk
¼ cup orange juice
2 tablespoons honey

- Place all ingredients in blender and process until smooth, stopping to scrape down sides. Serve immediately. Serves 4. *Pasadena, California*

Fruit Smoothie

1 cup orange juice
1 ripe banana, peeled, thickly sliced
1 ripe peach, cut into chunks
1 cup strawberries

- Pour orange juice into blender and add banana, peach, strawberries and 1 cup ice cubes.

- Blend on high speed until creamy. Serves 3 to 4. *Melbourne, Florida*

Strawberry-Banana Smoothie

1 (16 ounce) bag frozen strawberries, semi-thawed
1 ripe banana
¾ cup plain yogurt
3 tablespoons sugar

- Place all ingredients in blender and blend until smooth. Serve immediately. Serves 4. *Moultrie, Georgia*

Tropicana Smoothie

1 (20 ounce) can crushed pineapple with juice
1 ripe banana, cut into 1-inch pieces
2 tablespoons honey
1 cup pineapple sherbet

- Place all ingredients in blender and process until thick and smooth. Serve immediately. Serves 4. *Aiken, South Carolina*

Tropical Smoothie

1½ heaping cups peeled, seeded ripe papaya
1 very ripe large banana
1½ heaping cups ripe cantaloupe, cut into chunks
1 (6 ounce) carton coconut cream pie yogurt
¼ cup milk

• Cut papaya into chunks. Place all ingredients in blender and puree until smooth.

• Pour into glasses and serve immediately. Serves 4. *Chapel Hill, North Carolina*

Tropical Fruit Smoothie

2 (8 ounce) cartons vanilla yogurt
1 cup fresh frozen blueberries
1 cup fresh frozen peach slices
1 (8 ounce) can pineapple chunks, drained

• Process all ingredients in blender until smooth. (Scrape sides once or twice.)

• Serve immediately. Serves 4. *Jasper, Alabama*

Strawberry Lemonade

1 (16 ounce) package frozen strawberries, thawed
1 (10 ounce) jar maraschino cherries (without stems) with juice
2 cups sugar
1 cup lemon juice

• Place all ingredients in blender; blend until smooth, stopping to scrape down sides.

• Pour mixture through strainer and pour into pitcher, discarding solids.

• Stir in 3 cups cold water, mixing well and serve over chipped ice. Serves 8. *Laurel, Mississippi*

Lemonade Tea

2 family-size tea bags
½ cup sugar
1 (12 ounce) can frozen lemonade
1 quart ginger ale, chilled

- Steep tea in 3 quarts water and mix with sugar and lemonade. Refrigerate.

- Add ginger ale just before serving. Serves 8. *La Grange, Georgia*

Raspberry Lemonade

1 cup lemonade
2 tablespoons raspberry syrup
2 - 3 fresh raspberries

- Fill tall glass with lemonade, raspberry syrup and ice and stir. Garnish with fresh raspberries. Serves 1. *Pine Bluff, Arkansas*

Limeade Cooler

1½ pints lime sherbet
1 (6 ounce) can frozen limeade concentrate
3 cups milk
Lime slices

- Beat lime sherbet in bowl and add concentrated limeade and milk. Blend all ingredients.

- Pour into 5 glasses and top each with additional scoop lime sherbet. Garnish with lime slices. Serve immediately. Serves 5. *Great Bend, Kansas*

Victorian Iced Tea

4 individual tea bags
¼ cup sugar
1 (11 ounce) can frozen cranberry-raspberry juice concentrate, thawed

- Place tea bags in teapot and add 4 cups boiling water. Cover and steep for 5 minutes. Remove and discard tea bags. Add sugar and mix. Refrigerate.

- Just before serving, combine cranberry-raspberry concentrate and 4 cups cold water in 2½-quart pitcher and stir in tea. Serve with ice cubes. Serves 8. *Belfast, Maine*

Banana-Strawberry Shake

1 (10 ounce) package frozen strawberries, partially thawed
2 bananas, sliced in 1-inch pieces
1 cup half-and-half cream
½ cup sugar
1 quart vanilla ice cream

- Combine fruit, half-and-half cream and sugar in blender. Cover and blend at high speed for about 30 seconds.

- Add ice cream and blend for about 45 seconds. Serve immediately. Serves 4. *Toppenish, Washington*

Peanut Power Shake

2 bananas, cut up
½ cup frozen orange juice concentrate, thawed
¼ cup peanut butter
¼ cup milk

- Combine all ingredients in blender container. Cover and blend until smooth.

- Add 1 cup ice cubes and blend until smooth. Serves 2. *Big Rapids, Michigan*

Pineapple-Strawberry Cooler

2 cups milk
1 (20 ounce) can crushed pineapple, chilled
½ pint vanilla ice cream
1 pint strawberry ice cream

- Combine milk, pineapple and vanilla ice cream in bowl. Mix just until they blend well. Pour into tall glasses and top with scoop of strawberry ice cream. Serves 3 to 4. *North Platte, Nebraska*

Berry Delight

1 (8 ounce) carton vanilla yogurt
1 ripe banana, cut in 1-inch pieces
1 cup fresh raspberries
2 cups raspberry sherbet

- Place all ingredients in blender and process until thick and smooth. Serve immediately. Serves 2 to 4. *Burley, Idaho*

Lemon-Banana Shake

1 (6 ounce) can frozen lemonade concentrate, thawed
1 cup diced bananas
1 quart vanilla ice cream
3 cups milk

- Combine lemonade concentrate and bananas in bowl. Beat until it is a heavy consistency.

- For each milkshake, add 1 scoop vanilla ice cream and ¼ cup lemon-banana mixture in bottom of glass.

- Fill glass two-thirds full milk and stir until it blends.

- Top off with 1 more scoop of ice cream. Serves 4. *Fort Dodge, Iowa*

Banana Split Float

2 ripe bananas, mashed
3 cups milk
1 (10 ounce) package frozen sweetened strawberries, thawed
1½ pints chocolate ice cream, divided

- Place bananas in blender and add milk, strawberries and ½ pint chocolate ice cream. Beat just until they blend well.

- Pour into tall, chilled glasses and top each with scoop of chocolate ice cream. Serves 3 to 4. *Jamestown, North Dakota*

Strawberry Spritzer

1 (10 ounce) package sweetened strawberries, thawed
1 liter lemon-lime soda, chilled
2 (12 ounce) can cream soda, chilled
1 (12 ounce) can frozen pink lemonade concentrate, thawed

- Place strawberries in blender and process until smooth and transfer to large pitcher. Add lemon-lime soda, cream soda and lemonade concentrate, stirring well.

- Quickly pour over small amount of crushed ice in each glass. Serve immediately. Serves 4 to 6. *Salina, Kansas*

Orange Lush

2 (6 ounce) cans frozen orange juice concentrate, thawed
1 pint cranberry juice
½ cup sugar
1 quart club soda, chilled

- Combine orange juice, cranberry juice and sugar in bowl and mix thoroughly. Refrigerate

- Just before serving, pour into punch bowl and stir in chilled club soda. Serves 12 to 15. *Springville, Utah*

Orange Slush

2 cups orange juice
½ cup instant, non-fat dry milk
¼ teaspoon almond extract
8 ice cubes

- Add all ingredients in blender and process on high until mixture combines and thickens. Serve immediately. Serves 3. *Mesa, Arizona*

Creamy Orange Drink

1¾ cups milk
½ pint vanilla ice cream
⅓ cup frozen orange juice concentrate
1 teaspoon non-dairy creamer

- Combine all ingredients in blender and blend until smooth. Serves 2. *Old Town, Maine*

Oreo Ice Cream Crush

3 scoops chocolate ice cream
½ cup milk
5 Oreo® cookies, 4 crushed and 1 whole
1 scoop vanilla ice cream

- Place chocolate ice cream and milk in blender; pulse until smooth and stir in crushed cookies.

- Pour into a tall 16-ounce glass. Top with scoop of vanilla ice cream and 1 whole cookie. Serves 1. *Brookings, South Dakota*

Strawberry Fizz

2 (10 ounce) boxes frozen strawberries, thawed
2 (6 ounce) cans frozen pink lemonade concentrate
2 (2 liter) bottles ginger ale, chilled
Fresh strawberries

- Process frozen strawberries through blender.

- Pour lemonade into punch bowl and stir in processed strawberries.

- Add chilled ginger ale and fresh strawberries and stir well. Serve immediately. Serves 6 to 10. *Fremont, Nebraska*

TIP: It would be nice to make an ice ring with another bottle of ginger ale.

Kid's Cherry Sparkler

2 (6 ounce) jars red maraschino cherries, drained
2 (6 ounce) jars green maraschino cherries, drained
½ gallon distilled water
1 (2 liter) bottle cherry lemon-lime drink, chilled

- Place 1 red or green cherry in each compartment of 4 ice cube trays.

- Fill trays with distilled water and freeze for 8 hours. Serve soft drink over ice cubes. Serves 8 to 12. *Charlottesville, Virginia*

Mexican Coffee

1 ounce Kahlua® liqueur
1 cup hot, black coffee
Ground cinnamon
Sweetened whipped cream

- Pour Kahlua® and coffee into tall mug.

- Sprinkle with cinnamon and stir.

- Top with whipped cream. (You can substitute frozen whipped topping, thawed). Serves 1. *Baytown, Texas*

Spiced Coffee

1 cup instant coffee granules
4 teaspoons grated lemon peel
4 teaspoons ground cinnamon
1 teaspoon ground cloves

- Combine all ingredients in small jar and cover tightly.

- For each serving, spoon 2 teaspoons coffee mix into coffee cup and stir in ¾ cup boiling water. Sweeten to taste. Serves 24. *Willmar, Minnesota*

Praline Coffee

3 cups hot brewed coffee
¾ cup half-and-half cream
¾ cup light packed brown sugar
2 tablespoons butter
¾ cup praline liqueur
Whipped cream

- Cook coffee, half-and-half cream, brown sugar and butter in large saucepan over medium heat, stirring constantly. Do not boil.

- Stir in liqueur and serve with sweetened whipped cream. Serves 4. *Abbeville, Louisiana*

Frosted Chocolate Milk

2 pints coffee ice cream
½ cup chocolate syrup
¼ cup instant coffee granules
2 quarts milk, divided

- Beat ice cream, chocolate syrup, coffee granules and half milk in blender. Beat until they blend.

- Combine remaining milk and refrigerate before serving.

- Serve in frosted glasses. Serves 8. *Harrington, Delaware*

Instant Cocoa Mix

1 (8 quart) box dry milk powder
1 (12 ounce) jar non-dairy creamer
1 (16 ounce) can instant chocolate-flavored drink mix
1¼ cups powdered sugar

- Combine all ingredients in bowl and store in airtight container.

- To serve, use ¼ cup cocoa mix per cup of hot water.
  Frederick, Maryland

Amaretto

3 cups sugar
1 pint vodka
3 tablespoons almond extract
1 tablespoon vanilla (not imitation)

- Combine sugar and 2¼ cups water in large pan. Bring mixture to boil.
  Reduce heat. Simmer for 5 minutes and stir occasionally. Remove
  from stove.

- Add vodka, almond extract and vanilla. Stir to mix. Store in airtight
  jar. Yields 1 quart. *San Marcos, Texas*

Amaretto Cooler

1¼ cups amaretto liqueur
2 quarts orange juice
1 (15 ounce) bottle club soda, chilled
Orange slices

- Combine all ingredients in bowl and stir well. Serve over ice.
  Serves 8. *Ardmore, Oklahoma*

Chocolate-Mint Fizz

¼ cup creme de menthe liqueur
¼ cup creme de cacao liqueur
1 pint vanilla ice cream
1 pint chocolate ice cream

- Place liqueurs into blender container. Add ice creams gradually and
  blend until smooth after each addition.

- Pour into glasses and serve immediately. Serves 4. *Camden, Arkansas*

Party Orange Sipper

2½ cups vodka
4 cups orange juice
2 (12 ounce) cans lemon-lime drink
⅓ cup maraschino cherry juice

- Combine vodka, orange juice and lemon-lime drink in pitcher. Fill 8 glasses with crushed ice and pour vodka-orange juice mixture over ice.

- Spoon about 2 teaspoons cherry juice into each glass, but do not stir. Serve immediately. Yields 2½ quarts; 20 (4 ounce) servings. *Cocoa, Florida*

White Sangria

4 cups dry white wine
1 cup silver rum
½ cup orange liqueur
Thin slices of lemon and limes
2 cups club soda, chilled

- Combine wine, rum and orange liqueur in 3-quart pitcher and add lemon and lime slices. Cover and refrigerate.

- When ready to serve, stir in club soda and about 2 cups ice cubes. Yields 3¾ pints; 12 (5 ounce) servings. *Socorro, New Mexico*

Southwest Pina Colada

1 (8 ounce) can crushed pineapple with juice
1 (7 ounce) can cream of coconut
1 cup rum

- Combine all ingredients in blender and mix. Add enough ice for desired consistency and process until liquid is "slushy". Serve while ice cold. Serves 6. *Safford, Arizona*

Pina Colada Icy

3 scoops pineapple sherbet, divided
1 scoop coconut sorbet
½ cup canned coconut milk
1 tablespoon light rum

- Place 2 scoops pineapple sherbet, coconut sorbet, coconut milk and rum in blender; pulse until smooth.

- Pour into tall glass and top with another scoop of pineapple sherbet. Serve with straw. Serves 1. *McDonough, Georgia*

Margarita Freeze

Great for the freezer and instant margaritas!

1 (16 ounce) container sweet-and-sour liquid bar mix
3 (6 ounce) cans limeade frozen concentrate
12 ounces tequila
6 ounces triple sec liqueur

- Mix all ingredients in large plastic container with lid and freeze. Liquid will be slushy.

- Dip or pour into margarita glasses. Yields 3¼ pints; 16 (3 ounce) servings. *Bay City, Texas.*

Easy Frozen Strawberry Margarita

1 (10 ounce) package frozen strawberries
1 (6 ounce) can frozen limeade concentrate
1 (6 ounce) can tequila

- Pour strawberries, limeade, tequila and ice into blender and process until smooth.

- Add enough ice to fill blender. Pour into margarita glasses. Serves 6. *Ruston, Louisiana*

Kahlua

1 cup instant coffee granules
4 cups sugar
1 quart vodka
1 vanilla bean, split

- Combine 3 cups hot water and coffee in large saucepan and mix well.

- Add sugar and bring to a boil. Boil for 2 minutes, turn off heat
  and cool.

- Add vodka and vanilla bean. Pour into bottle or jar, set for
  30 days before serving and shake occasionally. Yields 3½ pints.
  Cleburne, Texas

*TIP: If you happen to have some Mexican vanilla, you can make "instant"
Kahlua by using 3 tablespoons of Mexican vanilla instead of the
vanilla bean and you do not have to wait 30 days.*

Quick Kahlua

10 tablespoons instant coffee granules
2½ cups sugar
¼ cup Mexican vanilla
1½ cups bourbon
Ice cream

- Combine coffee granules with 8 cups water in large saucepan. Add
  sugar and bring to boil. Lower heat and simmer for about 45 minutes.

- Add vanilla, cool to room temperature, then add bourbon. This may be
  stored in jars at room temperature. Serve in cordial glasses or over ice
  cream. Yields 3 pints. *Corsicana, Texas*

Kahlua Frosty

1 cup Kahlua® liqueur
1 pint vanilla ice cream
1 cup half-and-half cream
¼ teaspoon almond extract

- Combine all ingredients and 1 heaping cup ice cubes in blender.

- Blend until smooth. Serve immediately. Yields 1 quart; 8 (4 ounce)
  servings. *McAlester, Oklahoma*

Holiday Eggnog

1 gallon eggnog
1 pint whipping cream
1 quart brandy
½ gallon vanilla ice cream, softened
Ground nutmeg

- Mix eggnog, cream, brandy and ice cream in bowl.

- Serve in individual cups, sprinkle with nutmeg and serve immediately. Yields 7½ quarts; 60 (4 ounce) servings.. *Newport, Vermont*

★ ★ ★
Breakfast & Brunch

Nothing whets the appetite like aromas from breakfasts and tempting brunch entrees and 49 recipes make variety easy!

**1001
Community
Recipes**

Breakfast & Brunch Contents

Breakfast Bake

*This is a favorite for overnight guests
or special enough for Christmas morning.*

1 pound hot sausage, cooked, crumbled
1 cup shredded cheddar cheese
1 cup biscuit mix
5 eggs, slightly beaten
2 cups milk

- Preheat oven to 350°.

- Place cooked, crumbled sausage in sprayed 9 x 13-inch baking dish and sprinkle with cheese.

- Combine biscuit mix, a little salt and eggs in bowl and beat well. Add milk and stir until fairly smooth. Pour over sausage mixture.

- Bake for 35 minutes. You can mix this up the night before and refrigerate. To bake the next morning, add 5 minutes to baking time. Serves 6. *Maryville, Tennessee*

Bacon-Sour Cream Omelet

2 eggs
5 strips bacon, fried, drained, crumbled
⅓ cup sour cream
3 green onions, chopped
1 tablespoon butter

- Combine eggs with 1 tablespoon water in bowl with fork.

- Combine bacon and sour cream. Saute onions in remaining bacon drippings and mix with bacon-sour cream.

- Melt butter in omelet pan. Pour in egg mixture and cook. When omelet is set, spoon sour cream mixture along center and fold omelet onto warm plate. Serves 1. *Elizabethtown, Kentucky*

Baked Eggs

4 eggs
4 tablespoons cream, divided
4 tablespoons cracker crumbs, divided
4 tablespoons shredded cheddar cheese, divided

- Preheat oven to 325°.

- Spray 4 muffin cups and place 1 egg in each.

- Sprinkle with a little salt and pepper. Add 1 tablespoon each of cream, crumbs and cheese for each egg.

- Bake for 12 to 20 minutes until eggs are set. Serves 4. *Brunswick, Maine*

TIP: As many eggs as required may be prepared at the same time.

Breakfast Frittata

2 medium zucchini, diced, drained
1 cup finely diced fresh mushrooms
Oil
2 ripe avocados, peeled, cubed
5 eggs
1½ cups shredded Swiss cheese

- Cook zucchini and mushrooms in large skillet with a little oil over medium heat for 4 to 5 minutes or just until tender. Remove from heat and sprinkle with a little salt and pepper.

- Place cubed avocado over top of vegetable mixture. Beat eggs and about 1 cup water or milk in bowl until frothy and pour over ingredients in skillet.

- Return skillet to medium heat, cover and cook for 5 minutes or until eggs set. Top with cheese, cover and cook for an additional 1 minute or just until cheese melts.

- Cut in wedges to serve. Serves 8. *Bend, Oregon*

Breakfast Wake-Up

2 (7 ounce) cans chopped green chilies
12 eggs
2 (16 ounce) packages shredded cheddar cheese, divided
Salsa

- Preheat oven to 350°.

- Drain green chilies and save juice.

- In separate bowl, beat eggs with juice of green chilies and add a little salt and pepper.

- Spread half cheese in sprayed 9 x 13-inch pan and layer chilies over this. Top with remaining cheese.

- Pour eggs over top and bake for 45 minutes. Serve with salsa. Serves 8. *Grants, New Mexico*

Breakfast-Ready Casserole

6 English muffins, halved
1 pound hot sausage, cooked, drained
1 (8 ounce) package shredded cheddar-Jack cheese, divided
5 eggs, beaten
1 (10 ounce) can cream of mushroom soup
2½ cups milk

- Preheat oven to 325°.

- Place English muffin halves and cooked sausage in sprayed 9 x 13-inch baking dish.

- In separate bowl combine half cheese, eggs, soup and milk and mix well.

- Gently pour cheese-soup mixture over sausage and muffins. Sprinkle remaining cheese over top of casserole.

- Bake for 65 to 70 minutes. Test to be sure center of casserole sets.

- Let stand for 10 or 15 minutes before slicing and serving. Serves 8. *Junction City, Kansas*

Christmas Breakfast

12 - 14 eggs, slightly beaten
1 pound sausage, cooked, drained, crumbled
2 cups milk
1½ cups shredded cheddar cheese
1 (5 ounce) box seasoned croutons

- Preheat oven to 350°.

- Mix all ingredients in bowl and pour into 9 x 13-inch baking dish.

- Bake for 40 minutes. Let stand for about 10 minutes before serving. Serves 8 to 10. *Jackson, Missouri*

Creamy Eggs on Toast

¼ cup (½ stick) butter
¼ cup flour
2 cups milk
6 eggs, hard-boiled, sliced

- Melt butter in skillet, stir in flour and add milk.

- Cook over medium heat and stir constantly until sauce thickens.

- Gently fold in egg slices. Serve over 6 slices toasted bread. Serves 6. *Spencer, Iowa*

Mexican Breakfast Eggs

¼ cup (½ stick) butter
9 eggs
3 tablespoons milk
5 tablespoons salsa
1 cup crushed tortilla chips

- Melt butter in skillet.

- Beat eggs in bowl and add milk and salsa.

- Pour egg mixture into skillet and stir until eggs cook lightly.

- Stir in tortilla chips and serve hot. Serves 6 to 8. *Palestine, Texas*

Sunday Night Eggs

2 tablespoons butter, melted
¾ cup shredded Swiss cheese, divided
5 eggs
2 tablespoons half-and-half cream
¼ cup milk

- Preheat oven to 350°.

- Pour butter into 8-inch baking dish and turn dish from side to side to spread butter. Sprinkle half of cheese over butter.

- Carefully crack eggs and pour into dish without breaking yolks. Pour half-and-half cream and milk around outside of eggs to keep from breaking yolks.

- Season with a little salt and pepper and sprinkle remaining cheese over top.

- Bake for about 10 minutes or until whites set and cheese melts. Serves 6. *Beckley, West Virginia*

Sunrise Eggs

6 eggs
2 cups milk
1 pound sausage, cooked, browned
¾ cup shredded Velveeta® cheese
6 slices white bread, trimmed, cubed

- Preheat oven to 350°.

- Beat eggs in bowl and add milk, sausage and cheese. Pour over bread and mix well.

- Pour into sprayed 9 x 13-inch baking pan.

- Cover and bake for 20 minutes. Remove cover, turn oven up to 375° and bake for an additional 10 minutes. Serves 8. *Elko, Nevada*

An Apple for Breakfast

*This is a really neat breakfast casserole and a delicious
way to serve fruit with breakfast or brunch!*

4 - 5 tart cooking apples, peeled, sliced
¾ cup chopped pecans
½ cup golden raisins
6 tablespoons brown sugar
½ teaspoon ground cinnamon
¼ cup (½ stick) butter
6 eggs
1½ cups orange juice
1 cup flour
3 tablespoons sugar
Ground cinnamon
Maple syrup

- Preheat oven to 400°.

- Saute apples, pecans, raisins, brown sugar, cinnamon and butter
  in large skillet, until apples begin to soften, about 6 minutes, and
  stir often.

- Place in sprayed 9 x 13-inch inch baking dish.

- Combine eggs, orange juice, flour and ¾ teaspoon salt in bowl, beat
  slowly until mixture is smooth and scrape around edges of bowl.

- Pour over apple mixture. Sprinkle with sugar and a little cinnamon.

- Bake for about 20 to 25 minutes or until knife inserted in center comes
  out clean.

- Serve with maple syrup. Serves 8 to 10. *Port Washington, Wisconsin*

Quick Breakfast Sandwiches

8 slices white bread*
Butter, softened
2 cups cooked, finely chopped ham
1 cup shredded Swiss cheese
3 eggs, beaten
1⅔ cups milk
1 tablespoon dried, minced onion flakes
1 teaspoon mustard

- Trim crusts off bread slices. Spread butter on 1 side of each slice of bread. Place 4 slices in sprayed 8-inch square baking pan.

- Top bread slices with chopped ham and remaining bread slices, buttered-side up. Sprinkle with shredded Swiss cheese.

- Combine eggs, milk, onion flakes, mustard with a little salt and mix well. Slowly pour over bread slices. Cover and refrigerate for at least 8 hours.

- When ready to bake, preheat oven to 325°.

- Remove baking pan from refrigerator about 10 minutes before cooking. Uncover and bake for 30 minutes or until center sets. To serve, cut into 4 sandwiches. Serves 4. *Chambersburg, Pennsylvania*

TIP: Use regular bread slices, not thin sandwich slices.

Corned Beef Hash Bake

2 (15 ounce) cans corned beef hash, slightly warmed
Butter
6 - 8 eggs
⅓ cup half-and-half cream

- Preheat oven to 350°.

- Spread corned beef hash in sprayed 9 x 13-inch pan. Pat down with back of spoon and make 6 to 8 deep hollows in hash large enough for egg to fit.

- Place tiny dab of butter in each hollow

- Pour eggs into each hollow and cover with about 1 tablespoon half-and-half cream.

- Bake for 15 to 20 minutes or until eggs set as desired. Divide into squares to serve. Serves 8. *Anniston, Alabama*

Cinnamon Souffle

1 loaf cinnamon-raisin bread
1 (20 ounce) can crushed pineapple with juice
1 cup (2 sticks) butter, melted
½ cup sugar
5 eggs, slightly beaten

- Preheat oven to 350°.

- Slice very thin portion of bread crusts off. Tear bread into small pieces and place in sprayed 9 x 13-inch baking dish. Pour pineapple with juice over bread and set aside.

- Cream butter and sugar in bowl. Add eggs to creamed mixture and mix well.

- Pour creamed mixture over bread and pineapple. Bake for 40 minutes. Serves 6 to 8. *Cortland, New York*

TIP: One-half cup chopped pecans could be added, if you like.

Homemade Egg Substitute

6 egg whites
¼ cup instant nonfat dry milk powder
2 teaspoons oil
¼ teaspoon ground turmeric

- Combine all ingredients and 2 teaspoons water in electric blender and process for 30 seconds and refrigerate. (¼ cup is the equivalent to one egg.) *Escondido, California*

Glazed Bacon

1 pound bacon
⅓ cup packed brown sugar
1 teaspoon flour
½ cup finely chopped pecans

- Preheat oven to 350°.

- Arrange bacon slices close together, but not overlapping, on wire rack over drip pan.

- Combine brown sugar, flour and pecans in bowl and sprinkle evenly over bacon.

- Bake for about 30 minutes. Drain on paper towels. *Shenandoah, Iowa*

Pecan Waffles

2 cups self-rising flour
½ cup oil
½ cup milk
⅔ cup finely chopped pecans

- Preheat waffle iron.

- Combine flour, oil and milk in bowl. Beat until they mix well. Stir in chopped pecans.

- Pour approximately ¾ cup batter into hot waffle iron and bake until brown and crispy. Serves 6. *Milford, Delaware*

Light and Crispy Waffles

2 cups biscuit mix
1 egg
½ cup oil
1⅓ cups club soda

- Preheat waffle iron.

- Combine all ingredients in bowl and stir with spoon. Pour just enough batter to cover waffle iron. Serves 6. *Wakefield, Rhode Island*

TIP: *To have waffles for a "company weekend", make up waffles in advance. Freeze separately on baking sheet and place in large resealable baggies. To heat, warm in oven at 350° for about 10 minutes.*

Waffle Flash

2 eggs
1 cup milk
½ teaspoon vanilla
8 slices stale bread
Butter
Syrup

- Heat waffle iron according to directions.

- Beat eggs in bowl, slowly add milk and vanilla and beat well. Remove crust from bread and butter both sides of bread.

- When waffle iron is ready, dip bread in egg mixture and place in waffle iron. Close lid and grill until light brown. Serve with butter and syrup. Serves 4. *Orangeburg, South Carolina*

Oven Pancakes

⅔ cup flour
⅔ cup milk
¼ cup sugar
5 large eggs, beaten
Oil
Syrup
Fresh berries

- Preheat oven to 425°.

- Combine flour, milk, sugar and beaten eggs in bowl and mix very well. Place a little oil on large baking sheet, rubbing oil to cover whole surface of pan. Place in oven for 5 minutes to heat.

- Pour mixture onto pan, making several pancakes. Bake for about 18 minutes or until puffy and golden.

- Serve with syrup or fresh berries. Serves 2 to 3. *Chapel Hill, North Carolina*

Biscuits and Sausage Gravy

*This is about as down-home as you can get and
it is every bit as good as you can imagine.*

3 cups biscuit mix
4 cups milk, divided
½ pound pork sausage
2 tablespoons butter
⅓ cup flour

- Preheat oven to 400°.

- Combine biscuit mix and ¾ cup milk in bowl and stir. Roll dough on floured wax paper to ¾-inch thickness and cut with biscuit cutter. Place on sprayed baking sheet. Bake for 12 to 15 minutes or until golden.

- For gravy, brown sausage in skillet, drain and reserve pan drippings in skillet. Set sausage aside.

- Add butter to drippings and melt. Add flour and cook for 1 minute, stirring constantly. Gradually add remaining milk, cook over medium heat, stirring constantly until mixture thickens. Stir in ½ teaspoon each of salt and pepper and add sausage.

- Cook until hot and stir constantly. Serve sausage gravy over cooked biscuits. Serves 6. *Fredericksburg, Texas*

French Toast

Oil
4 eggs
1 cup whipping cream
2 thick slices bread, cut into 3 strips
Powdered sugar

- Preheat oven to 325°.

- Place a little oil in skillet. Beat eggs, cream and pinch of salt.

- Dip bread into batter and allow batter to soak in.

- Fry bread in skillet until brown, turn and fry on other side. Transfer to baking sheet. Bake for about 4 minutes or until they puff. Sprinkle with powdered sugar. Serves 2. *Houma, Louisiana*

Sticky Pecan Rolls

1 (12 count) package brown-and-serve dinner rolls
¼ cup butter, melted
⅔ cup packed brown sugar
24 pecan halves

- Preheat oven to 400°.

- Place 1 roll in each of 12 sprayed muffin cups. Cut an "X" in top of each roll.

- Combine butter and brown sugar and mix well. Spoon mixture over rolls.

- Tuck 2 pecan halves in "X" on each roll. Bake for 10 to 15 minutes or until slightly brown. Serves 6. *Bogalusa, Louisiana*

Breakfast Ready Oatmeal

1½ cups old-fashioned oats
3½ cups milk
½ cup chopped pecans
⅓ cup packed brown sugar

- Combine and cook all ingredients and a dash of salt in saucepan over medium heat. Bring to a boil, lower heat and simmer for 6 minutes, stirring occasionally.

- Let stand for several minutes before serving. Serves 4. *Nampa, Idaho*

Cherry-Pecan Oatmeal

2 cups cooked oatmeal
½ cup dried cherries, chopped
½ cup packed brown sugar
¼ cup (½ stick) butter, softened
½ teaspoon ground cinnamon
½ cup chopped pecans, toasted

- Combine cherries, brown sugar, butter and cinnamon in bowl. Stir into cooked oatmeal.

- Spoon into individual serving bowls and sprinkle toasted pecans over top of each serving. Serves 2. *Beatrice, Nebraska*

TIP: Toasting brings out the flavors of nuts and seeds. Place nuts on baking sheet and bake at 225° for 10 minutes. Be careful not to burn them.

Ranch Sausage-Grits

1 cup quick-cooking grits
1 pound pork sausage
1 onion, chopped
1 cup salsa
1 (8 ounce) package shredded cheddar cheese, divided

- Preheat oven to 350°.

- Cook grits according to directions and set aside. Cook and brown sausage and onion in skillet and drain well.

- Combine grits, sausage mixture, salsa and half of cheese. Spoon into sprayed 2-quart baking dish.

- Bake for 15 minutes. Remove from oven and add remaining cheese. Bake for an additional 10 minutes. Serve hot. Serves 6 to 8. *Riverton, Wyoming*

Baked Grits

2 cups quick-cooking grits
2 cups milk
¾ cup (1½ sticks) butter
4 eggs, beaten

- Preheat oven to 350°.

- Stir grits in 4 cups water in saucepan over medium heat for about 5 minutes. Add milk and butter, cover and cook for an additional 10 minutes.

- Remove from heat and add beaten eggs.

- Pour in sprayed 9 x 13-inch baking dish and bake for 30 minutes. Serves 8. *Sumter, South Carolina*

Breakfast Shake

1 banana, cut into 1-inch slices
1 mango, peeled, cubed
1½ cups pineapple juice or orange juice, chilled
1 (8 ounce) container vanilla yogurt

- Process all ingredients in blender until smooth. Scrape sides of blender and mix. Serve immediately. Serves 2. *Plant City, Florida*

Pineapple Coffee Cake

1 (18 ounce) box butter cake mix
½ cup oil
4 eggs, slightly beaten
1 (20 ounce) can pineapple pie filling

- Preheat oven to 350°.

- Combine cake mix, oil and eggs in bowl. Beat until they mix well. Pour batter into sprayed, floured 9 x 13-inch baking pan.

- Bake for 45 to 50 minutes or when toothpick inserted in center comes out clean.

- With knife, punch holes in cake about 2 inches apart. Spread pineapple pie filling over cake while cake is still hot. Serves 12 to 15. *Petersburg, Virginia*

Blueberry Coffee Cake

1 (16 ounce) package blueberry muffin mix with blueberries
⅓ cup sour cream
1 egg
⅔ cup powdered sugar

- Preheat oven to 400°.

- Stir muffin mix, sour cream, egg and ½ cup water in bowl.

- Rinse blueberries and gently fold into batter. Pour into non-stick, sprayed 7 x 11-inch baking dish.

- Bake for about 25 minutes.

- Mix powdered sugar and 1 tablespoon water and drizzle over coffee cake. Serves 9. *Laconia, New Hampshire*

Ambrosia Spread

1 (11 ounce) can mandarin orange sections, drained
1 (8 ounce) container soft cream cheese with pineapple, softened
¼ cup flaked coconut, toasted
¼ cup slivered almonds, chopped, toasted

- Chop orange sections and set aside.

- Combine cream cheese, coconut and almonds in bowl and blend well. Gently fold in orange sections. Refrigerate.

- Spread on date-nut bread, banana bread, etc. Yields 1 pint. *Ft. Smith, Arkansas*

TIP: *This may also be used as a dip for fruits. Toasting brings out the flavors of nuts and seeds. Place nuts or seeds on baking sheet and bake at 225° for 10 minutes. Be careful not to burn them.*

Orange Butter

Great on biscuits and hot rolls.

⅔ cup (1⅓ sticks) butter, room temperature
¼ cup frozen orange juice concentrate, thawed
1 (16 ounce) box powdered sugar
1 teaspoon dried orange peel

- Combine all ingredients in bowl and blend well. Store in refrigerator. Yields 1 pint. *Monmouth, Illinois*

Honey Butter

Wonderful with hot biscuits!

½ cup (1 stick) butter, softened
¼ cup honey
2 tablespoons lemon juice
1 tablespoon brown sugar

- Cream butter in bowl until fluffy and add honey in fine stream while stirring.

- Add lemon juice and brown sugar and stir until all ingredients blend evenly.

- Refrigerate until ready to serve. Yields ½ cup. *Wooster, Ohio*

Apple Butter 🍁

2 cups apple cider
8 - 9 cups peeled, sliced apples
¾ cup sugar
1 teaspoon ground cinnamon
¼ teaspoon ground nutmeg

- Bring apple cider to a boil in large saucepan; reduce heat to medium and simmer for about 10 minutes to reduce liquid.

- Add apples, stirring often and simmer until mixture is thick and mushy.

- Stir in sugar, cinnamon and nutmeg and cool. Store in refrigerator. Serves 8. *Bracebridge, Ontario, Canada*

TIP: Apple butter and apple sauce are traditional foods often served at every meal on Canadian tables.

Cranberry Jam 🍁

The Northwest Territories is the third largest land division in Canada, but is very sparsely populated. The first inhabitants were the Inuit and Dene Indians. This Arctic region looks harsh, but its forests were home to fur-bearing animals and supported settlers as they came north. Meat was their most important source of food; there was plenty of caribou, deer, buffalo and fish as well as many varieties of berries in the spring. The hospitality in this area decrees one's door must always be open to all who pass with food for everyone.

4 cups cranberries
3 cups sugar
1 teaspoon ground cinnamon

• Place cranberries, sugar and 1 cup water in large saucepan; bring to a boil, reduce heat to medium and let simmer, stirring often, until mixture is thick and mushy.

• Refrigerate and serve with toast or muffins. Serves 6. *Yellowknife, Northwest Territories, Canada*

Apricot Bake

4 (15 ounce) cans apricot halves, drained, divided
1 (16 ounce) box light brown sugar, divided
2 cups round, buttery cracker crumbs, divided
½ cup (1 stick) butter, sliced

• Preheat oven to 300°.

• Place 2 cans drained apricots in sprayed 9 x 13-inch baking dish.

• Sprinkle half brown sugar and half cracker crumbs over apricots. Dot with half butter and repeat layers.

• Bake for 1 hour. Serves 12. *Ephrata, Washington*

Curried Fruit Medley

1 (29 ounce) can sliced peaches
2 (15 ounce) cans pineapple chunks
1 (10 ounce) jar maraschino cherries
1 cup packed brown sugar
1 teaspoon curry powder
¼ cup (½ stick) butter, cut into pieces

- Preheat oven to 350°.

- Drain fruits and place in 9 x 13-inch baking dish.

- Combine brown sugar and curry powder in bowl and stir well. Sprinkle over fruit and dot with butter.

- Cover and bake for 30 minutes or until thoroughly hot. Serves 12. *Bozeman, Montana*

Spiced Pears

1 (15 ounce) can pear halves with syrup
⅓ cup packed brown sugar
¾ teaspoon ground nutmeg
¾ teaspoon ground cinnamon

- Drain pears, reserve syrup and set pears aside.

- Place syrup, brown sugar, nutmeg and cinnamon in saucepan and bring to a boil. Reduce heat and simmer for 5 to 8 minutes, stirring frequently.

- Add pears and simmer for an additional 5 minutes or until thoroughly hot. Serves 3 to 4. *Roseburg, Oregon*

Pineapple-Cheese Casserole

*This is really a different kind of recipe – but so good. It can be
served at brunch and it's great with sandwiches at lunch.*

1 cup sugar
5 tablespoons flour
2 (20 ounce) cans unsweetened pineapple chunks, drained
1½ cups shredded cheddar cheese
1 stack buttery crackers, crushed
½ cup (1 stick) butter, melted

- Preheat oven to 350°.

- Mix sugar and flour in bowl.

- Layer in following order: pineapple, sugar-flour mixture, cheese and
  cracker crumbs in sprayed 9 x 13-inch baking dish. Drizzle butter over
  casserole.

- Bake for 25 minutes or until bubbly. Serves 12. *Sedalia, Missouri*

Pineapple Brunch Slices

1 cup cooked ground ham
1 teaspoon mustard
2 tablespoons mayonnaise
5 slices pineapple, drained

- Preheat oven to 375°.

- Combine ham, mustard and mayonnaise in bowl and mix well.

- Spread on pineapple slices.

- Bake in baking pan for about 15 minutes or until thoroughly hot.
  Serves 5. *Stillwater, Oklahoma*

Peachy Fruit Dip

1 (15 ounce) can sliced peaches, drained
½ cup marshmallow creme
1 (3 ounce) package cream cheese, cubed
⅛ teaspoon ground nutmeg
Fresh fruit

- Blend all ingredients in blender or food processor until smooth.

- Serve with assorted fresh fruit. Serves 4. *Cleveland, Tennessee*

Melon Boats

2 cantaloupes, chilled
4 cups red and green seedless grapes, chilled
1 cup mayonnaise
⅓ cup frozen concentrated orange juice, slightly thawed

- Cut each melon in 6 lengthwise sections and remove seeds and peel. Place on separate salad plates on lettuce leaves.

- Heap grapes over and around cantaloupe slices.

- Combine mayonnaise and juice concentrate in bowl and mix well. Ladle over fruit. Serves 6 to 12. *Sarasota, Florida*

Crabmeat Quiche

3 eggs, beaten
1 (8 ounce) carton sour cream
1 (6 ounce) can crabmeat, rinsed, drained, flaked
½ cup shredded Swiss cheese
1 (9 inch) piecrust
Garlic salt

- Preheat oven to 350°.

- Combine eggs and sour cream in bowl. Blend in crabmeat and cheese and add a little garlic salt and pepper.

- Pour into piecrust.

- Bake for 35 minutes. Serves 6. *Lancaster, South Carolina*

Green Chili Squares

1 (7 ounce) can chopped green chilies
1 (8 ounce) package shredded sharp cheddar cheese
8 eggs, beaten
½ cup half-and-half cream

- Preheat oven to 350°.

- Place green chilies in 9 x 13-inch baking pan and cover with cheese.

- Combine eggs, half-and-half cream, and a little salt and pepper in bowl. Pour over chilies and cheese.

- Bake for 30 minutes. Let stand at room temperature for a few minutes before cutting into squares. Serves 9 to 12. *Globe, Arizona*

Hot Tamale-Cheese Fiesta

2 (13 ounce) jars beef tamales with sauce
1 (8 ounce) package shredded Mexican 4-cheese blend, divided
1 (10 ounce) can cream of mushroom soup
2 teaspoons taco seasoning

- Preheat oven to 350°.

- Drain sauce from tamales into cup and set aside. Remove wrappers from tamales. Place tamales side by side in baking dish. Sprinkle one-fourth cheese over top of tamales.

- Combine ½ cup sauce from tamales, mushroom soup and taco seasoning in bowl and mix well.

- Pour sauce mixture over tamales and cheese.

- Bake for 5 to 10 minutes to heat tamales thoroughly.

- Remove from oven and sprinkle remaining cheese over top and bake until cheese melts. Serves 8. *New Braunfels, Texas*

Quesadilla Pie

1 (4 ounce) can chopped green chilies
½ pound sausage, cooked, crumbled
2 cups shredded cheddar cheese
3 eggs, well beaten
1½ cups milk
¾ cup biscuit mix
Hot salsa

- Preheat oven to 350°.

- Sprinkle green chilies in sprayed 9-inch pie pan. Add layer of sausage and layer of cheddar cheese.

- In separate bowl, combine eggs, milk and biscuit mix and mix well. Slowly pour over chilies, sausage and cheese.

- Bake for 35 minutes or until center sets. Serve with salsa on top of each slice. Serves 6. *Tucumcari, New Mexico*

TIP: To give this "pie" a little more zip, use hot sausage and a few drops of hot sauce!

Chiffon Cheese Souffle

Wow! Is this ever good! It is light and fluffy, but still very rich.

12 slices white bread with crusts trimmed
2 (5 ounce) jars sharp processed cheese spread, softened
6 eggs, beaten
3 cups milk
¾ cup (1½ sticks) butter, melted

- Cut each bread slice into 4 triangles. Place dab of cheese on each triangle and place triangles evenly in layers in sprayed 9 x 13-inch baking dish. (You could make this in a souffle dish if you have one.)

- Combine eggs, milk, butter and a little salt and pepper in bowl. Pour over bread layers. Cover and refrigerate for 8 hours.

- Remove from refrigerator 10 to 15 minutes before baking.

- When ready to bake, preheat oven to 350°.

- Uncover and bake for 1 hour. Serves 10 to 12. *Winchester, Kentucky*

Chile Rellenos

2 (7 ounce) cans chopped green chilies, drained
1 (16 ounce) package shredded Monterey Jack cheese
4 eggs, beaten
½ cup milk

- Preheat oven to 350°.

- Layer half green chilies, half cheese, then remaining chilies and cheese in 7 x 11-inch baking dish.

- Combine eggs, milk, and a little salt and pepper in small bowl and mix well.

- Pour over layers of cheese and green chilies.

- Bake for 30 minutes or until light brown and set. Cool for 5 minutes before cutting into squares. Serves 6 to 8. *Seguin, Texas*

★ ★ ★
Breads

Hot breads and biscuits add a special attraction to any meal. Decide on 32 easy recipes from breadsticks to corn bread!

1001
Community
Recipes

Breads Contents

Quick Sour Cream Biscuits

⅓ cup club soda
⅓ cup sour cream
½ tablespoon sugar
2 cups biscuit mix

- Preheat oven to 400°.

- Combine all ingredients in bowl with fork just until dry ingredients are moist. Turn bowl out onto lightly floured board and knead gently several times.

- Roll dough into 1 inch thickness and cut with biscuit cutter. Place biscuits in sprayed 9 x 13-inch baking pan. Bake for 12 to 14 minutes or until golden brown. Serves 6 to 8. *Alamo, Tennessee*

Quick Onion Biscuits

2 cups biscuit mix
¼ cup milk
1 (8 ounce) container French onion dip
2 tablespoons finely minced green onion

- Preheat oven to 400°.

- Combine all ingredients in bowl and mix until soft dough forms. Drop heaping teaspoonfuls of dough onto sprayed baking sheet. Bake for 10 to 12 minutes or until golden brown. Serves 6 to 8. *Anthony, Kansas*

Maple Syrup Biscuits

2¼ cups biscuit mix
⅔ cup milk
1½ cups maple syrup
Butter

- Preheat oven to 425°.

- Combine baking mix and milk in bowl. Stir just until moist. On floured surface, roll dough into ½-inch thickness. Cut with 2-inch biscuit cutter.

- Pour syrup into 7 x 11-inch baking dish. Place biscuits on top of syrup.

- Bake for 13 to 15 minutes or until biscuits are golden brown. Serve with butter. Serves 8 to 10. *Bellows Falls, Vermont*

Hot Biscuits

1⅓ cups flour
1 (8 ounce) carton whipping cream
2 tablespoons sugar
Butter

- Preheat oven to 400°.

- Combine all ingredients in bowl and stir until they blend well. Drop teaspoonfuls of biscuits onto sprayed baking sheet.

- Bake for 10 minutes or until light brown. Serve with plan or flavored butters. Serves 4. *Allendale, New Jersey*

French Onion Biscuits

2 cups biscuit mix
¼ cup milk
1 (8 ounce) container French onion dip
2 tablespoons finely minced green onion

- Preheat oven to 400°.

- Mix all ingredients in bowl until soft dough forms. Drop dough onto sprayed baking sheet.

- Bake for 10 minutes or until light golden brown. Serves 6 to 8. *Afton, Minnesota*

Speedy Biscuits

6 tablespoons shortening
3 cups flour
1 cup milk
Butter

- Preheat oven to 400°.

- Cut shortening into flour in bowl with pastry cutter or with spoon. Add milk and mix until dough forms a ball. Knead until dough is smooth.

- Place on floured surface and flatten slightly. Cut with floured biscuit cutter; place in sprayed pan.

- Bake for 10 to 12 minutes. Serve with butter. Serves 8 to 10. *Albany, Kentucky*

Come and Get 'Em Biscuits

2 cups flour
¼ cup mayonnaise
1 cup milk
Butter

- Preheat oven to 425°.

- Mix flour, mayonnaise and milk in bowl and drop teaspoonfuls of dough onto baking sheet.

- Bake until biscuits are golden brown.

- Serve with plain or flavored butters. Serves 6. *Abbeville, Georgia*

Sour Cream Biscuits

2 cups plus 1 tablespoon flour
1 tablespoon baking powder
½ teaspoon baking soda
½ cup shortening
1 (8 ounce) carton sour cream

- Preheat oven to 400°.

- Combine dry ingredients in bowl, add a little salt and cut in shortening.

- Gradually add sour cream and mix lightly. Turn on lightly floured board and knead a few times.

- Roll to ½ inch thickness. Cut with biscuit cutter and place onto sprayed baking sheet.

- Bake for 15 minutes or until light brown. Serves 4 to 6. *Aliceville, Alabama*

Orange French Toast

1 egg, beaten
½ cup orange juice
5 slices raisin bread
1 cup crushed graham crackers
2 tablespoons butter

- Combine egg and orange juice in bowl. Dip bread in mixture and then in cracker crumbs.

- Fry in butter until brown. Serves 4 to 5. *Addis, Louisiana*

Sticky Sweet Rolls

1 (12 count) package frozen dinner rolls, partially thawed
¼ cup (½ stick) butter, melted
¾ cup packed brown sugar
½ teaspoon ground cinnamon
1 cup chopped pecans

- Place 1 roll in each of 12 sprayed muffin cups and cut a deep "X" in top of each roll. Spray tops of rolls with cooking spray and place sheet of plastic wrap over rolls.

- Let rise for about 3 hours or until double in size.

- When ready to bake, preheat oven to 350°.

- Combine butter, brown sugar and cinnamon in bowl and mix well.

- Stir in pecans and spoon sugar mixture over rolls. Pull "X" open and let sugar mixture seep into rolls.

- Bake for 15 to 20 minutes or until light brown. Serve 6 to 8.
  Ashland, Missouri

Filled Muffins

1(16 ounce) box blueberry muffin mix with blueberries
1 egg
⅓ cup red raspberry jam
¼ cup sliced almonds

- Preheat oven to 375°.

- Rinse blueberries and drain.

- Combine muffin mix, egg and ½ cup water in bowl. Stir until moist and break up lumps in mix.

- Place paper liners in 8 to 12 muffin cups. Fill cups half full of batter.

- In separate bowl, combine raspberry jam with blueberries. Spoon mixture on top of batter. Cover with remaining batter and sprinkle almonds over batter.

- Bake for about 18 minutes or until light brown. Serves 8.
  Amherst, Virginia

Blueberry-Orange Muffins

1 (16 ounce) package blueberry muffin mix with blueberries
2 egg whites
½ cup orange juice
Orange marmalade

- Preheat oven to 375°.

- Rinse blueberries and drain.

- Stir muffin mix, egg whites and orange juice in bowl and break up any lumps.

- Fold blueberries gently into batter.

- Pour into muffin cups (with paper liners) about half full.

- Bake for 18 to 20 minutes or until toothpick inserted in center comes out clean.

- Spoon orange marmalade over top of hot muffins. Serves 8.
  Arnold, Maryland

Cheesy Breadsticks

1 loaf thick sliced bread
¾ cup (1½ sticks) butter, melted
1 cup shredded cheddar cheese
1 teaspoon Italian seasoning
1 teaspoon paprika

- Preheat oven to 325°.

- Remove crust from bread (discard crusts) and slice into 1-inch sticks. Brush or roll each stick in melted butter and place close together on large baking sheet.

- Sprinkle cheese, Italian seasoning and paprika over sticks and separate sticks so that all sides of stick will toast.

- Bake for 20 minutes or until sticks are slightly brown and lightly toasted. Serves 6 to 12. *Amelia, Louisiana*

Cheesy Herb Bread

1 loaf French bread
½ teaspoon garlic powder
1 teaspoon marjoram leaves
1 tablespoon dried parsley leaves
½ cup (1 stick) butter, softened
1 cup parmesan cheese

- Preheat oven to 375°.

- Slice bread into 1-inch slices but do not go through bottom. Combine garlic, marjoram, parsley and butter in bowl. Spread mixture in between slices and sprinkle with cheese.

- Wrap in foil and bake for 20 minutes. Unwrap and bake for an additional 5 minutes. Serves 8 to 12. *Battlefield, Missouri*

Deluxe Parmesan Bread

1 (16 ounce) loaf Italian bread
½ cup refrigerated creamy Caesar salad dressing
2 tablespoons mayonnaise
⅓ cup grated parmesan cheese
3 tablespoons finely chopped green onions

- Cut 24 (½ inch) thick slices from bread. Combine dressing, mayonnaise, parmesan cheese and onions in small bowl and spread 1 heaping teaspoon dressing mixture on each slice of bread.

- Place bread on baking sheet and broil 4 inches from heat until golden brown. Watch closely so that toast does not burn. Serve immediately. Serves 6 to 12. *Ada, Ohio*

Green Chili-Cheese Bread

1 loaf Italian bread
½ cup (1 stick) butter, melted
1 (4 ounce) can diced green chilies, drained
¾ cup shredded Monterey Jack cheese

- Preheat oven to 350°.

- Slice bread almost all the way through.

- Combine melted butter, green chilies and cheese in bowl. Spread between bread slices. Cover loaf with foil. Bake for 25 minutes. Serves 8 to 12. *Adobe Acres, New Mexico*

Swiss Bread Slices

1 (16 ounce) loaf French bread
1 (8 ounce) package shredded Swiss cheese
⅓ cup mayonnaise
2 teaspoons minced fresh basil
1 tablespoon finely grated onion
1 tablespoon olive oil
1 teaspoon cider vinegar

- Preheat oven to 375°.

- Cut bread in half lengthwise. Combine cheese, mayonnaise, basil, onion, olive oil and vinegar in bowl.

- Spread over cut sides of bread and place on baking sheet.

- Bake for 8 to 10 minutes or until cheese melts and bread is light brown.

- When ready to serve, cut loaf into 8 equal portions. Serves 6 to 8.
  Basalt, Colorado

Cheese-Toasted French Bread

1 (16 ounce) loaf French bread
1 (3 ounce) package bacon bits
1 (8 ounce) package shredded mozzarella cheese
½ cup (1 stick) butter, melted

- Preheat oven to 350°.

- Slice loaf of bread into 1-inch slices and place sliced loaf on large piece of foil.

- Combine bacon bits and cheese in bowl and sprinkle mixture in between slices of bread.

- Drizzle melted butter over loaf and let some drip down in between slices.

- Wrap loaf tightly in foil. Bake for 20 to 25 minutes or until thoroughly hot. Serves 8 to 12. *Anchorage, Kentucky*

Buttered Ranch-Style Bread

1 (16 ounce) loaf French bread
½ cup (1 stick) butter, softened
1 tablespoon dry ranch-style dressing mix
2 tablespoons mayonnaise
3 tablespoons bacon bits

- Preheat oven to 350°.

- Cut loaf in half horizontally.

- Combine butter, dressing mix, mayonnaise and bacon bits in bowl and mix well. Spread mixture on both cut sides of bread.

- Place top back on bottom of loaf, wrap securely with heavy foil and bake for 20 to 25 minutes. Serves 8 to 12. *Colstrip, Montana*

Herb Pull-Apart Bread

½ cup (1 stick) butter
1 teaspoon dried basil leaves
1½ teaspoons parsley flakes
½ teaspoon dried thyme leaves
½ teaspoon cilantro leaves
1 teaspoon garlic powder
1 (3 pound) package frozen, white dinner roll dough, thawed

- Combine butter, basil, parsley, thyme, cilantro and garlic powder in saucepan and heat on low heat until herbs blend with melted butter.

- Divide dough into 24 balls.

- Place 12 dough balls in sprayed 12-cup bundt pan and generously brush with half butter mixture.

- Layer 12 more dough balls in pan and brush with remaining butter mixture. Cover and let stand in warm place for about 4 hours or until double in size.

- When ready to bake, preheat oven to 350°.

- Bake for 24 to 27 minutes or until bread sounds hollow when tapped and top is golden brown.

- Cool for for 5 minutes and turn upside down onto serving plate. Serves 10 to 14. *Arcadia, Florida*

Cheese Bread

1 (16 ounce) package shredded, sharp cheddar cheese
1 cup mayonnaise
1 (1 ounce) packet ranch-style dressing mix
10 (1 inch) slices French bread

- Preheat oven to 350°.

- Combine cheese, mayonnaise and dressing mix in bowl.

- Spread on bread slices and heat in oven until brown. Serves 8 to 10.
  Bennett, Colorado

Strawberry Bread

*Great for finger food at parties or as sandwiches with
cream cheese and pecans – and red is always "in"!*

3 cups flour
1 teaspoon baking soda
1 teaspoon ground cinnamon
2 cups sugar
2 (10 ounce) cartons frozen strawberries, thawed
1¼ cups oil
4 eggs, beaten
1 teaspoon red food coloring

- Preheat oven to 350°.

- Combine flour, baking soda, cinnamon, ½ teaspoon salt and sugar
  in bowl.

- With spoon, make a "well" in dry ingredients, add strawberries, oil and
  eggs and mix well. Add food coloring and mix well.

- Pour into 2 sprayed, floured loaf pans.

- Bake for 1 hour. Serves 12 to 14. *Blanding, Utah*

Popovers

1 cup flour
2 eggs
1 cup milk
1 tablespoon melted shortening

- Preheat oven to 425°.

- Combine all ingredients in bowl and mix until smooth.

- Fill 6 sprayed custard cups about half-full.

- Bake for 40 to 45 minutes or until puffed and light brown. Serves 4 to 6. *Albany, Indiana*

Seasoned Breadsticks

1 (11 ounce) package refrigerated breadsticks
¼ cup (½ stick) butter, melted
2 tablespoons prepared pesto
¼ teaspoon garlic powder
3 tablespoons grated parmesan cheese

- Preheat oven to 375°.

- Unroll, separate breadsticks and place on baking pan.

- Combine melted butter, pesto and garlic powder in bowl and brush over breadsticks.

- Twist each breadstick 3 times. Sprinkle with parmesan cheese.

- Bake for about 12 minutes or until golden brown. Serves 6 to 8. *Antlers, Oklahoma*

Breadsticks

1½ cups shredded Monterey Jack cheese
¼ cup poppy seeds
2 tablespoons dry onion soup mix
2 (11 ounce) packages breadstick dough

- Preheat oven to 375°.

- Spread cheese evenly in 9 x 13-inch baking dish. Sprinkle poppy seeds and soup mix evenly over cheese.

- Separate breadstick dough into sticks. Stretch strips slightly until each strip is about 12 inches long.

- Roll strips one at a time in cheese mixture and coat all sides.

- Cut into 3 or 4-inch pieces. Place on baking sheet and bake for 12 minutes. Serves 8. *Acton, California*

Jack's Breadsticks

1 (11 ounce) package refrigerated breadstick dough
⅓ cup finely shredded Monterey Jack cheese with jalapenos
½ teaspoon ground cumin
½ teaspoon garlic powder

- Preheat oven to 375°.

- Place dough on flat surface and cut along perforations to form 12 breadsticks.

- Combine cheese, cumin and garlic powder in bowl and sprinkle over breadsticks, pressing into dough.

- Twist each breadstick and place on sprayed baking sheet.

- Bake for 14 minutes or until light brown. Serves 8 to 12.
Camden, Delaware

Corny Sausage Squares

½ pound pork sausage
1 (10 ounce) can golden corn soup
2 eggs
¼ cup milk
1 (8 ounce) package corn muffin mix

- Preheat oven to 350°.

- Brown sausage in skillet and stir until sausage is crumbly. Drain and set aside.

- Combine soup, eggs and milk in medium bowl. Stir in corn muffin mix until it blends well.

- Fold in sausage and pour into sprayed 9-inch square baking pan.

- Bake for 25 minutes or until golden brown and cut into squares to serve. Serves 8. *Albion, Indiana*

Corn Sticks

2 cups biscuit mix
2 tablespoons minced green onions
1 (8 ounce) can cream-style corn
Melted butter

- Preheat oven to 400°.

- Combine biscuit mix, green onions and cream-style corn in bowl.

- Place dough on floured surface and cut into 3 x 1-inch strips. Roll in melted butter.

- Bake for 15 to 16 minutes. Serves 6. *Barbourville, Kentucky*

Crunchy Corn Sticks

2 cups biscuit mix
2 tablespoons cornmeal
⅛ teaspoon cayenne pepper
3 tablespoons finely minced green onions
1 (8 ounce) can cream-style corn
½ cup (1 stick) butter, melted

- Preheat oven to 400°.

- Combine biscuit mix, cornmeal, cayenne pepper, green onions and cream-style corn in bowl and mix until they blend well.

- Place dough on floured surface and pat out to ½ inch thickness. Cut into strips and roll in melted butter.

- Place on baking sheet and bake for 15 to 16 minutes or until light brown. Serves 6 to 10. *Burgaw, North Carolina*

Spicy Cornbread Twists

3 tablespoons butter
⅓ cup cornmeal
¼ teaspoon cayenne pepper
1 (11 ounce) can refrigerated soft breadsticks

- Preheat oven to 350°.

- Place butter in pie pan and melt in oven. Remove from oven.

- Mix cornmeal and cayenne pepper on wax paper.

- Roll breadsticks in butter, then cornmeal mixture.

- Twist breadsticks according to package directions and place on baking sheet. Bake for 15 to 18 minutes. Serves 6. *Baldwyn, Mississippi*

Hot Water Cornbread

1½ cups cornmeal
1 egg, beaten
¼ cup (½ stick) butter, melted
Oil
Butter

- Pour 1¼ cups boiling water over cornmeal and 1 teaspoon salt in bowl, stir very well and cool.

- Stir in egg and butter.

- Drop tablespoonfuls of mixture into skillet with a little oil and form into small patty shapes with spoon.

- Brown on both sides and drain on paper towels. Serve hot with butter. Serves 6. *Abernathy, Texas*

Texas Cornbread

1 cup yellow cornmeal
⅔ cup flour
¼ teaspoon baking soda
1¼ cups buttermilk*
1 large egg, beaten

- Preheat oven to 400°.

- Combine cornmeal, flour and baking soda in center of bowl and stir in buttermilk and egg just until moist.

- Pour into sprayed 7 x 11-inch baking pan and bake for 15 minutes or until golden brown. Serves 6 to 8. *Aledo, Texas*

TIP: To make buttermilk, mix 1 cup milk with 1 tablespoon lemon juice or vinegar and let milk stand for about 10 minutes.

★ ★ ★

Soups
& Stews

"Comfort" comes immediately to mind
when we think of warm and hearty soups
and stews from 31 delicious recipes!

1001
Community
Recipes

Soups & Stews Contents

Zesty Creamy Chicken Soup

This is a really easy way to whip up a fast chicken soup.

2 tablespoons butter
½ onion, finely chopped
1 carrot, grated
1 (10 ounce) can cream of celery soup
1 (10 ounce) can cream of mushroom soup
1 (10 ounce) can cream of chicken soup
1 (14 ounce) can chicken broth
2 soup cans milk
1 tablespoon dried parsley flakes
¼ teaspoon garlic powder
1 (16 ounce) package, cubed Mexican Velveeta® cheese
4 boneless, skinless chicken breast halves, cooked, diced

- Melt butter in large saucepan or roasting pan and saute onion and carrots for 10 minutes, but do not brown.

- Add remaining ingredients and heat but do not boil.

- Reduce heat to low, cook until cheese melts and stir constantly.

- Serve piping hot. Serves 8 to 12. *Breckenridge, Colorado*

TIP: *This is really the easy way to make chicken soup and if you are in an absolute rush, you could even use 2 (12 ounce) cans chicken. Leftover turkey could be substituted for chicken.*

Zesty Chicken Stew

8 boneless, skinless chicken thighs
¼ cup flour
3 tablespoons olive oil
¾ teaspoon dried oregano
¾ teaspoon dried basil
1 large onion, chopped
1 cup white cooking wine
1 (14 ounce) can chicken broth
3 medium red potatoes, peeled, diced
1 (15 ounce) can diced tomatoes, drained
1 (8 ounce) can sliced carrots, drained
3 tablespoons chopped fresh cilantro
Brown rice, cooked

- Lightly dredge chicken in flour and shake to remove excess.

- Brown chicken in hot oil in large heavy pan over medium-high heat for 4 minutes on each side and set aside.

- Combine oregano, basil and a little salt and pepper in bowl and sprinkle mixture evenly over chicken.

- Saute onion in remaining oil, stir in wine and cook for 2 minutes. Return chicken to pan and add broth, potatoes, tomatoes and carrots.

- Reduce heat and simmer, stirring occasionally, for 45 minutes. Stir in cilantro and serve over rice. Serves 6 to 8. *Arkoma, Oklahoma*

Speedy Taco Soup

1 (12 ounce) can chicken with juice
1 (14 ounce) can chicken broth
1 (16 ounce) jar mild thick-and-chunky salsa
1 (15 ounce) can ranch-style beans

- Combine chicken, broth, salsa and beans in large saucepan.

- Bring to a boil, reduce heat and simmer for 15 minutes. Serves 8. *Bayard, New Mexico*

TIP: A 15-ounce can whole kernel corn may also be added.

Tempting Tortilla Soup

*Don't let the number of ingredients keep you
from serving this. It's really easy.*

3 large boneless, skinless chicken breast halves, cooked, cubed
1 (10 ounce) package frozen corn, thawed
1 onion, chopped
3 (14 ounce) cans chicken broth
2 (10 ounce) cans tomatoes and green chilies
2 teaspoons ground cumin
1 teaspoon chili powder
1 clove garlic, minced
6 corn tortillas

- Combine all ingredients except tortillas in large soup pot. Bring to a boil, reduce heat and simmer for 35 minutes.

- Preheat oven to 350°.

- While soup simmers, cut tortillas into 1-inch strips and place on baking sheet. Bake for about 5 minutes or until crisp.

- Serve tortilla strips with each serving of soup. Serves 6 to 8. *Black Canyon City, Arizona*

Creamy Chicken-Spinach Soup

1 (9 ounce) package refrigerated cheese tortellini
2 (14 ounce) cans chicken broth, divided
1 (10 ounce) can cream of chicken soup
1 (12 ounce) can white chicken meat with liquid
1 (10 ounce) package frozen chopped spinach
2 cups milk
½ teaspoon dried thyme

- Cook tortellini in soup pot with 1 can chicken broth according to package directions.

- Stir in remaining broth, soup, chicken, spinach, milk, 1 teaspoon salt, ½ teaspoon pepper and thyme. Bring to a boil, reduce heat to low and simmer for 10 minutes. Serves 8. *Abingdon, Illinois*

Speedy Creamy Broccoli-Rice Soup

1 (6 ounce) package chicken and wild rice mix
1 (10 ounce) package frozen chopped broccoli
2 (10 ounce) cans cream of chicken soup
1 (12 ounce) can chicken breast chunks

- Combine rice mix, seasoning packet and 5 cups water in soup pot. Bring to a boil, reduce heat and simmer for 15 minutes.

- Stir in broccoli, chicken soup and chicken. Cover and simmer for an additional 5 minutes. Serves 8. *Amberely, Ohio*

Chicken-Noodle Soup

1 (3 ounce) package chicken-flavored ramen noodles, broken
1 (10 ounce) package frozen green peas, thawed
1 (4 ounce) jar sliced mushrooms
3 cups cooked, cubed chicken or deli turkey

- Heat 2¼ cups water in large saucepan to boiling and add ramen noodles, contents of seasoning packet and peas. (It's even better if you add 2 tablespoons butter.)

- Heat to boiling, reduce heat to medium and cook for about 5 minutes. Stir in mushrooms and chicken and continue cooking over medium heat until all ingredients heat through. Serves 8. *Algona, Washington*

TIP: Garnish with about 1 cup lightly crushed potato chips, if desired.

Cheesy Chicken Soup

1 (10 ounce) can fiesta nacho cheese soup
1 (10 ounce) can cream of chicken soup
1 (10 ounce) soup can milk
1 chicken bouillon cube or 1 teaspoon bouillon granules

- Mix all ingredients in saucepan and stir until smooth. Serve hot. Serves 4. *Atoka, Oklahoma*

All-American Soup

3 boneless, skinless chicken breast halves, cut into strips
1 onion, chopped
Oil
1 (10 ounce) can tomatoes and green chilies
2 (14 ounce) cans chicken broth
3 large baking potatoes, peeled, cubed
1 (10 ounce) can cream of celery soup
1 cup milk
1 teaspoon dried basil
1 (8 ounce) package shredded Velveeta® cheese
½ cup sour cream

- Brown and cook chicken strips and onion in large saucepan with a little oil for about 10 minutes.

- Add tomatoes and green chilies, chicken broth, and potatoes. Boil and cook for 15 minutes or until potatoes are tender.

- Stir in soup, milk, basil and 1 teaspoon salt. Cook on medium heat and stir constantly until thoroughly hot.

- Stir in cheese until cheese melts. Remove from heat and stir in sour cream. Serves 6 to 10. *Belle View, Virginia*

Tasty Turkey Soup

1 (16 ounce) package frozen chopped onions and bell peppers
Oil
2 (3 ounce) packages chicken-flavored ramen noodles
2 (10 ounce) cans cream of chicken soup
1 cup cubed turkey

- Cook onions and bell peppers in soup pot with a little oil just until tender but not brown.

- Add ramen noodles, seasoning packets and 2 cups water. Cook for 5 minutes or until noodles are tender.

- Stir in chicken soup and cubed turkey. Heat, stirring constantly, until thoroughly hot. Serves 6 to 8. *Bay Ridge, Maryland*

Supper-Ready Potato Soup

1 (18 ounce) package frozen hash-brown potatoes with onions
    and peppers, thawed
2 (14 ounce) cans chicken broth
3 ribs celery, finely chopped
2 (10 ounce) cans cream of chicken soup
2 cups milk
2 cups chopped ham
2 teaspoons minced garlic
1 teaspoon dried parsley flakes

• Combine hash-brown potatoes, broth and celery in large soup pot and
  boil. Reduce heat and simmer for 25 minutes.

• Pour in soup and milk and stir until mixture is smooth. Add ham,
  garlic, parsley and ½ teaspoon pepper. Bring to a boil, stir constantly,
  immediately reduce heat and simmer for 10 minutes. Serves 12.
  American Falls, Idaho

Navy Bean Soup

3 (15 ounce) cans navy beans with liquid
1 cup chopped ham
1 large onion, chopped
½ teaspoon garlic powder

• Combine beans, ham, onion and garlic powder in large saucepan.

• Add 1 cup water and bring to a boil. Simmer until onion is
  tender-crisp. Serve hot with cornbread. Serves 6 to 8. *Ada, Michigan*

Easy Pork Tenderloin Stew

This is a great recipe for leftover pork or beef.

2 - 3 cups cooked, cubed pork
1 (12 ounce) jar pork gravy
¼ cup chili sauce
1 (16 ounce) package frozen stew vegetables

• Combine pork, gravy, chili sauce, stew vegetables and ½ cup water in
  soup pot.

• Bring to a boil and boil for 2 minutes; reduce heat and simmer for
  10 minutes. Serve with cornbread or hot biscuits. Serves 8.
  Anandale, Louisiana

Spaghetti Soup

1 (7 ounce) package precut spaghetti
1 (18 ounce) package frozen, cooked meatballs, thawed
1 (28 ounce) jar spaghetti sauce
1 (15 ounce) can Mexican stewed tomatoes

- Cook spaghetti in soup pot with 3 quarts boiling water and a little salt for about 6 minutes (no need to drain).

- When spaghetti is done, add meatballs, spaghetti sauce and stewed tomatoes and cook until mixture heats through. Serves 8 to 10. *Agua Fria, New Mexico*

TIP: To garnish each soup bowl, sprinkle with 2 tablespoons mozzarella cheese or whatever cheese you have.

Meatball Stew

1 (18 ounce) package frozen, cooked Italian meatballs
1 (14 ounce) can beef broth
2 (15 ounce) cans Italian stewed tomatoes
1 (16 ounce) package frozen stew vegetables

- Place meatballs, beef broth and stewed tomatoes in large saucepan. Bring to a boil, reduce heat and simmer for 10 minutes or until meatballs are thoroughly hot.

- Add vegetables and cook on medium heat for 10 minutes. Mixture will be fairly thin.

- If you like thicker stew, mix 2 tablespoons cornstarch in ¼ cup water and stir into stew, bring to a boil and stir constantly until stew thickens. Serves 8 to 10. *Bar Harbor, Maine*

Easy Meaty Minestrone

2 (20 ounce) cans minestrone soup
1 (15 ounce) can pinto beans with juice
1 (18 ounce) package frozen Italian meatballs, thawed
1 (5 ounce) package grated parmesan cheese

- Combine soup, beans, meatballs and ½ cup water in large saucepan. Bring to a boil, reduce heat to low and simmer for about 15 minutes.

- To serve, sprinkle each serving with parmesan cheese. Serves 8. *Akron, New York*

Italian Vegetable Soup

1 pound lean ground beef
2 teaspoons minced garlic
1 green bell pepper, seeded, chopped
2 (14 ounce) cans beef broth
1 (15 ounce) can Italian stewed tomatoes
2 small zucchini, sliced
1 (15 ounce) can cannellini beans, rinsed, drained
1 (10 ounce) package frozen chopped spinach, thawed

- Brown and cook beef and garlic in soup pot for 5 minutes or until beef crumbles.

- Stir in bell pepper, broth, tomatoes, zucchini and beans and cook on medium heat for 15 minutes.

- Add spinach and continue cooking for an additional 10 minutes. Serves 6 to 8. *Fair Haven, Vermont*

Down-Home Beefy Soup

1½ pounds lean ground beef
1 (16 ounce) package frozen onions and peppers
2 teaspoons minced garlic
2 (14 ounce) cans beef broth
2 (15 ounce) cans Italian stewed tomatoes
1 tablespoon Italian seasoning
1½ cups macaroni
Shredded cheddar cheese

- Brown and cook beef, onions and peppers, and garlic in soup pot on medium heat. Add beef broth, 2 cups water, stewed tomatoes and Italian seasoning and boil for 2 minutes.

- Add macaroni and cook, stirring occasionally on medium heat for about 15 minutes.

- When serving, sprinkle cheese over each serving. Serves 8. *Acton, Massachusetts*

Chunky Beefy Noodle Soup

1 pound beef round steak, cubed
1 onion, chopped
2 ribs celery, sliced
1 tablespoon oil
1 tablespoon chili powder
½ teaspoon dried oregano
1 (15 ounce) can stewed tomatoes
2 (14 ounce) cans beef broth
½ (8 ounce) package egg noodles
1 green bell pepper, seeded, chopped

- Cook and stir steak, onion and celery in soup pot with oil for 15 minutes or until beef browns.

- Stir in 2 cups water, 1 teaspoon salt, chili powder, oregano, stewed tomatoes and beef broth. Bring to a boil, reduce heat and simmer for 1 hour 30 minutes to 2 hours or until beef is tender.

- Stir in noodles and bell pepper and heat to boiling. Reduce heat and simmer for 10 to 15 minutes or until noodles are tender. Serves 8.
Benton City, Washington

Cadillac Chili

1½ pounds lean ground beef
2 pounds chili ground beef
1 onion, chopped
Oil
1 (15 ounce) can tomato sauce
1 (10 ounce) can diced tomatoes and green chilies
¼ cup ground cumin
1 teaspoon oregano
2 tablespoons chili powder
1 (15 ounce) can pinto beans with liquid, optional

- Combine meats and onion in a little oil in large roasting pan and brown. Add tomato sauce, tomatoes and green chilies, cumin, oregano, chili powder, 2 cups water and a little salt. Bring to a boil, reduce heat and simmer for 2 hours.

- Add beans, if you like, and heat until thoroughly hot. Serves 8 to 10.
Anahuac, Texas

Blue Norther Stew

*Cold fronts in the south are called northers. This is
a great choice for one of those cold, winter days.*

1½ pounds lean ground beef
1 onion, chopped
1 (1 ounce) packet taco seasoning
1 (1 ounce) packet ranch dressing mix
1 (15 ounce) can whole kernel corn, drained
1 (15 ounce) can kidney beans with liquid
2 (15 ounce) cans pinto beans with liquid
2 (15 ounce) cans Mexican stewed tomatoes
1 (10 ounce) can tomatoes and green chilies

• Brown ground beef and onion in large roasting pan. Add both packets
  seasonings and mix well.

• Add corn, both beans, stewed tomatoes, tomatoes and green chilies,
  and 1 cup water, mix well and simmer for about 30 minutes. Serves
  10 to 14. *Baldwin, Louisiana*

Chili Soup Warmer

1 (10 ounce) can tomato bisque soup
1 (10 ounce) can chili
1 (10 ounce) can fiesta chili-beef soup
1(15 ounce) can chicken broth
Crackers

• Combine tomato bisque soup, chili, fiesta chili-beef soup and broth in
  saucepan. Add amount of water to produce desired thickness of soup.

• Heat and serve hot with crackers. Serves 4. *Ashville, Alabama*

Rich Cheddar Chowder

2 (14 ounce) cans chicken broth
4 baking potatoes, peeled, diced
1 onion, chopped
1 cup shredded carrots
1 green bell pepper, seeded, chopped
1 red bell pepper, seeded, chopped
¼ cup (½ stick) butter
⅓ cup flour
1 (1 pint) carton half-and-half cream
1½ cups milk
1 (16 ounce) package shredded sharp cheddar cheese
⅛ - ¼ teaspoon hot sauce

- Combine broth, potatoes, onion, carrots and bell peppers in large soup pot. Bring to a boil, reduce heat and simmer for 15 minutes.

- Melt butter in large saucepan, add flour and stir until smooth. Cook for 1 minute and stir constantly. Gradually add half-and-half cream and milk; cook over medium heat and stir constantly until sauce thickens.

- Add sauce and cheese to vegetable mixture and cook just until thoroughly hot; do not boil. Serves 8 to 10. *Algoma, Wisconsin*

Yellow Squash Soup

2 pounds fresh, yellow squash, thinly sliced
1 onion, chopped
1 (14 ounce) can chicken broth
1 (8 ounce) carton sour cream

- Simmer squash and onions in broth in saucepan until very tender. Refrigerate. Just before serving, add sour cream and a little salt and pepper. Serve cold. Serves 6. *Akron, Pennsylvania*

Swiss-Vegetable Soup

1 (1 ounce) packet dry vegetable soup mix
1 cup half-and-half cream
1½ cups shredded Swiss cheese
Crackers

- Combine soup mix and 3 cups water in saucepan and boil. Lower heat and simmer for about 10 minutes. Add half-and-half cream and cheese and serve hot. Serve with crackers. Serves 6. *Alburtis, Pennsylvania*

Tomato-French Onion Soup

1 (10 ounce) can tomato bisque soup
2 (10 ounce) cans French onion soup
Croutons
Grated parmesan cheese

- Combine soups and 2 soup cans water in saucepan. Heat until thoroughly hot.

- Serve in bowls topped with croutons and a sprinkle of parmesan cheese. Serve 3 to 4. *Ball, Louisiana*

Easy Spinach Soup

2 (10 ounce) packages frozen chopped spinach, cooked
2 (10 ounce) cans cream of mushroom soup
1 cup half-and-half cream
1 (14 ounce) can chicken broth

- Place spinach, mushroom soup and half-and-half cream in blender and puree until smooth.

- Place spinach mixture and chicken broth in saucepan and heat on medium heat until hot.

- Reduce heat to low and simmer for 20 minutes. Serve hot or cold. Serves 6 to 8. *Ardmore, Indiana*

Avocado-Cream Soup

4 ripe avocados, peeled, diced, divided
1½ cups whipping cream, divided
2 (14 ounce) cans chicken broth
¼ cup dry sherry

- Blend half avocados and half cream in bowl. Repeat with remaining avocados and cream.

- Bring broth to a boil in saucepan, reduce heat and stir in avocado puree.

- Add 1 teaspoon salt and sherry and refrigerate thoroughly. Serves 6 to 8. *Beaver Dam, Kentucky*

Crunchy Peanut Soup

2 (10 ounce) cans cream of chicken soup
2 soup cans milk
1¼ cups crunchy peanut butter
½ teaspoon celery salt

- Blend soup and milk in saucepan on medium heat.

- Stir in peanut butter and celery salt and heat until they blend well.
  Serves 4. *Adairsville, Georgia*

Spiked Crab Soup

1 (1 ounce) packet dry onion soup mix
1 (6 ounce) can crabmeat with juice, flaked
1 (8 ounce) carton whipping cream
½ cup white wine

- Dissolve soup mix with 2 cups water in saucepan.

- Add crabmeat with crab juice and whipping cream. Season with
  a little salt and pepper.

- Heat, but do not boil, and simmer for 20 minutes.

- Stir in wine, heat and serve warm. Serves 6. *Allendale,
  South Carolina*

"Fish of the Day" Chowder 🍁

Nova Scotia, Canada, attracted the social traditions of the British. They feasted on mutton pies, beef stew, berries and fried oysters; and they enjoyed an abundance of molasses, which they called treacle.

2 pounds cod fillets (can use haddock or other white fish)
6 bacon slices, cut into 1-inch pieces
1 onion, chopped
2 ribs celery, sliced
½ red bell pepper, seeded, chopped
2 tablespoons flour
1 (14 ounce) can chicken broth
2 cups peeled, diced potatoes
1 (1 pint) carton half-and-half cream

- Cut fillets into medium size pieces and set aside. Cook bacon in skillet until crisp and brown; set aside. Add onion, celery and bell pepper to remaining fat and saute until tender.

- Stir in flour on medium-high heat and slowly add chick broth, potatoes and a little salt and pepper. Cook for about 10 minutes or until potatoes are tender.

- Stir in fish pieces, bring to a boil; reduce heat to medium-low heat and simmer for about 10 minutes or until fish flakes. Stir in half-and-half cream and heat for about 10 minutes, but do not bring to a boil.

- Serve in individual bowls with bacon pieces on top. Serves 6.
  Antigonish, Nova Scotia, Canada

★ ★ ★

Salads

Many easy to assemble salads (there
are 124 plus 30 dressings) with fruit,
pasta, veggies or meat can be a main dish!

**1001
Community
Recipes**

Salads Contents

Salads Contents

Sunday Special Apple Salad

1 (20 ounce) can crushed pineapple with juice
⅔ cup sugar
1 tablespoon flour
1 tablespoon white vinegar
1 (12 ounce) carton whipped topping, thawed
3 red delicious apples with peels, diced
1 (10 ounce) package miniature marshmallows
½ cup roasted peanuts

- Drain pineapple, save juice and set pineapple aside. Combine juice, sugar, flour and vinegar in saucepan, mix well.

- Place on medium heat and cook, stirring constantly, until mixture thickens. Set aside to cool.

- Transfer to large salad bowl and fold in whipped topping, pineapple, apples and marshmallows and refrigerate. To serve, sprinkle peanuts over top of salad. Serves 8. *Amery, Wisconsin*

Stained-Glass Fruit Salad

2 (20 ounce) cans peach pie filling
3 bananas, sliced
1 (16 ounce) package frozen unsweetened strawberries, drained
1 (20 ounce) can pineapple tidbits, drained

- Mix all ingredients in bowl. Cover and refrigerate overnight.

- When ready to serve, place in pretty crystal bowl. Serves 8 to 10. *Almont, Michigan*

Pistachio Salad or Dessert

1 (20 ounce) can crushed pineapple with juice
1 (3 ounce) package instant pistachio pudding
2 cups miniature marshmallows
1 cup chopped pecans
1 (8 ounce) carton whipped topping, thawed

- Place pineapple in large bowl and sprinkle with pudding mix.

- Add marshmallows and pecans and fold in whipped topping.

- Pour into crystal serving dish and refrigerate. Serves 12. *Bethany, Missouri*

Pink Salad

1 (6 ounce) package raspberry gelatin
1 (20 ounce) can crushed pineapple with juice
1 cup small curd cottage cheese
1 (8 ounce) carton whipped topping, thawed
¼ cup chopped pecans

- Place gelatin in large bowl.

- Combine juice from pineapple and, if necessary, enough water to make 1¼ cups liquid in saucepan. Heat, pour over gelatin and mix well.

- Refrigerate just until gelatin begins to thicken.

- Fold in cottage cheese, whipped topping and pecans.

- Pour into molds or 9 x 13-inch dish and refrigerate. Serves 12.
  Angier, North Carolina

Pear Mousse

2 (15 ounce) cans sliced pears with juice
1 (6 ounce) package lemon gelatin
1 (8 ounce) package cream cheese, softened
1 (8 ounce) carton whipped topping, thawed

- Drain pears and set aside juice. Add enough water to juice to equal ¾ cup and heat in saucepan. Heat juice to boiling point. Add gelatin. Mix well and cool.

- Place pears and cream cheese in blender and process until smooth.

- Place in large bowl and fold in cooled but not congealed gelatin mixture and whipped topping. Mix until smooth.

- Pour into individual dessert dishes. Cover with plastic wrap and refrigerate. Serves 6 to 8. *Belvedere, Virginia*

TIP: *To garnish, place a slice of kiwifruit on top of mousse.*

Peachy Fruit Salad

2 (20 ounce) cans peach pie filling
1 (20 ounce) can pineapple chunks, drained
1 (11 ounce) can mandarin oranges, drained
1 (8 ounce) jar maraschino cherries, drained
1 cup miniature marshmallows

- Combine all ingredients in large bowl, fold together gently and refrigerate.

- Serve in pretty crystal bowl. (Bananas may be added, if you like.) Serves 10 to 12. *Alamo, Georgia*

Orange-Pear Salad

1 (15 ounce) can sliced pears with juice
1 (6 ounce) package orange gelatin
1 (8 ounce) package cream cheese, softened
1 (8 ounce) carton whipped topping, thawed

- Boil juice from pears with ½ cup water in saucepan. Add gelatin and dissolve. Mix thoroughly and refrigerate until partially set.

- Blend pears and cream cheese in blender. Fold in pear mixture and whipped topping into gelatin mixture and blend well.

- Pour into 7 x 11-inch shallow dish and refrigerate. Serves 9. *Berryville, Virginia*

Orange Glow

1 (6 ounce) package orange gelatin
1 cup finely grated carrots
1 (15 ounce) can crushed pineapple with juice
¾ cup chopped pecans

- Combine gelatin with 1 cup boiling water in bowl and mix well until it dissolves. Add carrots, pineapple and pecans.

- Pour into 7 x 11-inch glass dish. Refrigerate until congealed. Serves 9. *Barboursville, West Virginia*

Mango Salad

1 (3 ounce) package apricot gelatin
2 (3 ounce) packages lemon gelatin
1 (8 ounce) package cream cheese, softened
2 (15 ounce) cans mangoes with juice

- Dissolve gelatins in 1¾ cups boiling water in bowl.

- In separate bowl, beat cream cheese until creamy. Add mangoes and juice and beat (canned mangoes are soft and will beat well) until mangoes are in pieces.

- Add mango mixture to gelatin and pour into sprayed 2-quart mold. It will make 12 to 14 little individual molds if you prefer. Serves 12.
  Buena Vista, Colorado

TIP: This could make a delightful light dessert molded in a sherbet dish with a little shortbread cookie placed on the dessert plate.

Tropical Mango Salad

2 (15 ounce) cans mangoes with juice
1 (6 ounce) package orange gelatin
1 (8 ounce) package cream cheese, softened
½ (8 ounce) carton whipped topping, thawed

- Drain juice from mangoes and set aside. Cut mango slices in bite-size pieces; set aside. Place ½ cup mango juice and 1 cup water in saucepan and bring to boiling. (If needed, add more water to equal total liquid of 1½ cups.

- Pour over gelatin in bowl and mix well until gelatin dissolves.

- Add cream cheese and start mixer very slowly. Gradually increase speed until cream cheese mixes into gelatin. Add to mango pieces.

- Place in refrigerator until it congeals slightly. Fold in whipped topping.

- Pour into 7 x 11-inch dish and refrigerate. Serves 8.
  Alturas, California

Cream Cheese-Mango Salad

2 (15 ounce) cans mangoes with juice
1 (6 ounce) package lemon gelatin
2 (8 ounces) cream cheese, softened
1 (8 ounce) can crushed pineapple with juice

- Drain juice from mangoes. Combine juice and enough water to make ¾ cup liquid in saucepan. Bring to a boil and add gelatin. Stir until it dissolves.

- Cream mangoes and cream cheese in bowl. Fold in pineapple. Mix into hot gelatin and pour into mold or individual dishes. Serves 6. *Alma, Arkansas*

Mandarin Fluff

2 (11 ounce) cans mandarin oranges, well drained
1 (14 ounce) can pineapple tidbits, well drained
1 cup miniature marshmallows
1 (8 ounce) carton whipped topping, thawed
½ cup chopped pecans

- Place oranges and pineapple in bowl and stir in marshmallows. (Make sure marshmallows are not stuck together.) Fold in whipped topping and pecans and refrigerate.

- Serve in individual sherbet glasses. Serves 6. *Attica, Indiana*

Luscious Strawberry Salad

1 (6 ounce) package strawberry gelatin
2 (10 ounce) boxes frozen strawberries, thawed
3 bananas, sliced
1 (8 ounce) carton sour cream

- Dissolve gelatin in 1 cup boiling water in bowl and mix well. Add strawberries and bananas.

- Pour half mixture in 9 x 13-inch dish and leave all bananas in bottom layer. Refrigerate until firm.

- Spread sour cream over firm gelatin.

- Add remaining gelatin over sour cream. Refrigerate until firm. Serves 6. *Andrews, South Carolina*

Fantastic Fruit Salad

2 (11 ounce) cans mandarin oranges
2 (15 ounce) cans pineapple chunks
1 (16 ounce) carton frozen strawberries, thawed
1 (20 ounce) can peach pie filling
1 (20 ounce) can apricot pie filling

• Drain oranges, pineapple and strawberries.

• Combine all ingredients in bowl and fold together gently. Serves 10 to 14. *Castle Hills, Delaware*

TIP: If you have several bananas, add them too.

Divinity Salad

1 (6 ounce) package lemon gelatin
1 (8 ounce) package cream cheese, softened
¾ cup chopped pecans
1 (15 ounce) can crushed pineapple with juice
1 (8 ounce) carton whipped topping, thawed

• Blend gelatin with 1 cup boiling water in bowl with mixer until it dissolves.

• Add cream cheese, beat slowly and increase speed until smooth. Add pecans and pineapple and cool in refrigerator until nearly set.

• Fold in whipped topping. Pour into 9 x 13-inch dish and refrigerate. Serves 9 to 12. *Boonsboro, Maryland*

Creamy Salad Supreme

1 (6 ounce) package orange gelatin
1 (8 ounce) package cream cheese, softened
2 (15 ounce) cans mangoes with juice
2 (10 ounce) cans mandarin oranges, drained

• Place gelatin in bowl and pour ¾ cup boiling water over gelatin and mix well until gelatin dissolves. Let partially cool and add cream cheese. At very slow speed at first, beat in cream cheese until it mixes well.

• Fold in mangoes and mandarin oranges. Pour into 8-cup mold. Refrigerate for several hours. Serves 8. *Angels Camp, California*

Cold Cola Salad

1 (6 ounce) package cherry gelatin
1 (10 ounce) bottle maraschino cherries, drained
1 cup cola soda
1 cup chopped pecans

- Dissolve gelatin in ¾ cup boiling water in bowl.

- Chop cherries into 4 slices each. Add cherries, cola and pecans to gelatin. Pour into 8-cup mold.

- Refrigerate until firm. Serves 6. *Andalusia, Pennsylvania*

Cinnamon Salad

2 (6 ounce) packages cherry gelatin
⅓ cup cinnamon red-hot candies
1 (25 ounce) jar applesauce
2 teaspoons lemon juice

- Heat 3 cups water in large saucepan to boil, add gelatin and stir until it dissolves. Reduce heat to moderately low and add candies. Continue to heat and stir until candies dissolve. Remove mixture from heat and add in applesauce and lemon juice.

- Pour half gelatin mixture into 9 x 13-inch baking dish and set aside remaining gelatin mixture at room temperature. Place first layer in freezer for 1 hour or until set.

Filling:

2 (8 ounce) packages cream cheese, softened
1 cup mayonnaise
1 cup chopped walnuts
Lettuce leaves

- Beat cream cheese and mayonnaise in bowl and beat until fairly smooth and mix in walnuts. When first layer of gelatin sets, spread cream cheese mixture over top.

- Refrigerate for 30 minutes and pour remaining gelatin mixture over cream cheese layer. Refrigerate for several hours. Serve on lettuce leaves. Serves 12. *Blackstone, Virginia*

Coconut-Orange Salad

1 (6 ounce) package orange gelatin
1 pint vanilla ice cream, softened
½ cup flaked coconut
1 (11 ounce) can mandarin oranges, drained

- Dissolve gelatin in 1 cup boiling water in bowl and cool slightly. Fold in ice cream, coconut and oranges.

- Pour into 7 x 11-inch dish and freeze. Serves 6. *Ayer, Massachusetts*

Cherry Squares

1 (6 ounce) package cherry gelatin
1 (20 ounce) can cherry pie filling
1 (8 ounce) can crushed pineapple with juice
1 cup lemon-lime soda, chilled
Shredded lettuce

- Dissolve gelatin in 1 cup boiling water in bowl, mixing well. Stir in cherry pie filling and crushed pineapple. Slowly stir in soda (mixture will foam a little). Pour into 9-inch square dish; cover and refrigerate for several hours until firm.

- Cut into squares to serve and place on bed of shredded lettuce. Serves 9. *Arcadia, Wisconsin*

Cherry Salad

1 (20 ounce) can cherry pie filling
1 (20 ounce) can crushed pineapple, drained
1 (14 ounce) can sweetened condensed milk
1 cup miniature marshmallows
1 cup chopped pecans
1 (8 ounce) carton whipped topping, thawed

- Combine pie filling, pineapple, sweetened condensed milk, marshmallows and pecans in large bowl.

- Fold in whipped topping, refrigerate and serve in pretty crystal bowl. Serves 10. *Argentine, Michigan*

TIP: Add a couple drops of red food coloring if you like a brighter color.

Watergate Salad

1 (20 ounce) can crushed pineapple with juice
2 (3 ounce) packages pistachio instant pudding mix
¾ cup chopped pecans
1 (12 ounce) carton whipped topping, thawed

- Mix pineapple with instant pudding mix in bowl until it thickens slightly. Add pecans.

- Mix well and fold in whipped topping.

- Pour into pretty crystal bowl and refrigerate. Serves 8. *Black Diamond, Washington*

TIP: *One cup miniature marshmallows may be added.*

Butter-Mint Salad

1 (6 ounce) box lime gelatin
1 (20 ounce) can crushed pineapple with juice
½ (10 ounce) bag miniature marshmallows
1 (8 ounce) carton whipped topping, thawed
1 (8 ounce) bag butter mints, crushed

- Mix gelatin with pineapple in bowl. Stir in marshmallows and refrigerate overnight.

- Fold in whipped topping and butter mints. Pour into 9 x 13-inch dish and freeze. Serves 9 to 12. *Amelia, Ohio*

Frozen Dessert Salad

1 (8 ounce) package cream cheese, softened
1 cup powdered sugar
1 (10 ounce) box frozen strawberries, thawed
1 (15 ounce) can crushed pineapple, drained
1 (8 ounce) carton whipped topping, thawed

- Beat cream cheese and powdered sugar in bowl and fold in strawberries, pineapple and whipped topping. (This will be even better if you stir in ¾ cup chopped pecans.)

- Pour into 9 x 9-inch pan and freeze.

- Cut into squares to serve. Serves 9 to 12. *Goffstown, New Hampshire*

Cottage Cheese-Fruit Salad

1 (6 ounce) package orange gelatin
1 (16 ounce) carton small curd cottage cheese
2 (11 ounce) cans mandarin oranges, drained
1 (20 ounce) can chunk pineapple, drained
1 (8 ounce) carton whipped topping, thawed

- Sprinkle gelatin over cottage cheese in bowl and mix well. Add oranges and pineapple and mix well.

- Fold in whipped topping, refrigerate and serve in pretty crystal bowl. Serves 10. *Devonshire, Delaware*

Chilled Cranberry Salad

1 (14 ounce) can sweetened condensed milk
⅓ cup lemon juice
1 (20 ounce) can crushed pineapple, drained
1 (16 ounce) can whole cranberry sauce
3 cups miniature marshmallows
Dash of red food coloring, optional
1 (8 ounce) carton whipped topping, thawed

- Combine sweetened condensed milk and lemon juice in large bowl and mix well. Add pineapple, cranberry sauce and marshmallows and stir until they blend well. Add food coloring for a brighter color.

- Fold in whipped topping and spoon into 9 x 13-inch dish and refrigerate. Let dish stand for about 15 minutes before cutting into squares. Serves 10 to 12. *Bridgton, Maine*

Cranapple Wiggle

A family friend made this recipe a tradition.

1 (6 ounce) package cherry gelatin
1 (16 ounce) can whole cranberry sauce
1 (15 ounce) can crushed pineapple with juice
1 cup chopped apples
1 cup chopped pecans

- Dissolve gelatin in 1½ cups boiling water in bowl and mix well. Add cranberry sauce, pineapple, apples and pecans.

- Pour into sprayed 9 x 13-inch glass dish and refrigerate. Stir about the time it begins to set so the apples will not all stay on top. Serves 12. *Bessemer, Michigan*

Cranberry Mousse

1 (15 ounce) can jellied cranberry sauce
1 (8 ounce) can crushed pineapple, drained
1 (8 ounce) carton sour cream
1 tablespoon mayonnaise

- Place cranberry sauce and crushed pineapple in saucepan. Cook until cranberry sauce liquefies.

- Fold in sour cream and mayonnaise.

- Pour into molds or muffin pan and freeze. Serves 6.
  Randolph, Vermont

Cranberry Salad

1 (6 ounce) package cherry gelatin
1 (16 ounce) can whole cranberry sauce
1 pint sour cream
¾ cup chopped pecans

- Dissolve gelatin in 1¼ cups boiling water in bowl. When it mixes, add cranberry sauce.

- Mix well and refrigerate until it begins to congeal. Add sour cream and pecans and mix well.

- Pour into 7 x 11-inch baking dish. Refrigerate for several hours before serving. Serves 6 to 8. *Bonners Ferry, Idaho*

Cranberry Waldorf Salad

3 red delicious apples with peel, cubed
⅔ cup coarsely chopped pecans
¾ cup Craisins®
⅓ cup shredded cheddar cheese
Dressing:
⅓ cup mayonnaise
2 tablespoons sugar

- Combine apples, pecans and Craisins® in salad bowl.

- In separate bowl, combine mayonnaise and sugar; add to salad mixture and toss. Refrigerate for at least 1 to 2 hours.

- When ready to serve, sprinkle cheese over top of salad. Serves 4.
  Alden, New York

Festive Cranberry Salad

1 (6 ounce) package raspberry gelatin
1 (20 ounce) can crushed pineapple
1 (16 ounce) can whole cranberries
⅔ cup chopped walnuts

- Place gelatin in bowl and pour in 1½ cups boiling water, mixing well until it dissolves. Stir in pineapple, cranberries and walnuts.

- Transfer to 7 x 11-inch glass baking dish. Refrigerate for several hours.

- Cut into squares to serve. Serves 8. *Brewster, Washington*

Classic Apple-Cranberry Salad

½ cup mayonnaise
2 tablespoons peanut butter
1 teaspoon lemon juice
½ teaspoon sugar
2 gala apples with peel, chopped
2 celery ribs, chopped
⅓ cup cherry-flavored Craisins®
1 cup shredded lettuce
¼ cup chopped pecans

- Whisk mayonnaise, peanut butter, lemon juice and sugar in bowl.

- Add apples, celery and Craisins® and toss to coat well. Cover and refrigerate for 1 hour.

- Arrange lettuce on serving platter, top with chilled apple mixture and sprinkle evenly with pecans. Serves 4 to 6. *Aitkin, Minnesota*

Frozen Holiday Salad

2 (3 ounce) packages cream cheese, softened
3 tablespoons mayonnaise
¼ cup sugar
1 (16 ounce) can whole cranberry sauce
1 (8 ounce) can crushed pineapple, drained
1 cup chopped pecans
1 cup miniature marshmallows
1 (8 ounce) carton whipped topping, thawed

- Beat cream cheese, mayonnaise and sugar in bowl until smooth.

- Add cranberry sauce, pineapple, pecans and marshmallows and fold in whipped topping.

- Pour into sprayed 9 x 13-inch glass dish and freeze.

- When ready to serve, take salad out of freezer a few minutes before cutting into squares. Serves 9 to 12. *Alma, Georgia*

Chicken-Artichoke Salad

4 cups cooked, chopped chicken breasts
1 (14 ounce) can artichoke hearts, drained chopped
½ cup chopped walnuts
1 cup chopped, seeded red bell pepper
⅔ cup mayonnaise

- Combine all ingredients with a little salt and pepper in bowl.

- Cover and refrigerate until ready to serve. Serves 4 to 6.
  Baldwin City, Kansas

TIP: *This can be a hot salad if you place a lot of salad on slices of toasted Texas toast. Sprinkle it with shredded cheddar cheese and bake at 400° for 10 minutes. A hot salad for a cold night!*

Chicken Salad

3 cups boneless, skinless chicken breast halves, cooked, chopped
1½ cups chopped celery
½ cup sweet pickle relish
2 eggs, hard-boiled, chopped
¾ cup mayonnaise

- Combine all ingredients and a little salt and pepper in bowl. Serves 4.
  Anson, Texas

Light Chicken Salad Supper

1 rotisserie-cooked chicken
1 cup halved red and green grapes
2 cups chopped celery
⅔ cup walnut halves
⅔ cup sliced onion

- Skin chicken, cut chicken breast in thin strips and place in bowl. Add remaining ingredients.

Dressing:

½ cup mayonnaise
1 tablespoon orange juice
2 tablespoons red wine vinegar
1 teaspoon chili powder
1 teaspoon paprika

- Combine all dressing ingredients in bowl, add a little salt and pepper and mix well. Spoon over salad mixture and toss.

- Cover and refrigerate. Serves 8 to 10. *Bethel Acres, Oklahoma*

Hawaiian Chicken Salad

3 cups cooked, diced chicken breasts
1 (20 ounce) can pineapple tidbits, well drained
1 cup halved red grapes
3 ribs celery, sliced
1 large ripe banana, sliced

- Combine chicken, pineapple, grapes and celery in bowl and toss. Cover and refrigerate.

- When ready to serve, add banana. Top with dressing and toss.

Dressing:

½ cup mayonnaise
¾ cup poppy seed dressing
½ cup salted peanuts

- Combine mayonnaise, poppy seed dressing and a little salt in bowl.

- Just before serving, sprinkle peanuts over top of salad. Serves 6. *Angwin, California*

Derby Chicken Salad

3 - 4 boneless, skinless chicken breast halves, cooked, cubed
¼ pound bacon, cooked, crumbled
2 avocados, peeled, diced
2 tomatoes, diced, drained
Italian dressing

- Combine chicken, bacon, avocados and tomatoes in bowl.

- When ready to serve, pour dressing over salad and toss. Refrigerate. Serves 4 to 6. *Brooks, Kentucky*

Apple-Walnut Chicken Salad

3 - 4 boneless skinless chicken breast halves, cooked, cubed
2 tart green apples, peeled, chopped
½ cup chopped pitted dates
1 cup finely chopped celery

- Mix all ingredients in bowl. Toss with dressing.

Dressing:

½ cup chopped walnuts
⅓ cup sour cream
⅓ cup mayonnaise
1 tablespoon lemon juice

- Toast walnuts at 300° for 10 minutes. Mix sour cream, mayonnaise and lemon juice. Mix with walnuts. Pour over chicken salad and toss. Refrigerate. Serves 4. *Burbank, Washington*

Chicken Caesar Salad

4 boneless, skinless chicken breast halves, grilled
1 (10 ounce) package romaine salad greens
½ cup shredded parmesan cheese
1 cup seasoned croutons
¾ cup Caesar dressing

- Cut chicken breasts into strips.

- Combine chicken, salad greens, parmesan cheese and croutons in large bowl.

- When ready to serve, toss with dressing. Serves 4 to 6. *Bucksport, Maine*

Chicken-Waldorf Salad

1 pound boneless, skinless chicken breast, halves
1 red apple with peel, sliced
1 green apple with peel, sliced
1 cup sliced celery
¾ cup chopped walnuts
2 (6 ounce) cartons orange yogurt
½ cup mayonnaise
1 teaspoon seasoned salt
Shredded lettuce

- Place chicken in large saucepan and cover with water. Cook for about 15 minutes on high heat, drain and cool. Cut into 1-inch chunks and season with salt and pepper. Place in large salad bowl.

- Add apples, celery and walnuts.

- In separate bowl, combine yogurt, mayonnaise and seasoned salt and mix well. Toss with chicken-apple mixture.

- Serve at room temperature or refrigerate for several hours. Serve over shredded lettuce. Serves 8. *Westport, Connecticut*

Brown Rice-Chicken Salad

1 (8.8 ounce) package whole grain brown ready rice
1 (12 ounce) can premium chunk chicken breasts, drained
⅔ cup sun-dried tomatoes, chopped
2 ripe avocados, peeled, diced
¾ cup dijon-style mustard vinaigrette dressing

- Prepare rice according to package directions. Combine rice, chicken, tomatoes, avocados and a little salt and pepper in bowl. Spoon dressing over salad and gently toss to mix well. Refrigerate for at least 2 hours before serving. Serves 6. *Ashville, Ohio*

Broccoli-Chicken Salad

3 - 4 boneless, skinless chicken breast halves, cooked, cubed
2 cups fresh broccoli florets
1 red bell pepper, seeded, chopped
1 cup chopped celery
Honey-mustard dressing

- Combine chicken, broccoli, bell pepper and celery in bowl.

- Toss with dressing and refrigerate. Serves 6. *Aledo, Illinois*

Black Bean Chicken Salad

3 - 4 boneless skinless chicken breasts, cooked, cubed
1 (15 ounce) can black beans, drained
1 bunch green onions, chopped
1 cup chopped celery

- Blend all ingredients in bowl and toss with dressing.

Dressing:

¾ cup virgin olive oil
¼ cup lemon juice
2 teaspoons dijon-style mustard
2 teaspoons ground cumin

- Combine all ingredients in bowl. Toss with salad and refrigerate.
  Serves 6. *Gooding, Idaho*

Barbecue-Chicken Salad

Here's a quickie with that "it-takes-a-long-time" flavor.

Dressing:

¾ cup ranch dressing
3 tablespoons barbecue sauce
2 tablespoons salsa

- Combine all dressing ingredients in bowl and refrigerate.

Salad:

3 grilled boneless, skinless chicken breast halves
1 (9 ounce) package romaine lettuce, cut up
1 (15 ounce) can seasoned black beans, rinsed, drained
12 - 15 cherry tomatoes

- Cut chicken breasts in strips and place in oven just long enough to
  warm thoroughly.

- Place chicken strips, romaine, black beans and cherry tomatoes
  in bowl. Toss with enough dressing to lightly coat. Serves 4.
  Alvarado, Texas

TIP: *The next time you grill, just grill some extra chicken breasts and
     freeze them to use for this dish. Or, if you don't have time to grill
     chicken, just use deli smoked turkey.*

Chicken Salad with Fruit

1 (12 ounce) package spring salad mix
1 (6 ounce) package frozen, ready-to-serve chicken strips, thawed
½ cup fresh raspberries
½ cup fresh strawberries
1 fresh peach, peeled, sliced
1 (8 ounce) bottle raspberry salad dressing

• Combine salad mix, chicken strips, berries and peach in salad
  bowl. Toss with just enough salad dressing to coat salad. Serve
  immediately. Serves 6. *Baldwin, Georgia*

Great Chicken 'n Greens Salad

2 cups skinned, diced rotisserie chicken
1 (10 ounce) package mixed greens
½ cup chopped sun-dried tomatoes
1 red bell pepper, seeded, chopped
3 tablespoons sunflower seeds

• Combine chicken, greens, tomatoes and bell pepper in salad bowl
  and toss.

Dressing:

½ (8 ounce) bottle vinaigrette salad dressing
2 tablespoons refrigerated honey-mustard salad dressing

• Combine vinaigrette dressing and honey-mustard dressing in
  bowl, pour over salad and toss. (Use more dressing if needed.)
  Sprinkle sunflower seeds over salad and serve. Serves 6 to 8.
  Armona, California

Noodle-Turkey Salad

1 (3 ounce) package oriental-flavor ramen noodle soup mix
1 (16 ounce) package finely shredded coleslaw mix
¾ pound deli smoked turkey, cut into strips
½ cup vinaigrette salad dressing

• Coarsely crush noodles and place in bowl with lid. Add coleslaw mix
  and turkey strips.

• Combine vinaigrette salad dressing and seasoning packet from noodle
  mix in small bowl and pour over noodle-turkey mixture and toss to
  coat mixture well. Refrigerate. Serves 6. *Cathcart, Washington*

Asian Turkey Salad

¾ pound turkey breasts, julienned
1 (9 ounce) package coleslaw mix
¼ cup chopped fresh cilantro
1 sweet red bell pepper, seeded, julienned
1 bunch fresh green onions, sliced

• Combine all ingredients in salad bowl.

Dressing:

¼ cup olive oil
2 tablespoons lime juice
1 tablespoon sugar
1 tablespoon peanut butter
1 tablespoon soy sauce

• Combine all dressing ingredients in jar with lid, seal jar and shake
until dressing blends well. Spoon over salad and toss. Serve
immediately. Serves 6. *Bandon, Oregon*

Fiesta Holiday Salad

This is great for that leftover holiday turkey!

1 (10 ounce) package torn romaine lettuce
3 cups diced smoked turkey
1 (15 ounce) can black beans, rinsed, drained
2 tomatoes, quartered, drained

• Combine lettuce, turkey, beans and tomatoes in large bowl.

Dressing:

⅔ cup mayonnaise
¾ cup salsa

• Combine mayonnaise and salsa in bowl.

• When ready to serve, spoon dressing over salad and toss.
If you like, a sliced red onion can be added to salad. Serves 8.
Blanchard, Oklahoma

*TIP: For a little extra touch, you might sprinkle crumbled bacon over
top of salad. You can buy the real, cooked, crumbled bacon in the
grocery store if you don't have time to fry some.*

Broccoli-Pepperoni Salad

1 (1 pound) bunch broccoli
½ pound fresh mushrooms, sliced
6 ounces Swiss cheese, diced
1 (3 ounce) package sliced pepperoni, chopped
Italian dressing

- Cut off broccoli florets and combine florets, mushrooms, cheese and pepperoni in bowl. Toss with dressing.

- Refrigerate for at least 8 hours before serving. Serves 6.
  Bridgeport, Alabama

Supper-Ready Beef and Bean Salad

¾ pound deli roast beef, cut in strips
2 (15 ounce) cans kidney beans, rinsed, drained
1 cup chopped onion
1 cup chopped celery
3 eggs, hard-boiled, chopped
Shredded lettuce

- Combine all salad ingredients except lettuce in salad bowl.

Dressing:

⅓ cup mayonnaise
⅓ cup chipotle chili GourMayo®
¼ cup ketchup
¼ cup sweet pickle relish
2 tablespoons olive oil

- Combine dressing ingredients in small bowl and mix well. Spoon over beef-bean mixture and toss. Refrigerate for several hours before serving.

- When ready to serve, place shredded lettuce on serving plate and spoon beef-bean salad over lettuce to serve. Serves 8.
  Evansville, Wyoming

Roasted Beef Salad Supper

¾ pound sliced roast beef
1½ cups deli potato salad
1 cup roasted red bell peppers, cut in strips
1 seedless cucumber, sliced
1 small red onion, sliced into rings

- Arrange roast beef slices and potato salad on platter and top with bell pepper, cucumber slices, onion rings and a little salt and pepper.

- Cover and refrigerate overnight.

Dressing:

⅓ cup oil
⅓ cup honey
3 tablespoons red wine vinegar
2 teaspoons minced parsley
¼ teaspoon dill weed

- Combine all dressing ingredients in bowl, mix well and pour over salad just before serving. Serves 8. *Annandale, Minnesota*

Beefy Green Salad

⅓ pound deli roast beef
1 (15 ounce) can 3-bean salad, chilled, drained
½ pound mozzarella cheese, cubed
1 (8 ounce) bag mixed salad greens with Italian dressing

- Cut beef in thin strips. Lightly toss beef, 3-bean salad and cheese in large salad bowl.

- Pour in just enough salad dressing to moisten greens. Serves 4 to 6. *Aldan, Pennsylvania*

TIP: Substitute turkey or ham for beef and Swiss cheese for mozzarella.

Wacky Tuna Salad

1 (7 ounce) package cooked light tuna in water, drained
1 red apple with peel, chopped
1 (10 ounce) package frozen green peas, thawed, drained
1 red bell pepper, chopped

- Place tuna in bowl, add apple, green peas and bell pepper, mix well.

Dressing:

½ (8 ounce) bottle sweet honey Catalina salad dressing
½ cup mayonnaise
Shredded lettuce

- Combine dressing and mayonnaise in bowl, pour over tuna salad and stir to blend well.

- Refrigerate at least 2 hours and serve over bed of shredded lettuce. Serves 6 to 8. *Beechwood, Michigan*

Crunchy Potato Salad

10 - 12 small new (red) potatoes, cut in wedges
1 (10 ounce) package red-tip lettuce
6 ounces feta cheese
½ cup pecan halves
⅓ cup chopped onion
¼ cup honey
¼ cup lemon juice
½ cup oil
3 eggs, hard-boiled, cut in wedges

- Cook potatoes in salted water in saucepan for about 15 minutes or until tender. Drain and cool. Combine lettuce, crumbled feta cheese, pecans and onions in salad bowl.

- In separate bowl, combine honey, lemon juice and oil and mix well. Pour over salad and toss. Garnish with egg wedges. Serves 10. *Benton, Louisiana*

Bacon Potato Salad

5 medium size potatoes, baked, cooled
1 (4.3 ounce) package, cooked, real crumbled bacon
3 ribs celery, finely chopped
1 bunch green onions, sliced

- Cut potatoes into cubes and place in salad bowl; add crumbled bacon, celery and green onions.

Dressing:

½ cup mayonnaise
½ cup sour cream
1 (2 ounce) can chopped pimentos
1 tablespoon lemon juice

- Combine mayonnaise, sour cream, pimentos, lemon juice and a generous amount of salt and pepper in bowl. Spoon over salad and toss. Refrigerate. Serves 4. *Burlington, Kansas*

Ranch Potato Salad

2 pounds red (new) potatoes
1 (8 ounce) block mozzarella cheese, cubed
2 ribs celery, sliced
1 red bell pepper, seeded, chopped
1 (2.8 ounce) package bacon bits
1 (8 ounce) bottle ranch salad dressing

- Place potatoes in large saucepan with water to cover and bring to a boil. Reduce heat and simmer for about 20 minutes or until potatoes are tender. Drain and allow to cool just enough to be able to cube.

- Place potatoes in large salad bowl and add cheese, celery, bell pepper, bacon bits and a little salt and pepper. Pour salad dressing over salad and toss. Refrigerate for at least 2 hours before serving. Serves 10 to 12. *Arlington, Tennessee*

Special Macaroni Salad

1 (16 ounce) carton prepared macaroni salad
1 (8 ounce) can whole kernel corn, drained
2 small zucchini, diced
⅔ cup chunky salsa

- Combine all ingredients in salad bowl, mixing well. Cover and refrigerate until ready to serve. Serves 8. *Cache, Oklahoma*

Rainbow Pasta Salad

1 (16 ounce) package tri-color spiral pasta
1 red bell pepper, thinly sliced
1 yellow bell pepper, thinly sliced
4 small zucchini, with peel, sliced
3 ribs celery, sliced diagonally
Lettuce
Breadsticks

- Cook pasta according to package direction; rinse in cold water and drain well. Combine pasta, bell peppers, zucchini and celery in large bowl.

Dressing:

1 (14 ounce) can sweetened condensed milk
1 cup white vinegar
1¼ cups mayonnaise

- Combine sweetened condensed milk, vinegar, mayonnaise and 2 teaspoons pepper in small bowl. Pour dressing over salad. Toss well, cover and refrigerate overnight.

- Serve over bed of lettuce with breadsticks. Serves 12 to 14. *Auberry, California*

Tri-color Pasta Salad

3 cups tri-color spiral pasta
1 tablespoon olive oil
1 large bunch broccoli, cut into small florets
1 cup chopped celery
1 cup peeled, thinly sliced cucumber
1 (1 pound) block Swiss cheese, cubed
1 (8 ounce) bottle ranch dressing

- Cook pasta according to package directions and drain. Stir in olive oil and transfer to large salad bowl. Add broccoli florets, celery, cucumber, cheese and a little salt and pepper.

- Pour dressing over salad and toss. Refrigerate for several hours for flavors to blend. Serves 10. *Bay Pines, Florida*

Pasta-Turkey Salad Supper

1 (12 ounce) package tri-color spiral pasta
1 (4 ounce) can sliced ripe olives, drained
2 cups fresh broccoli florets, chopped
2 small yellow squash, sliced
1 (8 ounce) bottle cheddar-parmesan ranch dressing
1 (3 pound) package hickory-smoked cracked pepper turkey
   breast, sliced

- Cook pasta according to package directions, drain and rinse in cold
  water. Place in large salad bowl and add olives, broccoli and squash.

- Pour dressing over salad mixture and toss. Place turkey on top of
  salad. Serves 8. *Avalon, California*

*TIP: You won't need all the turkey, but what's left will make
   great sandwiches!*

Pasta Toss

1 (8 ounce) package bow-tie pasta
1 tablespoon oil
2 cups diagonally sliced carrots
2 cups broccoli florets
1 red bell pepper, julienned
1 yellow bell pepper, julienned

- Cook pasta according to package directions. Drain and add olive oil;
  cool. Add carrots, broccoli and bell peppers.

Dressing:

¾ cup creamy Italian salad dressing
2 tablespoons balsamic vinegar
1 tablespoon sugar

- Combine dressing ingredients with ½ teaspoon each of salt and pepper
  and pour over vegetables; toss. Refrigerate for several hours before
  serving. Serves 8. *Cedaredge, Colorado*

Pasta Salad Bowl

1 (16 ounce) package bow-tie pasta
1 (16 ounce) package frozen green peas, thawed
½ cup sliced fresh green onions
1 seedless cucumber, thinly sliced
2 cups deli ham, cut in strips

• Cook pasta according to package directions and drain. Rinse with cold water and drain again.

• Transfer to serving bowl and add peas, onions, cucumber and ham.

Dressing:

⅔ cup mayonnaise
¼ cup cider vinegar
1 teaspoon sugar
2 teaspoons dried dill

• Combine dressing ingredients in small bowl and spoon over salad.

• Toss to coat well and refrigerate. Serves 8 to 10. *Battle Mountain, Nevada*

Pasta Plus Salad

1 (16 ounce) package bow-tie pasta
1 (10 ounce) package frozen green peas, thawed
1 red bell pepper, seeded, cut in strips
1 (8 ounce) package cubed Swiss cheese
1 small yellow summer squash, sliced

• Cook pasta according to package directions and add peas last 2 minutes of cooking time. Drain pasta and peas, rinse in cold water and drain again.

• Transfer to large salad bowl and add bell pepper, cheese and squash.

Dressing:

¾ cup mayonnaise
2 tablespoons lemon juice
1 tablespoon sugar
½ cup whipping cream

• Combine dressing ingredients and a little salt and pepper in bowl and mix well. Spoon over salad. Toss salad and refrigerate for several hours before serving. Serves 8. *Carefree, Arizona*

Fusilli Pasta Salad

1 (16 ounce) package fusilli or corkscrew pasta
1 (16 ounce) package frozen broccoli-cauliflower combination
1 (8 ounce) package cubed mozzarella cheese
1 (8 ounce) bottle of Catalina salad dressing

- Cook pasta according to package directions. Drain and cool.

- Cook vegetables in microwave according to package directions. Drain and cool.

- Combine pasta, vegetables and cheese chunks in large bowl.

- Toss with Catalina dressing. Refrigerate for several hours before serving. Serves 8 to 10. *Ashland, Nebraska*

Color-Coded Salad

1 (16 ounce) package tri-colored macaroni, cooked, drained
1 red bell pepper, julienned
1 cup chopped zucchini
1 cup broccoli florets
1 cup Caesar salad dressing

- Combine all ingredients in bowl.

- Toss with Caesar salad dressing. Refrigerate. Serves 6 to 8. *Bourg, Louisiana*

Spinach-Pecan Salad

1 (10 ounce) package baby spinach
2 eggs, hard-boiled, sliced
½ cup pecans, toasted
1 (6 ounce) package cooked bacon, crumbled
¼ cup crumbled blue cheese
1 (8 ounce) bottle Italian salad dressing

- Combine spinach, eggs, pecans, bacon and blue cheese in salad bowl and toss.

- Drizzle with salad dressing. Serves 4. *Brusly, Louisiana*

Spinach-Orange Salad

1 (10 ounce) package spinach, stems removed
2 (10 ounce) cans mandarin oranges, drained
⅓ small jicama, peeled, julienned
⅓ cup slivered almonds, toasted
Vinaigrette dressing

• Combine spinach, oranges, jicama and almonds in large bowl.

• Toss with vinaigrette dressing. Serves 6. *Belleair Bluffs, Florida*

TIP: *Toasting brings out the flavors of nuts and seeds. Place nuts or seeds on baking sheet and bake at 225° for 10 minutes. Be careful not to burn them.*

Spinach-Bacon Salad

1 (10 ounce) package fresh spinach
3 eggs, hard-boiled, chopped
8 fresh mushroom caps, sliced
1 (11 ounce) can sliced water chestnuts, drained

• Mix all ingredients in bowl and serve with dressing.

Dressing:

½ pound bacon, chopped
1 cup sugar
1⅓ cups white vinegar
5 teaspoons cornstarch

• Fry bacon in skillet until crisp, drain and leave bacon drippings in skillet.

• Add sugar and vinegar to skillet and stir well.

• Add 1 cup water and bring to a boil.

• Mix cornstarch with ⅔ cup water and stir until it dissolves. Pour cornstarch mixture into skillet with sugar-vinegar mixture. Return to boil and simmer for 5 minutes.

• Add bacon. Remove from heat and toss salad with dressing while hot. Serves 6. *Blue Ridge, Virginia*

Spinach-Apple Salad

1 (10 ounce) package fresh spinach
⅓ cup frozen orange juice concentrate, thawed
¾ cup mayonnaise
1 red apple
5 slices bacon, fried, crumbled

- Tear spinach into small pieces. Mix orange juice concentrate and mayonnaise in bowl.

- When ready to serve, peel and chop apple and mix with spinach. Pour orange juice-mayonnaise mixture over salad and top with bacon. Serves 6. *Benson, North Carolina*

Spinach Salad

1 (10 ounce) bag baby spinach
1 cup fresh sliced strawberries
1 (3 ounce) package silvered almonds, toasted
½ cup crumbled feta cheese

- Combine all ingredients in salad bowl and toss with dressing.

Dressing:

½ cup sugar
¼ cup white wine vinegar
⅓ cup olive oil
2 teaspoons poppy seeds

- Combine all ingredients in bowl and toss with salad. Serves 6 to 8. *Cadiz, Kentucky*

Special Spinach Salad

1 (10 ounce) package fresh spinach
1 (15 ounce) can bean sprouts, drained
8 slices bacon, cooked crisp
1 (11 ounce) can water chestnuts, chopped
Olive oil
Red wine vinegar

- Combine spinach and bean sprouts in bowl.

- When ready to serve, add crumbled bacon and water chestnuts. Toss with vinaigrette made from 3 parts olive oil and 1 part red wine vinegar. Serves 6. *Cashmere, Washington*

Spinach Salad Oriental

1 (10 ounce) package fresh spinach
2 eggs, hard-boiled, sliced
1 (14 ounce) can bean sprouts, drained
1 (8 ounce) can water chestnuts, chopped

- Combine all ingredients in bowl. Top with dressing.

Dressing:

¾ cup olive oil
⅓ cup sugar
¼ cup ketchup
3 tablespoons red wine vinegar

- Combine all ingredients in bowl and mix well. Use desired amount of dressing and refrigerate remaining salad dressing. Serves 8. *Boardman, Oregon*

Colorful Salad Toss

2 (8 ounce) packages baby spinach without stems
1 small head cauliflower, cut into small florets
1 red bell pepper, seeded, chopped
¾ cup walnut halves
½ cup roasted sunflower seeds
1 (8 ounce) bottle wild berry vinaigrette salad dressing

- Combine spinach, cauliflower, bell pepper, walnuts, sunflower seeds and generous amount of salt in large salad bowl. Refrigerate.

- When ready to serve, pour about half salad dressing over salad and toss; add more dressing if needed. Serves 12. *Carlin, Nevada*

Oriental-Spinach Salad

1 (10 ounce) package fresh spinach
1 (15 ounce) can bean sprouts, drained
8 slices bacon, cooked crisp, drained
1 (11 ounce) can water chestnuts, chopped
Vinaigrette salad dressing

- Combine spinach and bean sprouts in bowl. When ready to serve, add crumbled bacon and water chestnuts. Toss with vinaigrette salad dressing. Serves 8. *Belleville, Kansas*

TIP: If you don't have vinaigrette on hand, you can make it with 3 parts olive oil and 1 part red wine vinegar.

Green Salad with Candied Pecans

Candied Pecans:

1⅓ cups pecan halves
¼ cup honey
3 tablespoons light corn syrup

- Preheat oven to 325°.

- Combine pecans, honey and corn syrup in bowl and stir until pecans are well coated. Spread out on rimmed baking sheet and bake for 12 minutes or until pecans toast.

- Remove to piece of foil, separate clumps with fork and cool.

Salad:

1 (10 ounce) package baby spinach
4 cups young salad greens
1 tart apple, thinly sliced
1 cup crumbled blue cheese
1 (8 ounce) bottle zesty Italian salad dressing

- Combine spinach, greens, apple slices and blue cheese in salad bowl; toss with about half bottle of salad dressing. Add more if needed.

- Sprinkle candied pecans over top of salad when ready to serve. Serves 8 to 10. *Blackshear, Georgia*

Warm Spinach Salad

1 (10 ounce) package fresh spinach, stems removed
1 (15 ounce) can cannellini beans, rinsed, drained
1 (11 ounce) can Mexicorn®, drained
1 cup shredded Monterey Jack cheese

- Combine spinach, cannellini beans and corn in salad bowl.

Dressing:

1 (8 ounce) bottle zesty Italian salad dressing
1 sweet red bell pepper, seeded and chopped

- Combine salad dressing and chopped bell pepper in saucepan. Bring to a boil, reduce heat to low and cook for 2 minutes.

- Pour hot dressing over spinach mixture and toss. Sprinkle with cheese and serve warm. Serves 8. *Center, Colorado*

Red and Green Salad

2 (10 ounce) packages fresh spinach
1 quart fresh strawberries, halved
½ cup slivered almonds, toasted
Poppy seed salad dressing

- Tear spinach into small pieces and add strawberries and almonds in bowl. Refrigerate until ready to serve.

- Toss with dressing. Serves 8. *Black Hawk, South Dakota*

Wilted Spinach Salad

1 (10 ounce) package fresh baby spinach
1 (15 ounce) can cannellini beans, rinsed, drained
¾ cup zesty Italian salad dressing
¾ cup shredded Monterey Jack cheese

- Remove large stems from spinach and place in salad bowl and add cannellini beans; toss. Heat Italian salad dressing in saucepan to boiling and pour over spinach-bean mixture and toss.

- Sprinkle cheese over salad and serve immediately. Serves 6. *Alpha, New Jersey*

Chilled Spinach Couscous

⅓ cup olive oil
3 tablespoons lemon juice
½ teaspoon sugar
1 (10 ounce) package parmesan couscous with spice sack
1 (9 ounce) package fresh baby spinach
4 fresh green onions, sliced
2 tablespoons fresh chopped dill
⅓ cup crumbled feta cheese

- Whisk olive oil, lemon juice and sugar in bowl.

- Heat 1¼ cups water in large saucepan to boiling, adding spice sack. Remove from heat and stir in couscous; let stand for 5 minutes. Fluff with fork and toss with olive oil-sugar mixture; let cool completely.

- Tear stems from spinach and break spinach into smaller pieces. Stir sliced onions, chopped dill and torn spinach into couscous and toss. Cover and refrigerate for several hours.

- When ready to serve, sprinkle feta cheese over top of salad. Serves 6. *Dunleith, Delaware*

Merry Berry Salad

1 (10 ounce) package mixed salad greens
1 red with peel, diced
1 green apple with peel, diced
1 cup shredded parmesan cheese
½ cup Craisins®
½ cup slivered almonds, toasted
Poppy seed dressing

- Toss greens, apples, cheese, Craisins® and almonds in large salad
  bowl. Drizzle poppy seed dressing over salad and toss. Serves 6 to 8.
  Brookwood, Maryland

TIP: Toasting brings out the flavors of nuts and seeds. Place nuts or
seeds on baking sheet and bake at 225° for 10 minutes. Be careful
not to burn them.

Greens and Fruit

1 (10 ounce) package spring salad greens
1 (11 ounce) can mandarin oranges, drained
¼ cup sliced almonds
1 cup halved, green seedless grapes
1 (8 ounce) raspberry vinaigrette salad dressing
¼ cup precooked bacon bits

- Combine salad greens, oranges, almonds and grapes in salad bowl.

- Toss with half raspberry vinaigrette salad dressing, adding more if
  needed. Sprinkle with bacon bits. Serves 4 to 6. *Aracanum, Ohio*

Mandarin Salad

1 head red-tipped lettuce
2 (11 ounce) cans mandarin oranges, drained
2 avocados, peeled, diced
1 small red onion, sliced
Poppy seed dressing

- Combine lettuce, oranges, avocados and onion in salad bowl.

- When ready to serve, toss with poppy seed dressing. Serves 6.
  Blissfield, Michigan

Salad Delight with Apple Vinaigrette Dressing

2 (10 ounce) bags radicchio salad mix
2 golden delicious apples, cut in wedges
1¼ cups crumbled blue cheese
⅔ cup chopped walnuts

• Combine all ingredients in salad bowl.

Dressing:

⅔ cup applesauce
⅓ cup olive oil
⅓ cup cider vinegar
1 tablespoon dijon-style mustard

• Combine dressing ingredients in small bowl, mixing well and toss with salad. Serves 8. *Avon, New York*

TIP: *If slicing apple several minutes before serving, you might want to toss apple with 1 tablespoon or so of lemon juice.*

Berry Delicious Salad

1 (10 ounce) package mixed salad greens
2 cups fresh blueberries
⅔ cup crumbled gorgonzola cheese
⅓ cup chopped pecans, toasted
Raspberry vinaigrette dressing

• Combine salad greens, blueberries, cheese and pecans in salad bowl. Toss salad with raspberry vinaigrette and refrigerate. Serves 4. *Baldwin, Wisconsin*

Orange-Cranberry Salad

1 (10 ounce) package red-tipped lettuce, rinsed
1 seedless cucumber, halved lengthwise, sliced
1 (11 ounce) can mandarin oranges, drained
½ cup Craisins®
⅓ cup toasted slivered almonds, toasted
1 (12 ounce) bottle raspberry-vinaigrette dressing

• Combine lettuce, cucumber, oranges, Craisins® and almonds in salad bowl. Toss with about one-third of dressing; use more as needed. Serves 6 to 8. *Morrisville, Vermont*

Swiss Romaine

1 large head romaine lettuce, torn into bite-size pieces
1 bunch fresh green onions with tops, sliced
1 sweet red bell pepper, seeded, julienned
1 (8 ounce) package shredded Swiss cheese
⅓ cup sunflower seeds
Seasoned croutons

- Combine romaine, green onions, bell pepper and shredded cheese in salad bowl.

Dressing:

⅔ cup olive oil
⅓ cup red wine vinegar
2 teaspoons sugar

- Combine oil, vinegar and sugar in container with lid and shake well. Add sunflower seeds to salad and toss with vinaigrette dressing. Sprinkle croutons over top of salad. Serves 8. *Bronson, Michigan*

Swiss Salad

1 large head romaine lettuce
1 bunch fresh green onions with tops, chopped
1 (8 ounce) package shredded Swiss cheese
½ cup toasted sunflower seeds

- Tear lettuce into bite-size pieces in bowl. Add onions, cheese, sunflower seeds and toss. Serve with dressing.

Dressing:

⅔ cup oil
⅓ cup red wine vinegar

- Mix all dressing ingredients with 1 tablespoon salt and refrigerate. Serves 8. *Boxford, Massachusetts*

Italian Salad

1 (10 ounce) package mixed salad greens
1 cup shredded mozzarella cheese
1 (2 ounce) can sliced ripe black olives
1 (15 ounce) can cannellini beans, rinsed, drained
Zesty Italian dressing

- Combine greens, cheese, olives and cannellini beans in salad bowl. Toss with salad dressing. Serves 4 to 6. *Avilla, Indiana*

Veggie Salad

Crunchy and good!

5 zucchini, sliced paper thin
4 yellow squash, sliced paper thin
1 head cauliflower cut in bite-size pieces
1 red bell pepper, chopped
1 bunch green onions with tops, sliced
2 (2 ounce) packages slivered almonds, toasted
1 (8 ounce) bottle creamy Italian dressing

- Mix zucchini, squash, cauliflower, bell pepper, onions, almonds, ½ teaspoon salt and ¼ teaspoon pepper in bowl.

- Add dressing and toss. Refrigerate for several hours before serving. Serves 8. *Buckner, Missouri*

Veggie Salad with Lemon Dressing

1 (5.6 ounce) box toasted pine nut couscous
1 (15 ounce) can mixed vegetables, well drained
1 sweet red bell pepper, diced
⅔ cup crumbled feta cheese

- Cook couscous according to package directions and cool.

- Combine couscous, mixed vegetables, bell pepper and cheese in bowl, mixing well.

Dressing:

⅓ cup olive oil
2 tablespoons lemon juice
2 teaspoons sugar
1 teaspoon lemon pepper
Lettuce
Cherry tomatoes

- Combine oil, lemon juice, sugar and lemon pepper in jar with lid; shake well to blend ingredients. Pour over salad and toss.

- Serve on bed of lettuce and garnish with cherry tomatoes. Serves 6. *Dupont, Colorado*

Special Cauliflower Salad

1 head cauliflower, cut into bite-size pieces
1 (10 ounce) package frozen green peas, thawed
1 sweet red bell pepper, seeded, chopped
1 small purple onion, chopped
1 (8 ounce) carton sour cream
1 (1 ounce) packet dry ranch-style salad dressing

- Combine cauliflower, peas, bell pepper and purple onion in large salad bowl.

- In separate bowl, combine sour cream and ranch dressing and toss with vegetables. Refrigerate. Serves 8. *Carlin, Nevada*

Green and White Salad

1 (16 ounce) package frozen green peas, thawed
1 head cauliflower, cut into bite-size pieces
1 (8 ounce) carton sour cream
1 (1 ounce) packet dry ranch-style salad dressing

- Combine peas and cauliflower in large bowl.

- In separate bowl, combine sour cream and salad dressing mix. Toss with vegetables. Refrigerate. Serve 8 to 10. *Brundidge, Alabama*

TIP: Salad is even better if you add ½ purple onion, chopped.

Zippy Tossed Broccoli

2 large bunches broccoli
1 (8 ounce) package shredded pepper Jack cheese
1 small red onion, chopped
1 (4.3 ounce) package real crumbled bacon

- After washing and draining broccoli, cut into small florets and place in bowl with lid. Add cheese, onion and crumbled bacon.

Dressing:

1½ cups mayonnaise
⅔ cup sugar
3 tablespoons cider vinegar

- Combine mayonnaise, sugar, vinegar and 1 teaspoon salt in small bowl. Spoon over broccoli mixture and toss.

- Cover and refrigerate for several hours before serving. Serves 8. *Altamont, Illinois*

Broccoli-Noodle Crunch Salad

*Who thought up the idea of grating broccoli "stems" for a salad?
It was pure genius! This salad is different – and very good.
It will last and still be "crispy" in the refrigerator for days!*

1 cup slivered almonds, toasted
1 cup sunflower seeds, toasted
2 (.3 ounce) packages chicken-flavored ramen noodles
1 (12 ounce) package broccoli slaw

• Preheat oven to 275° (140° C).

• Toast almonds and sunflower seeds in oven for 15 minutes. Break
up ramen noodles (but do not cook) and mix with slaw, almonds and
sunflower seeds in bowl.

Dressing:

¾ cup oil
½ cup white vinegar
½ cup sugar
Ramen noodles seasoning packets

• Combine dressing ingredients and noodle seasoning packets in bowl.

• Pour over slaw mixture and mix well. Prepare at least 1 hour before
serving. Serves 10 to 12. *Bonham, Texas*

Choice Broccoli-Swiss Salad

2 large bunches fresh broccoli, washed, drained
1 (8 ounce) carton fresh mushrooms, sliced
1 (8 ounce) block Swiss cheese, diced
1 (3 ounce) package sliced pepperoni, chopped
1 (8 ounce) carton cherry tomatoes, halved, drained
1 (8 ounce) bottle zesty Italian salad dressing

• Cut broccoli into florets and place in plastic bowl with lid; discard
stems. Add mushrooms, cheese, pepperoni and tomatoes.

• Toss with Italian salad dressing, cover and refrigerate. Serves 8.
Adel, Iowa

Sweet Broccoli Salad

2 (12 ounce) packages broccoli slaw
½ cup Craisins®
¾ cup chopped pecans, toasted
6 sliced bacon, cooked, drained, crumbled

- Place broccoli slaw in large salad bowl. Add Craisins®, pecans and crumbled bacon and toss.

Dressing:

1 cup mayonnaise
½ cup sugar
¼ cup cider vinegar
1 small red onion, very finely chopped

- Combine mayonnaise, sugar, vinegar, onion, and salt and pepper in bowl, mixing until it blends well. Spoon over salad and toss.

- Cover and refrigerate for several hours before serving. Serves 8 to 10. *Baltic, Connecticut*

TIP: *Toasting brings out the flavors of nuts and seeds. Place nuts or seeds on baking sheet and bake at 225° for 10 minutes. Be careful not to burn them.*

Sesame-Broccoli Rabe Salad

¼ cup sesame seeds
Oil
1 (16 ounce) package broccoli rabe slaw
1 red bell pepper, seeded, chopped
2 (9 ounce) packages fresh tortellini, cooked
1 (8 ounce) bottle vinaigrette salad dressing
2 tablespoons olive oil

- Toast sesame seeds in skillet over medium-low heat in a little oil and set aside.

- Combine broccoli rabe, bell pepper and cooked tortellini in salad bowl. Drizzle salad dressing and olive oil over salad and toss.

- Refrigerate and just before serving, sprinkle sesame seeds over salad. Serves 12. *Amboy, Illinois*

Cabbage and Bean Salad

1 (16 ounce) package coleslaw mix
2 (15 ounce) cans garbanzo beans, rinsed, drained
1 (15 ounce) can kidney beans, rinsed, drained
1 (8 ounce) bottle zesty Italian salad dressing

- Combine coleslaw mix and all 3 cans beans in large salad bowl with lid. Pour salad dressing over mixture and toss.

- Cover and refrigerate for several hours before serving. Serve with slotted spoon. Serves 6. *Bethel, Ohio*

Bean and Onion Salad

1 (15 ounce) can whole green beans, drained
1 (15 ounce) can yellow wax beans, drained
½ cup finely chopped red onion
¼ cup slivered almonds

- Combine all ingredients in bowl and mix with dressing.

Dressing:

¼ cup oil
1 tablespoon white vinegar
1 teaspoon sugar
2 teaspoons dijon-style mustard

- Combine all ingredients in bowl and add ½ teaspoon each of salt and pepper. Pour over salad.

- Refrigerate for at least 1 hour before serving. Serves 6. *Belcourt, North Dakota*

Cashew-Pea Salad

1 (16 ounce) package frozen green peas, thawed
¼ cup diced celery
1 bunch fresh green onions, with tops, chopped
1 cup cashew pieces
½ cup mayonnaise

- Combine peas, celery, onions and cashews in bowl.

- Toss with mayonnaise seasoned with ½ teaspoon each of salt and pepper. Serves 4 to 6. *Bean Station, Tennessee*

Colorful English Pea Salad

2 (16 ounce) packages frozen green peas, thawed, drained
1 (12 ounce) package cubed mozzarella cheese
1 red bell pepper, chopped
1 orange bell pepper, chopped
1 onion, chopped
1¼ cups mayonnaise

- Combine peas, cheese, bell peppers and onion in large salad bowl and toss to mix. Stir in mayonnaise and a little salt and pepper.

- Refrigerate before serving. Serves 10 to 12. *Bloomingdale, Georgia*

Marinated Corn Salad

3 (15 ounce) cans whole kernel corn, drained
1 red bell pepper, chopped
1 cup chopped walnuts
¾ cup chopped celery
1 (8 ounce) bottle Italian salad dressing

- Combine corn, bell pepper, walnuts and celery in bowl with lid. (For a special little zip, add several dashes hot sauce.)

- Pour salad dressing over vegetables; cover and refrigerate for several hours before serving. Serves 8. *Arcola, Illinois*

Zesty Bean Salad

1 (15 ounce) can kidney beans, rinsed, drained
1 (15 ounce) can pinto beans, rinsed, drained
1 (15 ounce) can whole kernel corn, drained
1 red bell pepper, seeded, chopped
1 red onion, chopped
1 (7 ounce) can chopped green chilies
1 (12 ounce) package cubed Mexican 4-cheese blend

- Combine all ingredients in large bowl; mix well.

Dressing:

1 (8 ounce) bottle cheddar-parmesan ranch dressing
2 tablespoons lemon juice
1 teaspoon Creole seasoning

- Pour ranch dressing into bowl and stir in lemon juice and Creole seasoning. Pour over salad and toss. Refrigerate for several hours before serving for flavors to blend. Serves 10 to 12. *Delta, Utah*

Marinated Brussels Sprouts

2 (10 ounce) packages brussels sprouts, cooked
½ cup oil
¼ cup white wine vinegar
¼ cup sugar

• Mix all ingredients in bowl and marinate overnight in refrigerator.
  Serve cold. Serves 8. *Atco, New Jersey*

Carrot Salad

3 cups finely grated carrots
1 (8 ounce) can crushed pineapple, drained
¼ cup flaked coconut
1 tablespoon sugar
⅓ cup mayonnaise

• Combine all ingredients in bowl and mix well. Refrigerate. Serves 4.
  Conrad, Montana

Winter Salad

1 (15 ounce) can cut green beans, drained
1 (15 ounce) can English peas, drained
1 (15 ounce) can whole kernel corn, drained
1 (15 ounce) can jalapeno black-eyed peas, drained
1 (8 ounce) bottle Italian salad dressing

• Combine all vegetables in large bowl. (Add some chopped onion and
  chopped bell pepper if you have it.)

• Pour Italian dressing over vegetables. Cover and refrigerate.
  Serves 12. *Atkins, Arkansas*

Special Rice Salad

1 (6 ounce) package chicken-flavored rice and macaroni
¾ cup chopped green pepper
1 bunch fresh green onion with tops, chopped
2 (6 ounce) jars marinated artichoke hearts
½ - ⅔ cup mayonnaise

• Cook rice and macaroni according to package directions (but without
  butter), drain and cool. Add green pepper, onions, artichoke hearts
  and mayonnaise, toss and refrigerate. Serves 8 to 10. *Dexter, Maine*

Nutty Rice Salad

1 (6 ounce) package long grain-wild rice mix
1 (6 ounce) jar marinated artichoke hearts, drained, chopped
1 cup golden raisins
4 fresh green onions with tops, chopped
¾ cup pecan halves, toasted

- Prepare rice mix according to package directions, drain and cool. Place in salad bowl and add artichoke hearts, raisins and green onions.

Dressing:

⅓ cup orange juice
¼ cup olive oil
1 tablespoon lemon juice
1 tablespoon sugar

- Combine orange juice, oil, lemon juice and sugar in bowl. Stir until they blend well, spoon over salad and toss.

- Cover and refrigerate for at least 2 hours; top with pecans before serving. Serves 6 to 8. *Chauvin, Louisiana*

TIP: *Toasting brings out the flavors of nuts and seeds. Place nuts or seeds on baking sheet and bake at 225° for 10 minutes. Be careful not to burn them.*

Couscous Salad

1 (5.6 ounce) box parmesan couscous
¾ cup chopped fresh mushrooms
1 (4 ounce) can sliced ripe olives, drained
½ cup chopped green bell pepper
½ cup chopped red bell pepper
½ cup Italian salad dressing

- Cook couscous according to package directions. Cover and let stand for 5 minutes, then fluff with fork. Cool completely.

- Combine couscous, mushrooms, olives and bell peppers in salad bowl.

- Stir in salad dressing, cover and refrigerate for 30 minutes before serving. Serves 6. *Bayview, California*

Chunky Egg Salad

12 eggs, hard-boiled, quartered
⅓ cup sun-dried tomato GourMayo®
2 ribs celery, sliced
½ cup sliced, stuffed green olives
Lettuce leaves
Crackers

- Combine eggs, GourMayo®, celery and olives in salad bowl and add a little salt and pepper.

- Gently toss and serve over bed of lettuce leaves with crackers. Serves 6. *Boiling Springs, North Carolina*

TIP: This is also great stuffed in hollowed-out tomato, bell pepper or melon. And if you are really in a hurry, just put it between 2 slices of dark bread.

Terrific Tortellini Salad

2 (14 ounce) packages frozen cheese tortellini
1 green bell pepper, diced
1 red bell pepper, diced
1 cucumber, chopped
1 (14 ounce) can artichoke hearts, rinsed, drained
1 (8 ounce) bottle creamy Caesar salad dressing

- Prepare tortellini according to package directions and drain. Rinse with cold water, drain again and refrigerate.

- Combine tortellini, bell peppers, cucumber, artichoke hearts and dressing in large bowl.

- Cover and refrigerate for at least 2 hours before serving. Serves 12. *Calvert City, Kentucky*

Marinated Cucumbers

3 cucumbers, thinly sliced
2 (4 ounce) jars chopped pimentos, drained
⅔ cup oil
¼ cup white wine vinegar
1 (8 ounce) carton sour cream

- Mix cucumber and pimentos in bowl.

- In separate bowl, combine oil, vinegar and ½ teaspoon salt. Pour over cucumbers and refrigerate for 1 hour.

- To serve, drain well and pour sour cream over cucumbers and pimentos and toss. Serves 6 to 8. *Arial, South Carolina*

Cucumbers in Sour Cream 🍁

Fur trading began as early as the 1800's in British Columbia, Canada. Forts and trading posts were soon established and British gentry made the long voyage to establish fine homes on Vancouver Island. Salmon was the star along the west coast for both the early Indians and later for the settlers, but the discovery of gold brought ship loads of men and changed the history and the foods of British Colombia.

3 cucumbers, peeled, thinly sliced
1½ tablespoons vinegar
1 (8 ounce) carton sour cream
1 tablespoon sugar
½ teaspoon paprika
Sliced green onions for garnish

- Place sliced cucumbers in bowl (with lid) and sprinkle with 2 teaspoons salt. Cover and refrigerate for 3 to 4 hours.

- When ready to serve, drain cucumbers well. Combine vinegar, sour cream, sugar, a little pepper and paprika in bowl.

- Spoon mixture over drained cucumbers and sprinkle with several sliced green onions. Serves 6 to 8. *Summerland, British Columbia, Canada*

Cucumber-Onion Salad

2 -3 seedless cucumbers, peeled, sliced
2 onions, sliced
1 tablespoon white vinegar
½ cup sour cream

- Sprinkle ½ teaspoon salt over cucumbers in bowl and let stand for 20 minutes; drain. Add onions and vinegar; toss. Refrigerate.

- When ready to serve, stir in sour cream. Serves 6.
  Chickamauga, Georgia

Chilled Cucumbers

2 cucumbers, peeled, sliced
½ onion, sliced
¼ cup vinegar
⅓ cup sugar

- Place cucumbers and onion in bowl with lid.

- In separate bowl, combine vinegar and sugar. Pour over cucumbers and onions.

- Cover and refrigerate for 2 to 3 hours before serving. Serves 4.
  Arthur, Illinois

Red Hot Onions

Great with barbecue!

3 large purple onions
2 tablespoons hot sauce
3 tablespoons olive oil
3 tablespoons red wine vinegar

- Slice onions thinly. Pour 1 cup boiling water over onions in shallow bowl, let stand for 1 minute and drain.

- In separate bowl, mix hot sauce, oil and vinegar and pour over onion rings.

- Cover and refrigerate for at least 3 hours. Drain to serve. Serves 6 to 8. *Cottonport, Louisiana*

Spicy Coleslaw

1 (16 ounce) package coleslaw mix
1 sweet onion, diced
1 seedless cucumber, peeled and diced
1 red bell pepper, seeded, diced

- Combine coleslaw, onion, cucumber and bell pepper in bowl.

Dressing:

1 cup mayonnaise
⅓ cup cider vinegar
⅓ cup sugar
1 teaspoon hot sauce

- Combine mayonnaise, vinegar, sugar, hot sauce and 1 teaspoon salt in bowl. Spoon over coleslaw mixture and toss. Cover and refrigerate for several hours before serving. Serves 6 to 8. *Argyle, Texas*

Nutty Slaw

1 (16 ounce) package shredded carrots
3 cups shredded cabbage
2 red delicious apples, diced
¾ cup raisins
¾ cup chopped walnuts
1 (8 ounce) bottle coleslaw dressing

- Combine carrots, cabbage, apples, raisins and walnuts in plastic bowl with lid. Pour about three-fourths bottle of dressing over mixture and increase dressing as needed. Cover and refrigerate for several hours before serving. Serves 8. *Bluefield, Virginia*

Hawaiian Slaw

2 (1 ounce) packages of unflavored gelatin
3 cups orange juice, divided
1 (8 ounce) can crushed pineapple with juice
2 cups finely shredded cabbage

- Sprinkle gelatin over 1 cup orange juice in saucepan. Heat until gelatin dissolves. Stir in remaining orange juice and refrigerate until slightly thick. Fold in pineapple and cabbage and blend well.

- Pour into 8 x 8-inch dish and refrigerate until set. Serves 9. *Castle Rock, Washington*

Creamy Coleslaw 🍁

Quebec, Canada, has retained its French culture, history and foods. They dined on a variety of wild game and domestic farm animals, a variety of vegetables, and desserts of fruits, walnuts, grapes and berries of all kinds.

2 (9 ounce) packages shredded cabbage
1 red apple with peel, thinly sliced
3 ribs celery, thinly sliced
½ cup shredded carrots
1¼ cups mayonnaise
2 teaspoons mustard
¼ cup sugar
2 tablespoons vinegar

- Combine cabbage, apple, celery and carrots in large bowl.

- In separate bowl, combine mayonnaise, mustard, sugar, vinegar and 1 teaspoon salt. Stir into vegetables and mix well. Cover and refrigerate until serving time. Serves 6 to 8. *Pont-Rouge, Quebec, Canada*

Cabbage-Carrot Slaw

1 (16 ounce) package shredded carrots
3 cups shredded cabbage
2 red delicious apples with peels, diced
¾ cup raisins
¾ cup chopped walnuts
1 (8 ounce) bottle coleslaw dressing

- Combine carrots, cabbage, apples, raisins and walnuts in bowl.

- Add about three-fourths bottle of coleslaw dressing and increase dressing if needed. Cover and refrigerate for several hours before serving. Serves 8. *Chandler, Oklahoma*

Broccoli Slaw

1 (16 ounce) package broccoli slaw
1 cup small fresh broccoli florets
¾ cup Craisins®
1 Granny Smith apple with peel, diced
1 (11 ounce) can mandarin oranges, well drained
1 (8 ounce) bottle poppy seed dressing
½ cup slivered almonds, toasted

• Combine broccoli slaw, broccoli florets, Craisins®, apple and oranges in salad bowl. Toss with poppy seed dressing.

• Sprinkle almonds on top of salad. Refrigerate for at least 2 hours before serving. Serves 8. *Ashland, Pennsylvania*

★ ★ ★

Sandwiches

A delicious sandwich can be the center
of a simple meal or a yummy after-school
snack; select from 26 different ones!

1001
Community
Recipes

Sandwiches Contents

Chicken-Bacon Sandwiches

1 (12 ounce) can chicken breast, drained
⅓ cup mayonnaise
1 tablespoon dijon-style mustard
1 celery rib, finely chopped
3 tablespoons finely diced green onions
¼ cup cooked, crumbled bacon
Whole wheat bread
Shredded lettuce

- Combine chicken chunks, mayonnaise, mustard, celery, green onions, bacon and a little salt and pepper in medium bowl.

- Spread chicken mixture on whole wheat bread (crust removed) and top with shredded lettuce. Place second slice of bread on top and cut to make 4 little "bites". Serves 4 to 8. *Box Elder, South Dakota*

Spinach Sandwiches

1 (10 ounce) package chopped spinach, thawed, well drained
1 cup mayonnaise
1 (8 ounce) carton sour cream
½ cup finely minced onion
1 (1 ounce) packet dry vegetable soup mix
White bread

- Squeeze spinach between paper towels to completely remove excess moisture.

- Combine all ingredients in bowl and mix well. (If you like, ¾ cup finely chopped pecans may be added.)

- Refrigerate for 3 to 4 hours before making sandwiches.

- To make sandwiches, use thin slices of white bread. Yield 1 pint. *Baxter Springs, Kansas*

Reuben Sandwiches

12 slices dark rye bread
6 slices Swiss cheese
12 thin deli slices corned beef
4 cups deli coleslaw, drained

- On 6 slices of rye bread, layer cheese, 2 slices corned beef and lots of coleslaw. Top with remaining bread slices. Serves 6. *Balmville, New York*

Pizza Sandwich

1 (14 ounce) package English muffins
1 pound bulk sausage, cooked, drained
1½ cups pizza sauce
1 (4 ounce) can mushrooms, drained
1 (8 ounce) package shredded mozzarella cheese

- Split muffins and layer ingredients on each muffin half ending with cheese.

- Broil until cheese melts. Serves 8. *Auburn, Illinois*

Hot Roast Beef Sandwich

1 (12 ounce) loaf French bread
¼ cup creamy dijon-style mustard
¾ pound sliced deli roast beef
8 slices American cheese

- Preheat oven to 325°.

- Split French bread horizontally and spread mustard on bottom slice. Layer slices of beef over mustard and cheese slices over beef with cheese on top. Add top bread slice.

- Cut loaf in quarters and place on baking sheet. Heat for about 5 minutes or until cheese just partially melts. Serves 4. *Bargersville, Indiana*

Grilled Bacon-Banana Sandwiches

Peanut butter
8 slices English muffins
2 bananas
8 slices bacon, cooked crispy
Butter, softened

- Spread peanut butter over 8 muffin slices. Slice bananas and arrange on top of 4 slices.

- Place 2 strips bacon on each of 4 slices. Top with remaining muffin slices. Spread top slice with butter.

- Brown sandwiches butter-side down in skillet. Spread butter on other side, turn and cook other side until golden brown. Serve hot. Serves 4. *Big Coppitt Key, Florida*

Green Chili Grilled Cheese

4 slices cheddar cheese
4 slices bread
1 (4 ounce) can chopped green chilies, drained
3 tablespoons butter, softened

- Place 1 slice cheese on each of 2 slices bread. Sprinkle with green chilies.

- Top with remaining slices cheese and remaining slices bread.

- Butter outside of sandwiches.

- Brown sandwiches in large skillet over medium heat on both sides until golden brown and cheese melts. Serves 2. *Bath, New Mexico*

Italian Sausage Sandwiches

1 pound sweet Italian sausage, casing removed
1 red bell pepper, chopped
1 onion, chopped
1⅔ cups Italian-style spaghetti sauce
6 hoagie rolls

- Cook sausage, bell pepper and onion in skillet over medium heat until sausage browns.

- Stir in spaghetti sauce and heat until boiling. Simmer for 5 minutes and stir constantly.

- Pour mixture over split hoagie rolls. Serves 6. *Belmar, New Jersey*

Turkey-Cranberry Croissants

1 (8 ounce) package cream cheese, softened
½ cup orange marmalade
6 large croissants, split
Shredded lettuce
1 pound thinly sliced deli turkey
1 cup whole cranberry sauce

- Beat cream cheese, orange marmalade and 1 tablespoon water in bowl. Spread small amount evenly on cut sides of croissants.

- Top with lettuce and slices of turkey. Place cranberry sauce in bowl and stir for easy spreading. Spread 2 or 3 tablespoons cranberries over turkey and place top of croissant over cranberry sauce. Serves 6. *Ballinger, Texas*

Luncheon Sandwiches

1 loaf thinly-sliced sandwich bread
1 cup (2 sticks) butter, softened
1 (5 ounce) jar cheese spread, softened
½ teaspoon Worcestershire sauce

- Trim crust on bread.

- Beat butter and cheese spread in bowl until smooth and creamy and add Worcestershire sauce.

- Spread mixture on 3 slices bread to make triple-decker sandwich.

- Place fourth slice bread on top. Cut into finger sandwiches. Serves 6 to 10. *Childersburg, Alabama*

TIP: These sandwiches may be served cold or warmed at 300° for 5 or 10 minutes.

Olive Tea Sandwiches

Loaf of thinly-sliced white bread
1 (8 ounce) package cream cheese, softened
1 cup finely diced salad olives
⅓ cup chopped pecans, toasted
⅔ cup mayonnaise

- Cut crust off each slice of bread. Flatten each slice with rolling pin.

- Beat cream cheese in bowl until cheese is creamy and stir in olives, toasted pecans and mayonnaise.

- Spread 2 tablespoons of this mixture on 1 side of each bread slice. Roll tightly, place in dish, cover and refrigerate for at least 4 hours.

- When ready to serve, cut each roll into 4 slices. Refrigerate any leftovers. Yields 2 cups. *Belltown, California*

TIP: Toasting brings out the flavors of nuts and seeds. Place nuts or seeds on baking sheet and bake at 225° for 10 minutes. Be careful not to burn them.

Party Sandwiches

½ pound bacon, cooked, crumbled
½ cup coarsely chopped ripe olives
½ cup chopped pecans
1¼ cups mayonnaise
White bread

- Mix all ingredients in bowl. Spread on thinly sliced white bread.

- Cut sandwiches into 3 strips. Yields 2½ cups filling. *Branford, Connecticut*

Cream Cheese Sandwiches

2 (8 ounce) packages cream cheese, softened
1 (4 ounce) can black olives, chopped
¾ cups finely chopped pecans
Pumpernickel rye bread

- Beat cream cheese in bowl until creamy. Fold in olives and pecans.

- Trim crusts on bread. Spread cream cheese on bread. Top with another slice.

- Slice sandwich into 3 finger strips. Yields 1 pint filling. *Esmond, Rhode Island*

Turkey on a Muffin

4 slices Swiss cheese
2 English muffins, split, toasted
½ pound thinly sliced deli turkey
1 (15 ounce) can asparagus spears, well drained
1 (1 ounce) packet hollandaise sauce mix

- Place cheese slice on each muffin half and top with turkey slices.

- Cut asparagus spears to fit muffin halves and top each sandwich with 3 or 4 asparagus spears. (Use remaining asparagus for something else.)

- Prepare hollandaise sauce in bowl according to package directions and pour generous amount over each open-face sandwich. Serve immediately. Serves 4. *Middlebury, Vermont*

Open-Face Apple-Ham Sandwiches

You will need some kaiser rolls or whatever
you have in the pantry for these sandwiches.

Mayonnaise and mustard
Kaiser rolls, split horizontally
16 slices American cheese
8 thin slices deli ham
1 red delicious apple with peel, finely chopped

- Spread a little mayonnaise and mustard on top and bottom of 4 kaiser rolls and place on baking sheet.

- Top each with 1 slice of cheese, slice ham and about 2 tablespoons chopped apple. Top with remaining slice of cheese.

- Broil 4 to 5 inches from heat just until top slice of cheese melts. Serve immediately. Serves 8. *Bayside, Wisconsin*

"Honey Do" Open-Face Sandwich

⅓ cup honey-mustard dressing
4 kaiser rolls, split
8 thin slices deli honey ham
8 slices Swiss cheese

- Preheat oven to 400°.

- Spread honey-mustard on each split roll. Top each with ham and cheese slices. Place on baking sheet and bake for 4 to 5 minutes or until cheese melts. Serves 8. *Buffalo, Wyoming*

Provolone Pepper Burgers

⅓ cup finely cubed provolone cheese
¼ cup diced roasted red peppers
¼ cup finely chopped onion
1 pound lean ground beef
4 hamburger buns, split

- Combine cheese, red peppers, onion and a little salt and pepper in bowl. Add beef, mix well and shape into 4 patties.

- Grill patties over medium-hot heat for 5 minutes on each side or until meat is no longer pink.

- Add your favorite lettuce, tomatoes, etc. and serve on hamburger buns. Serves 4. *Big Bear City, California*

Southwest Burgers

2 pounds lean ground beef
1 (1 ounce) packet taco seasoning mix
1 cup salsa, divided
8 kaiser buns
8 slices hot pepper Jack cheese

- Combine beef, taco seasoning and ¼ cup salsa in large bowl. Shape mixture into 8 patties.

- If you are grilling, cook patties for about 12 minutes or until they cook thoroughly and turn once. To broil in oven, place patties on broiler pan 4 to 5 inches from heat and broil until they cook thoroughly. Turn once during cooking

- When patties are almost done, place buns cut-side down on grill and heat for 1 or 2 minutes.

- Place patties on bottom half of buns, top with cheese and cook for an additional 1 minute or until cheese melts.

- Top with heaping tablespoon salsa and top half of bun. Serves 8.
  Clarkdale, Arizona

Meatball Hoagies

1 small onion, diced
1 small green bell pepper, diced
1 tablespoon oil
1 (15 ounce) can sloppy Joe sauce
30 - 32 frozen cooked meatballs
4 hoagie buns

- Saute onion and bell pepper in oil in skillet.

- Add sauce and meatballs, cook for 10 minutes or until thoroughly hot and stir often.

- Spoon evenly onto hoagie buns. Serves 4. *Brunswick, Maryland*

Hot Bunwiches

8 hamburger buns
8 slices Swiss cheese
8 slices ham
8 slices turkey
8 slices American cheese

- Lay out all 8 buns and place slices of Swiss cheese, ham, turkey and American cheese on bottom buns.

- Place top bun over American cheese, wrap each bunwich individually in foil and place in freezer. Remove from freezer 2 to 3 hours before serving.

- When ready to bake, preheat oven to 325°.

- Bake for about 30 minutes and serve hot. Serves 8. *Albia, Iowa*

Wrap-That-Turkey Burger

1 pound ground turkey
⅓ cup shredded 4-cheese blend
¼ cup finely grated onion, drained
1 teaspoon Creole spicy seasoning
4 fajita-size flour tortillas, warmed
2 cups shredded lettuce
⅔ cup guacamole

- Combine ground turkey, cheese, onion and Creole spicy seasoning in bowl.

- Shape into 4 patties (make patties a little longer than round) and refrigerate for about 30 minutes before cooking.

- Grill patties about 5 inches from heat for about 8 minutes or until thermometer reads 165°.

- Place tortillas on flat surface and arrange one-fourth lettuce on each tortilla. Place 1 patty on each tortilla and spread with guacamole. Fold tortilla in half to cover filling. Serves 4. *Bishop, California*

TIP: If you don't want to buy spicy seasoning, use 1 teaspoon seasoned salt and ¼ teaspoon cayenne pepper.

Guacamole-Ham Wrap

¾ cup guacamole
4 (8 inch) spinach tortillas
¾ cup salsa
½ (8 ounce) package shredded 4-cheese blend
¾ pound deli ham, cut in thin strips
Shredded lettuce

- Spread guacamole over half of each tortilla and layer salsa, cheese, ham strips and lettuce to within 2 inches of edges. Roll tightly. Refrigerate. Serves 4. *Bowie, Texas*

Easy Dog Wraps

8 wieners
8 slices cheese
1 (8 ounce) package refrigerated crescent rolls
Mustard

- Preheat oven to 375°.

- Split wieners lengthwise and fill with folded cheese slice.

- Wrap in crescent dough roll and bake for about 12 minutes. Serve with mustard. Yields 8 wraps. *Bayberry, New York*

Hot Reuben Spread

1 (8 ounce) package shredded Swiss cheese
¾ cup drained sauerkraut, rinsed, drained
1 (8 ounce) package cream cheese, softened, cubed
2 (2.5 ounce) packages sliced corned beef, chopped
3-inch rye bread

- Combine Swiss cheese, sauerkraut, cream cheese and corned beef in bowl and spoon into sprayed, small slow cooker.

- Cover and cook on LOW for 1 hour.

- Serve on slices of rye bread. Serves 8. *Bridgeport, Texas*

Cream Cheese Sandwich Spread

2 (8 ounce) packages cream cheese, softened
1 (2 ounce) jar dried beef, finely chopped
1 bunch fresh green onions with tops, chopped
¾ cup mayonnaise
Whole wheat bread

- Combine all ingredients and ½ teaspoon salt in bowl and blend until mixture spreads smoothly.

- Trim crust off bread and spread cream cheese mixture on half of the bread slices.

- Top with another slice of bread and slice into 3 strips or 4 quarters. Yields 1 pint. *Brookings, Oregon*

TIP: *The best way to chop dried beef is to use scissors to cut into small pieces.*

Hot-and-Sweet Mustard

This is great to keep in refrigerator for ham sandwiches.

4 ounces dry mustard
1 cup vinegar
3 eggs
1 cup sugar

- Soak dry mustard in vinegar overnight.

- Beat eggs and sugar in bowl and add to vinegar-mustard mixture.

- Cook in double boiler over low heat for about 15 minutes and stir constantly. Mixture will resemble custard consistency.

- Pour immediately into jars. Store in refrigerator. Serve with ham. Yields 2 cups. *Canton, South Dakota*

★ ★ ★
Side Dishes

Side dishes can make an everyday
dinner into something special
and 156 choices allow plenty of variety!

**1001
Community
Recipes**

Side Dishes Contents

Side Dishes Contents

Creamy Macaroni and Cheese

Yes, this is more trouble than opening that "blue box", but it is well worth the time to make this macaroni and cheese.

1 (12 ounce) package macaroni
6 tablespoons (¾ stick) butter
¼ cup flour
2 cups milk
1 (1 pound) package cubed Velveeta® cheese

- Preheat oven to 350°.

- Cook macaroni in saucepan according to package directions and drain.

- In separate saucepan, melt butter and stir in flour and ½ teaspoon each of salt and pepper until they blend well.

- Slowly add milk, stirring constantly, and heat until it begins to thicken. Add cheese and stir until cheese melts.

- Pour cheese sauce over macaroni and mix well.

- Pour into sprayed 2½-quart baking dish. Cover and bake for 30 minutes or until bubbly. Serves 4 to 6. *Brookshire, Texas*

A Different Macaroni

1 (8 ounce) package shell macaroni
½ cup whipping cream
1 (8 ounce) carton shredded gorgonzola cheese
1 (10 ounce) package frozen green peas, thawed
2 cups cubed ham

- Cook macaroni in saucepan according to package directions and drain. Add cream and gorgonzola cheese and stir until cheese melts.

- Fold in peas and ham and cook on low heat, stirring constantly, 5 minutes or until mixture is thoroughly hot.

- Spoon into serving bowl and serve hot. Serves 10. *Broyhill Park, Virginia*

Macaroni and Cheese

1 cup macaroni
1½ cups small curd cottage cheese
1½ cups shredded cheddar or American cheese
¼ cup grated parmesan cheese

- Preheat oven to 350°.

- Cook macaroni in saucepan according to package directions and drain.

- Combine remaining ingredients in bowl. Combine macaroni with cheese mixture.

- Spoon into sprayed 2-quart baking dish.

- Cover and bake for 35 minutes. Serves 4 to 6. *Belzoni, Mississippi*

Worth-It Macaroni

2 cups macaroni
2 cups milk
¼ cup flour
Seasoned salt
1 (12 ounce) package shredded sharp cheddar cheese
¼ cup (½ stick) butter, melted
1 cup soft breadcrumbs

- Preheat oven to 350°.

- Cook macaroni in saucepan according to package directions, drain and set aside.

- Combine milk, flour and an ample amount of seasoned salt in container with lid; shake to mix well.

- Combine macaroni, flour-milk mixture and cheese in large bowl.

- Pour into sprayed 9 x 13-inch baking dish. Pour melted butter over breadcrumbs in bowl, toss and sprinkle over top.

- Cover and bake for 35 minutes, remove cover and return to oven for 10 minutes. Serves 8. *Bremen, Georgia*

Macaroni and Cheese Deluxe

1 (8 ounce) package small shell macaroni
3 tablespoons butter, melted
1 (15 ounce) can stewed tomatoes
1 (8 ounce) package shredded Velveeta® cheese
1 cup crushed potato chips, optional

- Preheat oven to 350°.

- Cook macaroni in saucepan according to package directions, drain and place in bowl.

- While macaroni is still hot, stir in butter, tomatoes, cheese and a little salt and pepper and mix well.

- Pour into sprayed 2-quart baking dish, cover and bake for 25 minutes.

- Remove from oven, uncover and sprinkle with crushed potato chips. Bake for an additional 10 minutes or until potato chips are light brown. Serves 8. *Citronelle, Alabama*

Macaroni, Cheese and Tomatoes

2 cups elbow macaroni
1 (14 ounce) can stewed tomatoes with liquid
1 (8 ounce) package shredded cheddar cheese
2 tablespoons sugar
1 (6 ounce) package cheese slices

- Preheat oven to 350°.

- Cook macaroni in saucepan according to package directions and drain.

- Combine macaroni, tomatoes, shredded cheese, sugar, ¼ cup water and a little salt in large bowl and mix well.

- Pour into 9 x 13-inch baking dish and place cheese slices on top.

- Bake for 30 minutes or until bubbly. Serves 6 to 8. *Bellevue, Kentucky*

Special Macaroni and Cheese

1 (8 ounce) package small macaroni shells
1 (15 ounce) can stewed tomatoes
1 (8 ounce) package cubed Velveeta® cheese
3 tablespoons butter, melted

- Preheat oven to 350°.

- Cook shells in saucepan according to package directions and drain.

- Combine shells, tomatoes, cheese cubes and butter in large bowl. Pour into sprayed 2-quart baking dish.

- Cover and bake for 35 minutes. Serves 4 to 6. *Belle Meade, Tennessee*

Spiced-Up Macaroni

Macaroni:

1 (8 ounce) package spiral pasta
⅓ cup (⅔ stick) butter

- Cook macaroni in saucepan according to package directions, drain and add butter, stir until butter melts.

- Cover, set aside and keep warm.

Spicy Tomatoes:

1 (8 ounce) package shredded Mexican Velveeta® cheese
1 (10 ounce) can tomatoes and green chilies with liquid
½ yellow onion, finely diced
1 (8 ounce) carton sour cream

- Preheat oven to 325°.

- Combine cheese, tomatoes and green chilies, and onion in large saucepan. Stir in macaroni, heat on low for 5 minutes and stir occasionally.

- Fold in sour cream and pour into 2-quart baking dish. Cover and bake for 20 minutes. Serves 8. *Chaparral, New Mexico*

Sensational Spaghetti

Forget the tomato sauce. This is spaghetti to love!

1 (12 ounce) package thin spaghetti
½ cup (1 stick) butter
1½ teaspoons minced garlic
1 cup grated parmesan cheese
1 pint whipping cream
1 teaspoon dried parsley flakes
10 - 12 strips bacon, fried crisp, crumbled

- Preheat oven to 325°.

- Cook spaghetti in saucepan according to package directions and drain. Melt butter in large skillet and saute garlic until slightly brown.

- Add spaghetti, parmesan cheese, cream, parsley flakes, and ½ teaspoon each of salt and pepper to garlic and mix well.

- Spoon into sprayed 2-quart baking dish. Cover and bake just until warm, about 15 minutes.

- Uncover and sprinkle crumbled bacon over casserole. Serves 4 to 6. *Greenville, Rhode Island*

Ranch Spaghetti

1 (12 ounce) package spaghetti
¼ cup (½ stick) butter, cut in 3 pieces
¾ cup sour cream
¾ cup bottled ranch dressing
½ cup grated parmesan cheese

- Cook spaghetti in saucepan according to package directions, drain and return to saucepan. Stir in butter, sour cream and ranch dressing and toss.

- Spoon into serving bowl and sprinkle with grated parmesan cheese. Serves 8. *Batesville, Indiana*

TIP: You can make a main dish with this recipe just by adding 1 to 2 cups cubed ham or turkey.

Penne Pasta in Creamy Pesto

1 (16 ounce) package penne rigate pasta
1 (8 ounce) package Neufchatel cheese, softened
2 tablespoons butter
1 (6 ounce) jar basil pesto

- Cook pasta in saucepan according to package directions. Drain, leaving a little pasta water (about ½ cup) in pan. While pasta is still hot, cut cheese into chunks and stir cheese and butter into pasta, stirring until both have melted.

- Gently stir in basil pesto, adding 1 to 2 tablespoons water if mixture is too stiff. Serve hot. Serves 4 to 6. *Broad Brook, Connecticut*

Favorite Pasta

4 ounces spinach linguine
1 cup whipping cream
1 cup chicken broth
½ cup freshly grated parmesan cheese
½ cup frozen green peas

- Cook linguine in medium saucepan according to package directions, drain and keep warm.

- In separate saucepan, combine whipping cream and chicken broth and bring to a boil. Reduce heat and simmer mixture for 25 minutes or until it thickens and reduces to 1 cup. Remove from heat, add cheese and peas and stir until cheese melts.

- Toss with linguine and serve immediately. Serves 4 to 6. *Benton Heights, Michigan*

Creamy Seasoned Noodles

1 (8 ounce) package wide egg noodles
1 (1 ounce) packet Italian salad dressing mix
½ cup whipping cream
¼ cup (½ stick) butter, cut in chunks
¼ cup grated parmesan cheese

- Cook noodles in saucepan according to package directions and drain.

- Add butter and stir until it melts. Add remaining ingredients and toss lightly to blend thoroughly. Serve hot. Serves 4. *Appleton, Minnesota*

Cheesy Noodle Casserole

1 (8 ounce) package egg noodles
1 (16 ounce) package frozen broccoli florets, thawed
1 red bell pepper, seeded, chopped
1 (8 ounce) package shredded Velveeta® cheese
1 cup milk
¾ cup coarsely crushed bite-size cheese crackers

- Preheat oven to 350°.

- Cook noodles in large saucepan according to package directions. Add broccoli and bell pepper for last 2 minutes of cooking time. Drain and set aside.

- In same saucepan, combine cheese and milk over low heat and stir until cheese melts.

- Stir in noodle-broccoli mixture and spoon into sprayed 3-quart baking dish.

- Sprinkle with crushed crackers and bake for 25 to 30 minutes or until top is golden brown. Serves 10. *Albertville, Montana*

Creamy Pasta

8 ounces pasta
1 (8 ounce) jar roasted red peppers, drained
1 (15 ounce) can chicken broth
1 (3 ounce) package cream cheese

- Cook pasta according to package directions. Drain and keep warm.

- Combine red peppers and broth in blender and mix well. Pour into saucepan and heat to boiling. Turn heat down and whisk in cream cheese.

- Serve over pasta. Serves 4. *Enoch, Utah*

Pasta Frittata

1 onion, chopped
1 green bell pepper, chopped
1 red bell pepper, chopped
2 tablespoons butter
1 (7 ounce) box thin spaghetti, slightly broken, cooked
1 (8 ounce) package shredded mozzarella cheese
5 eggs
1 cup milk
⅓ cup shredded parmesan cheese
1 tablespoon dried basil
1 teaspoon oregano

- Preheat oven to 375°.

- Saute onion and bell peppers in butter in skillet over medium heat for about 5 minutes, but do not brown.

- Combine onion-pepper mixture and spaghetti in large bowl and toss. Add mozzarella cheese and toss.

- In separate bowl, beat eggs, milk, parmesan cheese, basil, oregano and ½ teaspoon each of salt and pepper. Add spaghetti mixture and pour into sprayed 9 x 13-inch baking dish.

- Cover with foil and bake for about 15 to 20 minutes. Uncover and make sure eggs are set. If not, bake for an additional 2 to 3 minutes. Serves 6 to 8. *Bethlehem, West Virginia*

TIP: *This can be put together, refrigerated and baked later. Let it get to room temperature before placing in oven. Cut into squares to serve. It is a great dish for a luncheon or late night supper.*

Spinach Fettuccine

1 (6 ounce) can tomato paste
1 (5 ounce) can evaporated milk
½ cup (1 stick) butter
1 (12 ounce) package spinach fettuccine

- Combine tomato paste, evaporated milk and butter in saucepan and cook until butter melts.

- Season with a little salt and pepper.

- Cook fettuccine in saucepan according to package directions. Serve sauce over fettuccine. Serves 4. *Barrington Hills, Illinois*

Wonderful Fettuccine Alfredo

1 (16 ounce) package fettuccine
2 tablespoons butter
¾ cup grated fresh parmesan cheese
1¼ cups whipping cream

- Cook fettuccine in saucepan according to package directions.

- Melt butter in large saucepan over medium heat and stir in parmesan cheese, cream and a little pepper. Cook for 1 minute and stir constantly. Reduce heat and pour in fettuccine, tossing gently to coat fettuccine. Serves 4. *Heyburn, Idaho*

Artichoke Fettuccine

1 (12 ounce) package fettuccine
1 (14 ounce) can water-packed artichoke hearts, drained, chopped
1 (10 ounce) box frozen green peas, thawed
1 (16 ounce) jar alfredo sauce
2 heaping tablespoons crumbled blue cheese

- Cook fettuccine in saucepan according to package directions. Drain and place in serving bowl and keep warm.

- Combine artichoke hearts, peas and alfredo sauce in large saucepan and heat. Stir well, spoon into bowl with fettuccine and toss.

- Sprinkle with blue cheese and serve hot. Serves 10. *Concord, Massachusetts*

Tasty Rice Bake

1½ cups rice
½ cup (1 stick) butter, melted
1 (10 ounce) can French onion soup
1 (8 ounce) can sliced water chestnuts, drained

- Preheat oven to 350°.

- Combine all ingredients and 1¼ cups water in bowl. Pour into sprayed 2-quart baking dish.

- Cover and bake for 1 hour. Serves 4 to 6. *Sitka, Alaska*

Pecan-Mushroom Rice

1 cup pecan halves
1½ cups instant rice
2 cups chicken broth
2 tablespoons butter
2 (8 ounce) cans whole mushrooms, drained
2 teaspoons minced garlic
3 cups baby spinach leaves without stems
½ cup grated parmesan cheese

- Cook and stir pecans in large saucepan over medium heat for 5 minutes. Remove from pan and cool slightly.

- Cook rice with chicken broth and butter in saucepan according to package directions. Gently stir in mushrooms, garlic, spinach, parmesan cheese and pecans. Serves 8. *Paipa, Hawaii*

Mushroom Rice

1 (6 ounce) package chicken Rice-a-Roni®
1 (4 ounce) can sliced mushrooms, drained
⅓ cup slivered almonds
1 (8 ounce) carton sour cream

- Preheat oven to 350°.

- Prepare rice in saucepan according to package directions. Fold in mushrooms, almonds and sour cream. Place in sprayed 3-quart baking dish.

- Cover and bake for 25 to 30 minutes. Serves 6 to 8. *Bicknell, Indiana*

Green Chile-Rice

1 cup instant rice, cooked
1 (12 ounce) package shredded Monterey Jack cheese
1 (7 ounce) can chopped green chilies
2 (8 ounce) cartons sour cream
½ teaspoon garlic powder

- Preheat oven to 350°.

- Mix all ingredients in large bowl and add a little salt, if you like.

- Spoon into sprayed 9 x 13-inch baking dish and bake for 30 minutes. Serves 6 to 8. *Ely, Nevada*

Dinner Rice

2 cups cooked rice
1 onion, chopped
¼ cup (½ stick) butter, melted
1 (8 ounce) package shredded Mexican Velveeta® cheese

- Preheat oven to 325°.

- Combine all ingredients in bowl and mix well. Spoon mixture into sprayed 2-quart baking dish.

- Cover and bake for 30 minutes. Serves 4 to 6. *Checotah, Oklahoma*

Creamy Rice Bake

1 cup finely chopped green onions with tops
¼ cup (½ stick) butter
3 cups cooked rice
1 (8 ounce) carton sour cream
¾ cup small curd cottage cheese
1¼ cups shredded Monterey Jack cheese

- Preheat oven to 350°.

- Saute onion with butter in large skillet. Remove from heat and add rice, sour cream, cottage cheese, ½ teaspoon each of salt and pepper, and Monterey Jack cheese.

- Toss lightly to mix and spoon into sprayed 2-quart baking dish. Cover and bake for 35 minutes. Serves 4 to 6. *Athens, Pennsylvania*

Colorful Bacon-Rice

¾ pound bacon
2½ cups cooked rice
1 (15 ounce) can sliced carrots, drained
1 (10 ounce) package frozen green peas, thawed

- Fry bacon in large skillet until crisp. Drain bacon on paper towels, leaving about ½ cup bacon drippings in skillet. Crumble bacon and set aside.

- Add rice, carrots and peas to skillet and cook, stirring occasionally until mixture is thoroughly hot. Stir in bacon and serve hot. Serves 4. *Belton, South Carolina*

Broccoli and Wild Rice

2 (10 ounce) packages frozen chopped broccoli
1 (6 ounce) box long grain-wild rice
1 (8 ounce) jar processed cheese spread
1 (10 ounce) can cream of chicken soup

- Preheat oven to 350°.

- Cook broccoli and rice in saucepan according to package directions.

- Combine all ingredients in bowl and pour into sprayed 2-quart baking dish.

- Bake for 25 to 30 minutes or until bubbly. Serves 4 to 6.
  Holbrook, Arizona

Baked Rice

2 cups rice
½ cup (1 stick) butter, melted
1 (10 ounce) can cream of celery soup
1 (10 ounce) can cream of onion soup

- Preheat oven to 350°.

- Combine rice, butter, soups and 1½ cups water in bowl.

- Pour into sprayed 3-quart baking dish.

- Bake for 1 hour. Serves 6 to 8. *Clio, Alabama*

Hoppin' John

4 slices bacon
1 onion, chopped
1 cup rice
1 (15 ounce) can black-eyed peas with liquid

- Fry bacon in skillet, drain, crumble and set aside.

- Saute onion in bacon grease.

- Combine onion, bacon grease, a little salt, rice and 2½ cups water in large saucepan. Bring to a boil. Cover, lower heat and simmer for 30 minutes.

- Add bacon and black-eyed peas and simmer for 5 more minutes. Remove from heat and allow to stand for 5 more minutes until liquid absorbs. Serves 4. *Carthage, Mississippi*

Supper Frittata

2 cups cooked rice
1 (10 ounce) box frozen green peas, thawed
1 cup cooked, cubed ham
Oil
8 large eggs, beaten
1 cup shredded pepper Jack cheese, divided
1 teaspoon dried thyme

- Heat rice, peas and ham in large, heavy ovenproof skillet with a little oil for 3 to 4 minutes or until mixture is thoroughly hot.

- In separate bowl, whisk eggs, three-fourths cheese, thyme and a little salt.

- Add to mixture in skillet and shake pan gently to distribute evenly.

- Cover and cook on medium heat, without stirring until set on bottom and sides. (Eggs will still be runny in center.)

- Sprinkle remaining cheese over top. Place ovenproof skillet in oven and broil for about 5 minutes or until frittata is firm in center. Serves 8 to 10. *Augusta, Arkansas*

Couscous and Veggies

1 (6 ounce) box herbed chicken-flavored couscous
¼ cup (½ stick) butter
1 red bell pepper, seeded, chopped
1 medium yellow squash, seeded, cubed
1 cup broccoli florets, coarsely chopped

- Preheat oven to 325°.

- Cook couscous in saucepan according to package directions, but omit butter. Melt butter in saucepan and saute bell pepper, squash and broccoli. Cook for about 10 minutes or until vegetables are almost tender.

- Combine couscous and vegetables and add a little salt and pepper. Spoon into sprayed 2-quart baking dish.

- Cover and bake for about 15 minutes or just until mixture is thoroughly hot. Serves 8. *Bonsall, California*

Carnival Couscous

Take a back seat rice! Couscous is here! Couscous is an ideal side dish for any entree because it absorbs flavors as it soaks up liquid. Couscous is a tiny Middle Eastern pasta that is often thought of as a grain.

1 (6 ounce) box herbed-chicken couscous
¼ cup (½ stick) butter
1 red bell pepper, minced
1 yellow squash, seeded, minced
1 cup fresh broccoli florets, finely chopped
1 cup celery, chopped

- Cook couscous in saucepan according to package directions, but omit butter.

- Melt butter in saucepan and saute bell pepper, squash, broccoli and celery. Cook for about 10 minutes or until vegetables are almost tender.

- Combine couscous, vegetables, and ½ teaspoon each of salt and pepper and serve. Serves 4 to 6. *Central Park, Washington*

TIP: If you want to make this in advance, place couscous and vegetables in sprayed baking dish and mix well. Cover and bake at 325° for about 20 minutes.

Parmesan-Garlic Orzo

1 (10 ounce) box original plain couscous
1 tablespoon minced garlic
¼ cup olive oil
½ cup grated parmesan cheese
¼ cup milk
1 tablespoon dried parsley
1 (8 ounce) can green peas, drained

- Bring 2 cups water in large saucepan to a boil, stir in couscous and cover. Let stand for 5 minutes.

- Stir in garlic, oil, parmesan cheese, milk, parsley, peas, and a little salt and pepper.

- Cook and stir until thoroughly hot. Serves 8. *Dacono, Colorado*

TIP: You might want to garnish with 3 sliced green onions.

Confetti Orzo

*This is really good. The alfredo sauce gives it a very
mild, pleasing flavor. (Sure beats "buttered rice".)*

8 ounces orzo pasta
½ cup (1 stick) butter
3 cups broccoli florets, stemmed
1 bunch green onions with tops, chopped
1 red bell pepper, seeded, chopped
2 cups celery, chopped
1 clove garlic, minced
½ teaspoon cumin
2 teaspoons chicken bouillon granules
1 (8 ounce) carton sour cream
1 (16 ounce) jar creamy alfredo sauce

• Preheat oven to 325°.

• Cook orzo in saucepan according to package directions; it is best to stir orzo several times during cooking time. Drain.

• While orzo is cooking, melt butter in skillet and saute broccoli, onions, bell pepper, celery, garlic and cumin and cook just until tender-crisp.

• Add chicken bouillon to vegetables.

• Spoon into large bowl and fold in sour cream, alfredo sauce, 1 teaspoon each of salt and pepper, and orzo.

• Spoon into sprayed 9 x 13-inch baking dish.

• Cover and bake for 30 minutes. Serves 6 to 8. *Colchester, Connecticut*

TIP: *You can refrigerate this and bake later. Let it come to room
    temperature before baking. This can easily be made into a main
    dish by adding 3 to 4 cups chopped, cooked chicken or turkey.*

The Perfect Potato

4 large baking potatoes, baked, warm
Stuffing:
¼ cup (½ stick) butter
¼ cup sour cream
1 cup finely chopped ham
1 (10 ounce) package frozen broccoli florets, coarsely chopped
1 cup shredded sharp cheddar cheese

* Preheat oven to 400°.

* Slit potatoes down center, but not through to bottom. For each potato, use one-fourth each of butter and sour cream. Work in one-fourth each of ham, broccoli and cheese with fork.

* Just before serving, place potatoes on baking sheet and heat for 10 minutes. Serves 4. *Dalton Gardens, Idaho*

Loaded Baked Potatoes

6 medium - large potatoes
1 (1 pound) package hot sausage
1 (16 ounce) package cubed Velveeta® cheese
1 (10 ounce) can tomatoes and green chilies, drained

* Preheat oven to 375°.

* Wrap potatoes in foil and bake for 1 hour or until done.

* Brown sausage in skillet and drain. Discard grease.

* Add cheese to sausage and heat until cheese melts. Add tomatoes and green chilies.

* Serve sausage-cheese mixture over baked potatoes. Serves 6. *Edgemoor, Delaware*

Ham-Baked Potatoes

4 potatoes, baked, hot
1 cup cooked, diced ham
1(10 ounce) can cream of mushroom soup
1 cup shredded cheddar cheese

- Place hot potatoes on microwave-safe plate. Cut in half lengthwise. Fluff up potatoes with fork and top each potato with one-fourth ham.

- Heat soup with ¼ cup water in saucepan and heat just until spreadable.

- Spoon soup over potatoes and top with cheese.

- Microwave on HIGH for 4 minutes or until hot. Serves 4. *Big Pine Key, Florida*

Creamy Potato Bake

6 - 8 baked potatoes
1 (8 ounce) carton sour cream
1 (8 ounce) package cream cheese, softened
1½ cups shredded cheddar cheese

- Preheat oven to 325°.

- Cut potatoes in half lengthwise. Scoop flesh out of potatoes and place in bowl.

- Add a little salt, sour cream and cream cheese and whip until all mix well.

- Spoon mashed potatoes back into potato skins and bake until potatoes are hot.

- Sprinkle cheddar cheese on top of potatoes. Serves 6 to 8. *Claxton, Georgia*

Broccoli-Topped Potatoes

4 hot baked potatoes, halved
1 cup diced, cooked ham
1 (10 ounce) can cream of broccoli soup
½ cup shredded cheddar cheese

- Place hot baked potatoes on microwave-safe plate. Carefully fluff up potatoes with fork. Top each potato with ham.

- Stir soup in can until smooth. Spoon soup over potatoes and top with cheese. Microwave on HIGH for 4 minutes. Serves 4. *Emmett, Idaho*

Broccoli-Cheese Potato Topper

1 (10 ounce) can fiesta nacho cheese soup
2 tablespoons sour cream
½ teaspoon dijon-style mustard
1 (10 ounce) box frozen broccoli flowerets, cooked
4 medium potatoes, baked, halved

- Combine soup, sour cream, mustard and broccoli in 1-quart microwave-safe baking dish. Heat in microwave for 2 to 2½ minutes.

- Fluff potatoes with fork; leave skins intact. Spoon broccoli mixture over potato halves. Serves 4. *Bartonville, Illinois*

Baked Potato Toppers

1 cup shredded cheddar cheese
½ cup sour cream
¼ cup (½ stick) butter, softened
¼ cup chopped green onions

- Mix all ingredients in bowl and serve on baked potatoes. Serves 4. *Fruitland, Idaho*

Cheddar Potatoes

1 (10 ounce) can cheddar cheese soup
⅓ cup sour cream
2 fresh green onions, chopped
3 cups instant seasoned mashed potatoes, prepared

- Preheat oven to 350°.

- Heat soup in saucepan and add sour cream, green onions and a little pepper. Stir in potatoes until they blend well.

- Pour into sprayed 2-quart baking dish and bake for 25 minutes. Serves 4 to 6. *Coushatta, Louisiana*

Dinner-Bell Mashed Potatoes

8 medium - large potatoes
1 (8 ounce) carton sour cream
1 (8 ounce) package cream cheese, softened
Butter

- Preheat oven to 325°.

- Peel, cut up and boil potatoes in saucepan until tender and drain.

- Whip hot potatoes and add sour cream, cream cheese, 1 teaspoon salt and ½ teaspoon pepper. Continue whipping until cream cheese melts.

- Pour in sprayed 3-quart baking dish. Dot generously with butter.

- Cover and bake for about 20 minutes. Serves 6 to 8. *Beulah, North Dakota*

TIP: *This may be made the day before and refrigerated. Bake for 30 minutes, if refrigerated.*

Whipped Potato Bake

4 pounds potatoes, peeled, cubed
½ cup (1 stick) butter, softened
1 (8 ounce) carton whipping cream
1 (8 ounce) carton cream cheese with chives
1½ teaspoons garlic salt
1 cup slivered almonds

- Preheat oven to 325°.

- Place potatoes and a little salt in large saucepan and cover with water. Bring to a boil, reduce heat and cook for about 15 minutes or until potatoes are tender. Drain.

- Beat potatoes until smooth and add butter, whipping cream, cream cheese and garlic salt. Beat until butter melts and mixture blends well.

- Pour into sprayed 9 x 13-inch baking dish and bake for 20 minutes.

- Remove from oven and sprinkle almonds over top of casserole.

- Bake for an additional 20 minutes or until potatoes are light brown. Serves 10 to 12. *Baxter, Minnesota*

Supreme Mashed Potatoes

1 (8 ounce) package cream cheese, softened
½ cup sour cream
2 tablespoons butter, softened
1 (1 ounce) packet ranch salad dressing mix
8 cups prepared instant mashed potatoes, warm

- Preheat oven to 325°.

- Combine cream cheese, sour cream, butter and ranch salad dressing mix in bowl, beat until smooth. Stir in warm potatoes and mix well.

- Transfer to sprayed 3-quart baking dish, cover and bake for 25 minutes or until mixture is thoroughly hot. Serves 8. *Black Jack, Missouri*

Scalloped Potatoes 🍁

Vast herds of buffalo roamed the great prairies of Saskatchewan, Canada. Dried buffalo was plentiful in the fur trading posts and was carried great distances by canoe. Settlers from all over Europe were lured to Saskatchewan with the promise of $10.00 parcels of land to grow fields of grains. It took huge numbers of people to harvest the grain and housewives had to feed hungry men with vegetables from their gardens and meat from their cattle, pigs and chickens.

6 - 8 potatoes, peeled, thinly sliced
2 onions, chopped
¼ cup flour
4 cups milk
½ cup (1 stick) butter, melted, divided
1 cup breadcrumbs

- Preheat oven to 325°.

- Combine sliced potatoes, onions and flour in large bowl. Carefully toss until potatoes and onions are evenly coated with flour; spoon into sprayed 9 x 13-inch baking dish.

- Combine milk with 2 teaspoons salt and a little pepper in bowl; slowly pour over potato mixture. Spoon half melted butter over mixture.

- In separate bowl, combine remaining butter with breadcrumbs and sprinkle over top of potato mixture. Bake for 1 hour 35 to 45 minutes. Serves 12. *Moose Jaw, Saskatchewan, Canada*

Potato Souffle

2⅔ cups instant mashed potatoes
2 eggs, beaten
1 cup shredded cheddar cheese
1 (3 ounce) can french-fried onion rings

- Preheat oven to 325°.

- Prepare mashed potato mix according to package directions. Add eggs and cheese and stir until they blend well.

- Spoon mixture into sprayed 2-quart baking dish. Sprinkle with onion rings.

- Bake for 25 minutes. Serves 4 to 6. *Cherryvale, Kansas*

Scalloped Potato Casserole

6 medium potatoes
½ cup (1 stick) butter
1 tablespoon flour
2 cups shredded cheddar cheese
¾ cup milk

- Preheat oven to 350°.

- Peel and slice potatoes. Place half potatoes in sprayed 3-quart baking dish.

- Slice half butter over potatoes, sprinkle with half flour and cover with half cheese. Repeat layers with cheese on top.

- Pour milk over casserole and sprinkle with a little pepper. (Prepare as fast as you can so potatoes will not turn dark.)

- Cover and bake for 1 hour. Serves 6 to 8. *Bloomfield, Indiana*

Company Potatoes

5 potatoes, peeled, sliced
2 (8 ounce) cartons whipping cream
2 tablespoons dijon-style mustard
2 tablespoons butter
Garlic powder
½ cup grated parmesan cheese

- Preheat oven to 350°.

- Layer potatoes and a little salt and pepper in sprayed 9 x 13-inch baking dish.

- Combine cream, mustard, butter and a little garlic powder in saucepan and heat to boiling. Pour over potatoes.

- Cover and bake for 1 hour.

- Uncover and top with parmesan cheese. Bake for an additional 10 minutes or until potatoes are tender. Serves 5. *Cold Spring, Kentucky*

Pretty Parsley Potatoes

2 pounds small new (red) potatoes with peels, quartered
¼ cup vegetable oil
1 (1 ounce) packet ranch dressing mix
¼ cup fresh chopped parsley

- Place potatoes, vegetable oil, dressing mix and ¼ cup water in 4 to 5-quart slow cooker and toss to coat potatoes.

- Cover and cook on LOW for 3 to 4 hours or until potatoes are tender.

- When ready to serve, sprinkle parsley over potatoes and toss. Serves 6 to 8. *Delphi, Louisiana*

Parslied Potatoes 🍁

1 pound small new (red) potatoes
½ cup (1 stick) butter
¼ cup chopped, fresh parsley

- Scrub potatoes well and place in large saucepan covered with salted, boiling water. Cook potatoes on medium-high heat for about 10 minutes or until potatoes are tender.

- Drain and let potatoes cool slightly and rub potatoes with butter and a little salt and pepper. Place in serving bowl and garnish with chopped parsley. Serves 6. *Prince Rupert, British Columbia, Canada*

Cheesy Potatoes

10 - 12 new potatoes with peels
1 (8 ounce) carton sour cream
¼ cup (½ stick) butter, melted
1 (16 ounce) package Velveeta® cheese, sliced

- Preheat oven to 400°.

- Rinse and scrub potatoes. Cut into ¼-inch slices, place in large saucepan and cover with water. Cook for 25 minutes until slightly tender and drain.

- Place half potatoes in 9 x 13-inch baking dish. Sprinkle with a little salt and pepper. Spread half sour cream and half melted butter over top of potatoes. Put half sliced cheese on top.

- Repeat layers. Bake for about 20 minutes or until bubbly. Serves 6 to 8. *Dover-Foxcroft, Maine*

Potatoes au Gratin

1 (8 ounce) package cubed Velveeta® cheese
1 (16 ounce) carton half-and-half cream
1 cup shredded cheddar cheese
½ cup (1 stick) butter
1 (32 ounce) package frozen hash-brown potatoes, thawed

• Preheat oven to 350°.

• Melt Velveeta® cheese, half-and-half cream, cheddar cheese and butter in double boiler.

• Place hash browns in sprayed 9 x 13-inch baking dish and pour cheese mixture over potatoes.

• Bake for 1 hour. Serves 6 to 8. *Bryans Road, Maryland*

Potatoes Supreme

1 (32 ounce) package frozen hash-brown potatoes, thawed
1 onion, chopped
2 (10 ounce) cans cream of chicken soup
1 (8 ounce) carton sour cream

• Preheat oven to 350°.

• Combine all ingredients in large bowl. Pour into sprayed 9 x 13-inch baking dish.

• Cover and bake for 1 hour. Serves 6 to 8. *Brewster, Massachusetts*

TIP: This recipe is also good with ½ cup shredded parmesan or cheddar cheese sprinkled on top for the last 5 minutes of baking.

Potatoes with a Zip

1 (32 ounce) bag frozen hash-brown potatoes, thawed
1 (16 ounce) package cubed Velveeta® cheese
2 cups mayonnaise
1 (7 ounce) can chopped green chilies

• Preheat oven to 325°.

• Combine all ingredients in large bowl.

• Spoon into sprayed 9 x 13-inch baking dish. Cover and bake for 1 hour. Stir twice during baking to prevent burning. Serves 6 to 8. *Boyne City, Michigan*

Golden Potato Casserole

1 (2 pound) bag frozen hash-brown potatoes, thawed
1 (1 pint) carton sour cream
1 (8 ounce) package shredded cheddar cheese
1 bunch fresh green onions with tops, chopped

• Preheat oven to 325°.

• Combine all ingredients in large bowl and thoroughly mix. Pour into sprayed 9 x 13-inch baking dish. Cover and bake for 55 minutes. Serves 6 to 8. *Chamberlain, South Dakota*

Creamy Cheesy Potatoes

1 (32 ounce) bag frozen hash-brown potatoes, thawed
1 (16 ounce) package cubed Velveeta® cheese
1 (10 ounce) can cream of chicken soup
1 (8 ounce) carton sour cream

• Preheat oven to 325°.

• Combine all ingredients in large bowl. (You may want to add ½ teaspoon salt.) Spoon into sprayed 9 x 13-inch baking dish. Cover and bake for 1 hour.

• Stir twice during baking to prevent burning. Serves 6 to 8. *Auburn, Nebraska*

Cheddar-Potato Casserole

This is a "winner" for the easiest and best potato dish!

1 (2 pound) bag frozen hash-brown potatoes, thawed
1 onion, finely chopped
¾ cup (1½ sticks) butter, melted, divided
1 cup sour cream
1 (10 ounce) can cream of chicken soup
2 cups shredded cheddar cheese
1½ cups crushed corn flakes

• Preheat oven to 350°.

• Combine hash browns, onion, ½ cup butter, sour cream, soup and cheese in large bowl and mix well.

• Pour into sprayed 9 x 13-inch baking dish. Combine corn flakes and remaining butter in bowl, sprinkle over mixture and bake for 45 minutes. Serves 6 to 8. *Broken Bow, Nebraska*

Potato Pancakes

3 pounds white potatoes, peeled, grated
1 onion, finely minced
3 eggs, beaten
½ cup seasoned dry breadcrumbs
Oil

• Combine potatoes, onions, eggs, a little salt and pepper and breadcrumbs in large bowl and mix well.

• Drop spoonfuls of mixture in hot oil in skillet and brown on both sides. Serves 4 to 6. *Collins, Nebraska*

Whipped Sweet Potatoes

2 (15 ounce) cans sweet potatoes
¼ cup (½ stick) butter, melted
¼ cup orange juice
1 cup miniature marshmallows

• Preheat oven to 350°.

• Combine sweet potatoes, butter, orange juice and ½ teaspoon salt in bowl. Beat until fluffy. Fold in marshmallows.

• Spoon into sprayed 2-quart baking dish. Bake for 25 minutes. Serves 4 to 6. *Bowling Green, Missouri*

TIP: You could also sprinkle additional marshmallows and broil until light brown.

Sweet Potatoes and Pecans

2 (17 ounce) cans sweet potatoes, drained, divided
1½ cups packed brown sugar
¼ cup (½ stick) butter, melted
1 cup chopped pecans

• Preheat oven to 350°.

• Slice half sweet potatoes and place in sprayed 2-quart baking dish.

• Mix brown sugar, butter and pecans in bowl and sprinkle half mixture over sweet potatoes. Repeat layers. Bake for 30 minutes. Serves 4 to 6. *DeQuincy, Louisiana*

Sweet Potato Casserole

1 (29 ounce) can sweet potatoes, drained
⅓ cup evaporated milk
¾ cup sugar
2 eggs, beaten
¼ cup (½ stick) butter, melted
1 teaspoon vanilla

- Preheat oven to 350°.

- Place sweet potatoes in bowl and mash slightly with fork.
  Add remaining ingredients and mix well. Pour mixture into sprayed
  7 x 11-inch baking dish.

Topping:

1 cup packed light brown sugar
⅓ cup (⅔ stick) butter, melted
½ cup flour
1 cup chopped pecans

- Mix topping ingredients in bowl and sprinkle over top of casserole.

- Bake for 35 minutes or until crusty on top. Serves 8. *Bucknell Manor, Virginia*

Sweet Potato Bake

2 (15 ounce) cans sweet potatoes, drained, divided
1½ cups packed brown sugar
¼ cup (½ stick) butter, melted
¾ cup chopped pecans
1 cup miniature marshmallows

- Preheat oven to 350°.

- Place 1 can sweet potatoes in sprayed 2-quart baking dish

- Combine brown sugar, butter and pecans in bowl and sprinkle
  half of mixture over sweet potatoes. Repeat layers of sweet
  potatoes and brown sugar mixture. Cover and bake for 25 minutes.

- Sprinkle marshmallows on top and return to oven for 10 to
  15 minutes or until marshmallows are light brown. Serves 8 to 10.
  Bells, Tennessee

Chili-Baked Beans

2 (16 ounce) cans pork and beans, drained
1 (15 ounce) can chili with beans
¼ cup molasses
1 teaspoon chili powder

- Preheat oven to 350°.

- Combine pork and beans, chili, molasses, and chili powder in 2-quart baking dish. Bake until bubbly. Serves 4 to 6. *Hampton, New Hampshire*

Western Baked Beans 🍁

Alberta, Canada, was at first one big open cattle range, but when the railroad came in 1883, immigrants came from Britain and all over Europe wanting land to farm. Towns were formed with lumberyards, blacksmith shops and grain elevators to serve the farms.

But above all, Albertans were proud of their ranch legacy. Wild game was plentiful, lush fields of grains were available, but beef was king (and still is) as the favorite food for the settlers.

1 (28 ounce) can baked beans
1 (28 ounce) can kidney beans
3 (15 ounce) cans lima beans
2 onions, finely chopped
1 cup packed brown sugar
1 teaspoon dry mustard
½ teaspoon garlic powder
½ teaspoon hot sauce, optional
½ cup ketchup
⅔ cup vinegar

- Preheat oven to 350°.

- Place all beans and onions in large stew pot.

- Combine brown sugar, mustard, garlic powder, hot sauce, ketchup and vinegar in bowl and stir into beans.

- Cover and bake for 35 minutes. Remove lid and continue baking for an additional 35 minutes. Serves 8 to 10. *Rocky Mountain House, Alberta, Canada*

Classic Baked Bean Stand-By

3 (18 ounce) cans baked beans
½ cup chili sauce
⅓ cup packed brown sugar
4 slices bacon, cooked, crumbled

- Preheat oven to 325°.

- Combine baked beans, chili sauce and brown sugar in sprayed 3-quart baking dish.

- Bake for 40 minutes.

- When ready to serve, sprinkle bacon on top. Serves 6 to 8. *Belvidere, New Jersey*

Instant Beans and Rice

1 (8.8 ounce) package (microwaveable) rice
1 (15 ounce) can pinto beans with liquid
½ cup hot thick-and-chunky salsa
1 teaspoon ground cumin

- Microwave rice in package for 90 seconds; transfer to saucepan and add beans, salsa, cumin and a little salt. Heat on medium heat just until thoroughly hot. Serves 4. *Clayton, New Mexico*

Onion Rings

1 yellow onion, sliced
2⅓ cups biscuit mix, divided
1 cup beer
2 eggs, slightly beaten
Oil

- Separate onion rings and toss with ⅓ cup biscuit mix. In separate bowl, stir together remaining biscuit mix, beer, eggs and a little salt.

- Prepare deep fryer or very large saucepan with hot oil to 375° (oil must be very hot or onion rings will not be crisp). Dip onion rings, a few at a time into batter, letting excess drip into bowl.

- Fry for about 2 minutes and turn with fork, fry until golden brown and drain on paper towels. Serves 4. *Big Lake, Texas*

Festive Cranberry Stuffing

1 (14 ounce) can chicken broth
1 rib celery, chopped
½ cup fresh or frozen cranberries
1 small onion, chopped
4 cups herb-seasoned stuffing

- Preheat oven to 325°.

- Mix broth, dash of pepper, celery, cranberries and onion in saucepan and heat to a boil. Cover and cook over low heat for 5 minutes.

- Add stuffing, mix lightly and spoon into baking dish.

- Bake until thoroughly hot. Serves 4 to 6. *Buena Vista, Virginia*

Festive Cranberries

What a great dish for Thanksgiving or Christmas!

2 (20 ounce) cans pie apples (pie apples, not apple pie filling)
1 (16 ounce) can whole cranberries
¾ cup sugar
½ cup packed brown sugar

Topping:

¼ cup (½ stick) butter
1½ cups crushed corn flakes
⅔ cup sugar
½ teaspoon ground cinnamon
1 cup chopped pecans

- Preheat oven to 325°.

- Combine pie apples, cranberries, sugar and brown sugar in bowl and mix well. Spoon into sprayed 2-quart baking dish.

- Melt butter in saucepan and mix in corn flakes, sugar, cinnamon and pecans. Sprinkle over apples and cranberries.

- Bake for 1 hour. This can be served hot or at room temperature. Serves 4 to 6. *Berlin, Wisconsin*

Cinnamon Baked Apples

6 Granny Smith apples
¾ cup mixed nuts
1 cup packed light brown sugar
1 teaspoon ground cinnamon

- Preheat oven to 350°.

- Core apples without cutting through to bottom. Using a potato peeler, peel 1-inch strip around top of apple.

- Combine nuts, brown sugar and cinnamon in bowl and stuff cavities and place apples in sprayed 2-quart baking dish. Drizzle 2 tablespoons water over apples and bake for about 45 minutes or until apples are tender when pierced with knife.

- Serve warm or at room temperature. Serves 4 to 6.
  Castlewood, Virginia

Artichoke Squares

2 (6 ounce) jars marinated artichoke hearts, with liquid
1 onion, finely chopped
½ teaspoon minced garlic
4 eggs, beaten
⅓ cup breadcrumbs
1 (8 ounce) package cheddar cheese
1 tablespoon dried parsley flakes

- Preheat oven to 325°.

- Drain liquid (marinade) from 1 jar artichoke hearts into skillet, heat and cook onion and garlic in liquid. (Discard liquid from remaining jar artichoke hearts.)

- Chop artichoke hearts and set aside.

- In separate bowl, combine eggs, breadcrumbs, and ¼ teaspoon each of salt and pepper. Fold in cheese and parsley. Add artichokes and onions and mix well.

- Spoon into sprayed 9-inch square baking dish.

- Bake for 30 minutes. Allow several minutes before cutting into squares to serve. Serves 6 to 8. *Erda, Utah*

TIP: *These artichoke squares are perfect for a brunch because they can be served hot or at room temperature. They can also be made ahead of time and reheated when ready to serve.*

Asparagus Casserole

3 (15 ounce) cans cut asparagus, drained
3 eggs, hard-boiled, sliced
½ cup chopped pecans
1 (10 ounce) can cream of asparagus soup
½ cup milk
1 cup shredded Swiss cheese

- Preheat oven to 350°.

- Place asparagus in sprayed 7 x 11-inch baking dish and top with sliced eggs and pecans.

- Combine soup, milk and Swiss cheese in saucepan and heat over medium heat, stirring constantly, just until cheese melts and mixture blends well.

- Pour over asparagus mixture and spread to cover. Cover and bake for 25 minutes or until casserole is bubbly around edges. Serves 8. *Byron, Georgia*

Swiss Asparagus

3 (15 ounce) cans asparagus spears, drained
1½ cups sour cream
½ cup shredded Swiss cheese
2 tablespoons minced onion flakes
¼ teaspoon dry mustard
¼ teaspoon garlic powder
1 cup fresh breadcrumbs
3 tablespoons butter, melted

- Preheat oven to 325°.

- Place asparagus in sprayed 1½-quart baking dish.

- Combine sour cream, Swiss cheese, onion flakes, ¾ teaspoon salt, ¼ teaspoon pepper, dry mustard and garlic powder in bowl and mix well to blend.

- Spoon sour cream mixture over asparagus.

- In separate bowl, toss breadcrumbs with melted butter and sprinkle over casserole.

- Bake for 30 minutes. Serves 4 to 6. *Edwardsville, Kansas*

Asparagus Bake

2 (15 ounce) cans cut asparagus spears with liquid
3 eggs, hard-boiled, chopped
½ cup chopped pecans
1 (10 ounce) can cream of asparagus soup

- Preheat oven to 350°.

- Arrange asparagus spears in sprayed 2-quart baking dish. Top with eggs and pecans.

- Heat asparagus soup in saucepan and add liquid from asparagus spears.

- Spoon over eggs and pecans. Cover and bake for 25 minutes. Serves 4 to 6. *Bushnell, Illinois*

Asparagus Caesar

3 (15 ounce) cans asparagus spears, drained
¼ cup (½ stick) butter, melted
3 tablespoons lemon juice
½ cup grated parmesan cheese

- Preheat oven to 400°.

- Place asparagus in 2-quart baking dish. Drizzle on butter and lemon juice. Sprinkle cheese (and a little paprika if you like).

- Bake for 15 to 20 minutes. Serves 4 to 6. *Belle Plaine, Iowa*

Sesame Asparagus

6 fresh asparagus spears, trimmed
1 tablespoon butter
1 teaspoon lemon juice
1 teaspoon sesame seeds

- Place asparagus in skillet. Sprinkle with salt, if desired. Add ¼ cup water and bring to a boil. Reduce heat. Cover and simmer for about 4 minutes.

- Melt butter in saucepan and add lemon juice and sesame seeds.

- Drain asparagus and drizzle with butter mixture. Serves 4. *Columbia, Kentucky*

Cheddar-Broccoli Bake

1 (10 ounce) can cheddar cheese soup
½ cup milk
1 (16 ounce) package frozen broccoli florets, cooked, drained
1 (3 ounce) can french-fried onion rings

- Preheat oven to 350°.

- Mix soup, milk and broccoli in 2-quart baking dish.

- Bake for 25 minutes.

- Stir broccoli mixture and sprinkle onions over top.

- Bake for an additional 5 minutes or until onions are golden. Serves 4 to 6. *Garyville, Louisiana*

Impossible Broccoli Pie

1 (16 ounce) package frozen broccoli florets, thawed
1 (12 ounce) package shredded cheddar cheese, divided
½ cup chopped onion
3 eggs, slightly beaten
¾ cup buttermilk biscuit mix
1½ cups milk

- Preheat oven to 350°.

- Cut large chunks of broccoli into smaller pieces and discard some stems.

- Combine broccoli, two-thirds of cheese and onion in large bowl and mix well. Spoon into sprayed 10-inch, deep-dish pie pan.

- In same bowl, mix eggs and biscuit mix and beat for several minutes. Add milk and mix until fairly smooth. Pour over broccoli and cheese mixture.

- Bake for 35 to 40 minutes or until knife inserted in center comes out clean.

- Top with remaining cheese and bake just until cheese melts. Let stand for 5 minutes before slicing into wedges to serve. Serves 10. *Gardiner, Maine*

Crunchy Broccoli

2 (10 ounce) packages frozen broccoli florets
1 (8 ounce) can sliced water chestnuts, drained, chopped
½ cup (1 stick) butter, melted
1 (1 ounce) packet dry onion soup mix

- Place broccoli in microwave-safe dish, cover and microwave for 5 minutes.

- Turn dish and cook for an additional 4 minutes.

- Add water chestnuts.

- Combine melted butter and soup mix, blend well and toss with broccoli. Serves 4 to 6. *Capitol Heights, Maryland*

Broccoli Frittata

3 tablespoons butter
½ cup chopped onion
4 cups fresh broccoli florets without stems
6 large eggs, slightly beaten
1 (1 ounce) packet cream of broccoli soup mix
¾ cup shredded cheddar cheese
½ cup milk

- Preheat oven to 350°.

- Melt butter in skillet and saute onion. Add broccoli and 1 tablespoon water. Cook, stirring occasionally, on low heat for about 5 minutes until tender-crisp, but still bright green.

- In separate bowl, whisk eggs, soup mix, cheese, milk and a little salt and pepper. Fold in broccoli-onion mixture.

- Pour into sprayed 10-inch deep-dish pie pan and bake for 20 to 25 minutes or until center is set.

- Let frittata stand for 5 to 10 minutes before cutting into wedges. Serves 8. *Chelsea, Massachusetts*

Broccoli-Cauliflower Casserole

1 (10 ounce) package frozen broccoli florets, thawed
1 (10 ounce) package frozen cauliflower, thawed
1 egg, beaten
⅔ cup mayonnaise
1 (10 ounce) can cream of chicken soup
¼ cup milk
1 cup shredded Swiss cheese
1½ cups seasoned breadcrumbs
2 tablespoons butter, melted

- Preheat oven to 350°.

- Cook broccoli and cauliflower in microwave according to package directions. Drain well and place in large bowl.

- Combine egg, mayonnaise, soup, milk and cheese in saucepan and mix well. Heat just enough to be able to mix.

- Add to broccoli-cauliflower mixture and gently mix. Pour into sprayed 2½-quart baking dish.

- Combine breadcrumbs and butter in bowl, sprinkle over mixture and bake for 35 minutes. Serves 6 to 8. *Charlotte, Michigan*

Cauliflower Con Queso

1 large head cauliflower, broken into florets
¼ cup (½ stick) butter
½ onion, chopped
2 tablespoons flour
1 (15 ounce) can Mexican-stewed tomatoes
1 (4 ounce) can chopped green chilies, drained
1½ cups shredded Monterey Jack cheese

- Preheat oven to 325°.

- Cook cauliflower florets in water in saucepan until just tender-crisp, drain and place in sprayed 2-quart baking dish.

- Melt butter in medium saucepan. Saute onion just until clear, but not brown. Blend in flour and stir in tomatoes. Cook, stirring constantly, until mixture thickens.

- Add green chilies and ¾ teaspoon each of salt and pepper. Fold in cheese and stir until it melts. Pour sauce over cauliflower.

- Cover and bake for about 15 minutes. Serves 4 to 6. *Grantsville, Utah*

Souper Cauliflower

1 (16 ounce) package frozen cauliflower, cooked, drained
1 (10 ounce) can cream of celery soup
¼ cup milk
1 cup shredded cheddar cheese

- Preheat oven to 350°.

- Place cauliflower in sprayed 2-quart baking dish.

- Combine soup, milk and cheese in saucepan and heat just enough to mix well. Pour over cauliflower.

- Bake for 15 minutes. Serves 4 to 6. *Benson, Minnesota*

Savory Cauliflower

1 head cauliflower
1 (1 ounce) packet hollandaise sauce mix
Fresh parsley to garnish
Lemon slices to garnish, optional

- Cut cauliflower into small florets. Cook in salted water in saucepan until barely tender. Do not overcook.

- Mix sauce according to package directions.

- Drain cauliflower, top with sauce and sprinkle with parsley. Garnish with lemon slices, if you like. Serves 4. *Drew, Mississippi*

Best Cauliflower

1 (16 ounce) package frozen cauliflower
1 (8 ounce) carton sour cream
1½ cups shredded American or cheddar cheese
4 teaspoons sesame seeds, toasted

- Preheat oven to 350°.

- Cook cauliflower according to package directions.

- Drain and place half cauliflower in 2-quart baking dish. Sprinkle a little salt and pepper on cauliflower.

- Spread half sour cream and half cheese; top with half sesame seeds and repeat layers.

- Bake for about 15 to 20 minutes. Serves 4 to 6. *Buffalo, Missouri*

Cauliflower Medley

1 head cauliflower, cut into florets
1 (14 ounce) can Italian stewed tomatoes with juice
1 bell pepper, chopped
1 onion, chopped
¼ cup (½ stick) butter
1 cup shredded cheddar cheese

- Preheat oven to 350°.

- Place cauliflower, stewed tomatoes, bell pepper, onion and butter in large saucepan with about 2 tablespoons water and a little salt and pepper.

- Cover and cook in saucepan until cauliflower is done, about 10 to 15 minutes. (Do not let cauliflower get mushy.)

- Place in 2-quart baking dish and sprinkle cheese on top.

- Bake just until cheese melts. Serves 4 to 6. *Evergreen, Montana*

Fiesta Corn

1 (15 ounce) can cream-style corn
1 (15 ounce) can whole kernel corn
1 green bell pepper, seeded, chopped
1 (4 ounce) can chopped green chilies
¼ cup (½ stick) butter, melted
2 eggs, beaten
¼ teaspoon cayenne pepper
¼ teaspoon sugar
1½ cups buttery cracker crumbs, divided
1 cup shredded 4-cheese blend

- Preheat oven to 350°.

- Combine both cans of corn, bell pepper, green chilies, butter, eggs, cayenne pepper, sugar, ½ cup cracker crumbs, cheese and a little salt and pepper in large bowl.

- Spoon into sprayed 3-quart baking dish and sprinkle remaining crumbs on top. Bake for 35 minutes. Serves 6 to 8. *El Jebel, Colorado*

Wild West Corn

3 (15 ounce) cans whole kernel corn, drained
1 (10 ounce) can tomatoes and green chilies, drained
1 (8 ounce) package shredded Monterey Jack cheese
1 cup cheese cracker crumbs

- Preheat oven to 350°.

- Combine corn, tomatoes and green chilies, and cheese in large bowl and mix well. Pour into sprayed 2½-quart baking dish.

- Sprinkle cracker crumbs over top. Bake for 25 minutes. Serves 4 to 6. *Douglas, Wyoming*

Stuffed Corn

1 (15 ounce) can cream-style corn
1 (15 ounce) can whole kernel corn, drained
½ cup (1 stick) butter, melted
1 (6 ounce) package chicken stuffing mix

- Preheat oven to 350°.

- Combine all ingredients plus seasoning packet and ½ cup water in bowl and mix well.

- Spoon into sprayed 9 x 13-inch baking pan. Bake for 30 minutes. Serves 6 to 8. *Cozad, Nebraska*

Hot Corn Bake

3 (15 ounce) cans whole kernel corn, drained
1 (10 ounce) can cream of corn soup
1 cup salsa
1 (8 ounce) package shredded Mexican 4-cheese blend, divided

- Preheat oven to 350°.

- Combine corn, corn soup, salsa and half cheese in bowl and mix well.

- Pour into sprayed 3-quart baking dish and sprinkle remaining cheese on top.

- Bake for 20 to 30 minutes. Serves 6 to 8. *Gardnerville, Nevada*

Fantastic Fried Corn

Yes, I know this has too many calories, but it's my grandkids'
favorite vegetable. And who can turn down grandkids?

2 (16 ounce) packages frozen whole kernel corn
½ cup (1 stick) butter
1 cup whipping cream
1 tablespoon sugar

- Place corn in large skillet over medium heat and add butter, whipping cream, sugar and 1 teaspoon salt.

- Stir constantly and heat until most of whipping cream and butter absorbs into corn. Serves 4 to 6. *Canton, Texas*

Everybody's Favorite Corn

1 (15 ounce) can whole kernel corn
1 (15 ounce) can cream-style corn
½ cup (1 stick) butter, melted
2 eggs, beaten
1 (8 ounce) carton sour cream
1 (6 ounce) package jalapeno cornbread mix
½ cup shredded cheddar cheese

- Preheat oven to 350°.

- Mix all ingredients, except cheese in large bowl and pour into sprayed 9 x 13-inch baking dish.

- Cover and bake for 35 minutes or until light brown on top. Uncover, sprinkle cheese on top and return to oven for 5 minutes. Serves 8 to 10. *Hanover, New Hampshire*

Atomic Salsa-Corn

1 (8 ounce) jar hot salsa
1 (16 ounce) package frozen whole kernel corn, thawed
¼ teaspoon garlic powder
½ cup shredded Monterey Jack cheese

- Combine hot salsa, corn, garlic powder and ¼ cup water in saucepan. Cook on medium-low heat, stirring occasionally, for 5 to 7 minutes.

- Pour into serving bowl and sprinkle with cheese. Serves 4 to 6. *Eunice, New Mexico*

Corn Pudding ✹

Settlers came to Ontario, Canada, from England, Ireland, Scotland and the United States. The preparation of their foods became part of their social life with logging bees, corn husking bees and quilting bees. Ontario soon became the most heavily populated province in Canada. The cities flourished and their foods became exotic international cuisine while the hard working farm folks favored roast pork, vegetables and desserts made with apples, mincemeat and pumpkins.

3 eggs, lightly beaten
5 tablespoons flour
2 (15 ounce) cans cream-style corn
1 (15 ounce) can whole kernel corn
½ cup shredded carrots
1½ cups milk or light cream
1 cup shredded cheddar cheese
½ teaspoon white pepper

- Preheat oven to 325°.

- Combine eggs and flour in large bowl and whisk until well blended. Stir in all cans of corn, carrots, milk, cheese, white pepper and 1½ teaspoons salt.

- Pour into sprayed 2-quart baking dish and bake for 1 hour 15 minutes or until pudding is set. Serves 8. *Hawkesbury, Ontario, Canada*

TIP: *White pepper is used to avoid black specks in the pudding. Black pepper may be used, if you like.*

Glazed Carrots

1 (16 ounce) package frozen baby carrots
¼ cup apple cider
¼ cup apple jelly
1½ teaspoons dijon-style mustard

- Combine carrots and apple cider in saucepan and bring to boil. Reduce heat. Cover and simmer for about 8 minutes or until carrots are tender.

- Remove cover and cook on medium heat until liquid evaporates. Stir in jelly and mustard. Cook until jelly melts and carrots glaze. Serves 4. *Cherryville, North Carolina*

Krazy Karrots

1 (16 ounce) package baby carrots
¼ cup (½ stick) butter, melted
⅔ cup packed brown sugar
1 (1 ounce) packet ranch dressing mix

- Combine carrots, melted butter, brown sugar, ranch dressing mix and ¼ cup water in 4-quart slow cooker and stir well.

- Cover and cook on LOW for 3 to 4 hours and stir occasionally. Serves 6 to 8. *Bellport, New York*

Sunny Day Carrots

2½ cups finely shredded carrots
2 cups cooked white rice
2 eggs, beaten
1 (8 ounce) package shredded Velveeta® cheese
1 (15 ounce) can cream-style corn
¼ cup whipping cream
2 tablespoons butter, melted
2 tablespoons dried minced onion
1 teaspoon seasoned salt
½ teaspoon white pepper

- Preheat oven to 350°.

- Combine all ingredients in large bowl. Spoon into sprayed 3-quart baking dish. Bake for 40 minutes or until set. Serves 8. *Beverly, New Jersey*

TIP: *White pepper is used to avoid black specks in the dish. Black pepper may be used, if you like.*

Brown Sugar Carrots

2 (15 ounce) cans carrots
¼ cup (½ stick) butter
3 tablespoons brown sugar
½ teaspoon ground ginger

- Drain carrots but set aside 2 tablespoons liquid.

- Combine 2 tablespoons liquid with butter, brown sugar and ginger in saucepan. Heat thoroughly.

- Add carrots, stirring gently and cook for 3 minutes. Serve hot. Serves 4 to 6. *Beecher, Illinois*

Sunshine on the Table

*This is absolutely the prettiest casserole you will place on
your table! And it is not only pretty, but it is also tasty,
delicious, delectable, savory, appetizing, classic and elegant.
Need I go on? You'll never want a simple buttered carrot again!*

**2½ cups carrots, finely shredded
2 cups cooked rice
2 eggs, beaten
2 cups cubed Velveeta® cheese
1 (15 ounce) can cream-style corn
¼ cup half-and-half cream
2 tablespoons butter, melted
2 tablespoons dried minced onion**

- Preheat oven to 350°.

- Combine all ingredients and ½ teaspoon each of salt and pepper in
  large bowl.

- Spoon into sprayed 3-quart baking dish.

- Bake for 40 minutes or until set. Serves 6 to 8. *Devils Lake,
  North Dakota*

Creamy Cabbage Bake

**1 head cabbage, shredded
1 (10 ounce) can cream of celery soup
⅔ cup milk
1 (8 ounce) package shredded cheddar cheese**

- Preheat oven to 325°.

- Place cabbage in sprayed 2-quart baking dish.

- Mix celery soup with milk and pour over top of cabbage. Cover and
  bake for 30 minutes.

- Remove from oven, sprinkle with cheese and bake uncovered for an
  additional 5 minutes. Serves 4 to 6. *Ballville, Ohio*

Sweet-and-Sour Red Cabbage ❧

2 heads red cabbage, shredded (enough for 6 - 8 cups)
½ cup finely chopped onion
½ cup packed brown sugar
⅓ cup vinegar

- Place cabbage and onion in large skillet. Add just enough water to cover bottom of pan. Stir in brown sugar, vinegar and a little salt and pepper; mix well.

- Cover and cook on medium heat for about 10 minutes, stirring often. The cabbage should be slightly crisp when cooking is done. Serves 6. *Brandon, Manitoba, Canada*

Hearty Maple Beans

½ pound Polish sausage, thinly sliced
1 onion, very finely chopped
1 (15 ounce) can pork and beans
1 (15 ounce) can pinto beans, drained
1 (15 ounce) can navy beans, drained
¾ cup maple syrup
2 tablespoons vinegar
3 tablespoons ketchup
1 tablespoon mustard
¼ cup bacon bits

- Preheat oven to 350°.

- Combine all ingredients except bacon bits in large bowl and stir to blend well. Pour into 3-quart baking dish and bake for 25 minutes. Remove from oven, sprinkle bacon bits over top and return to oven for 5 minutes. Serves 10 to 12. *Commerce, Oklahoma*

Baked Beans and Corn

1 (15 ounce) can ranch-style beans
1 (15 ounce) can pork and beans
1 (15 ounce) whole kernel corn, drained
1 (15 ounce) can chili without beans

- Preheat oven to 300°.

- Combine all ingredients in bowl. Spoon into sprayed 3-quart baking dish. Bake for 1 hour. Serves 6 to 8. *Coquille, Oregon*

Eggplant Casserole

1 large eggplant
1 cup cracker crumbs
1 cup shredded cheddar cheese, divided
1 (10 ounce) can tomatoes and green chilies

- Preheat oven to 350°.

- Peel and slice eggplant.

- Place eggplant in saucepan and cover with water. Cook for 10 minutes or until tender. Drain well on paper towels.

- Mash eggplant. Stir in crackers, ¾ cup cheese, and tomatoes and green chilies and mix well.

- Spoon mixture into sprayed 1-quart baking dish. Sprinkle with remaining cheese. Bake for 30 minutes. Serves 4. *Bangor, Pennsylvania*

Cheesy Baked Eggplant

1 eggplant
½ cup mayonnaise
⅔ cup seasoned breadcrumbs
¼ cup grated parmesan cheese

- Preheat oven to 400°.

- Peel eggplant and slice ½ inch thick.

- Spread both sides with mayonnaise and dip in mixture of breadcrumbs and cheese. Coat both sides well.

- Place in single layer in shallow baking dish. Bake for 20 minutes. Serves 4. *Lonsdale, Rhode Island*

Baked Eggplant

1 medium eggplant
¼ cup (½ stick) butter, melted
1 (5 ounce) can evaporated milk
1½ cups cracker crumbs

- Preheat oven to 350°.

- Peel, slice and boil eggplant in saucepan until just tender enough to mash. Mash and season with a little salt and pepper.

- Add remaining ingredients.

- Pour into sprayed 2-quart baking dish. Bake for 25 minutes. Serves 4 to 6. *Bishopville, South Carolina*

Eggplant Frittata

This is a delicious way to serve eggplant for a light lunch and it is rich enough to be served as the main course. You could put it together the day before the lunch, then cook just before serving.

3 cups peeled, finely chopped eggplant
½ cup green bell pepper, chopped
3 tablespoons extra light olive oil
1 (8 ounce) jar roasted red peppers, drained, chopped
10 eggs
½ cup half-and-half cream
1 teaspoon Italian seasoning
⅓ cup grated parmesan cheese

- Preheat oven to 325°.

- Cook eggplant and bell pepper in oil in skillet for 2 to 3 minutes, just until tender. Stir in roasted red peppers.

- Combine eggs, half-and-half cream, 1 teaspoon salt, Italian seasoning and ¼ teaspoon pepper in bowl and beat just until they blend well.

- Add eggplant-pepper mixture to egg-cream mixture. Pour into sprayed 10-inch pie pan.

- Cover and bake for about 15 minutes or until center sets.

- Uncover and sprinkle parmesan cheese over top. Return to oven for about 5 minutes, just until cheese melts slightly.

- Cut into wedges to serve. Serves 6 to 8. *St. Albans, Vermont*

Sunday Green Beans

3 (15 ounce) cans whole green beans, drained
1 (16 ounce) package shredded Mexican Velveeta® cheese
1 (8 ounce) can sliced water chestnuts, drained, chopped
½ cup slivered almonds
¾ cup chopped roasted red bell pepper
1½ cups cracker crumbs
¼ cup (½ stick) butter, melted

- Preheat oven to 350°.

- Place green beans in sprayed 9 x 13-inch baking dish and cover with shredded cheese. Sprinkle with water chestnuts, almonds and roasted bell peppers.

- Place casserole in microwave and heat just until cheese begins to melt. (Watch closely.)

- Combine cracker crumbs and melted butter in bowl, sprinkle over casserole and bake for 30 minutes. Serves 10 to 12. *Cordell, Oklahoma*

Green Bean Revenge

3 (16 ounce) cans green beans, drained
1 (8 ounce) can sliced water chestnuts, drained, chopped
2 (8 ounce) jars jalapeno processed cheese spread
1½ cups cracker crumbs
¼ cup (½ stick) butter, melted

- Preheat oven to 350°.

- Place green beans in sprayed 9 x 13-inch baking dish and cover with water chestnuts.

- Heat both jars cheese in microwave just until they can be poured (take lids off). Pour cheese over green beans and water chestnuts.

- Combine cracker crumbs and butter in bowl and sprinkle over casserole.

- Bake for 30 minutes. Serves 6 to 8. *Carrizo Springs, Texas*

Green Bean Delight

¼ cup (½ stick) butter, divided
½ cup onion, chopped
½ cup celery, chopped
1 tablespoon flour
1 teaspoon sugar
1 cup half-and-half cream
3 (15 ounce) cans French-style green beans, drained
¾ cup crushed corn flakes
1 cup shredded Swiss cheese

- Preheat oven to 325°.

- Melt 2 tablespoons butter in skillet and saute onion and celery. Stir in flour, sugar, ½ teaspoon each of salt and pepper. Cook for 1 minute on medium heat and stir constantly.

- Reduce heat, slowly add half-and-half cream and stir until smooth. Cook and stir over low heat for about 2 minutes until mixture thickens, but do not boil.

- Fold in green beans. Spread into sprayed 9 x 13-inch baking dish.

- Melt remaining butter and toss with corn flake crumbs, mix in cheese and sprinkle over top of casserole.

- Bake for about 25 minutes or until hot. Serves 6 to 8.
  Ellsworth, Kansas

Crunchy Green Beans

3 (15 ounce) cans whole green beans
2 (10 ounce) cans cream of mushroom soup
2 (11 ounce) cans water chestnuts, chopped
2 (3 ounce) cans french-fried onion rings

- Preheat oven to 350°.

- Combine green beans, mushroom soup, water chestnuts, ½ teaspoon salt and a little pepper in bowl.

- Pour mixture into 2-quart baking dish. Cover and bake for 30 minutes.

- Remove casserole from oven and sprinkle onion rings over top and bake for an additional 10 minutes. Serves 4 to 6. *Kayenta, Arizona*

Fancy Green Beans

2 (16 ounce) package frozen French-style green beans, thawed
½ cup (1 stick) butter
1 (8 ounce) package fresh mushrooms, sliced
2 (10 ounce) cans cream of chicken soup
⅔ cup sliced roasted red bell peppers
2 teaspoons soy sauce
1 cup shredded white cheddar cheese
⅔ cup chopped cashews
⅔ cup chow mein noodles

- Preheat oven to 325°.

- Cook green beans according to package directions, drain and set aside. Melt butter in large saucepan and saute mushrooms for about 5 minutes, but do not brown.

- Stir in soups, ¼ cup water, roasted peppers, soy sauce and cheese and gently mix.

- Fold in green beans and spoon into sprayed 9 x 13-inch deep baking pan.

- Combine cashews and chow mein noodles in bowl, sprinkle over top of casserole and bake for 30 minutes or until edges are hot and bubbly. Serves 10 to 12. *Beebe, Arkansas*

Onion Casserole

5 - 6 medium mild onions, thinly sliced
3 tablespoons butter
1 cup milk
4 eggs

- Preheat oven to 325°.

- Melt butter in skillet, add onions, cover and saute for about 30 minutes and cool.

- Beat milk and eggs in bowl. Stir in onions and transfer to sprayed baking dish.

- Bake for 45 to 50 minutes or until light golden. Serves 5 to 6. *Dell Rapids, South Dakota*

Cheesy Onion Casserole

5 sweet onions, sliced
½ cup (1 stick) butter
1 cup shredded cheddar cheese
22 saltine crackers, crushed

- Preheat oven to 325°.

- Saute onions in butter in skillet until soft.

- Layer half onions, half cheese, half crackers in sprayed 2-quart baking dish and repeat layers.

- Bake for 35 minutes. Serves 4 to 6. *Blountville, Tennessee*

Cheesy Baked Onions

4 yellow onions, peeled, sliced
½ cup (1 stick) butter
25 round, buttery crackers, crushed
⅓ cup grated parmesan cheese

- Preheat oven to 325°.

- Saute onions in butter in skillet until transparent.

- Spread half onions in sprayed 2-quart baking dish. Top with half crackers and half cheese. Repeat layers.

- Bake for 30 minutes. Serves 4 to 6. *Gunnison, Utah*

Baked Onions

4 large onions, thinly sliced
1½ cups crushed potato chips
1 cup shredded cheddar cheese
1 (10 ounce) can cream of chicken soup
¼ cup milk or water

- Preheat oven to 300°.

- Layer one-half onion, one-half potato chips and one-half cheese in 9 x 13-inch baking dish. Repeat layers.

- Spoon soup over last layer and pour milk or water on top. Sprinkle with a little cayenne or black pepper.

- Bake for 1 hour. Serves 6 to 8. *Cornelia, Georgia*

Creamed Onions and Peas

1 (10 ounce) can cream of celery soup
½ cup milk
3 (15 ounce) jars tiny white onions, drained
1 (10 ounce) package frozen peas
½ cup slivered almonds
3 tablespoons grated parmesan cheese

- Preheat oven to 350°.

- Combine soup and milk in large saucepan; heat and stir until bubbly. Gently stir in onions, peas and almonds and mix well.

- Spoon into sprayed 2-quart baking dish. Cover and bake for 30 minutes. Sprinkle parmesan cheese over top of casserole before serving. Serves 8. *Newport, Vermont*

Creamed Green Peas

1 (16 ounce) package frozen English peas
2 tablespoons butter
1 (10 ounce) can cream of celery soup
1 (3 ounce) package cream cheese
1 (8 ounce) can water chestnuts, drained

- Cook peas in microwave for 8 minutes and turn dish after 4 minutes.

- Combine butter, soup and cream cheese in large saucepan. Cook on medium heat and stir until butter and cream cheese melt. Add peas and water chestnuts and mix.

- Serve hot. Serves 4 to 6. *Deep River, Connecticut*

Swiss Cheesy Peas

3 (15 ounce) cans green peas and onions, drained
1 (8 ounce) carton sour cream
1 (8 ounce) package shredded Swiss cheese
2 cups crushed corn flakes

- Preheat oven to 350°.

- Combine peas and onions, sour cream, Swiss cheese, and a little salt in large bowl. Spoon into sprayed 3-quart baking dish. Sprinkle corn flakes over top.

- Bake for 35 minutes. Serves 6 to 8. *Chase City, Virginia*

Parmesan Peas

2 (10 ounce) packages frozen green peas
3 tablespoons butter, melted
1 tablespoon lemon juice
⅓ cup grated parmesan cheese

- Microwave peas in 2 tablespoons water for 3 minutes. Rotate bowl half turn and cook for an additional 3 minutes.

- Stir in butter, lemon juice and parmesan cheese. Leave in oven for several minutes. Serve hot. Serves 4 to 6. *Clarkston, Washington*

Spinach-Artichoke Special

2 (16 ounce) packages frozen chopped spinach, thawed
1 onion, chopped
1 sweet red bell pepper, seeded, chopped
½ cup (1 stick) butter
1 (8 ounce) package cream cheese, cubed
1 teaspoon seasoned salt
1 (14 ounce) can artichokes, drained, chopped
¾ cup shredded parmesan cheese

- Preheat oven to 325°.

- Cook spinach according to package directions in saucepan, drain, squeeze spinach between paper towels to complete remove excess moisture and set aside.

- Saute onion and bell pepper in butter in skillet until onion is clear but not browned.

- On low heat add cream cheese and stir constantly until cheese melts. Stir in spinach, seasoned salt and artichokes and pour into sprayed 3-quart baking dish.

- Cover and bake for 30 minutes. Uncover, sprinkle parmesan cheese over top of casserole and return to oven for 5 minutes. Serves 10. *Black River Falls, Wisconsin*

Spinach-Artichoke Bake

1 (9 inch) frozen piecrust
1 (8 ounce) package cream cheese, softened
1 (10 ounce) package frozen chopped spinach, thawed, drained
1 (14 ounce) jar artichoke hearts, drained, chopped
1 (1.8 ounce) box dry vegetable soup mix
1 (8 ounce) package shredded mozzarella cheese, divided

- Preheat oven to 425°.

- Fit piecrust into 9-inch tart pan with removable bottom. Pierce dough with fork several times and line inside of piecrust with foil. Fill with dried beans, rice or pie weights to keep pastry from puffing up.

- Bake for 15 minutes. Remove foil and weights and bake for an additional 5 minutes.

- Reduce heat to 325°.

- Beat cream cheese in bowl until creamy. Squeeze spinach between paper towels to completely remove excess moisture. At low speed add spinach, artichokes, soup mix and half cheese. Spread evenly on crust.

- Sprinkle remaining cheese over top and bake for 35 minutes or until light brown. Cool for 15 minutes before serving and remove sides of pan. Serves 8. *Lovell, Wyoming*

TIP: Squeeze spinach between paper towels to completely remove excess moisture.

Spinach to Like

2 (10 ounce) packages frozen, chopped spinach
1 (8 ounce) carton sour cream
½ (1 ounce) packet dry onion soup mix
⅔ cup seasoned breadcrumbs

- Preheat oven to 350°.

- Cook spinach according to package directions in saucepan and drain well. Squeeze spinach between paper towels to completely remove excess moisture. Add sour cream and onion soup mix to spinach.

- Pour into 2-quart baking dish. Sprinkle breadcrumbs on top. Bake for 35 minutes. Serves 4 to 6. *Cordova, Alabama*

Super Spinach Bake

¼ cup (½ stick) butter
⅔ cup cracker crumbs
2 (10 ounce) packages frozen chopped spinach, thawed, drained
1 (8 ounce) package shredded cheddar cheese, divided
1 (8 ounce) carton sour cream
1 tablespoon dry onion soup mix

- Preheat oven to 325°.

- Melt butter in skillet over medium heat and add cracker crumbs. Cook, stirring often for 5 minutes or until crumbs are light brown; set aside.

- Squeeze spinach between paper towels to completely remove excess moisture. Combine spinach, 1 cup cheese, sour cream and soup mix in medium bowl. Spoon into sprayed 7 x 11-inch baking dish. Top with browned crumbs.

- Bake for 30 minutes. Remove from oven, sprinkle remaining cheese over top and return to oven for 5 minutes. Serves 8. *Buckhannon, West Virginia*

Spinach Delight

This great casserole may be made in advance and baked when ready to serve.

2 (10 ounce) boxes frozen, chopped spinach, thawed
1 (16 ounce) carton small curd cottage cheese
3 cups shredded white cheddar cheese
4 eggs, beaten
3 tablespoons flour
¼ cup (½ stick) butter, melted
½ teaspoon garlic salt
½ teaspoon celery salt
½ teaspoon lemon pepper
1 tablespoon dried onion flakes

- Preheat oven to 325°.

- Squeeze spinach between paper towels to completely remove excess moisture.

- Mix spinach, cottage cheese, cheddar cheese, eggs, flour, butter, seasonings and onion flakes in large bowl. Pour into sprayed 2½ -quart baking dish.

- Bake for 1 hour. Serves 4 to 6. *Carlisle, Arkansas*

Spinach Special

Eat something green on New Year's Day to have money in the New Year. It's a great tradition and this is the dish to go with the tradition.

3 (10 ounce) packages frozen chopped spinach
1 onion, chopped
½ cup (1 stick) butter
1 (8 ounce) package cream cheese, cubed
1 (14 ounce) can artichokes, drained, chopped
⅔ cup grated parmesan cheese

- Preheat oven to 325.

- Cook spinach according to package directions in saucepan. Drain thoroughly, squeeze spinach between paper towels to completely remove excess moisture and set aside.

- Saute onion in butter in skillet, stir and cook until onion is clear but not brown.

- On low heat add cream cheese and stir constantly until cheese melts.

- Stir in spinach, artichokes, and ½ teaspoon each of salt and pepper.

- Pour into sprayed 2-quart baking dish. Sprinkle parmesan cheese over top of casserole.

- Cover and bake for 30 minutes. Serves 4 to 6. *Cornville, Arizona*

Spinach Bake

2 (8 ounce) packages cream cheese, softened
1 (10 ounce) can cream of chicken soup
2 (16 ounce) packages frozen chopped spinach, thawed, drained
1 cup crushed round, buttery crackers

- Preheat oven to 325°.

- Beat cream cheese in bowl until smooth. Add soup and mix well.

- Squeeze spinach between paper towels to completely remove excess moisture. Stir into cream cheese mixture.

- Spoon into sprayed 3-quart baking dish.

- Sprinkle cracker crumbs over top. Bake for 35 minutes. Serves 6 to 8. *Burney, California*

Herbed Spinach

2 (16 ounce) packages frozen chopped spinach
1 (8 ounce) package cream cheese, softened
¼ cup (½ stick) butter, melted, divided
1 (6 ounce) package herbed-seasoned stuffing

• Preheat oven to 325°.

• Cook spinach according to package directions in saucepan. Drain and squeeze spinach between paper towels to completely remove excess moisture. Add cream cheese and half butter. Season with a little salt and pepper.

• Pour into sprayed baking dish. Spread herb stuffing on top and drizzle with remaining butter.

• Bake for 25 minutes. Serves 8 to 10. *Florence, Colorado*

Favorite Spinach

2 (10 ounce) packages frozen chopped spinach, thawed, drained
1 (1 ounce) package dry onion soup mix
1 (8 ounce) carton sour cream
⅔ cup shredded Monterey Jack cheese

• Preheat oven to 350°.

• Squeeze spinach between paper towels to completely remove excess moisture. Combine spinach, onion soup mix and sour cream in bowl. Pour into sprayed 2-quart baking dish. Bake for 20 minutes.

• Remove from oven, sprinkle cheese over top and bake for an additional 5 minutes. Serves 4 to 6. *Durham, Connecticut*

Cheese-Please Spinach

1 (16 ounce) package frozen chopped spinach
3 eggs
½ cup flour
1 (16 ounce) carton small curd cottage cheese
2 cups shredded cheddar cheese

• Preheat oven to 350°.

• Cook spinach in saucepan, drain, squeeze spinach between towels to completely remove excess moisture and set aside. Beat eggs in bowl and add flour, cottage cheese, and a little salt and pepper. Stir in spinach and cheddar cheese and pour into 1½-quart baking dish.

• Bake for 35 minutes. Serves 8. *Bunnell, Florida*

Creamed Spinach Bake

1 (16 ounce) package frozen chopped spinach
2 (3 ounce) packages cream cheese, softened
3 tablespoons butter
1 cup Italian-style seasoned breadcrumbs

- Preheat oven to 325°.

- Cook spinach with ¾ cup water in saucepan for 6 minutes, drain thoroughly and squeeze spinach between paper towels to completely remove excess moisture. Add cream cheese and butter and heat until they melt and mix well with spinach.

- Pour into sprayed 2-quart baking dish. Sprinkle a little salt over spinach and cover with breadcrumbs. Bake for 15 to 20 minutes. Serves 4 to 6. *Greenville, Delaware*

Squash with Maple Syrup 🍁

4 medium yellow squash
2 medium zucchini, sliced
¼ cup (½ stick) butter, melted
⅓ cup maple syrup
½ teaspoon ground cinnamon

- Peel yellow squash and cut in half lengthwise, remove seeds and cut in thin slices. Combine yellow squash and zucchini and steam in small amount of boiling water for about 15 minutes. Drain and mash well.

- Add butter, maple syrup, cinnamon and ½ teaspoon salt and whip with spoon until smooth. Serves 5 to 6. *New Maryland, New Brunswick, Canada*

TIP: This can be served immediately or placed in sprayed 2-quart baking dish and reheated for about 15 minutes at 375°.

Seasoned Squash and Onion

8 yellow squash, sliced
2 onions, chopped
¼ cup (½ stick) butter
1 cup shredded American cheese

- Cook squash and onion in small amount of water in saucepan until tender and drain. Add butter and cheese and toss. Serve hot. Serves 6 to 8. *Cumming, Georgia*

Posh Squash

8 medium yellow squash, sliced
½ green bell pepper, seeded, chopped
1 small onion, chopped
1 (8 ounce) package cubed Mexican Velveeta® cheese

- Preheat oven to 350°.

- Combine squash, bell pepper and onion in large saucepan and just barely cover with water. Cook just until tender, about 10 to 15 minutes.

- Drain and add cheese. Stir until cheese melts and pour into sprayed 2-quart baking dish.

- Bake for 15 minutes. Serves 4 to 6. *Kellogg, Idaho*

Chile-Cheese Squash

1 pound yellow squash
⅔ cup mayonnaise
1 (4 ounce) can diced green chilies, drained
⅔ cup shredded longhorn cheese
⅔ cup breadcrumbs

- Cook squash in salted water in saucepan just until tender-crisp and drain. Return squash to saucepan and stir in mayonnaise, green chilies, cheese and breadcrumbs.

- Serve hot. Serves 4 to 6. *Five Points, New Mexico*

Baked Squash

5 cups squash, cooked, drained
¾ cup shredded Monterey Jack cheese
1 (10 ounce) can cream of chicken soup
1 (6 ounce) box herb dressing mix

- Preheat oven to 375°.

- Place cooked squash in bowl and season with a little salt. Add cheese and soup and blend well. Mix dressing according to package directions.

- Place half dressing in sprayed 9 x 13-inch baking dish. Spoon squash mixture on top and sprinkle remaining dressing on top.

- Bake for 30 minutes. Serves 6 to 8. *Big Flats, New York*

Filled Summer Squash

5 large yellow squash
1 (16 ounce) package frozen chopped spinach
1 (8 ounce) package cream cheese, cubed
1 (1 ounce) packet dry onion soup mix
¾ cup shredded cheddar cheese

- Preheat oven to 325°.

- Steam squash whole until tender. Slit squash lengthwise and remove seeds with spoon.

- Cook spinach according to package directions in saucepan and drain. When spinach is done, remove pan from heat, add cream cheese and stir until cream cheese melts. Stir in soup mix and blend well.

- Place squash shells on large, sprayed baking pan. Fill shells with spinach mixture and top with heaping tablespoon of cheddar cheese.

- Bake for 10 to 15 minutes or until squash is thoroughly hot. Serves 5. *Brighton, Illinois*

Creamy Squash

6 - 8 medium yellow squash
1 (8 ounce) package cream cheese, cubed, softened
2 tablespoons butter
½ teaspoon sugar

- Cut squash in little pieces and place in large saucepan. Cover with water and boil for 10 to 15 minutes or until tender.

- Drain squash and add cream cheese, butter, sugar, and ¾ teaspoon each of salt and pepper.

- Cook over low heat and stir until cream cheese melts. Serve hot. Serves 6 to 8. *Bremen, Indiana*

Creamy Cheesy Zucchini

3 pounds zucchini, sliced
1 red bell pepper, finely diced
¼ cup (½ stick) plus 3 tablespoons butter, melted, divided
1 (10 ounce) can cream of celery soup
1 (8 ounce) package cubed Velveeta® cheese
1 teaspoon seasoned salt
2½ cups crushed buttery cheese crackers
⅓ cup slivered almonds

- Preheat oven to 325°.

- Boil zucchini and bell pepper with enough water to cover in saucepan just until barely tender and drain well. Do not overcook!

- Combine ¼ cup melted butter, soup, cheese, ¼ cup water and seasoned salt in bowl.

- Gently stir in zucchini mixture and spoon into 3-quart baking dish. Sprinkle crushed crackers and almonds over top and drizzle 3 tablespoons melted butter over crackers.

- Bake for 35 minutes or until hot and bubbly. Serves 8 to 10. *Comanche, Iowa*

Fried Zucchini

3 large zucchini, grated
5 eggs
⅓ (12 ounce) box round buttery crackers, crushed
½ cup grated parmesan cheese
Oil

- Squeeze zucchini between paper towels to completely remove excess moisture.

- Combine zucchini, eggs and cracker crumbs in bowl and mix well. Add cheese and a little salt and pepper.

- Drop spoonfuls of mixture into skillet with a little oil. Fry for about 15 minutes and brown on each side. Serves 4 to 6. *Fulton, Mississippi*

Speedy Zucchini and Fettuccine

1 (9 ounce) package refrigerated fresh fettuccine
⅓ cup extra-virgin olive oil, divided
1 tablespoon minced garlic
4 small zucchini, grated
1 tablespoon lemon juice
½ cup pine nuts, toasted
⅓ cup grated parmesan cheese

- Cook fettuccine according to package directions, drain and place in serving bowl.

- Heat large skillet over high heat and add 2 tablespoons oil, garlic and zucchini. Saute for 1 minute.

- Add zucchini mixture to pasta with lemon juice, pine nuts, and a little salt and pepper.

- Stir in remaining olive oil and toss to combine. Sprinkle parmesan cheese over top of dish to serve. Serves 8 to 10. *Clare, Michigan*

Zucchini Patties

1½ cups grated zucchini
1 egg, beaten
2 tablespoons flour
⅓ cup finely minced onion
3 tablespoons oil

- Squeeze zucchini between paper towels to completely remove excess moisture. Mix all ingredients in bowl and add ½ teaspoon salt.

- Heat oil in skillet. Drop tablespoonfuls of mixture into skillet on medium-high heat.

- Turn and brown both sides. Remove and drain on paper towels. Serves 4. *Hawthorne, Nevada*

Zucchini Bake

3 cups zucchini, grated
1½ cups shredded Monterey Jack cheese
4 eggs, beaten
¼ teaspoon garlic powder
2 cups cheese cracker crumbs

- Preheat oven to 350°.

- Squeeze zucchini between paper towels to completely remove excess moisture.

- Combine zucchini, cheese, eggs, garlic powder, and ½ teaspoon each of salt and pepper in bowl and mix well. Spoon into sprayed 2-quart baking dish.

- Sprinkle cracker crumbs over top.

- Bake for 35 to 40 minutes. Serves 4 to 6. *Blue Earth, Minnesota*

TIP: Zucchini is a popular summer squash that has a light and delicate flavor. When buying zucchini, select the smaller ones, which will have a thinner skin. This delicious vegetable can be cooked many different ways or eaten raw in salads. Try adding sliced or chopped raw zucchini to your next green salad. You'll love the addition.

Broccoli-Stuffed Tomatoes

4 medium tomatoes
1 (10 ounce) package frozen chopped broccoli
1 (6 ounce) roll garlic cheese, softened
½ teaspoon garlic salt

- Preheat oven to 375°.

- Cut tops off tomatoes and scoop out flesh.

- Cook broccoli according to package directions and drain well. Combine broccoli, cheese and garlic salt in saucepan. Heat just until cheese melts.

- Stuff broccoli mixture into tomatoes and place on baking sheet.

- Bake for about 10 minutes. Serves 4. *Cuthbert, Georgia*

Baked Tomatoes

2 (14 ounce) cans diced tomatoes, drained
1½ cups breadcrumbs, toasted, divided
¼ cup sugar
½ onion, chopped
¼ cup (½ stick) butter, melted

- Preheat oven to 325°.

- Combine tomatoes, 1 cup breadcrumbs, sugar, onion and butter.

- Pour into sprayed baking dish and cover with remaining breadcrumbs.

- Bake for 25 to 30 minutes or until crumbs are light brown. Serves 4 to 6. *Byron, Illinois*

Potato-Stuffed Bell Peppers

3 baking potatoes
6 large red bell peppers
Paprika

- Preheat oven at 425°.

- Pierce each potato 3 to 4 times and place on oven rack. Bake for 1 hour 20 to 30 minutes. Cool for about 20 minutes.

- While potatoes cook, cut bell peppers in half lengthwise through stem. Remove seed and membranes; rinse and pat dry. Set aside.

Stuffing:

1 (8 ounce) carton sour cream
1 cup shredded colby Jack cheese
¼ cup (½ stick) butter, melted
3 fresh green onions, finely chopped
2 teaspoons dried parsley

- Peel cooked potatoes and mash slightly with potato masher in bowl. Add sour cream, cheese, butter, green onions, parsley, and a little salt and pepper; mix well.

- Spoon potatoes into bell pepper halves and sprinkle with paprika.

- Bell peppers may be grilled for about 20 minutes or baked at 425° for about 10 to 15 minutes. Serves 6. *Buhl, Idaho*

Creamed Vegetable Bake

1 (16 ounce) package frozen broccoli, cauliflower and carrots
1 (10 ounce) package frozen green peas
1 (10 ounce) package frozen whole kernel corn
2 (10 ounce) can cream of mushroom soup
1 (8 ounce) package cream cheese, cubed
⅔ cup milk
2 cups seasoned croutons

- Preheat oven to 325°.

- Cook all vegetables according to package directions, drain and place in large bowl.

- Combine soup, cream cheese, milk, and a little salt and pepper in saucepan. Heat on medium-low heat and stir constantly until mixture blends well. Stir into vegetables in bowl and gently mix.

- Spoon into sprayed 3-quart baking dish and cover with croutons. Bake for 25 to 30 minutes or until croutons are light brown. Serves 10 to 12.
Chipley, Florida

Vegetables You'll Remember

A retired minister's wife brought this great dish to a church supper and it was an immediate hit. We requested it at every supper after that.

2 (15 ounce) cans mixed vegetables, drained
1 cup chopped celery
½ onion, chopped
1 (8 ounce) can sliced water chestnuts, drained
1 cup shredded sharp cheddar cheese
¾ cup mayonnaise
1½ cups round buttery crackers, crushed
6 tablespoons (¾ stick) butter, melted

- Preheat oven to 350°.

- Combine mixed vegetables, celery, onion, water chestnuts, cheese and mayonnaise in bowl and mix well. Spoon into sprayed 3-quart baking dish.

- In separate bowl, combine crushed crackers and melted butter and sprinkle over vegetable mixture.

- Bake for 30 minutes or until crackers are light brown. Serves 8 to 10.
Empire, Louisiana

Creamy Vegetable Casserole

1 (16 ounce) package frozen broccoli, carrots and cauliflower
1 (10 ounce) can cream of mushroom soup
1 (8 ounce) carton garden-vegetable cream cheese
1 cup seasoned croutons

- Preheat oven to 325°.

- Cook vegetables according to package directions, drain and place in large bowl.

- Combine soup and cream cheese in saucepan and heat just enough to mix easily. Pour into vegetable mixture and mix well.

- Pour into 2-quart baking dish and sprinkle with croutons. Bake for 25 minutes or until bubbly. Serves 6. *Butler, Indiana*

Buttered Vegetables

½ cup (1 stick) butter
2 yellow squash, sliced
1 (16 ounce) package frozen broccoli florets
1 (10 ounce) box frozen corn

- Melt butter in large skillet and add all vegetables.

- Saute vegetables for about 10 to 15 minutes or until tender-crisp. Add a little salt, if you like. Serve warm. Serves 8. *Eudora, Kansas*

Veggies to Love

1 (16 ounce) package frozen broccoli, cauliflower and carrots
1 (10 ounce) can cream of celery soup
⅓ cup milk
1 (3 ounce) can french-fried onion rings

- Preheat oven to 350°.

- Cook vegetables according to package directions in saucepan and drain. Add soup and milk; mix well.

- Pour into sprayed 2-quart baking dish and sprinkle french-fried onions over top.

- Bake for 30 minutes or until bubbly. Serves 4 to 6.
Centerville, Indiana

Roasted Vegetables

1½ pounds assorted fresh vegetables (squash, carrots, red bell
peppers, zucchini, cauliflower and/or broccoli)
1 (11 ounce) can water chestnuts, drained
2 tablespoons butter, melted
1 (1 ounce) packet savory herb with garlic soup mix

• Preheat oven to 400°.

• Cut all vegetables in uniform 2-inch pieces and place in sprayed
2-quart baking dish with water chestnuts.

• Combine melted butter and soup mix in bowl, drizzle over vegetables
and stir well.

• Cover and bake for 20 to 25 minutes or until tender and stir once.
Serves 4 to 6. *Bolivar, Tennessee*

Herb-Seasoned Vegetables

1 (14 ounce) can seasoned chicken broth with Italian herbs
½ teaspoon garlic powder
1 (16 ounce) package frozen vegetables
½ cup grated parmesan cheese

• Heat broth, garlic powder and vegetables in saucepan to a boil. Cover
and cook over low heat for 5 minutes or until tender-crisp and drain.

• Place in serving dish and sprinkle cheese over vegetables. Serves
4 to 6. *Houlton, Maine*

TIP: Use broccoli, cauliflower or your favorite vegetable.

Healthy Veggies

1 (16 ounce) package frozen broccoli, cauliflower and carrots
2 medium zucchini, halved lengthwise, sliced
1 (1 ounce) packet ranch dressing mix
2 tablespoons butter, melted

• Place broccoli, cauliflower, carrots and zucchini in 4-quart slow cooker.

• Combine ranch dressing mix, melted butter and ½ cup water in
bowl, spoon over vegetables and stir.

• Cover and cook on LOW for 2 to 3 hours. Serves 6 to 8.
Cabazon, California

Garden Casserole

1 pound yellow squash, sliced
1 pound zucchini, sliced
1 green bell pepper, seeded, chopped
1 red bell pepper, seeded, chopped
1 (15 ounce) can sliced carrots, drained
1 (10 ounce) can cream of chicken soup
1 (8 ounce) carton sour cream
½ cup (1 stick) plus 3 tablespoons butter, melted, divided
1 (6 ounce) box herb stuffing mix

- Preheat oven to 325°.

- Cook squash, zucchini and bell peppers in salted water in saucepan for 8 to 10 minutes or until just tender-crisp and drain well. (Do not overcook.) Stir in carrots, chicken soup and sour cream; mix well.

- Melt ½ cup butter in large saucepan and add stuffing mix, mix well and set aside 1 cup for topping. Add vegetable-soup mixture and mix gently, but well.

- Spoon into sprayed 9 x 13-inch baking dish and sprinkle remaining stuffing mix over top.

- Drizzle remaining 3 tablespoons melted butter over top and bake for 35 minutes. Serves 10. *Fort Lupton, Colorado*

★ ★ ★

Beef

Beef is a dinner-time favorite with
almost everyone. Decide from 50 variations
of roasts, steaks, briskets and more!

**1001
Community
Recipes**

Beef Contents

Tasty Taco Casserole

2 pounds lean ground beef
1 (10 ounce) can taco sauce
2 (15 ounce) cans Spanish rice
1 (8 ounce) can whole kernel corn, drained
1 (8 ounce) package shredded Mexican 4-cheese blend, divided
1 cup crushed tortilla chips

- Preheat oven to 350°.

- Brown beef in skillet and cook and stir until beef is crumbly. Add taco sauce, rice, corn and half cheese and mix well.

- Spoon into sprayed 9 x 13-inch baking pan, cover and bake for 35 minutes.

- Remove from oven, sprinkle remaining cheese and chips over top of casserole and continue baking for 5 minutes. Serves 8. *Carthage, Texas*

Taco Pie

1 pound lean ground beef
1 (11 ounce) can Mexicorn®, drained
1 (8 ounce) can tomato sauce
1 (1.25 ounce) packet taco seasoning
1 (9 inch) frozen piecrust
1½ cups shredded cheddar cheese, divided

- Preheat oven to 350°.

- Brown and cook ground beef in large skillet until no longer pink. Stir in corn, tomato sauce and taco seasoning. Keep warm.

- Place piecrust in pie pan, trim edges and bake for 5 minutes. Remove from oven and spoon ground beef mixture onto piecrust, spreading evenly.

- Sprinkle 1 cup cheese over top and bake for 20 minutes or until filling is bubbly. Remove from oven, cover with remaining cheese and return to oven for 5 minutes.

- When serving, cut pie in wedges. Serves 6 to 8. *Lordsburg, New Mexico*

Southern Taco Pie

1 pound lean ground beef
1 large bell pepper, seeded, chopped
2 jalapeno peppers, seeded, chopped
Oil
1 (15 ounce) can Mexican stewed tomatoes
1 tablespoon chili powder
1 (8 ounce) package shredded sharp cheddar cheese
1 (8 ounce) box corn muffin mix
1 egg
⅓ cup milk

- Preheat oven to 375°.

- Brown ground beef, bell pepper and jalapeno peppers in large skillet with a little oil; drain. Stir in tomatoes, chili powder, ½ cup water and a little salt.

- Cover and cook on medium heat for about 10 minutes or until most liquid cooks out, but it is not dry.

- Pour into sprayed 9 x 13-inch baking pan and sprinkle with cheese.

- Combine corn muffin mix with egg and milk in bowl and pour over pie. Bake for 20 to 25 minutes or until muffin mix is light brown. Serves 6.
  Hahnville, Louisiana

Smothered Beef Steak

2 pounds lean round steak
1 cup rice
1 (14 ounce) can beef broth
1 green bell pepper, seeded, chopped

- Cut steak into serving-size pieces and brown in very large skillet.

- Add rice, beef broth, bell pepper and 1 cup water to skillet. Bring to a boil. Reduce heat and cover and simmer for 1 hour. Serves 6 to 8.
  Charles Town, West Virginia

Smothered Beef Patties

1½ pounds lean ground beef
½ cup chili sauce
½ cup buttery cracker crumbs
1 (14 ounce) can beef broth

- Combine beef, chili sauce and cracker crumbs in bowl and form into 5 or 6 patties. Brown patties in skillet and pour beef broth over patties.

- Bring to a boil. Reduce heat and cover and simmer for about 40 minutes. Serves 5 to 6. *Crete, Nebraska*

Simple Casserole Supper

1 pound lean ground beef
¼ cup rice
1 (10 ounce) can French onion soup
1 (6 ounce) can french-fried onion rings

- Preheat oven to 325°.

- Brown ground beef in skillet, drain and place in sprayed 7 x 11-inch baking dish. Add rice, onion soup and ½ cup water.

- Cover and bake for 40 minutes. Uncover, sprinkle onion rings over top and return to oven for 10 minutes. Serves 4 to 6. *Blackwood, New Jersey*

Quick Skillet Supper

1½ pounds lean ground beef
⅔ cup stir-fry sauce
1 (16 ounce) package frozen stir-fry vegetables
2 (3 ounce) packages Oriental-flavor ramen noodles

- Brown and crumble ground beef in large skillet. Add 2½ cups water, stir-fry sauce, vegetables and seasoning packets from ramen noodles.

- Cook and stir on medium-low heat for about 5 minutes.

- Break noodles, add to beef-vegetable mixture and cook for about 6 minutes. Stir to separate noodles as they soften. Serves 4 to 6. *Blasdell, New Mexico*

Simple Spaghetti Bake

8 ounces spaghetti
1 (1 pound) lean ground beef
1 green bell pepper, seeded, finely chopped
1 onion, chopped
1 (10 ounce) can tomato bisque soup
1 (15 ounce) can tomato sauce
2 teaspoons Italian seasoning
1 (8 ounce) can whole kernel corn, drained
1 (4 ounce) can black sliced olives, drained
1 (12 ounce) package shredded cheddar cheese

- Cook spaghetti according to package directions, drain and set aside.

- Cook beef, bell pepper and onion in skillet and drain.

- Add remaining ingredients, ½ cup water and ½ teaspoon salt and spaghetti to beef mixture and stir well. Pour into sprayed 9 x 13-inch baking dish and cover.

- Refrigerate for 2 to 3 hours.

- When ready to bake, preheat oven to 350°.

- Cover and bake for 45 minutes. Serves 6 to 8. *Laughlin, Nevada*

Pinto-Beef Pie

1 pound lean ground beef
1 onion, chopped
2 (16 ounce) cans pinto beans with liquid
1 (10 ounce) can tomatoes and green chilies with liquid
1 (2.8 ounce) can french-fried onion rings

- Preheat oven to 350°.

- Brown beef and onion in skillet and drain.

- Layer 1 can beans, beef-onion mixture, and ½ can tomatoes and green chilies in 2-quart baking dish. Repeat layers.

- Top with onion rings and bake for 30 minutes. Serves 4 to 6. *Castle Hills, Texas*

Meatloaf Tonight

1½ pounds lean ground beef
1 (10 ounce) can golden cream of mushroom soup
1 (10 ounce) can cream of celery soup
1 (1 ounce) packet savory herb-garlic soup mix
1 cup cooked rice

• Preheat oven to 350°.

• Combine ground beef, both soups, soup mix and cooked rice in bowl.

• Place in sprayed 9 x 13-inch baking pan and form into loaf.

• Bake for 45 to 50 minutes or until loaf is golden brown. Serves 8.
  Haughton, Louisiana

TIP: Use cooked instant rice to cut preparation time.

Mac 'n Cheese Supper

1½ pounds lean ground beef
2 (7 ounce) packages macaroni and cheese dinners
1 (15 ounce) can whole kernel corn, drained
1½ cups shredded Monterey Jack cheese

• Brown ground beef with 1 teaspoon salt in large skillet, until no longer pink and drain.

• Prepare macaroni and cheese according to package directions.

• Spoon beef, macaroni and corn in sprayed 5-quart slow cooker;
  mix well.

• Cover and cook on LOW for 4 to 5 hours.

• When ready to serve, sprinkle cheese over top and leave in cooker until cheese melts. Serves 6 to 8. *Cairo, Illinois*

It's-Time-to-Eat

1 pound lean ground beef
1 onion, chopped
¼ cup steak sauce
1 tablespoon flour
1 (15 ounce) can baked beans with liquid
1 (8 ounce) can whole kernel corn, drained
1½ cups crushed garlic-flavored croutons

- Preheat oven to 325°.

- Brown beef and onion in large skillet and drain. Stir in all remaining ingredients except croutons.

- Pour into sprayed 9 x 13-inch baking dish and sprinkle crouton crumbs on top. Bake for 45 minutes or until bubbly around edges. Serves 6 to 8. *Charlestown, Indiana*

Enchilada Lasagna

1½ pounds lean ground beef
1 onion, chopped
1 teaspoon minced garlic
1 (15 ounce) can enchilada sauce
1 (15 ounce) can stewed tomatoes
1 teaspoon cumin
1 egg, beaten
1 (12 ounce) carton small curd cottage cheese
1 (12 ounce) package shredded 4-cheese blend, divided
8 (8-inch) corn tortillas, torn
1 cup shredded cheddar cheese

- Preheat oven to 325°.

- Cook beef, onion and garlic in large skillet until meat is no longer pink. Stir in enchilada sauce, tomatoes, cumin and ½ teaspoon salt. Bring mixture to boil, reduce heat and simmer for 20 minutes.

- Combine egg and cottage cheese in small bowl.

- Spread one-third of meat sauce in sprayed 9 x 13-inch baking dish. Top with half of 4-cheese blend, half tortillas and half cottage cheese mixture. Repeat layers. Top with remaining meat sauce and sprinkle cheddar cheese.

- Cover and bake for 25 minutes. Uncover and bake for 10 more minutes. Serves 6 to 8. *Celina, Texas*

Easy Winter Warmer

*This is such a good spaghetti sauce on noodles
and is a great substitute for cream sauce.*

1 (12 ounce) package medium egg noodles
Oil
3 tablespoons butter
1½ pounds lean ground round beef
**1 (10 ounce) package frozen seasoning blend (chopped onions and
     peppers), thawed**
1 (28 ounce) jar spaghetti sauce
1 (12 ounce) package shredded mozzarella cheese

• Preheat oven to 350°.

• Cook noodles according to package directions in pot of boiling water
  with a dab of oil and salt. Drain thoroughly, add butter and stir until
  butter melts.

• Brown beef and onions and peppers in skillet and drain thoroughly.

• Pour half of spaghetti sauce in sprayed 9 x 13-inch baking dish. Layer
  half noodles, half beef and half cheese. Repeat for second layer.

• Cover and bake for about 30 minutes or until dish is thoroughly hot.
  Serves 4 to 6. *Blackville, South Carolina*

Easy Salisbury Steak

1¼ pounds lean ground beef
½ cup flour
1 egg
1 (10 ounce) can beef gravy
Rice or noodles, cooked

• Preheat oven to 350°.

• Combine beef, flour and egg in large bowl. Add a little salt and pepper
  and mix well.

• Shape into 5 patties and place in shallow 7 x 11-inch baking dish.
  Bake for 20 minutes and drain off any fat.

• Pour beef gravy over patties. Bake for an additional 20 minutes.
  Serve with rice or noodles. Serves 4 to 6. *Chelsea Beach, Maryland*

Creamy Beef Casserole

1½ pounds lean ground beef
1 onion, chopped
1 green bell pepper, seeded, chopped
1 (15 ounce) can tomato sauce
1 (7 ounce) can chopped green chilies
1 (12 ounce) package medium noodles
1 (16 ounce) carton small curd cottage cheese
¾ cup mayonnaise
1 cup shredded 4-cheese blend

- Preheat oven to 350°.

- Brown beef, onion and bell pepper in large skillet over medium-high heat. Stir in tomato sauce, green chilies and a little salt and pepper. Reduce heat, stir well and simmer for 20 minutes.

- Cook noodles according to package directions and drain well.

- Combine cottage cheese and mayonnaise in bowl and fold into noodles. Spoon noodle mixture into sprayed 9 x 13-inch baking dish.

- Pour beef mixture over noodle mixture. Cover and bake for 30 minutes.

- Remove cover, sprinkle cheese on top and return to oven for an additional 5 minutes. Serves 8. *Benton, Kentucky*

Cheesy Beefy Gnocchi

1 pound lean ground beef
1 (10 ounce) can cheddar cheese soup
1 (10 ounce) can tomato bisque soup
2 cups gnocchi or shell pasta

- Cook beef in skillet until brown and drain.

- Add soups, 1½ cups water and pasta. Bring mixture to a boil.

- Cover and cook over medium heat for 10 to 12 minutes or until pasta is done and stir often. Serves 6. *Bath, Pennsylvania*

Beefy-Rice Casserole

1 pound lean ground beef
¾ cup white rice
1 (10 ounce) package frozen corn, thawed
1 (10 ounce) can French onion soup
1 (2.8 ounce) can french-fried onion rings

- Preheat oven to 325°.

- Brown ground beef in skillet, drain and place in sprayed 3-quart baking dish.

- Stir in rice, corn, onion soup and ½ cup water. Cover and bake for 30 minutes.

- Uncover and sprinkle onion rings over top of casserole and return to oven for 15 minutes. Serves 5 to 6. *Hot Springs, North Dakota*

Beef-Potato Casserole

1½ pounds lean ground beef
1 (15 ounce) can sloppy Joe sauce
1 (10 ounce) can beef broth
1 (20 ounce) package frozen hash-brown potatoes, thawed
1 (8 ounce) package shredded cheddar cheese

- Preheat oven to 375°.

- Cook beef in skillet over medium heat until no longer pink and stir to crumble. Add sloppy Joe sauce, beef broth and a little pepper.

- Place hash browns in sprayed 9 x 13-inch baking dish and top with beef mixture.

- Cover and bake for 30 minutes.

- Uncover, sprinkle cheese over top and continue baking for an additional 5 minutes. Serves 8. *Fairway, Kansas*

Beef Patties in Creamy Onion Sauce

1½ pounds lean ground beef
⅓ cup salsa
⅓ cup buttery cracker crumbs
1 (10 ounce) can cream of onion soup
Noodles, cooked

- Combine beef, salsa and cracker crumbs in bowl and form into 5 to 6 patties. Brown in skillet and reduce heat.

- Add ¼ cup water and simmer for 15 minutes. Combine onion soup and ½ cup water or milk in saucepan, heat and mix.

- Pour over beef patties. Serve over noodles. Serves 5 to 6.
  Cottondale, Alabama

Asian Beef and Noodles

1¼ pounds ground beef
1 (16 ounce) package frozen Oriental stir-fry vegetable mixture
2 (3 ounce) packages Oriental-flavored ramen noodles
½ teaspoon ground ginger
3 tablespoons thinly sliced green onions

- Brown ground beef in large skillet and drain.

- Add ½ cup water and a little salt and pepper; simmer for 10 minutes and transfer to separate bowl.

- In same skillet, combine 2 cups water, vegetables, noodles (broken up), ginger and both seasoning packets from noodles.

- Bring to a boil and reduce heat.

- Cover, simmer for 3 minutes or until noodles are tender and stir occasionally.

- Return beef to skillet and stir in green onions. Serve right from skillet. Serves 4 to 6. *Kearny, Arizona*

Black Bean-Chili Casserole

1 pound lean ground beef
1 onion, finely chopped
Oil
2 (15 ounce) cans black beans, drained
1 teaspoon ground cumin
1 teaspoon chili powder
1½ cups thick-and-chunky salsa
1 (6.5 ounce) package corn muffin mix
1 egg
¼ cup milk

- Preheat oven to 375°.

- Cook beef and onion in large skillet with a little oil on medium-high heat for 8 to 10 minutes. Stir in black beans (or pinto beans if you prefer), cumin, chili powder, salsa and a little salt. Bring to a boil and reduce heat to medium. Cook for 5 minutes and stir occasionally. Spoon into sprayed 3-quart round baking dish.

- Prepare muffin mix according to package directions with egg and milk in small bowl. Drop spoonfuls of batter onto bean-beef mixture around edge of baking dish.

- Bake for 20 to 25 minutes or until topping is golden brown. Serves 6 to 8. *Cherokee Village, Arkansas*

Good Night Casserole Supper

1 pound lean ground beef
1 onion, chopped
1 red bell pepper, seeded, chopped
1 green bell pepper, seeded, chopped
2 (10 ounce) cans golden cream of mushroom soup
⅔ cup rice
¼ cup soy sauce
1 (3 ounce) can french-fried onion rings

- Preheat oven to 350°.

- Brown beef and onion in large skillet and drain. Pour into sprayed 9 x 13-inch baking dish. Stir in bell peppers, soup, rice, soy sauce, ¾ cup water and a little salt and pepper. With paper towel, clean off edges of baking dish.

- Cover and bake for 45 minutes, remove dish from oven and sprinkle onion rings over top. Bake uncovered for 15 minutes. Serves 6 to 8. *Calimesa, California*

Pepper Steak

You can't beat this tender sirloin and
colorful peppers with a tasty beef sauce.

1½ pounds (¾ inch) thick boneless sirloin
3 tablespoons oil
1 green bell pepper, thinly sliced
1 red bell pepper, thinly sliced
1 onion, cut in wedges
1 teaspoon minced garlic
1 (14 ounce) can beef broth
2 tablespoons cornstarch
1 (10 ounce) can beefy mushroom soup
2 tablespoons soy sauce
4 cups cooked rice

- Preheat oven to 350°.

- Slice beef across grain into thin strips. Pour oil in large skillet and brown steak on high heat. Reduce heat and cook on low for 10 minutes.

- With slotted spoon, remove beef from skillet and place in 3-quart baking dish.

- Saute bell peppers, onion and garlic in skillet with remaining oil. Combine beef broth and cornstarch and mix well.

- Stir in beef broth, soup, soy sauce and ½ teaspoon salt and heat to boiling.

- Pour soup mixture over beef, cover and bake for about 65 minutes. Serve over rice. Serves 6 to 8. *Hamilton, Montana*

Shepherd's Pie

1 pound boneless sirloin, cut into 1-inch cubes
1 onion, sliced
1 (8 ounce) can sliced carrots, drained
1 (14 ounce) jar tomato-pasta sauce
½ (7.2 ounce) box (1 pouch) roasted-garlic mashed potatoes
⅔ cup milk
2 tablespoons butter

- Preheat oven to 375°.

- Heat large non-stick skillet over medium heat and add beef cubes, onion and a little salt and pepper. Cook for 10 minutes and stir frequently until beef browns.

- Stir in carrots, pasta sauce and ½ cup water and bring to a boil. Reduce heat to medium, cook for 10 minutes and stir occasionally. Spread in sprayed 3-quart round baking dish.

- Prepare potatoes according to package directions. Use 1 pouch potatoes, 1 cup water, milk and butter. Spoon 8 mounds around edge of hot beef mixture.

- Bake for 25 minutes or until bubbly and potatoes are light golden brown. Serves 6 to 8. *David City, Nebraska*

Beef and Broccoli

1 pound beef sirloin steak
1 onion, chopped
Oil
1 (10 ounce) can cream of broccoli soup
1 (10 ounce) package frozen chopped broccoli, thawed
Noodles, cooked

- Slice beef across grain into very thin strips. Brown steak strips and onion in a little oil in large skillet and stir several times.

- Reduce heat and simmer for 10 minutes. Stir in soup and broccoli and heat.

- When ready to serve, spoon beef mixture over noodles. Serves 4 to 6. *Frederick, Colorado*

Thai Beef, Noodles and Veggies

2 (4.4 ounce) packages Thai sesame noodles
1 pound sirloin steak, cut in strips
Oil
1 (16 ounce) package frozen stir-fry vegetables, thawed
½ cup chopped peanuts

- Cook noodles according to package directions, remove from heat and cover. Season sirloin strips with a little salt and pepper.

- Brown half sirloin strips in a little oil in skillet and cook for about 2 minutes. Remove from skillet and drain. Repeat with remaining sirloin strips.

- In same skillet, place vegetables and ½ cup water, cover and cook for 5 minutes or until tender-crisp. Remove from heat, add steak strips and toss to mix.

- To serve, sprinkle with chopped peanuts. Serves 4 to 6. *East Hampton, Connecticut*

Smothered Steak and Potatoes

1½ pounds round steak
Oil
2 (15 ounce) cans whole new potatoes, drained
1 (10 ounce) can golden mushroom soup
1 (1 ounce) packet dry onion soup mix
1½ cups milk

- Preheat oven to 325°.

- Cut steak into serving-size pieces and brown in skillet with a little oil on high heat.

- Transfer to sprayed 9 x 13-inch baking pan and place potatoes over steak.

- Combine mushroom soup, dry onion soup mix and milk in saucepan and heat just enough to be able to mix well. Pour over steak and potatoes.

- Cover and bake for 50 minutes. Serves 6. *Harrington, Delaware*

Steak-Bake Italiano

2 pounds lean round steak
2 teaspoons Italian seasoning
1 teaspoon garlic salt
2 (15 ounce) cans stewed tomatoes

• Preheat oven to 325°.

• Cut steak into serving-size pieces and brown in skillet.

• Place in 9 x 13-inch baking dish.

• Combine Italian seasoning, garlic salt and stewed tomatoes in bowl.
  Pour over steak pieces.

• Cover and bake for 1 hour. Serves 6 to 8. *Citrus Springs, Florida*

Spicy Onion-Mushroom Steak

1½ pounds tenderized round steak
Flour
Oil
1 (15 ounce) can Mexican stewed tomatoes
¾ cup picante sauce
1 (14 ounce) can beef broth
1 (6.4 ounce) package Mexican-style rice

• Cut round steak into serving-size pieces and dredge in flour.

• Brown steak in skillet with a little oil and stir in tomatoes, picante and
  beef broth. Bring to a boil, reduce heat to low, cover and simmer for
  50 to 60 minutes.

• Prepare rice according to package directions and spoon onto serving
  platter. Spoon steak and sauce over rice. Serves 8. *Dawson, Georgia*

Savory Steak

Great sauce with mashed potatoes.

1½ pounds lean round steak
1 onion, halved, sliced
2 (10 ounce) cans golden mushroom soup
1½ cups hot thick-and-chunky salsa

• Trim fat from steak and cut into serving-size pieces.

• Sprinkle with 1 teaspoon pepper and place in sprayed 5 to 6-quart slow cooker. Place onion slices over steak.

• Combine soup and salsa in bowl and mix well. Spoon over steak and onions. Cover and cook on LOW for 7 to 8 hours. Serves 4 to 6. *Litchfield Park, Arizona*

Red Wine Round Steak

2 pounds (¾ inch) thick round steak
Oil
1 (1 ounce) packet dry onion soup mix
1 cup dry red wine
1 (4 ounce) can sliced mushrooms

• Preheat oven to 325°.

• Remove all fat from steak and cut in serving-size pieces. Brown meat in skillet on both sides with a little oil. Place in sprayed 9 x 13-inch baking dish.

• In same skillet, combine onion soup mix, wine, 1 cup hot water and mushrooms. Pour over steak.

• Cover and bake for 1 hour 20 minutes or until steak is tender. Serves 6 to 8. *Clewistown, Florida*

Lean-Mean Round Steak

Flour
1 teaspoon paprika
2 pounds lean round steak, cut into strips
2 tablespoons canola oil
1 cup chopped onion
½ cup chopped green bell pepper
2 (15 ounce) cans Mexican stewed tomatoes
2 (8 ounce) cans tomato sauce
1 tablespoon chili powder
Shredded cheddar cheese
Fresh cilantro
Rice, cooked

- Combine flour, paprika and a little salt and pepper in bowl. Dredge steak strips in flour and set aside.

- Heat oil in large, heavy skillet over medium heat. Brown meat and add onions, bell pepper, tomatoes, tomato sauce, chili powder and 1 cup water. Reduce heat to medium-low, cover and simmer for 1 hour.

- To serve, arrange steak on hot ovenproof serving platter and cover with sauce. Sprinkle shredded cheese on top.

- Place under broiler for 1 to 2 minutes or until cheese melts. Garnish with fresh cilantro.

- Serve over rice. Serves 6 to 8. *Donalsonville, Georgia*

Cowpoke Steak and Gravy

1 - 1½ pounds tenderized round steak
Oil
1 (1 ounce) packet onion soup mix
1 (10 ounce) can golden mushroom soup

- Preheat oven to 325°.

- Cut round steak into serving-size pieces and season with a little salt and pepper. Lightly brown steak pieces in small amount of oil in skillet. Transfer steak to 9 x 13-inch baking pan. Sprinkle onion soup mix over steak.

- Combine mushroom soup and ¾ cup water in saucepan and heat just enough to mix well. Pour over steak pieces.

- Cover and bake for 1 hour. Serves 4 to 6. *Center, Texas*

Classy Beef and Noodles

2 pounds lean round steak, cut in strips
Oil
2 (10 ounce) cans golden mushroom soup
½ cup cooking sherry
1 (1 ounce) packet dry onion-mushroom soup mix
1 (12 ounce) package medium egg noodles
¼ cup (½ stick) butter

- Preheat oven to 325°.

- Brown steak strips in skillet with a little oil and drain off fat.
  Stir in mushroom soup, sherry, dry onion-mushroom soup mix
  and ¾ cup water.

- Spoon into sprayed 3-quart baking dish, cover and bake for 1 hour
  or until steak is tender.

- Cook noodles according to package directions, drain and stir in butter.
  Spoon onto serving platter and spoon steak mixture over noodles.
  Serves 8 to 10. *Kimberley, Idaho*

Cheesy Meatball Pie

2 cups shredded hash-brown potatoes, thawed
1 (10 ounce) box frozen green peas, thawed
18 frozen Italian meatballs, thawed, halved
¾ cup shredded cheddar cheese
½ cup biscuit mix
1 cup milk
2 large eggs

- Preheat oven to 375°.

- Toss hash-brown potatoes with a little salt and pepper in bowl and
  spread in sprayed deep-dish pie pan.

- Layer peas, meatballs and cheese over potatoes in pie pan.

- Whisk biscuit mix, milk and eggs in bowl until ingredients blend well.

- Pour over layers and bake for 35 minutes or until center sets and top
  is golden brown.

- Let stand for 10 minutes before cutting in wedges to serve. Serves
  8 to 10. *Calumet Park, Illinois*

Supper-Ready Beef

1 (3 - 4) pound rump roast
1 (10 ounce) can French onion soup
1 (14 ounce) can beef broth
1 teaspoon garlic powder

- Preheat oven to 350°.

- Place roast in roasting pan. Pour soup and broth over roast and sprinkle with garlic powder.

- Cover and bake for 3 hours 30 minutes. Gravy will be in pan. Serves 6 to 8. *Cicero, Indiana*

Savory Rib Roast

1 tablespoon dried thyme
1 tablespoon dried, crushed rosemary
1 teaspoon rubbed sage
1 (4 - 5 pound) rib roast

- Preheat oven to 350°.

- Combine thyme, rosemary and sage in small bowl and rub over roast.

- Place roast fat-side up on rack in large roasting pan. Bake for 2 hours to 2 hours 30 minutes or until meat reaches desired doneness.

- Remove roast to warm serving platter and let stand for 10 minutes before slicing. Serves 6 to 8. *Carlisle, Iowa*

Easy Roast

1 (4 pound) rump roast
1 (10 ounce) can cream of mushroom soup
1 (1 ounce) packet dry onion soup mix
½ cup white wine

- Preheat oven to 325°.

- Place roast in sprayed roasting pan.

- Combine mushroom soup, onion soup mix, white wine and ⅓ cup water in bowl. Pour over roast.

- Cover and bake for 3 to 4 hours. Serves 6 to 8. *Daleville, Alabama*

Dutch Oven Roast

1 (3 pound) rump roast
1 onion, sliced
1 (10 ounce) can golden mushroom soup
1 (1 ounce) packet brown gravy mix
2 teaspoons minced garlic

• Preheat oven to 325°.

• Place roast in sprayed Dutch oven or large, heavy pot and place onion slices on top of roast.

• Combine soup, gravy mix, garlic and ⅔ cup water in saucepan and heat just enough for mixture to blend well. Pour mixture over roast.

• Place lid on Dutch oven or pot and bake for 3 hours 30 minutes or until roast is tender. Serves 8 to 10. *Hardin, Montana*

Beef Roast

1 (4 pound) boneless rump roast
½ cup flour, divided
1 (1 ounce) packet brown gravy mix
1 (1 ounce) packet beefy onion soup mix

• If necessary, cut roast in half to fit into cooker.

• Rub half of flour over roast and place in 5 to 6-quart slow cooker.

• Combine remaining flour, gravy mix and soup mix in small bowl; gradually add 2 cups water and stir until it mixes well. Pour over roast.

• Cover and cook on LOW for 7 to 8 hours or until roast is tender. Serves 6 to 8. *Corning, Arkansas*

TIP: This makes a great gravy for mashed potatoes (use instant).

Sweet and Savory Brisket

1 (3 - 4 pound) trimmed beef brisket, halved
⅓ cup grape or plum jelly
1 cup ketchup
1 (1 ounce) packet dry onion soup mix

- Place half of brisket in slow cooker. Combine jelly, ketchup, onion soup mix and ¾ teaspoon pepper in saucepan and heat just enough to mix well. Spread half over brisket. Top with remaining brisket and jelly-soup mixture.

- Cover and cook on LOW for 8 to 9 hours. Slice brisket and serve with cooking juices. Serves 6 to 8. *Coweta, Oklahoma*

Next-Day Beef

1 (5 - 6 pound) trimmed beef brisket
1 (1 ounce) packet dry onion soup mix
1 (10 ounce) bottle steak sauce
1 (12 ounce) bottle barbecue sauce

- Preheat oven to 325°.

- Place brisket, cut-side up in roasting pan.

- Combine onion soup mix, steak sauce and barbecue sauce in bowl. Pour over brisket. Cover and roast for 4 to 5 hours or until tender. Remove brisket from pan and pour off liquid and set aside. Refrigerate both separately overnight.

- The next day, trim all fat from meat, slice and reheat. Skim fat off drippings and reheat. Serve over brisket. Serves 8 to 10. *Fruita, Colorado*

Easy Breezy Brisket

1 (4 - 5 pound) brisket
1 (1 ounce) packet dry onion soup mix
2 tablespoons Worcestershire sauce
1 cup red wine

- Preheat oven to 325°.

- Place brisket in shallow baking pan. Sprinkle onion soup mix over brisket. Pour Worcestershire and red wine in pan.

- Cover and bake for 5 to 6 hours. Serves 6 to 8. *Chandler, Texas*

Easy Brisket

1 (4 - 5 pound) trimmed brisket
1 (1 ounce) packet dry onion soup mix
1 (12 ounce) can cola
1 (10 ounce) bottle Heinz 57® sauce

- Place brisket fat-side up in slow cooker.

- Combine onion soup mix, cola and 57 sauce in bowl and stir well to remove lumps in soup mix. Pour over brisket.

- Cover and cook on LOW for 8 to 10 hours.

- When ready to serve, let brisket stand at room temperature for about 15 minutes. To serve, cut thin slices across grain of brisket. Serves 6 to 8. *Camdenton, Missouri*

Corned Beef Supper

1 (4 - 5 pound) corned beef brisket
4 large potatoes, peeled, quartered
6 carrots, peeled, halved
1 head cabbage

- Place corned beef in roasting pan, cover with water and bring to boil. Reduce heat, simmer for 3 hours and add water if necessary. Add potatoes and carrots.

- Cut cabbage into eights and lay over potatoes, carrots and brisket. Bring to a boil, reduce heat and cook for an additional 30 to 40 minutes or until vegetables are done.

- Slice corned beef across grain. Serves 6 to 8. *Hooksett, New Hampshire*

TIP: *Leftover corned beef is good for sandwiches.*

Winter Chili Supper

1 (40 ounce) can chili with beans
1 (7 ounce) can chopped green chilies
1 bunch fresh green onions, sliced
1 (8 ounce) package shredded Mexican 4-cheese blend
2½ cups crushed ranch-flavored tortilla chips, divided

- Preheat oven to 350°.

- Combine chili, green chilies, green onions, cheese and 2 cups crushed chips in bowl. Transfer to sprayed 3-quart baking dish and bake for 25 minutes.

- Remove from oven and sprinkle remaining chips over top of casserole and bake for an additional 10 minutes. Serves 6 to 8.
  Fort Scott, Kansas

Texas Chili Pie

2 (20 ounce) cans chili without beans
1 (16 ounce) package small corn chips
1 onion, chopped
1 (16 ounce) package shredded cheddar cheese

- Preheat oven to 325°.

- Heat chili in saucepan.

- Layer one-third each of corn chips, chili, onion and cheese in 9 x 13-inch baking dish. Repeat layers twice more. Bake for 20 minutes or until cheese bubbles. Serves 6 to 8. *Childress, Texas*

Reuben Casserole Supper

1 (20 ounce) bag frozen hash-brown potatoes, thawed
1½ pounds (¼-inch) thick deli corned beef slices
1 (8 ounce) bottle Russian salad dressing
1 (15 ounce) can sauerkraut, drained
8 slices Swiss cheese

- Preheat oven to 400°.

- Place hash-brown potatoes in sprayed 9 x 13-inch baking dish and season with a little salt and pepper. Bake for 30 minutes.

- Place corned beef slices, overlapping, on top of potatoes; spoon dressing over top of beef and arrange sauerkraut on top. Cover with slices of cheese, reduce heat to 350° and bake for an additional 15 minutes. Serves 8 to 10. *Bloomingdale, New Jersey*

Quick-Friday-Night-Game Supper

2 (15 ounce) cans chili without beans
2 (15 ounce) cans pinto beans with liquid
2 (15 ounce) cans beef tamales
1 (8 ounce) package shredded Mexican 4-cheese blend, divided
Tortilla chips

- Preheat oven to 350°.

- Spoon both cans chili in pan in sprayed 9 x 13-inch baking pan and spread out with back of large spoon.

- Spread beans with liquid over chili. Remove wrappers from tamales and place tamales over beans. Sprinkle about ½ cup cheese over top, cover and bake for 30 minutes.

- Remove from oven and sprinkle remaining cheese over top of casserole. Return to oven for just 5 minutes.

- Serve with lots of tortilla chips. Serves 6 to 8. *Cisco, Texas*

TIP: You might want to serve some hot thick-and-chunky salsa along with this dish.

★ ★ ★

Chicken

Chicken is always a family
favorite. And there are 80 tasty
recipes to choose from!

1001
Community
Recipes

Chicken Contents

Chicken Contents

Chicken a la Orange

1 (11 ounce) can mandarin oranges, drained
1 (6 ounce) can frozen orange juice concentrate
1 tablespoon lemon juice
1 tablespoon cornstarch
6 boneless, skinless chicken breast halves
2 tablespoons garlic-and-herb seasoning
2 tablespoons butter
Rice, cooked

- Combine oranges, orange juice concentrate, lemon juice, ⅔ cup water and cornstarch in saucepan. Stir constantly over medium heat until mixture thickens. Set aside.

- Sprinkle chicken breasts with herb seasoning and place in skillet with butter. Cook for about 7 minutes on each side until brown.

- Lower heat and spoon orange juice mixture over chicken, cover and simmer for about 20 minutes. Add a little water if sauce gets too thick.

- Serve over rice. Serves 6. *Chelan, Washington*

Alfredo Chicken

5 - 6 boneless, skinless chicken breast halves
Oil
1 (16 ounce) package frozen broccoli florets, thawed
1 red bell pepper, seeded, chopped
1 (16 ounce) jar alfredo sauce

- Preheat oven to 325°.

- Brown and cook chicken breasts in large skillet with a little oil until juices run clear. Transfer to sprayed 9 x 13-inch baking dish.

- Microwave broccoli according to package directions and drain. (If broccoli stems are extra long, trim and discard.) Spoon broccoli and bell pepper over chicken.

- Heat alfredo sauce with ¼ cup water in small saucepan. Pour over chicken and vegetables. Cover and bake for 15 to 20 minutes. Serves 5 to 6. *Blennerhassett, West Virginia*

TIP: This chicken-broccoli dish can be "dressed up" a bit by sprinkling a little shredded parmesan cheese over the top after baking.

Almond Crusted Chicken

1 egg
¼ cup seasoned breadcrumbs
1 cup sliced almonds
4 boneless, skinless chicken breast halves
1 (5 ounce) package grated parmesan cheese

- Preheat oven to 350°.

- Place egg and 1 tablespoon water in shallow bowl and beat. In separate shallow bowl, combine breadcrumbs and almonds.

- Dip each chicken breast in egg, then in almond mixture and place in sprayed 9 x 13-inch baking pan.

- Bake for 20 minutes. Remove from oven and sprinkle parmesan cheese over top and bake for an additional 15 minutes or until almonds and cheese are golden brown.

Sauce:

1 teaspoon minced garlic
⅓ cup finely chopped onion
2 tablespoons oil
1 cup white wine
¼ cup teriyaki sauce

- Saute garlic and onion in oil in saucepan. Add wine and teriyaki sauce, bring to a boil and reduce heat. Simmer for about 10 minutes or until mixture reduces by half.

- Serve sauce over chicken. Serves 4. *Glenrock, Wyoming*

Apricot Chicken

6 boneless, skinless chicken breast halves
1 (12 ounce) jar apricot preserves
1 (8 ounce) bottle Catalina dressing
1 (1 ounce) packet dry onion soup mix

- Place chicken in sprayed 6-quart slow cooker.

- Combine apricot preserves, Catalina dressing, onion soup mix and ¼ cup water in bowl and stir well. Cover chicken breasts with sauce mixture.

- Cover and cook on LOW for 5 to 6 hours. Serves 6.
Columbiana, Alabama

Apricot-Ginger Chicken

2 teaspoons ground ginger
½ cup Italian dressing
4 boneless, skinless chicken breast halves
⅔ cup apricot preserves

- Preheat oven to 350°.

- Combine ginger and Italian dressing and place in large resealable plastic bag. Add chicken to bag and marinate in refrigerator for 8 to 10 hours, turning occasionally.

- When ready to bake, preheat oven to 350°.

- Remove chicken from marinade and set aside ¼ cup marinade; discard remaining marinade. Place chicken in shallow baking dish.

- Pour ¼ cup marinade into saucepan, bring to a boil and cook for 1 minute. Remove from heat, stir in preserves and set aside.

- Bake chicken for 45 minutes and brush with marinade mixture last 10 minutes of cooking. Serves 4. *Colorado City, Arizona*

Bacon-Wrapped Chicken

6 boneless, skinless chicken breast halves
1 (8 ounce) carton whipped cream cheese with onion and chives
Butter
6 bacon strips

- Preheat oven to 325°.

- Flatten chicken to ½-inch thickness. Spread 3 tablespoons cream cheese over each.

- Dot with butter and a little salt and roll up each chicken breast. Wrap each with bacon strip.

- Place seam-side down in sprayed 9 x 13-inch baking dish.

- Bake for 40 to 45 minutes or until juices run clear.

- To brown, broil 6 inches from heat for about 3 minutes or until bacon is crisp. Serves 6. *Barling, Arkansas*

Busy Day Chicken Casserole

6 boneless, skinless chicken breast halves, cooked
1 (1 pint) carton sour cream
1 (7 ounce) package ready-cut spaghetti
2 (10 ounce) cans cream of chicken soup
1 (4 ounce) can mushrooms, drained
½ cup (1 stick) butter, melted
1 cup fresh grated parmesan cheese

- Preheat oven to 350°.

- Cut chicken into strips and combine with ⅛ teaspoon pepper and remaining ingredients, except parmesan cheese, in bowl and mix well.

- Pour into sprayed 9 x 13-inch baking dish and sprinkle cheese on top. Cover and bake for 50 minutes. Serves 6. *Borrego Springs, California*

Chicken and Beef

1 (2.25 ounce) jar sliced dried beef, separated
6 strips bacon
6 boneless, skinless chicken breast halves
1(10 ounce) can cream of chicken soup

- Preheat oven to 325°.

- Place dried beef in sprayed 9 x 13-inch baking dish. Wrap bacon strip around each chicken breast and place over beef.

- Heat chicken soup and ¼ cup water in saucepan and pour over chicken. Cover and bake for 1 hour 10 minutes. Serves 6. *Coventry, Connecticut*

Chicken and Vegetables

4 - 5 boneless, skinless chicken breast halves
1 (16 ounce) package frozen broccoli, cauliflower and
    carrots, thawed
1 (10 ounce) can cream of celery soup
1 (8 ounce) package shredded cheddar-Jack cheese

- Cut chicken into strips and place chicken strips sprinkled with 2 teaspoons salt in sprayed slow cooker.

- Combine vegetables, celery soup and half cheese in large bowl and mix well. Spoon over chicken breasts. Cover and cook on LOW for 4 to 5 hours.

- About 10 minutes before serving, sprinkle remaining cheese on top of casserole. Serves 4 to 5. *Elsmere, Delaware*

Cashew Chicken and Veggies

1 pound boneless, skinless chicken breast halves
2 tablespoons cornstarch
1 tablespoon soy sauce
1 teaspoon grated fresh ginger
1 (16 ounce) package frozen broccoli florets, thawed
1 (10 ounce) package frozen green peas, thawed
Oil
1 (1 ounce) packet savory herb-garlic soup mix
⅔ cup whole cashews
1 (6 ounce) package chicken and herb-flavored rice, cooked
Rice, cooked

- Cut chicken crosswise into ¼-inch wide strips. Combine cornstarch, soy sauce and ginger in medium bowl and mix well. Add chicken strips and stir to coat well.

- Stir-fry broccoli and peas in large skillet with a little oil for 3 minutes and remove to warm plate.

- In same skillet with a little oil, stir-fry chicken until all pieces change color. Stir in ½ cup water and soup mix.

- Cook on medium heat for about 5 minutes until soup mix coats chicken well.

- Return cooked vegetables to skillet, add cashews and cook until thoroughly hot. Serve chicken and vegetables over rice. Serves 12. *Delta, Colorado*

Chicken Bake

6 boneless, skinless chicken breast halves
6 slices Swiss cheese
1 (10 ounce) can cream of chicken soup
1 (8 ounce) box chicken stuffing mix

- Preheat oven to 325°.

- Flatten each chicken breast with rolling pin and place in sprayed 9 x 13-inch baking dish.

- Place cheese slices over chicken. Combine chicken soup and ½ cup water in bowl and pour over chicken.

- Mix stuffing mix according to package directions and sprinkle over chicken. Bake for 1 hour. Serves 6. *Biscayne Park, Florida*

Chicken Breasts Supreme

6 boneless, skinless chicken breast halves
¼ cup (½ stick) butter
1 (10 ounce) can cream of chicken soup
¾ cup sauterne or chicken broth
1 (8.5 ounce) can sliced water chestnuts, drained
1 (4 ounce) can sliced mushrooms, drained
2 tablespoons chopped green bell pepper
¼ teaspoon crushed thyme leaves

• Preheat oven to 350°.

• Brown chicken breasts in butter on all sides in skillet. Arrange in 9 x 13-inch baking pan. Sprinkle with ½ teaspoon salt and dash of pepper.

• Add soup to butter that is left in skillet and slowly stir in sauterne or broth. Add remaining ingredients and heat to boil.

• Pour soup mixture over chicken. Cover and bake for 45 minutes.

• Remove cover and bake for an additional 15 minutes. Serves 6.
  Brookhaven, Georgia

Chicken Crunch

4 - 6 boneless, skinless chicken breast halves
½ cup Italian salad dressing
½ cup sour cream
2½ cups crushed corn flakes

• Place chicken in resealable plastic bag and add salad dressing and sour cream. Seal and refrigerate for 1 hour.

• When ready to bake, preheat oven to 375°.

• Remove chicken from marinade and discard marinade.

• Dredge chicken in corn flakes and place in sprayed 9 x 13-inch baking dish.

• Bake for 45 minutes. Serves 4 to 6. *Ammon, Idaho*

Chicken Divan

2 (10 ounce) packages frozen broccoli
4 - 6 boneless, skinless chicken breast halves, cooked, sliced
2 (10 ounce) cans cream of chicken soup
1 cup mayonnaise
1 teaspoon lemon juice
½ teaspoon curry powder or Worcestershire sauce
1½ cups shredded sharp cheese, divided
½ cup seasoned breadcrumbs
1 teaspoon butter, melted

- Preheat oven to 350°.

- Cook broccoli in saucepan until tender and drain. Arrange broccoli in sprayed 9 x 13-inch baking dish. Place chicken slices on top.

- Combine soup, mayonnaise, lemon juice, curry or Worcestershire sauce and half cheese in bowl and spread over chicken.

- In separate bowl, combine breadcrumbs and butter; layer over chicken.

- Sprinkle remaining cheese over top and bake for 25 to 30 minutes. Serves 4 to 6. *Berrys Chapel, Tennessee*

Chicken Oriental

1 (6 ounce) jar sweet-and-sour sauce
1 (1 ounce) packet dry onion soup mix
1 (16 ounce) can whole cranberry sauce
6 boneless, skinless chicken breast halves

- Preheat oven to 325°.

- Combine sweet-and-sour sauce, onion soup mix and cranberry sauce in bowl.

- Place chicken breasts in sprayed 9 x 13-inch shallow baking dish. Pour cranberry mixture over chicken breasts.

- Cover and bake for 30 minutes.

- Uncover and bake for an additional 25 minutes. Serves 6. *Burns, Oregon*

Chicken Linguine

1 pound boneless, skinless chicken breast halves, cut into strips
Oil
1 (28 ounce) can garlic-onion spaghetti sauce
1 (16 ounce) package frozen broccoli, carrots and cauliflower,
    thawed
1 bell pepper, seeded, chopped
⅓ cup grated parmesan cheese
1 (12 ounce) package linguine, cooked, drained

- Cook half chicken strips in a little oil in large skillet over medium heat until light brown. Remove and set aside. Repeat with remaining chicken and set aside.

- In same skillet combine spaghetti sauce, vegetables, bell pepper and cheese and bring to a boil. Reduce heat to medium-low, cover and cook for 10 minutes or until vegetables are tender. Stir occasionally.

- Return chicken to skillet and heat thoroughly.

- Place cooked linguine on serving platter and spoon chicken mixture over linguine. Serves 12. *Beardstown, Illinois*

TIP: *Break linguine into thirds before cooking to make serving a little easier.*

Chicken Parmesan

1½ cups biscuit mix
⅔ cup grated parmesan cheese
6 - 8 boneless, skinless chicken breast halves
½ cup (1 stick) butter, melted

- Preheat oven to 325°.

- Combine biscuit mix and parmesan cheese in shallow bowl.

- Dip chicken in butter and in biscuit-cheese mixture.

- Place in large, sprayed baking dish. Bake for 1 hour or until light brown. Serves 6 to 8. *Beme, Indiana*

Chicken Souffle

16 slices white bread, crusts removed
Butter, softened
5 boneless, skinless, chicken breast halves, cooked, thinly sliced
    diagonally
½ cup mayonnaise
1 cup shredded cheddar cheese, divided
5 large eggs
2 cups milk
1 (10 ounce) can cream of mushroom soup

- Butter 8 slices of bread on 1 side. Place butter-side down in sprayed 9 x 13-inch baking dish. Cover with sliced chicken.

- Spread chicken slices with mayonnaise and sprinkle with ½ cup cheese. Top with remaining 8 slices bread.

- Beat eggs, milk, and ½ teaspoon each of salt and pepper in bowl and pour over entire casserole. Refrigerate for 8 hours.

- When ready to bake, preheat oven to 350°.

- Spread mushroom soup with back of large spoon over top of casserole. Cover and bake for 45 minutes.

- Uncover, sprinkle with remaining cheddar cheese, return to oven and bake for an additional 15 minutes. Serves 4 to 6. *Asbury, Iowa*

TIP: *You could use deli-sliced chicken instead of cooking chicken breasts to save time.*

Chicken Supper

5 boneless, skinless chicken breast halves
5 slices onion
5 potatoes, peeled, quartered
1(10 ounce) can cream of celery soup

- Preheat oven to 325°.

- Place chicken breasts in sprayed 9 x 13-inch baking dish. Top chicken with onion slices and place potatoes around chicken.

- Heat soup in saucepan with ¼ cup water just enough to mix well and pour over chicken and vegetables.

- Cover and bake for 1 hour 10 minutes. Serves 5. *Colby, Kansas*

Chicken Spaghetti

3 boneless, skinless chicken breasts, boiled
1 (10 ounce) can tomatoes and green chilies
1 (10 ounce) can cream of mushroom soup
1 (8 ounce) package shredded cheddar cheese
1 (8 ounce) package shredded Velveeta® cheese
1 (12 ounce) package spaghetti

- Preheat oven to 350°.

- Shred cooked chicken into large bowl. Add tomatoes and green chilies, soup, cheddar cheese, and Velveeta® cheese.

- Cook spaghetti according to package directions and drain.

- Add to chicken mixture and mix well. Pour into 3-quart baking dish, cover and bake at for 35 minutes. Serves 6. *Batesville, Alabama*

Chicken-Taco Pie

1 pound boneless, skinless chicken breast halves
Oil
1 (1 ounce) packet taco seasoning mix
1 green bell pepper, seeded, finely chopped
1 red bell pepper, seeded, finely chopped
1 (8 ounce) package shredded Mexican 4-cheese blend
1 (8 ounce) package corn muffin mix
1 egg
⅓ cup milk

- Preheat oven to 400°.

- Cut chicken into 1-inch chunks and cook on medium-high heat in large skillet with a little oil. Cook for about 10 minutes and drain.

- Stir in taco seasoning, bell peppers and ¾ cup water. Reduce heat, cook for an additional 10 minutes and stir several times. Spoon into sprayed 9-inch deep-dish pie pan and sprinkle with cheese.

- Prepare corn muffin mix with egg and milk in bowl and mix well.

- Spoon over top of pie and bake for 20 minutes or until top is golden brown. Let stand for about 5 minutes before serving. Serves 8 to 10. *Buckner, Kentucky*

Cola Chicken

4 - 6 boneless, skinless chicken breast halves
1 cup ketchup
1 cup cola
2 tablespoons Worcestershire sauce

• Preheat oven to 350°.

• Place chicken in 9 x 13-inch baking dish. Sprinkle with a little salt and pepper.

• Mix ketchup, cola and Worcestershire sauce in bowl and pour over chicken.

• Cover and bake for 50 minutes. Serves 4 to 6. *DeRidder, Louisiana*

Chicken-Tortilla Dumplings

*This is a great recipe and using tortillas is
a lot easier than making real dumplings!*

6 large boneless, skinless chicken breast halves, cooked, cubed
2 ribs celery, chopped
1 onion, chopped
2 tablespoons chicken bouillon granules
1 (10 ounce) can cream of chicken soup
10 - 11 (8 inch) flour tortillas

• Place chicken breasts, 10 cups water, celery and onion in roasting pan. Bring to a boil, reduce heat and cook for about 30 minutes or until chicken is tender. Remove chicken and set aside to cool.

• Save broth in roasting pan (about 9 cups broth). Add chicken bouillon and taste to make sure it is rich and tasty. (Add more bouillon if needed and more water if you don't have 9 cups broth.) Add chicken soup to broth and bring to boil.

• Cut tortillas into 2 x 1-inch strips. Add strips, one at a time, to briskly boiling broth mixture and stir constantly.

• When all strips are in saucepan, pour in chicken, reduce heat to low and simmer for 5 to 10 minutes. Stir well but gently to prevent dumplings from sticking. The chicken and dumplings will be very thick.

• Pour into very large serving bowl and serve hot. Serves 6.
Brownfield, Texas

Creamy Salsa Chicken

4 - 5 skinless, boneless skinless chicken breast halves
1 (1 ounce) packet dry taco seasoning mix
1 cup salsa
½ cup sour cream

- Place chicken breasts in sprayed 5 to 6-quart slow cooker and add ¼ cup water.

- Sprinkle taco seasoning mix over chicken and top with salsa.

- Cook on LOW for 5 to 6 hours.

- When ready to serve, remove chicken breasts and place on platter. Stir sour cream into salsa and spoon over chicken breasts. Serves 4 to 5. *Ellsworth, Maine*

Creamy Tarragon Chicken

1½ cups flour
6 boneless, skinless chicken breast halves
2 tablespoons oil
1 (10 ounce) can chicken broth
1 cup milk
2 teaspoons dried tarragon
1 (4 ounce) can sliced mushrooms, drained
2 (8 ounce) packages microwave roasted chicken-flavored rice

- Mix flour and a little salt and pepper on wax paper, coat chicken and save extra flour. Heat oil in large skillet over medium-high heat and cook chicken breasts, turning once, for about 10 minutes or until light brown. Transfer to plate.

- In same skillet, stir in 2 tablespoons flour-salt mixture. Whisk in chicken broth, milk and tarragon, heat and stir constantly until it bubbles.

- Add mushrooms and return chicken to skillet. Cover and simmer for 10 to 15 minutes or until sauce thickens.

- Microwave rice according to package directions and place on serving platter. Spoon chicken and sauce over rice. Serves 6. *Burtonsville, Maryland*

Crispy Nutty Chicken

⅓ cup dry roasted peanuts, minced
1 cup corn flake crumbs
½ cup ranch-style buttermilk salad dressing
5 - 6 chicken breast halves

- Preheat oven to 350°.

- Combine peanuts and corn flake crumbs on wax paper.

- Pour salad dressing into pie pan.

- Dip each piece chicken in salad dressing and roll in crumb mixture to coat.

- Arrange chicken in 9 x 13-inch shallow baking dish.

- Bake for 50 minutes until light brown. Serves 5 to 6. *Buzzards Bay, Massachusetts*

Crunchy Baked Chicken

¼ pound (1 stick) butter, melted
2 tablespoons mayonnaise
2 tablespoons marinade for chicken (Lea & Perrins)
1 (6 ounce) can french-fried onions, crushed
6 boneless, skinless chicken breasts halves

- Preheat oven to 350°.

- Combine butter, mayonnaise and marinade for chicken in shallow bowl. In separate shallow bowl, place crushed onions.

- Dry chicken breasts with paper towels, dip first into butter mixture and dredge each chicken breast in crushed onions.

- Place in large baking pan and arrange so pieces do not touch.

- Bake for 30 minutes or until chicken juices run clear. Serves 6. *Brownlee Park, Michigan*

Encore Chicken

6 boneless, skinless chicken breast halves
Oil
1 (16 ounce) jar hot, thick-and-chunky salsa
1½ cups packed light brown sugar
1 tablespoon dijon-style mustard
Brown rice, cooked

- Preheat oven to 325°.

- Brown chicken breasts in large skillet with a little oil and place in sprayed 9 x 13-inch baking dish.

- Combine salsa, brown sugar, mustard and ½ teaspoon salt and pour over chicken.

- Cover and bake for 45 minutes. Serve over brown rice. Serves 6. *Becker, Minnesota*

Green Chile-Chicken Casserole

1 green bell pepper, seeded, chopped
3 ribs celery, chopped
¾ cup chopped green onions
½ cup (1 stick) butter
1 (7 ounce) can chopped green chilies
1½ cups rice
1 (8 ounce) carton sour cream
3 boneless, skinless chicken breast halves, cooked, sliced
1 (14 ounce) can chicken broth

- Preheat oven to 325°.

- Combine bell pepper, celery and green onions in skillet with butter and saute for 5 minutes. Transfer to bowl.

- Stir in green chilies, rice, sour cream, chicken, chicken broth, ¼ cup water and a little salt and pepper.

- Pour into sprayed 9 x 13-inch baking dish.

- Cover and bake for 40 minutes, uncover and continue to bake for 10 minutes. Serves 6 to 8. *Coolidge, Arizona*

Favorite Oven-Fried Chicken

Marinade:

2 cups buttermilk
2 tablespoons dijon-style mustard
2 teaspoons garlic powder
1 teaspoon cayenne pepper

Chicken:

6 - 8 boneless, skinless chicken breast halves
2½ cups crushed corn flakes
¾ cup breadcrumbs
2 tablespoons olive oil

- Combine marinade ingredients in large bowl and mix well. Place chicken pieces in bowl and turn to coat well.

- Place in refrigerator and marinate for 2 hours or overnight.

- When ready to bake, preheat oven to 400°.

- Line large baking pan with sprayed foil.

- Combine crushed corn flakes and breadcrumbs in large shallow bowl. Drizzle oil over crumbs and toss until they coat well.

- Take 1 piece chicken at a time, remove from marinade and dredge in crumb mixture. Press crumbs onto all sides of chicken and place in sprayed 9 x 13-inch baking pan. Do not let sides touch.

- Bake for 35 to 40 minutes. Serves 6 to 8. *Crystal Springs, Mississippi*

TIP: The easiest way to crush corn flakes is in a resealable plastic bag using the palm of your hand. You don't even have to get out the rolling pin if you don't want to or don't have one. Who needs a rolling pin anyway?

Here's the Stuff

5 boneless, skinless chicken breast halves
2 (10 ounce) cans cream of chicken soup
1 (6 ounce) box chicken stuffing mix
1 (16 ounce) package frozen green peas, thawed, drained

- Place chicken breasts in 6-quart slow cooker and spoon soup over chicken.

- Prepare stuffing mix according to package directions. Spoon over chicken and soup.

- Cover and cook on LOW for 5 to 6 hours.

- Sprinkle green peas over top of stuffing. Cover and cook for an additional 45 to 50 minutes. Serves 5. *Breckenridge Hills, Missouri*

TIP: Instead of 2 cans cream of chicken soup, use 1 can cream of chicken soup and 1 can fiesta nacho soup.

Imperial Chicken Casserole

5 boneless, skinless chicken breast halves, cooked, cubed
1 (1 pint) carton sour cream
1 (7 ounce) package ready-cut spaghetti
2 (10 ounce) cans cream of chicken soup
1 (4 ounce) can mushrooms, drained
½ cup (1 stick) butter, melted
1 cup fresh, grated parmesan cheese

- Preheat oven to 325°.

- Combine chicken, sour cream, spaghetti, chicken soup, mushrooms and butter in bowl.

- Pour into sprayed 9 x 13-inch baking dish, cover and bake for 50 minutes.

- Remove from oven and sprinkle cheese on top of casserole. Return to oven for 5 minutes. Serves 5. *Cut Bank, Montana*

Italian Chicken and Rice

3 boneless, chicken breast halves, cut into strips
1 (14 ounce) can chicken broth seasoned with Italian herbs
¾ cup rice
¼ cup grated parmesan cheese

- Cook chicken in non-stick skillet until brown and stir often. Remove chicken and set aside.

- Add broth and rice to skillet. Heat to boiling point. Cover and simmer over low heat for 25 minutes. (Check to see if it needs more water.) Stir in cheese. Return chicken to pan. Cover and cook for 5 minutes or until thoroughly heated. Serves 4. *Central City, Nebraska*

Italian Crumb Chicken

5 - 6 boneless, skinless chicken breast halves
¾ cup mayonnaise
⅓ cup grated parmesan cheese
½ cup Italian seasoned breadcrumbs

- Preheat oven to 400°.

- Place chicken breasts in foil-lined 9 x 13-inch baking pan. Combine mayonnaise, 2 teaspoons pepper and parmesan cheese in bowl and mix well. Spread mixture over chicken breasts and sprinkle on seasoned breadcrumbs.

- Bake for 20 to 25 minutes or until light brown. Breasts may be served whole or sliced diagonally. Serves 5 to 6. *Bithlo, Florida*

Jiffy Chicken

6 boneless, skinless chicken breast halves
¾ cup mayonnaise
2 cups crushed corn flake crumbs
½ cup grated parmesan cheese

- Preheat oven to 325°.

- Sprinkle chicken breasts with a little salt and pepper. Dip chicken in mayonnaise and spread mayonnaise over chicken with brush.

- Combine corn flakes and parmesan cheese in bowl. Dip mayonnaise-covered chicken in corn flake mixture (get plenty of crumbs on chicken) and place in sprayed 9 x 13-inch glass baking dish.

- Bake for 1 hour. Serves 6. *Fallon, Nevada*

Lemonade Chicken

6 boneless, skinless chicken breast halves
1 (6 ounce) can frozen lemonade, thawed
⅓ cup soy sauce
1 teaspoon garlic powder

- Preheat oven to 350°.

- Place chicken in sprayed 9 x 13-inch baking dish.

- Combine lemonade, soy sauce and garlic powder in bowl and pour over chicken.

- Cover and bake for 45 minutes.

- Uncover, spoon juices over chicken and bake for an additional 10 minutes. Serves 6. *Farmington, New Hampshire*

Mozzarella Cutlets

4 boneless, skinless chicken breast halves
1 cup Italian seasoned dry breadcrumbs
1 cup prepared spaghetti sauce
4 slices mozzarella cheese

- Preheat oven to 350°.

- Pound each chicken breast to flatten slightly.

- Coat chicken well in breadcrumbs. Arrange chicken breasts in sprayed 9 x 13-inch baking dish.

- Place one-fourth sauce over each chicken breast.

- Place 1 slice cheese over each and garnish with remaining breadcrumbs.

- Bake for 45 minutes. Serves 4. *Bernardsville, New Jersey*

One-Dish Chicken Bake

1 (6 ounce) package chicken stuffing mix
4 boneless, skinless chicken breast halves
1 (10 ounce) can cream of mushroom soup
½ cup sour cream

- Preheat oven to 375°.

- Toss contents of stuffing seasoning packet, stuffing mix and 1⅓ cups water into bowl and set aside.

- Place chicken in sprayed 9 x 13-inch baking dish.

- Mix soup and sour cream in saucepan and heat just enough to mix well and pour over chicken. Spoon stuffing evenly over top. Bake for 40 minutes. Serves 4. *Crownpoint, New Mexico*

Oven-Herb Chicken

2 cups crushed corn flakes
½ cup grated parmesan cheese
1 tablespoon rosemary
1 tablespoon thyme leaves
1 teaspoon oregano
1 tablespoon parsley flakes
½ teaspoon garlic powder
½ cup (1 stick) butter, melted
5 - 6 boneless, skinless chicken breast halves or 1 chicken, quartered

- Preheat oven to 325°.

- Combine corn flakes, parmesan cheese, rosemary, thyme, oregano, parsley, garlic powder, ½ teaspoon salt and 1 teaspoon pepper in medium bowl.

- Melt butter in small bowl in microwave. Dip chicken breasts in butter and corn flake mixture; coat well.

- Place chicken in sprayed 9 x 13-inch shallow baking dish. (Do not crowd pieces.)

- Bake for 1 hour. Serve 5 to 6. *Butner, North Carolina*

Orange Chicken

6 boneless, skinless chicken breasts halves
1 (12 ounce) jar orange marmalade
1 (8 ounce) bottle Russian salad dressing
1 (1 ounce) packet dry onion soup mix

- Place chicken breasts in oval slow cooker. Combine orange marmalade, dressing, soup mix and ¾ cup water in bowl and stir well. Spoon mixture over chicken breasts.

- Cover and cook on LOW for 4 to 6 hours. Serves 6. *Bayport, New York*

Perfect Chicken Breasts

1 (2.5 ounce) jar dried beef
6 small boneless, skinless chicken breast halves
6 slices bacon
2 (10 ounce) cans golden mushroom soup

- Line bottom of oval slow cooker with slices of dried beef and overlap some.

- Wrap each chicken breast with slice of bacon and secure with toothpick. Place in slow cooker, overlapping as little as possible.

- Combine mushroom soup and ½ cup water or milk in bowl and spoon over chicken breasts. Cover and cook on LOW for 6 to 8 hours. Serves 6. *Grafton, North Dakota*

TIP: When cooked, you will have a great "gravy" that is wonderful served over noodles or rice.

Quick-Fix Chicken

4 - 6 boneless, skinless chicken breast halves
1 (8 ounce) carton sour cream
¼ cup soy sauce
2 (10 ounce) cans French onion soup

- Place chicken in sprayed oval slow cooker.

- Combine sour cream, soy sauce and onion soup in bowl, stir and mix well. Pour over chicken.

- Cover and cook on LOW for 5 to 6 hours if chicken breasts are large, 3 to 4 hours if breasts are medium. Serves 4 to 6. *Cleveland, Oklahoma*

TIP: Serve chicken and sauce with rice or mashed potatoes.

Pimento Cheese Stuffed Fried Chicken

4 skinless, boneless chicken breast halves
½ cup milk
1 large egg, beaten
2 cups seasoned breadcrumbs
Oil
1 (16 ounce) carton pimento cheese

- Preheat oven to 350°.

- Dry chicken breasts with paper towels and sprinkle well with salt and pepper.

- Combine milk and egg in shallow bowl and mix well. In separate shallow bowl, place breadcrumbs. Dip chicken in milk mixture and dredge in breadcrumbs.

- Pour in a little oil to ⅛-inch depth in large skillet over medium-high heat and cook chicken for about 10 to 12 minutes on each side. Transfer to baking sheet.

- Hold chicken with tongs and cut slit in 1 side of each chicken breast to form a pocket. Spoon one-fourth pimento cheese into each pocket and secure chicken pocket with toothpick.

- Bake for about 3 minutes or until cheese melts. Serves 4.
  Archbold, Ohio

Reuben Chicken

4 boneless, skinless chicken breast halves
4 slices Swiss cheese
1 (15 ounce) can sauerkraut, drained
1 (8 ounce) bottle Catalina salad dressing

- Preheat oven to 350°.

- Arrange chicken breasts in sprayed, shallow baking pan.

- Place cheese over chicken and then sauerkraut. Cover with Catalina dressing.

- Cover and bake for 30 minutes. Uncover and bake for an additional 15 minutes. Serves 4. *Chenoweth, Oregon*

Rolled Chicken Florentine

6 boneless, skinless chicken breast halves
6 thin slices deli ham
6 thin slices Swiss cheese
1 (10 ounce) package frozen chopped spinach, thawed, drained
2 (10 ounce) cans cream of chicken soup
4 green onions, finely chopped
1 (10 ounce) box chicken-flavored rice mix

• Preheat oven to 325°.

• With flat side of meat mallet, pound chicken to ¼-inch thickness.

• Squeeze spinach between paper towels to completely remove excess moisture.

• Place ham slice, cheese slice and one-sixth spinach on each chicken piece and roll chicken from short end, jellyroll-style. Secure with wooden toothpicks.

• Place chicken in sprayed 9 x 13-inch glass baking dish. Cover with plastic wrap and microwave on HIGH for 4 minutes.

• Combine chicken soup, green onions, ⅔ cup water and a little pepper in bowl and mix well. Pour over chicken rolls, cover and bake for 25 minutes or until chicken is fork-tender.

• Cook rice mix according to package directions and place on serving platter. Spoon chicken and sauce over rice. Serves 6.
Avalon, Pennsylvania

Saucy Chicken

5 - 6 boneless, skinless chicken breast halves
2 cups thick-and-chunky salsa
⅓ cup packed light brown sugar
1½ tablespoons dijon-style mustard
Rice, cooked

• Preheat oven to 350°.

• Place chicken breasts in sprayed 9 x 13-inch baking dish.

• Combine salsa, brown sugar and mustard in bowl and pour over chicken.

• Cover and bake for 45 minutes. Serve over rice. Serves 5 to 6.
Kingston, Rhode Island

Sesame Chicken

½ cup (1 stick) butter, melted
2¼ teaspoons chili powder
4 boneless, skinless chicken breast halves
1 cup sesame seeds, lightly toasted

- Preheat oven to 325°.

- Combine butter and chili powder in bowl.

- Dip chicken in butter mixture then roll in sesame seeds.

- Place in sprayed 9 x 13- inch baking dish. Bake for 1 hour; turn after 30 minutes. Serves 4. *Bennettsville, South Carolina*

Summertime Limeade Chicken

6 large boneless, skinless chicken breast halves
1 (6 ounce) can frozen limeade concentrate, thawed
3 tablespoons brown sugar
½ cup chili sauce
Rice, cooked

- Sprinkle chicken breasts with a little salt and pepper and place in lightly sprayed skillet. Cook on high heat and brown on both sides for about 10 minutes. Remove from skillet, set aside and keep warm.

- Add limeade concentrate, brown sugar and chili sauce to skillet. Bring to boil and cook, stirring constantly for 4 minutes.

- Return chicken to skillet and spoon sauce over chicken. Reduce heat, cover and simmer for 15 minutes. Serve over rice. Serves 6. *Deadwood, South Dakota*

Sunday Chicken

5 - 6 boneless, skinless chicken breast halves
½ cup sour cream
¼ cup soy sauce
1 (10 ounce) can French onion soup

- Preheat oven to 350°.

- Place chicken in sprayed 9 x 13-inch baking dish.

- Combine sour cream, soy sauce and soup in saucepan and heat just enough to mix well. Pour over chicken breasts.

- Cover and bake for 55 minutes. Serves 5 to 6. *Clinton, Tennessee*

Supper-Ready Chicken

3 boneless, skinless chicken breasts, cooked
1 large onion, sliced
2 (15 ounce) cans new potatoes, drained, sliced
1 (10 ounce) can cream of celery soup
½ cup milk
1 cup shredded mozzarella cheese

- Preheat oven to 350°.

- Slice each chicken breast and place in sprayed 9 x 13-inch baking dish. Spread onion slices and potato slices over chicken.

- Combine soup and milk in saucepan and heat just until they mix well. Spoon over chicken-onion-potato slices, cover and bake for 25 minutes.

- Remove from oven, sprinkle cheese over top and return to oven for 5 minutes. Serves 8. *Buda, Texas*

Sweet 'n Spicy Chicken

1 pound boneless, skinless chicken breast halves
3 tablespoons taco seasoning
Oil
1 (11 ounce) jar chunky salsa
1 cup peach preserves
Rice or noodles, cooked

- Cut chicken into ½-inch cubes. Place chicken in large resealable plastic bag, add taco seasoning and toss to coat.

- Brown chicken in little oil in skillet.

- Combine salsa and preserves in bowl. Stir into chicken.

- Bring to a boil. Reduce heat, cover and simmer until juices run clear. Serve over rice or noodles. Serves 4 to 6. *Fillmore, Utah*

Three Cheers for Chicken

8 boneless, skinless chicken breast halves
6 tablespoons (¾ stick) butter
1 onion, chopped
½ bell pepper, chopped
1 (4 ounce) jar chopped pimentos, drained
1 cup rice
1 (10 ounce) can cream of chicken soup
1 (10 ounce) can cream of celery soup
1 (8 ounce) can sliced water chestnuts
1 cup shredded cheddar cheese

- Preheat oven to 350°.

- Salt and pepper chicken and place in sprayed 10 x 15-inch glass baking dish.

- Melt butter in medium saucepan and add onion, bell pepper, pimentos, rice, soups, 2 soup cans water and water chestnuts and pour over chicken.

- Cover and bake for 15 minutes, reduce temperature to 325° and cook for an additional 1 hour. Add cheese 5 minutes before dish is done and return to oven for last 5 minutes. Serves 8. *Swanton, Vermont*

Wine and Chicken

6 - 8 boneless, skinless chicken breast halves
Oil
1 (10 ounce) can cream of mushroom soup
1 (10 ounce) can cream of onion soup
1 cup white wine

- Preheat oven to 325°.

- Brown chicken in little bit of oil in skillet. Place in 9 x 13-inch baking dish.

- Combine soups and wine in bowl and pour over chicken.

- Cover and bake for 35 minutes. Uncover and bake for an additional 25 minutes. Serves 6 to 8. *Chesterfield, Virginia*

Skillet Roasted Chicken

1 (2½ - 3 pound) chicken, quartered
2 teaspoons sage
Oil
2 teaspoons minced garlic
2 (10 ounce) cans cream of chicken soup
Rice, cooked

- Dry chicken quarters with paper towels. Sprinkle with sage and a little salt and pepper.

- Place in large skillet with a little oil. Cook on both sides over medium-high heat for about 15 minutes until chicken is cooked.

- Combine garlic, chicken soup and ½ cup water in saucepan. Heat just enough to blend ingredients.

- Pour over chicken, cover and cook on low heat for 5 minutes or until chicken heats thoroughly. Serve over rice. Serves 4 to 6.
  Cheney, Washington

Finger Lickin' BBQ Chicken

1 (2 pound) chicken, quartered
½ cup ketchup
¼ cup (½ stick) butter, melted
2 tablespoons sugar
1 tablespoon mustard
½ teaspoon minced garlic
¼ cup lemon juice
¼ cup white vinegar
¼ cup Worcestershire sauce

- Preheat oven to 325°.

- Sprinkle chicken quarters with a little salt and pepper and brown in skillet.

- Place in sprayed 9 x 13-inch baking pan.

- Combine remaining ingredients in bowl. Pour over chicken, cover and bake for 50 minutes. Serves 4 to 6. *Burnet, Texas*

Company Chicken

2 chickens, quartered
2 (10 ounce) cans cream of mushroom soup
1 (1 pint) carton sour cream
1 cup sherry

- Preheat oven to 300°.

- Place chickens quarters in sprayed, large shallow baking dish.

- Combine soup, sour cream and sherry in saucepan. Pour mixture over chicken. (You might sprinkle a little paprika over top.)

- Cover and bake for 1 hour 15 minutes. Serves 8 to 10. *Bradley, West Virginia*

TIP: This is great served over rice.

Honey-Glazed Chicken

¾ cup flour
½ teaspoon cayenne pepper
1 broiler-fryer chicken, quartered, wing tips cut off
¼ cup (½ stick) butter, divided
⅓ cup packed brown sugar
⅓ cup honey
⅓ cup lemon juice
1 tablespoon light soy sauce

- Preheat oven to 350°.

- Combine flour, cayenne pepper and ½ teaspoon salt in shallow bowl. Dredge chicken quarters in flour mixture.

- Place 2 tablespoons butter in large, heavy skillet and brown chicken over high heat on both sides. Transfer to sprayed 9 x 13-inch baking dish.

- In same skillet, add remaining butter, brown sugar, honey, lemon juice and soy sauce and bring to a boil.

- Remove from heat and pour mixture over chicken quarters. Bake for 35 to 40 minutes; baste several times with pan drippings. Serves 4 to 6. *Deer Lodge, Montana*

Italian Chicken over Polenta

1 pound frozen chicken tenders, halved
1 onion, chopped
1 (15 ounce) can Italian stewed tomatoes
⅔ cup pitted kalamata olives

• Season chicken with a little salt and pepper. Place in large skillet with a little oil and cook over medium-high heat

• Add onion, cover and cook for about 8 minutes, and turn once. Add tomatoes and olives, cover and cook for an additional 8 minutes or until chicken is done.

Polenta:

¾ cup cornmeal
⅔ cup grated parmesan cheese

• Place 2½ cups water in saucepan and bring to boiling. Stir in cornmeal and ½ teaspoon salt and cook, stirring occasionally, until mixture starts to thicken.

• Stir in cheese. Spoon polenta onto serving plates and top with chicken and sauce. Serves 4 to 6. *Buchanan, Michigan*

Sweet-and-Sour Chicken

2 - 3 pounds boneless chicken pieces
Oil
1 (1 ounce) packet dry onion soup mix
1 (6 ounce) can frozen orange juice concentrate, thawed

• Preheat oven to 350°.

• Brown chicken in little oil in skillet. Place in 9 x 13-inch baking dish.

• Combine onion soup mix, orange juice concentrate and ⅔ cup water in small bowl and stir well. Pour over chicken.

• Bake for 50 minutes. Serves 6. *Boca Pointe, Florida*

Spicy Orange Chicken over Noodles

1 pound boneless, skinless chicken tenders
2 tablespoons oil
2 tablespoons soy sauce
1 (16 ounce) package frozen stir-fry vegetables, thawed
1 (6 ounce) package chow mein noodles

- Lightly brown chicken tenders in oil in large skillet over medium-high heat.

- Add soy sauce and stir-fry vegetables and cook for about 8 minutes or until vegetables are tender-crisp.

Sauce:

⅔ cup orange marmalade
1 tablespoon olive oil
2 teaspoons lime juice
½ teaspoon dried ginger
¼ teaspoon cayenne pepper

- Combine marmalade, oil, lime juice, ginger and cayenne pepper in saucepan and mix well. Heat and pour over chicken and vegetables and toss.

- Serve over chow mein noodles. Serves 10 to 12. *Captain Cook, Hawaii*

Roasted Chicken and Vegetables

3 pounds boneless chicken parts
1 cup lemon pepper marinade with lemon juice, divided
1 (16 ounce) package frozen mixed vegetables, thawed
¼ cup olive oil

- Preheat oven to 375°.

- Arrange chicken skin-side down in sprayed 10 x 15 inch baking pan. Pour ⅔ cup marinade over chicken.

- Bake for 30 minutes. Turn chicken over and baste with remaining marinade.

- Toss vegetables with oil and 1 tablespoon salt in bowl. Arrange vegetables around chicken and cover. Return pan to oven and bake for an additional 30 minutes. Serves 6 to 8. *Bluffton, Indiana*

Chicken Couscous

1¼ cups chicken broth
1 (5.6 ounce) package toasted pine nut couscous, cooked
1 rotisserie chicken, boned, cubed
1 (4 ounce) can chopped pimento
½ cup feta cheese
1 (16 ounce) package frozen green peas
1 tablespoon dried basil
1 tablespoon lemon juice

- Heat broth and seasoning packet from couscous in microwave on HIGH for 4 minutes or until broth begins to boil.

- Place couscous in large bowl and stir in broth. Cover and let stand for 5 minutes.

- Fluff couscous with fork and add remaining ingredients. Toss to blend well. Serve warm. Serves 10. *Breese, Illinois*

TIP: *Couscous is a quick alternative to rice or pasta and it couldn't be easier to make. All you have to do is add boiling water (or in this case, broth).*

Ranch Chicken To Go

1 (8 ounce) package pasta
½ cup (1 stick) butter, melted
1 (10 ounce) can cream of chicken soup
1 (1 ounce) packet ranch salad dressing mix
2 (15 ounce) cans peas and carrots, drained
3 cups cooked, cubed chicken
1 (2.8 ounce) can french-fried onion rings

- Preheat oven to 325°.

- Cook pasta according to package directions, drain and keep warm.

- Combine butter, soup, dressing mix, peas and carrots in saucepan. Stir occasionally over medium heat until all ingredients mix well and are thoroughly hot.

- Toss with cooked pasta and chicken and spoon into sprayed 3-quart baking dish. Cover and bake for 15 minutes.

- Remove from oven, sprinkle onion rings over top and bake uncovered for an additional 15 minutes. Serves 10 to 12. *Dalton, Massachusetts*

Supreme Chicken and Green Beans

1 (16 ounce) package frozen seasoning blend (onions and
    bell peppers)
Oil
3 cups cooked, diced chicken
1 (6 ounce) package long grain-wild rice, cooked
1 (10 ounce) can cream of chicken soup
1 (4 ounce) can chopped pimentos
1 (15 ounce) can French-style green beans, drained
½ cup slivered almonds
1 cup mayonnaise
3 cups lightly crushed potato chips

- Preheat oven to 350°.

- Saute onions and bell peppers in skillet with a little oil.

- Combine onions and bell peppers, chicken, rice, soup, pimentos, green
  beans, almonds, mayonnaise and a little salt and pepper in large bowl.
  Mix well.

- Spoon mixture into sprayed 9 x 13-inch deep baking dish.

- Sprinkle crushed potato chips over casserole and bake for 35 minutes
  or until chips are light brown. Serves 10 to 12. *Columbus, Kansas*

Chop Suey Veggies and Chicken

3 cups cooked, cubed chicken
2 (10 ounce) cans cream of chicken soup
2 (15 ounce) cans chop suey vegetables, drained
1 (8 ounce) can sliced water chestnuts, drained
1 (16 ounce) package frozen seasoning blend (onions and
    bell peppers)
½ teaspoon hot sauce
½ - 1 teaspoon curry powder
2 cups chow mein noodles

- Preheat oven to 350°.

- Combine chicken, soup, vegetables, water chestnuts, onions and bell
  peppers, hot sauce, curry powder, and a little salt and pepper in large
  bowl and mix well.

- Spoon into sprayed 9 x 13-inch baking dish. Sprinkle chow mein
  noodles over top and bake for 40 minutes. Serves 10 to 12.
  Florence, Mississippi

Mushrooms, Noodles and Chicken

½ cup (1 stick) butter
1 green bell pepper, seeded, chopped
1 red bell pepper, seeded chopped
½ cup flour
1½ teaspoons seasoned salt
1½ cups milk
1 (14 ounce) can beef broth
1 (10 ounce) can cream of mushroom soup
1 (12 ounce) package medium egg noodles, cooked, drained
3 - 4 cups cooked, cubed chicken
1 (8 ounce) package shredded cheddar cheese

- Preheat oven to 350°.

- Melt butter in large skillet on medium-high heat. Cook and stir bell peppers for 10 minutes. Stir in flour and seasoned salt and mix well.

- While still on medium-high heat, slowly stir in milk, beef broth and 1 teaspoon pepper. Cook until mixture is thick and pour into large bowl.

- Fold in mushroom soup, noodles and chicken and transfer to sprayed 10 x 15-inch baking pan. Cover and bake for 35 minutes or until thoroughly hot.

- Uncover, sprinkle cheese over casserole and bake for an additional 5 minutes. Serves 12. *Bedford Hills, New York*

Jalapeno Chicken

Even if you are not a spinach fan, you will find this to your liking!

2 cups chopped onion
2 tablespoons butter
1 (10 ounce) package frozen spinach, cooked, drained
6 jalapenos, seeded, chopped or 1 (7 ounce) can green chilies, drained
1 (8 ounce) carton sour cream
2 (10 ounce) cans cream of chicken soup
4 green onions with tops, chopped
1 (12 ounce) package corn tortilla chips, slightly crushed
4 cups diced turkey or chicken
1 (8 ounce) package shredded Monterey Jack cheese

• Preheat oven to 350°.

• Saute onion in butter in saucepan and blend in spinach, jalapenos, sour cream, soup, green onions and ½ teaspoon salt.

• Layer one-half chips, chicken, spinach mixture and cheese in large 10 x 15-inch baking dish or 2 (9 x 9-inch) dishes.

• Repeat layer with cheese on top. Bake for 35 minutes. Serves 8 to 10.
Cameron, Texas

TIP: Squeeze spinach between paper towels to completely remove excess moisture.

Cheesy Chicken Pie

1 (12 ounce) package shredded cheddar cheese, divided
1 (10 ounce) package frozen peas and carrots, thawed
1 red bell pepper, seeded, chopped
2 cups cooked, diced chicken breasts
1½ cups half-and-half cream
3 large eggs, beaten
¾ cup biscuit mix

- Preheat oven to 350°.

- Combine 2 cups cheese, peas and carrots, bell pepper and chicken in large bowl. Spread into sprayed 10-inch deep-dish pie pan.

- Combine half-and-half cream, eggs, biscuit mix and a little salt and pepper in bowl and mix well. Spoon mixture over cheese-vegetable mixture, but do not stir.

- Cover and bake for 35 minutes or until center of pie is firm. Remove from oven, sprinkle remaining cheese over top and bake for 5 minutes. Serves 8. *Eaton, Colorado*

Confetti Squash and Chicken

1 pound yellow squash, sliced
1 pound zucchini, sliced
2 cups cooked, cubed chicken
1 (10 ounce) can cream of chicken soup
1 (8 ounce) carton sour cream
1 (4 ounce) can chopped pimentos, drained
½ cup (1 stick) butter, melted
1 (6 ounce) box herb stuffing mix

- Preheat oven to 350°.

- Cook squash and zucchini in salted water in large saucepan for about 10 minutes. Drain, stir in chicken, soup, sour cream and pimentos and mix well.

- Combine melted butter and stuffing mix in bowl, add to vegetable-chicken mixture and mix well. Spoon into sprayed 9 x 13-inch baking dish.

- Cover and bake for 35 minutes. Serves 8. *Center Line, Michigan*

Chicken-Spaghetti Bake

1 (12 ounce) package spaghetti
1 (16 ounce) package frozen seasoning blend (onion and bell
    peppers)
3 ribs celery, sliced
Oil
1 (15 ounce) can Mexican stewed tomatoes
1 (10 ounce) can chicken broth
4 cups cooked, cubed chicken
1 (12 ounce) package shredded Velveeta® cheese, divided

- Preheat oven to 350°.

- Cook spaghetti according to package directions and drain.

- Saute onion and bell peppers and celery in large saucepan with a little oil. Add tomatoes, broth, chicken and a little salt and pepper. Stir in half cheese and spoon into sprayed 9 x 13-inch baking dish.

- Cover and bake for 40 minutes.

- Remove from oven and sprinkle remaining cheese over top of casserole. Bake for 5 minutes. Serves 12. *Dawson Springs, Kentucky*

Chicken-Cashew Bake

⅓ cup minced onion
1 cup minced celery
1 tablespoon butter, melted
1 (10 ounce) can cream of mushroom soup
½ cup chicken broth
1 tablespoon soy sauce
3 drops hot sauce
2 cups cooked, diced chicken
1 cup chow mein noodles
½ cup chopped cashews

- Preheat oven to 350°.

- Saute onion and celery in butter in saucepan. Add soup and chicken broth. Stir in soy sauce, hot sauce and chicken and simmer for about 5 minutes.

- Pour into 1-quart baking dish. Sprinkle noodles and nuts on top.

- Bake for 20 minutes or until thoroughly hot. Serves 6. *Franklin, Louisiana*

Chicken Pot Pie

1 (15 ounce) package refrigerated piecrust
1 (26 ounce) can cream of chicken soup
2 cups cooked, diced chicken breast
1 (10 ounce) package frozen mixed vegetables, thawed

- Preheat oven to 325°.

- Place 1 piecrust in 9-inch pie pan. Fill with chicken soup, chicken and mixed vegetables.

- Cover with second piecrust; fold edges under and crimp. Cut 4 slits in center of piecrust. Bake for 1 hour 15 minutes or until crust is golden. Serves 6. *Cochran, Georgia*

TIP: *When you're too busy to cook a chicken, get a rotisserie chicken from the grocery store. They are great.*

Chicken Pie 🍁

Settlers from Great Britain formed part of the early population in New Brunswick, Canada, and brought their English traditions in their foods. They enjoyed favorite chicken recipes, vegetables and many versions of the prolific blueberries.

1 (15 ounce) package frozen piecrust (2 crusts)
4 cups cooked, cubed chicken
¼ cup (½ stick) butter
2 onions, chopped
1 green bell pepper, seeded, chopped
8 - 10 slices bacon, cut into 1-inch slices
1 (4 ounce) can sliced mushrooms, drained
½ cup flour
1 (14 ounce) can chicken broth
1 (16 ounce) carton half-and-half cream
1 teaspoon ground sage

- Preheat oven to 375°.

- Place 1 piecrust in a 9-inch pie pan and spoon chopped chicken in bottom of piecrust.

- Melt butter in skillet and cook onions, bell pepper and bacon until light brown. Add mushrooms. Use slotted spoon to remove mixture from skillet and spread over chicken.

- Stir flour into remaining fat in skillet. Slowly add broth and half-and-half cream and cook on medium-high heat, stirring constantly, until mixture thickens. Stir in sage, 1 teaspoon salt and a little pepper and pour over chicken and vegetables.

- Place second piecrust over top and cut 3 to 4 slits in crust to allow steam to escape.

- Bake for 55 to 60 minutes or until bubbly around edges and crust is light brown. Serves 8. *Campbellton, New Brunswick, Canada*

Chicken Lasagna

1 (16 ounce) jar alfredo sauce
1 (4 ounce) can diced pimentos, drained
⅓ cup white cooking wine
1 (10 ounce) box frozen chopped spinach, thawed
1 (15 ounce) carton ricotta cheese
½ cup grated parmesan cheese
1 egg, beaten
8 lasagna noodles, cooked
3 cups cooked, shredded chicken
1 (12 ounce) package shredded cheddar cheese

- Preheat oven to 350°.

- Combine alfredo sauce, pimentos and wine in large bowl; set aside ½ cup sauce mixture for top of lasagna.

- Squeeze spinach between paper towels to completely remove excess moisture. Place in separate bowl and add ricotta, parmesan cheese and egg. Mix well.

- Place 4 noodles in sprayed 9 x 13-inch deep baking dish. Layer with half remaining sauce, half spinach-ricotta mixture and half chicken. (Spinach-ricotta mixture will be fairly dry so you will need to "spoon" it on and spread out.)

- Sprinkle with half cheese. For last layer, place noodles, remaining sauce, remaining spinach-rocotta mixture and remaining chicken. Top with the ½ cup sauce.

- Cover and bake for 45 minutes. Sprinkle remaining cheese and bake uncovered for 6 minutes. Let casserole stand for 10 minutes before serving. Serves 10 to 12. *Brinkley, Arkansas*

Chicken-Broccoli Skillet

3 cups cooked, cubed chicken
1 (16 ounce) package frozen broccoli florets
1 (8 ounce) package cubed Velveeta® cheese
⅔ cup mayonnaise
Rice, cooked

- Combine chicken, broccoli, cheese and ¼ cup water in skillet. Cover and cook over medium heat until broccoli is tender-crisp and cheese melts.

- Stir in mayonnaise and heat through, but do not boil. Serve over rice. Serves 6. *Brisbane, California*

Alfredo-Chicken Spaghetti

1 (8 ounce) package thin spaghetti, broken in thirds
2 teaspoons minced garlic
1 (16 ounce) jar alfredo sauce
¼ cup milk
1 (10 ounce) package frozen broccoli florets, thawed, drained
2 cups cooked, diced chicken
1 cup shredded mozzarella cheese

- Preheat oven to 350°.

- Cook spaghetti according to package directions and drain. Place back in saucepan and stir in garlic, alfredo sauce and milk; mix well.

- Add broccoli florets and cook on medium heat, stirring several times for about 5 minutes or until broccoli is tender; add more milk if needed.

- Stir in diced chicken and spoon into sprayed 7 x 11-inch baking dish. Cover and bake for 20 minutes.

- Remove from oven and sprinkle cheese over top. Return to oven for an additional 5 minutes. Serves 8. *Danielson, Connecticut*

Cranberry-Turkey and Stuffing

1 (6 ounce) package herb-seasoned chicken stuffing
2 tablespoons butter
1 onion, chopped
2 ribs celery, sliced
1 cup whole cranberry sauce
1 pound thick-sliced deli turkey
1 (12 ounce) can turkey gravy

- Preheat oven to 350°.

- Prepare stuffing mix according to package directions.

- Melt butter in skillet and saute onion and celery. Add onion, celery and cranberry sauce to stuffing mixture and mix well.

- Place turkey slices in sprayed 9 x 13-inch baking pan and pour gravy over turkey. Spoon stuffing-cranberry mixture over turkey and gravy.

- Bake for 20 minutes or until casserole is hot and bubbly. Serves 10 to 12. *Georgetown, Delaware*

Caribbean Turkey

Turkey tenderloins are wonderful. You will be glad you cooked them!

2 tablespoons jerk seasoning
1½ - 2 pounds turkey tenderloin
1 tablespoons fresh chopped rosemary
1½ cups raspberry-chipotle sauce

- Rub jerk seasoning evenly over tenderloins, sprinkle with rosemary and press into tenderloins. Cover and refrigerate for 1 to 2 hours.

- Grill tenderloins with lid closed, over medium-high heat for 5 to 10 minutes on each side. Baste with half raspberry-chipotle sauce.

- Let tenderloin stand for 10 minutes before slicing and serve with remaining raspberry-chipotle sauce. Serves 4 to 6. *Bunche Park, Florida*

TIP: *There are so many wonderful prepared meat sauces in the grocery stores that it's easy to be a genius cook. Try different ones and pick out your personal favorites.*

Baked Turkey and Dressing

1 (6 ounce) package turkey stuffing mix
3 cups cooked, diced turkey
1 red bell pepper, seeded, chopped
2 tablespoons dried parsley flakes
1 (10 ounce) can cream of chicken soup
1 (8 ounce) carton sour cream
¼ cup (½ stick) butter, melted
1 teaspoon ground cumin
1½ cups shredded mozzarella cheese

- Preheat oven to 350°.

- Combine all ingredients except mozzarella cheese in large bowl. Mix well and spoon into sprayed 9 x 13-inch baking dish.

- Cover and bake for 35 minutes. Uncover, sprinkle with cheese and bake for an additional 5 minutes. Serves 10 to 12. *Boonville, Indiana*

Turkey-Stuffing Casserole

3 - 4 cups cooked, chopped turkey
1 (16 ounce) package frozen broccoli florets, thawed
1 (10 ounce) can cream of chicken soup
⅔ cup sour cream
1 (8 ounce) package shredded Swiss cheese
1 (6 ounce) package turkey stuffing mix
½ cup chopped walnuts

- Preheat oven to 325°.

- Spread chopped turkey in 9 x 13-inch baking dish and top with broccoli florets.

- Combine soup, sour cream and cheese in bowl and spread over broccoli.

- In separate bowl, combine stuffing mix, walnuts and ¾ cup water and spread evenly over broccoli.

- Bake for 40 minutes or until hot and bubbly. Serves 12. *Homedale, Idaho*

★ ★ ★

Pork

Pork is full of flavor whether you're
preparing pork chops, tenderloins,
ham or ribs from these 59 ideas!

1001
Community
Recipes

Pork Contents

Sweet-and-Sour Pork Chops

¾ cup flour
8 (½ inch) thick boneless pork chops
¼ cup (½ stick) butter, divided
¾ cup orange juice
⅓ cup Craisins®
1 tablespoon dijon-style mustard
2 tablespoons brown sugar
2 (3.5 ounce) bags boil-in-bag rice

- Place flour in shallow bowl and dredge chops in flour. Brown pork chops, turning once, in heavy skillet with half butter.

- Add orange juice, Craisins®, mustard, brown sugar and remaining butter. Cook on high heat until mixture bubbles and reduce heat. Cover and simmer for 15 minutes.

- Cook rice according to package directions and place on serving platter. Place pork chops on top and serve with sauce. Serves 8. *Corbin, Kentucky*

Sweet and Savory Pork Chops

4 - 6 (1 inch) thick boneless pork chops, trimmed
½ cup grape, apple or plum jelly
½ cup chili sauce or hot ketchup
Soy sauce

- Preheat oven to 325°.

- Brown pork chops in skillet and season with a little salt and pepper. Transfer browned pork chops to shallow baking dish, place in oven and bake for 30 minutes.

- Combine jelly and chili sauce in bowl and spread over pork chops.

- Bake for 15 minutes, baste with sauce and bake for an additional 15 minutes or until pork chops are tender. Serve with soy sauce. Serves 4 to 6. *Kennebunk, Maine*

Stuffed Pork Chops

4 (¾ inch) thick boneless center-cut pork chops
Stuffing:
2 slices rye bread, diced
⅓ cup chopped onion
⅓ cup chopped celery
⅓ cup dried apples, diced
⅓ cup chicken broth
½ teaspoon dried thyme
Oil

- Preheat oven to 400°.

- Make 1-inch wide slit on side of each chop and insert knife blade to other side, but not through pork chop. Sweep knife back and forth and carefully cut pocket opening larger.

- Combine rye bread pieces, onion, celery, apples, broth and thyme in bowl and mix well. Stuff chops with stuffing mixture and press to use all stuffing mixture in pork chops.

- Place chops in heavy skillet with a little oil and saute each chop for about 3 minutes on each side. Transfer to non-stick baking dish and bake for 20 to 25 minutes. Serves 4. *Haynesville, Louisiana*

Smoky Grilled Pork Chops

1 cup mayonnaise (not light)
2 tablespoons lime juice
1 teaspoon ground cilantro
1 teaspoon chili powder
2 teaspoons minced garlic
8 (1 inch) thick bone-in, pork chops

- Combine mayonnaise, lime juice, cilantro, chili powder and garlic in bowl and mix. Set half aside.

- Grill or broil pork chops for 6 minutes on each side and brush with half sauce. Serve remaining sauce with chops. Serves 8. *Chevy Chase, Maryland*

Savory Pork Chops

6 (¾ inch) pork chops
1 cup pineapple juice
⅓ cup packed brown sugar
3 tablespoons cider vinegar
Noodles, cooked

- Brown pork chops in skillet on both sides and place in 5-quart slow cooker.

- Combine pineapple juice, brown sugar and vinegar in bowl and mix well. Pour over pork chops. Cover and cook on LOW for 4 to 5 hours. Serve over noodles. Serves 6. *Dennis, Massachusetts*

Saucy Pork Chops

4 (½ inch) thick pork chops
1 tablespoon oil
1 (10 ounce) can cream of onion soup
2 tablespoons soy sauce

- Brown pork chops in oil in skillet and cook chops for about 15 minutes and drain. Remove chops from skillet.

- Add soup and soy sauce to skillet. Heat to a boil. Return chops to skillet. Reduce heat to low. Cover and simmer for about 20 minutes. Serves 4. *Clinton, Michigan*

Pork Chops with Ginger Sauce

¾ cup chili sauce
2 teaspoons minced garlic
1 tablespoon minced fresh ginger
2 tablespoons Worcestershire sauce
1 large egg, beaten
½ cup seasoned breadcrumbs
2 tablespoons oil
4 (¾ inch) thick boneless pork chops

- Combine chili sauce, garlic, ginger and Worcestershire sauce in small bowl and set aside for flavors to blend.

- Whisk egg with 1 tablespoon water in shallow bowl. In separate shallow bowl, place breadcrumbs. Add oil in skillet on medium heat. Dip each chop in beaten egg and dredge in breadcrumbs to coat well. Cook in skillet for 5 minutes on each side. Serve with sauce. Serves 4. *Byron, Minnesota*

Pork Chops Deluxe

1 cup rice
¼ cup flour
1 teaspoon seasoned salt
6 pork chops with bone
3 tablespoons oil, divided
1 onion, chopped
1 green bell pepper, seeded, chopped
1 (15 ounce) can Mexican stewed tomatoes
1 (10 ounce) can chicken broth

- Preheat oven to 325°.

- Place rice in sprayed 9 x 13-inch baking dish.

- Combine flour and seasoned salt in shallow bowl and dredge pork chops in flour mixture. Brown pork chops in large skillet with half oil and place on top of rice.

- With remaining oil, saute onion and bell pepper in saucepan for about 4 minutes. Add stewed tomatoes and chicken broth and mix well.

- Pour over pork chops in baking dish. Cover and bake for 1 hour. Serves 6. *Hazlehurst, Mississippi*

Pork Chops and Gravy

6 (½ inch) thick pork chops
8 - 10 new (red) potatoes with peels, quartered
1 (16 ounce) package baby carrots
2 (10 ounce) cans cream of mushroom soup with roasted garlic

- Sprinkle salt and pepper on pork chops.

- Brown pork chops in skillet and place in 5 to 6-quart slow cooker. Place potatoes and carrots around pork chops.

- Heat mushroom soup with ½ cup water in saucepan and pour over chops and vegetables.

- Cover and cook on LOW for 6 to 7 hours. Serves 6. *Lead, South Dakota*

Pineapple-Pork Chops

6 - 8 thick, boneless pork chops
1 (6 ounce) can frozen pineapple juice concentrate, thawed
3 tablespoons brown sugar
⅓ cup wine or tarragon vinegar
⅓ cup honey
Rice, cooked

- Preheat oven to 325°.

- Place pork chops in a little oil in skillet and brown. Remove to shallow baking dish.

- Combine pineapple juice, brown sugar, vinegar and honey in bowl. Pour over pork chops.

- Cover and bake for about 50 minutes. Serve over rice. Serves 6 to 8.
  Brewerton, New York

Orange Pork Chops

6 (½ inch) thick boneless pork chops
2 tablespoons oil
1⅓ cups instant rice
1 cup orange juice
¼ teaspoon ground ginger
1 (10 ounce) can chicken and rice soup
½ cup chopped walnuts

- Preheat oven to 350°.

- Sprinkle a little salt and pepper over pork chops and brown in skillet with oil.

- Sprinkle rice into sprayed 7 x 11-inch baking dish. Add orange juice and arrange pork chops over rice.

- Add ginger to soup and stir right in can. Pour soup over pork chops. Sprinkle walnuts over top.

- Cover and bake for 25 minutes. Uncover and bake for an additional 10 minutes or until rice is tender. Serves 6. *Hazen, North Dakota*

Parmesan-Covered Pork Chops

½ cup grated parmesan cheese
⅔ cup Italian seasoned dried breadcrumbs
1 egg
4 - 5 thin-cut pork chops
Oil

- Combine cheese and dried breadcrumbs in shallow bowl. Beat egg with 1 teaspoon water on shallow plate.

- Dip each pork chop in beaten egg then into breadcrumb mixture.

- Cook over medium-high heat in skillet with a little oil for about 5 minutes on each side or until golden brown. Serves 4 to 5. *Conover, North Carolina*

Curried-Orange Pork Chops

¾ teaspoon curry powder, divided
½ teaspoon paprika
4 (½ inch) thick center-cut boneless pork chops
½ cup orange marmalade
1 heaping teaspoon horseradish
1 teaspoon balsamic vinegar
Rice or couscous, cooked

- Combine ¼ teaspoon curry powder, paprika and ½ teaspoon salt in bowl and sprinkle over pork chops.

- Place chops in skillet and cook over medium-high heat for 5 minutes on each side. Transfer chops to plate.

- In same skillet, combine remaining ½ teaspoon curry powder, marmalade, horseradish and vinegar. Cook for 1 minute.

- Place pork chops on rice or couscous. Spoon sauce over pork chops. Serves 4. *Creswell, Oregon*

Mission Pork Chops and Gravy

6 - 8 (½ inch) thick pork chops
Oil
1 (7 ounce) can chopped green chilies
8 - 10 new (red) potatoes with peels, quartered
2 (10 ounce) cans cream of mushroom soup with roasted garlic

- Preheat oven to 350°

- Sprinkle salt and pepper on pork chops. Brown pork chops in a little oil in skillet and place in sprayed 9 x 13-inch baking dish. Place green chilies and potatoes around and over pork chops.

- Heat mushroom soup with ½ cup water in saucepan and pour over chops and potatoes. Cover and bake for 1 hour. Serves 6 to 8. *Bluffton, Ohio*

"Giddy-Up" Pork Chops

6 boneless pork chops
½ cup salsa
½ cup honey or packed brown sugar
1 teaspoon soy sauce

- Preheat oven to 325°.

- Brown pork chops in ovenproof pan.

- Combine salsa, honey and soy sauce in bowl and heat for 20 to 30 seconds in microwave. Pour salsa mixture over pork chops; cover and bake for 45 minutes or until pork chops are tender. Serves 6. *Cushing, Oklahoma*

TIP: For variation, add ¼ teaspoon crushed red pepper flakes.

Chops and Stuffing

1 (6 ounce) box savory-herb stuffing mix
6 center-cut pork chops
Oil
3 onions, halved

- Preheat oven to 350°.

- Make stuffing according to package directions and set aside.

- Brown pork chops on both sides in skillet with little oil. Place in sprayed 9 x 13-inch baking dish. Divide stuffing and onions among pork chops and mound on top of each.

- Cover and bake for about 30 minutes. Serves 6. *Middletown, Rhode Island*

Crunchy Pork Chops

1 cup crushed saltine crackers
¼ cup biscuit mix
¾ teaspoon seasoned salt
1 egg, beaten
5 - 6 (½ inch) thick boneless pork chops
Oil

- Combine crushed crackers, biscuit mix and seasoned salt in shallow bowl. In separate shallow bowl, combine beaten egg and 2 tablespoons water.

- Dip pork chops into egg mixture and dredge in cracker mixture.

- Cook pork chops with a little oil in heavy skillet for about 15 minutes and turn once. Serves 5 to 6. *Beaver Falls, Pennsylvania*

Cranberries and Pork Chops

6 - 8 thick pork chops
Flour
Oil
2 cups fresh or frozen cranberries
1 cup sugar

- Preheat oven to 350°.

- Coat pork chops in flour and brown in small amount of oil in skillet. Place in shallow baking dish. Add cranberries, sugar and ½ cup water.

- Cover and bake for 30 minutes. Uncover and bake for an additional 30 minutes. Serves 6 to 8. *Lisbon, North Dakota*

Pork Chop Supper

6 smoked pork chops
Oil
1 (12 ounce) jar pork gravy
¼ cup milk
1 (12 ounce) package very small new (red) potatoes

- Brown pork chops in large skillet with a little oil. Pour gravy and milk (or water) into skillet and stir mixture around chops until they mix well.

- Add new potatoes around chops and gravy. Place lid on skillet and simmer on medium-low heat for about 15 minutes or until potatoes are tender. Serves 6. *Madison, South Dakota*

Spicy Glazed Pork Tenderloin

½ cup orange juice
¼ cup lime juice
½ cup packed brown sugar
1 teaspoon ground cumin
2 (1 pound) pork tenderloins
Oil

- Combine orange juice, lime juice, brown sugar and cumin in small bowl.

- Pat tenderloins dry with paper towels and season with a little salt and pepper. Place a little oil in large skillet over medium-high heat.

- Cook tenderloins, turn and brown on all sides, for about 9 to 10 minutes. Reduce heat to medium, add orange juice mixture and cook until mixture is thick and syrupy, about 10 minutes.

- Transfer to cutting board, cover tenderloins with foil and let stand for 10 minutes before slicing crosswise into ½-inch slices. Arrange on serving plate and pour glaze over slices. Serves 8. *Kuna, Idaho*

Tenderloin with Apricot Sauce

3 (1 pound) pork tenderloins
1 cup apricot preserves
⅓ cup lemon juice
⅓ cup ketchup
1 tablespoon soy sauce
Rice, cooked

- Preheat oven to 325°.

- Place tenderloins in roasting pan.

- Combine preserves, lemon juice, ketchup and soy sauce in bowl.

- Pour preserve mixture over pork; cover and bake for 1 hour 20 minutes. Baste once during baking.

- Serve over rice. Serves 6 to 8. *Boiling Springs, South Carolina*

Pork Picante

1 pound pork tenderloin, cubed
2 tablespoons taco seasoning
Oil
1 cup chunky salsa
⅓ cup peach preserves
Rice, cooked

- Toss pork with taco seasoning and brown with a little oil in skillet. Stir in salsa and preserves. Bring to a boil. Lower heat and simmer for 30 minutes. Pour over rice. Serves 4. *Cambridge, Illinois*

Spicy Grilled Tenderloin

2 tablespoons chili powder
¼ teaspoon ground thyme
¼ teaspoon ground ginger
2 (1 pound) pork tenderloins

- Combine chili powder, thyme, ginger and 1 teaspoon salt and rub over both tenderloins. Cover and refrigerate for about 3 hours.

- Grill for 15 minutes on each side. Slice to serve. Serves 8. *Camden, Tennessee*

Roasted Red Pepper Tenderloin

1 (1 pound) pork tenderloin
1 (1 ounce) packet ranch-style dressing mix
1 cup roasted red bell peppers, rinsed, chopped
1 (8 ounce) carton sour cream

- Brown tenderloins in skillet and place in 6-quart slow cooker.

- Combine ranch dressing mix, red bell peppers and ½ cup water in bowl and spoon over tenderloins.

- Cover and cook on LOW for 4 to 5 hours.

- When ready to serve, remove tenderloins from slow cooker. Stir sour cream into sauce and serve over tenderloin slices. Serves 4. *Harrisville, Utah*

Pork Tenderloin with Cranberry Sauce

2 (1 pound) pork tenderloins
½ cup chopped fresh cilantro
½ teaspoon ground cumin
2 teaspoons minced garlic

- Preheat oven to 375°.

- Season tenderloin with a little salt and pepper, cilantro, cumin and garlic.

- Place in foil-lined baking pan and bake for 15 minutes.

- Reduce heat to 325° and bake for an additional 35 minutes. Slice to serve.

Cranberry Sauce:

1 (16 ounce) can whole cranberries
1 cup orange marmalade
1 (8 ounce) can crushed pineapple, drained
¾ cup chopped pecans

- Combine cranberries, marmalade, pineapple and pecans in bowl and serve with tenderloin.

- Sauce may be served room temperature or warmed. Serves 8.
  Vergennes, Vermont

Peach Sweet Pork Tenderloin

3 tablespoons dijon-style mustard
1 tablespoon soy sauce
1 (12 ounce) jar peach preserves
2 (1 pound) pork tenderloins

- Preheat oven to 325°.

- Combine mustard, soy sauce and peach preserves in saucepan. Heat and stir just until mixture is well mixed.

- Place tenderloins in sprayed baking pan and spoon peach mixture over tenderloins. Sprinkle a little salt and pepper over tenderloins.

- Cover and bake for 1 hour. Uncover and bake for an additional 25 minutes. Let stand at room temperature for about 15 minutes before slicing. Serves 8. *Eastman, Georgia*

Marinated Garlic-Herb Tenderloin

2 (1 pound) pork tenderloins
1 (12 ounce) bottle roasted garlic and herb marinade, divided
1 (8 ounce) package medium egg noodles
¼ cup (½ stick) butter

- Butterfly pork lengthwise, being careful not to cut all the way through. Press open to flatten and place in large resealable plastic bag.

- Pour ¾ cup marinade into bag and close top securely. Marinate for 25 minutes and turn several times.

- Grill 4 to 5 inches from hot coals for 8 minutes.

- Turn pork over and brush with remaining marinade and cook for an additional 8 minutes.

- Cook noodles according to package directions and stir in butter. Serve tenderloin over noodles. Serves 8. *Cambridge, Minnesota*

Hawaiian Aloha Pork

This is great served over rice.

2 (1 pound) lean pork tenderloins
1 (15 ounce) can pineapple chunks with juice
1 (12 ounce) bottle chili sauce
1 teaspoon ground ginger
Rice, cooked

- Cut pork in 1-inch cubes. Season pork cubes with salt and pepper and brown on medium-high heat in skillet.

- Add pineapple with juice, chili sauce and ginger.

- Cover and simmer for 30 minutes. Serve over rice. Serves 4 to 6. *Cambria, California*

Choice Tenderloin Slices

2 (1 pound) pork tenderloins
1 (12 ounce) jar apricot preserves
⅓ cup lemon juice
⅓ cup ketchup
1 tablespoon light soy sauce
2 cups cooked rice

- Preheat oven to 325°.

- Place tenderloins in sprayed 7 x 11-inch baking pan.

- Combine preserves, lemon juice, ketchup and soy sauce in saucepan and heat just until mixture blends well.

- Spoon sauce over tenderloins, cover and bake for 1 hour. Baste twice during cooking.

- Let tenderloins stand for about 15 minutes before slicing. Place slices and sauce over rice. Serves 6 to 8. *Clifton Forge, Virginia*

Apple-Topped Tenderloin

1½ cups hickory marinade, divided
1 (1 pound) pork tenderloin
1 (20 ounce) can apple pie filling
¾ teaspoon ground cinnamon

- Combine 1 cup marinade and tenderloin and seal in resealable plastic bag. Marinate in refrigerator for at least 1 hour.

- When ready to bake, preheat oven to 325°.

- Remove tenderloin and discard used marinade.

- Bake tenderloin for 1 hour and baste twice with ¼ cup marinade. Let stand for 10 to 15 minutes before slicing.

- Combine pie filling, remaining ¼ cup marinade and cinnamon in saucepan and heat.

- Serve heated apples over sliced tenderloin. Serves 4 to 6. *Clyde Hill, Washington*

Sweet-and-Sour Pork Loin Roast

4 - 5 pound pork loin roast
Oil
1 (12 ounce) bottle chili sauce
1 (12 ounce) jar apricot preserves
1 (20 ounce) can chunk pineapple, drained
2 bell peppers, seeded, sliced

- Preheat oven to 325°.

- Season roast with salt and pepper and brown in a little oil in large heavy roasting pan. Add ½ cup water to pan. Cover and bake for 1 hour.

- Mix chili sauce and apricot preserves in bowl and pour over roast. Reduce heat to 275°; cover and bake for an additional 2 hours.

- Add pineapple and bell peppers and bake for 15 minutes. Serves 10 to 12. *Chester, West Virginia*

Plum Peachy Pork Roast

1 (4 - 5 pound) boneless pork loin roast
1 (12 ounce) jar plum jelly
½ cup peach preserves
½ teaspoon ground ginger

- Preheat oven to 325°.

- Place roast in shallow baking pan and bake for about 35 minutes.

- Turn roast to brown other side and bake for an additional 35 minutes.

- Heat jelly, peach preserves and ginger in saucepan. Brush roast generously with preserve mixture.

- Bake for an additional 15 minutes and baste again. Serves 8. *Bloomer, Wisconsin*

Nutty Pork Loin

1 (3 - 4 pound) boneless pork loin roast
1 teaspoon Creole seasoning
⅔ cup orange juice
⅔ cup orange marmalade
⅓ cup peanut butter

- Preheat oven to 350°.

- Place pork loin in roasting pan and season well with Creole seasoning. Cover and bake for 1 hour or until thermometer registers 160°.

- Combine orange juice, marmalade and peanut butter in saucepan. Heat just enough to mix well.

- Reduce oven to 325° and pour orange sauce over roast; cover and bake for an additional 1 hour 30 minutes.

- Brush occasionally with sauce during last hour of cooking time. To serve, slice roast, place in serving dish and cover with orange sauce. Serves 8 to 10. *Mills, Wyoming*

Apricot Baked Ham

This is the ham you will want for Easter dinner!

1 (12 - 15 pound) whole ham, fully cooked
Whole cloves
2 tablespoons dry mustard
1¼ cups apricot jam
1¼ cups packed light brown sugar

- Preheat oven to 450°.

- Place ham on rack in large roasting pan and insert cloves in ham every inch or so.

- Combine dry mustard and jam in bowl. Spread over entire surface of ham. Pat brown sugar over jam mixture.

- Place ham in hot oven and reduce heat to 325°. Bake for 15 minutes per pound. Serves 10 to 12. *Homer, Louisiana*

TIP: *Placing ham in very hot oven reduces total cooking time.*

Glazed Ham 🍁

1 (16 ounce) box brown sugar
2 tablespoons flour
⅓ cup dry mustard
1 cup white vinegar
1 (10 ounce) can beef broth
3 large egg yolks, beaten
1 (6 - 7 pound) ham

- Preheat oven to 400°.

- Combine brown sugar, flour, mustard and ½ teaspoon salt in saucepan and mix well. Stir in vinegar and beef broth and cook on medium heat for about 5 minutes.

- Stir little of hot mixture into beaten egg yolks. Add egg mixture back into flour-mustard mixture and cook, stirring constantly for about 2 minutes. Remove from heat and let cool slightly.

- Trim excess fat from ham and score ham in diamond pattern. Place ham in roasting pan and spoon glaze over surface. Bake for 45 minutes.

- Lower oven heat to 325° and continue baking for about 2 hours 30 minutes. Spoon glaze over ham several times during baking time. Serve ham with glaze. Serves 12. *North Battleford, Saskatchewan, Canada*

Ham and Sweet Potatoes

3 tablespoons dijon-style mustard, divided
1 (3 - 4 pound) boneless smoked ham
½ cup honey or packed brown sugar
1 (29 ounce) can sweet potatoes, drained or 4 cooked sweet
    potatoes, quartered

- Preheat oven at 325°.

- Spread 2 tablespoons mustard on ham. Place ham in sprayed, shallow baking pan and bake for 20 minutes.

- Combine remaining mustard with honey and spread over ham.

- Add sweet potatoes, baste with sauce and bake for 20 minutes. Serves 8. *Dresden, Tennessee*

Peach Glazed Ham

1 (5 pound) boneless ham
1 (12 ounce) jar peach preserves
3 tablespoons dijon-style mustard
¼ cup packed brown sugar

- Cook ham according to label directions. Combine preserves, mustard and brown sugar in bowl and mix well.

- About 30 minutes before cooking time ends, remove ham from oven and drain any liquid.

- Brush ham with half preserve-sugar mixture and return to oven for 30 minutes.

- Heat remaining preserve-sugar mixture in saucepan.

- Serve ham with heated preserve-sugar mixture. Serves 10 to 12.
  Crescent Springs, Kentucky

Peach-Pineapple Baked Ham

¼ cup dijon-style mustard, divided
1 (3 - 4) pound boneless smoked ham
1 cup peach preserves
1 cup pineapple preserves

- Preheat oven to 325°.

- Spread 2 tablespoons mustard on ham. Place ham in sprayed, shallow baking pan and bake for 20 minutes.

- Combine remaining mustard and both preserves in microwave-safe bowl and heat in microwave for 20 seconds (or in small saucepan at low heat for 2 to 3 minutes).

- Pour over ham and bake for about 15 minutes. Serves 8 to 10.
  Cresaptown, Maryland

Walnut-Ham Linguine

2 teaspoons minced garlic
½ cup coarsely chopped walnuts
1 red bell pepper, thinly sliced
¼ cup olive oil
½ pound cooked ham, cut in strips
1 (16 ounce) jar creamy alfredo sauce
¼ cup grated parmesan cheese
1 (12 ounce) package linguine, cooked al dente
1 cup seasoned breadcrumbs

- Preheat oven to 350°.

- Saute garlic, walnuts and bell pepper in oil in large skillet for 1 to 2 minutes.

- Combine garlic-bell pepper mixture, ham, alfredo sauce, parmesan cheese and linguine in large bowl and mix well.

- Spoon into sprayed 3-quart baking dish. Sprinkle breadcrumbs over top.

- Bake for 35 minutes or until breadcrumbs are light brown. Serves 6 to 8. *Hudson, New Hampshire*

Tortellini-Ham Supper

This is another great recipe for leftover ham.

2 (9 ounce) packages fresh tortellini
1 (10 ounce) package frozen green peas, thawed
1 (16 ounce) jar alfredo sauce
2 - 3 cups cubed ham

- Cook tortellini according to package directions. Add green peas about 5 minutes before tortellini are done and drain.

- Combine alfredo sauce and ham in saucepan and heat until thoroughly hot.

- Toss with tortellini and peas. Serve immediately. Serves 6 to 8. *Dover, Massachusetts*

Mac 'n Cheese Casserole

4 eggs
1½ cups milk
1 (12 ounce) package macaroni, cooked
1 (8 ounce) package shredded cheddar cheese
2 cups cubed ham
¾ cup seasoned breadcrumbs
¼ cup (½ stick) butter, cubed

- Preheat oven to 350°.

- Lightly beat eggs and milk with a little salt and pepper in large bowl.
  Stir in macaroni, cheese and ham.

- Spoon into sprayed 7 x 11-inch baking dish and bake for 20 minutes.

- Remove from oven, sprinkle with breadcrumbs and dot with
  butter. Continue baking for an additional 15 minutes. Serves 8.
  Fayette, Alabama

Ham and Potatoes Olé!

1 (24 ounce) package frozen hash browns with onion and
    peppers, thawed
3 cups cubed, cooked ham
1 (10 ounce) can cream of chicken soup
1 (10 ounce) can fiesta nacho cheese soup
1 cup hot salsa
1 (8 ounce) package shredded cheddar-Jack cheese

- Preheat oven to 350°.

- Combine hash browns, ham, both soups and salsa in large bowl and
  mix well.

- Spoon into sprayed 9 x 13-inch baking dish.

- Cover and bake for 40 minutes.

- Remove from oven, sprinkle cheese over casserole and bake uncovered
  for an additional 5 minutes. Serves 6 to 8. *Oracle, Arizona*

Ham-Vegetable Supper

1½ cups dry corkscrew macaroni
1 (16 ounce) package frozen broccoli, cauliflower and carrots
1 (10 ounce) can broccoli-cheese soup
1 (3 ounce) package cream cheese with chives, softened
¾ cup milk
1 (8 ounce) package cubed Velveeta® cheese
1 tablespoon dijon-style mustard
2 cups cooked, cubed ham

- Cook macaroni according to package directions in large saucepan. For last 5 minutes of cooking time, bring back to boiling, add vegetables, bring back to boiling and cook for remaining 5 minutes. Drain and set aside.

- In same saucepan, combine soup, cream cheese, milk, cheese and mustard over low heat and stir until cream cheese melts.

- Gently stir in ham, macaroni-vegetable mixture and a little salt and pepper. Heat thoroughly and stir often. Transfer to 3-quart serving dish. Serves 8. *Crossett, Arkansas*

Ham and Corn Casserole

*Ham and corn are always popular at church
suppers and this recipe is so easy to make.*

2 cups biscuit mix
2 cups finely chopped, cooked ham
1 cup shredded cheddar cheese
¼ cup (½ stick) butter, melted
1 small onion, chopped
1 bell pepper, seeded, finely chopped
3 large eggs, slightly beaten
1 (15 ounce) can cream-style corn
1 (11 ounce) can Mexicorn®
3 fresh green onions, finely chopped

- Preheat oven to 350°.

- Combine all ingredients except green onions in large bowl. Pour into sprayed 7 x 11-inch baking dish and bake for 50 minutes or until golden brown and set.

- Cut into squares to serve. Garnish with chopped green onions. Serves 8 to 10. *Charter Oak, California*

Broccoli, Rice and Ham Supper

1 (14 ounce) can chicken broth
1 (10 ounce) package frozen broccoli florets, thawed
1 carrot, shredded
1¼ cups instant rice
2 teaspoons lemon juice
1½ cups cooked ham, cut in strips
Lemon slices

- Pour broth in large saucepan over high heat and bring to a boil. Add broccoli and carrot and return to a boil. Reduce heat to low, cover and cook for 5 minutes.

- Remove from heat, stir in rice, lemon juice and ham. Cover and let stand for 5 minutes or until liquid absorbs. Fluff rice with fork and add a little salt and pepper.

- Transfer to serving bowl and garnish with twisted lemon slices. Serves 6. *Glendale, Colorado*

Ham and Pasta Bake

1 (10 ounce) can broccoli-cheese soup
½ cup grated parmesan cheese
1 cup milk
1 tablespoon spicy brown mustard
1 (16 ounce) package frozen broccoli florets, thawed
2 cups shell macaroni, cooked
8 ounces (deli) cooked ham, cut in bite-size chunks
Thin strips red bell pepper for garnish

- Combine soup, parmesan cheese, milk and mustard in large skillet and mix well. Add broccoli and stir over medium heat.

- Reduce heat to low, cover and cook for 5 minutes or until broccoli is tender-crisp.

- Stir in macaroni and ham and heat thoroughly. Transfer to sprayed 2-quart microwave dish, so it can be reheated, if needed.

- Garnish with very thin strips of bell pepper. Serves 8 to 10. *Colfax, Washington*

Sandwich Souffle

A fun lunch!

Butter, softened
8 slices white bread, crusts removed
4 slices ham
4 slices American cheese
2 cups milk
2 eggs, beaten

- Butter bread on both sides; make 4 sandwiches with ham and cheese.

- Place sandwiches in sprayed 8-inch square baking pan.

- Beat milk, eggs and a little salt and pepper in bowl. Pour over sandwiches and soak for 1 to 2 hours.

- When ready to bake, preheat oven to 375°.

- Bake for 45 to 50 minutes. Serves 4. *Essex, Connecticut*

Cherry Best Ham

1 (½ inch) thick center-cut ham slice
⅔ cup cherry preserves
½ teaspoon ground cinnamon
⅓ cup chopped walnuts

- Preheat oven to 325°.

- Place ham slice on foil-lined 9 x 13-inch glass baking dish. Spread preserves over ham and sprinkle cinnamon over preserves. Top with chopped walnuts.

- Bake for 20 minutes and the glass dish can be brought right to the table. Serves 4 to 6. *Brillion, Wisconsin*

Fruit-Covered Ham Slice

2 (15 ounce) cans fruit cocktail with juice
½ cup packed brown sugar
2 tablespoons cornstarch
1 (½ inch) thick center-cut ham slice

- Combine fruit cocktail, brown sugar and cornstarch in bowl and mix
  well. Cook on medium heat, stirring frequently, until sauce thickens.

- Place ham slice in large non-stick skillet on medium heat. Cook for
  about 5 minutes or just until ham thoroughly heats. Place on serving
  platter and spoon fruit sauce over ham. Serves 4 to 6. *Laurel, Delaware*

Honey-Ham Slice

⅓ cup orange juice
⅓ cup honey
1 teaspoon mustard
1 (1 inch) thick slice fully cooked ham

- Combine orange juice, honey and mustard in saucepan and cook slowly
  for 10 minutes, stirring occasionally.

- Place ham in broiling pan. Brush with orange glaze. Broil for
  8 minutes on first side about 3 inches from heat. Turn ham slice over.
  Brush with glaze again and broil for an additional 6 to 8 minutes.
  Serves 4. *Crystal River, Florida*

Peachy Glazed Ham

1 (15 ounce) can sliced peaches in light syrup
2 tablespoons dark brown sugar
2 teaspoons dijon-style mustard
1 (1 pound) center-cut ham slice
⅓ cup sliced green onions

- Drain peaches, pour ½ cup peach juice in large skillet and set peaches
  aside. Discard remaining juice.

- Add brown sugar and mustard to skillet, bring to a boil over medium-
  high heat and cook for 2 minutes or until slightly reduced. Add ham
  and cook for 2 minutes on each side.

- Add peaches and green onions, cover and cook over low heat for
  3 minutes or until peaches are thoroughly hot. Serves 4 to 6.
  Elberton, Georgia

Praline Ham

2 (½ inch) thick ham slices, cooked (about 2½ pounds)
½ cup maple syrup
3 tablespoons brown sugar
1 tablespoon butter
⅓ cup chopped pecans

- Preheat oven to 325°.

- Heat ham slices in ovenproof skillet for 10 minutes.

- Bring syrup, brown sugar and butter in small saucepan to a boil and stir often. Stir in pecans and spoon syrup mixture over ham.

- Bake for 20 minutes. Serves 8. *Jackson, Louisiana*

Sweet-and-Sour Spareribs

3 - 4 pounds spareribs
3 tablespoons soy sauce
⅓ cup mustard
1 cup packed brown sugar
½ teaspoon garlic salt

- Preheat oven to 325°.

- Place spareribs in roasting pan, bake for 45 minutes and drain.

- Make sauce with soy sauce, mustard, brown sugar and garlic salt in bowl and brush on ribs.

- Return to oven, reduce heat to 300° and bake for 2 hours or until ribs are tender. Baste several times while cooking. Serves 6 to 8. *McCall, Idaho*

Barbecued Spareribs

3 - 4 pounds pork spareribs or country-style pork ribs, trimmed
1 cup hot ketchup or chili sauce
½ cup honey or packed brown sugar
1 teaspoon liquid smoke

- Preheat oven to 350°.

- Place spareribs on sprayed broiler pan and bake for 1 hour 30 minutes.

- Combine ketchup, honey and liquid smoke in small saucepan and simmer for 2 to 3 minutes. Baste spareribs generously on both sides with ketchup mixture. Bake spareribs for an additional 1 hour 30 minutes or until tender and baste generously every 15 to 20 minutes. Serves 4 to 6. *Coleman, Texas*

Spunky Spareribs

5 - 6 pounds spareribs
1 (6 ounce) can frozen orange juice concentrate
2 teaspoons Worcestershire sauce
½ teaspoon garlic powder

- Preheat oven to 375°.

- Place spareribs in shallow baking pan, meat-side down. Sprinkle with a little salt and pepper. Roast for 30 minutes. Turn ribs and roast for an additional 30 minutes. Drain off fat.

- Combine remaining ingredients in bowl and brush mixture on ribs.

- Reduce heat to 300°. Cover ribs and roast for 2 hours or until tender, basting occasionally. Serves 4 to 6. *Carlinville, Illinois*

Finger Lickin' Baby Backs

2½ - 3 pounds baby back pork ribs
½ cup chili sauce
⅓ cup apple cider vinegar
½ cup packed brown sugar

- Cut ribs in serving-size pieces, sprinkle with pepper and place in sprayed 5 to 6-quart slow cooker. Combine chili sauce, vinegar, brown sugar and about ¾ cup water in bowl and pour over ribs.

- Cover and cook on LOW for about 6 to 7 hours. After about 3 hours, you might move ribs around in slow cooker so sauce is spread over all ribs. Serves 6 to 8. *Cassville, Missouri*

Creamy Sausage Fettuccine

1 (8 ounce) package fettuccine
1 pound Italian sausage
1 (10 ounce) can cream of mushroom soup
1 (16 ounce) carton sour cream

- Preheat oven to 325°.

- Cook fettuccine and drain.

- Cut sausage into 1-inch pieces, brown over medium heat and cook for about 8 minutes. Drain. Mix all ingredients and place in sprayed 2-quart baking dish.

- Bake for 30 minutes. Serves 6. *Minden, Nevada*

Colorful Sausage Supper

¼ cup olive oil, divided
1 pound Polish sausage, cut into ¼-inch slices
1 red bell pepper, seeded, julienned
3 small zucchini, sliced
3 small yellow squash, sliced
1 (12 ounce) package penne pasta
1 (26 ounce) jar spaghetti sauce, heated

- With 2 tablespoons oil, saute sausage, bell pepper, zucchini and squash in skillet until vegetables are tender-crisp. Keep warm.

- Cook pasta according to package directions and drain. Stir in remaining oil and add a little salt and pepper.

- Spoon into 9 x 13-inch baking dish and spread heated spaghetti sauce over pasta. Use slotted spoon to drain sausage-vegetable mixture and place on top. Serves 10 to 12. *Comstock, Michigan*

Sausage-Potato Bake

1 (10 ounce) can cream of celery soup
½ cup sour cream
1 teaspoon freeze-dried chives
1 cup shredded cheddar cheese
2 (15 ounce) cans whole new potatoes, drained, halved
1 (10 ounce) package frozen cut green beans, thawed
1 pound cooked Polish sausage, sliced
1 (2.8 ounce) can french-fried onions

- Preheat oven to 350°.

- Combine soup, sour cream, chives and cheese in large bowl. Stir in potatoes, green beans and sausage and spoon into sprayed 7 x 11-inch baking dish. Cover and bake for 30 minutes.

- Remove from oven and sprinkle onions over casserole. Bake uncovered for an additional 15 minutes or until onions are golden brown. Serves 8 to 10. *Hollandale, Mississippi*

★ ★ ★

Seafood

Add variety to your family meals
with gifts from the sea. They'll enjoy
30 selections from salmon to shrimp!

1001
Community
Recipes

Seafood Contents

Flounder au Gratin

½ cup fine dry breadcrumbs
¼ cup grated parmesan cheese
1 pound flounder
⅓ cup mayonnaise

- Preheat oven to 375°.

- Combine crumbs and cheese in shallow bowl. Brush both sides of fish with mayonnaise. Coat with crumb mixture.

- Arrange in single layer in shallow pan.

- Bake for 20 to 25 minutes or until fish flakes easily. Serves 4.
  Cloverdale, Virginia

Lemon-Dill Fillets

½ cup mayonnaise
2 tablespoons lemon juice
½ teaspoon finely grated lemon peel
1 teaspoon dill weed
1 pound cod or flounder fillets

- Combine mayonnaise, lemon juice, grated lemon peel and dill weed in bowl until they blend well.

- Place fish on sprayed grill or broiler rack and brush with half mayonnaise mixture. Grill or broil for 5 to 8 minutes, turn and brush with remaining mayonnaise mixture.

- Continue grilling or broiling for 5 to 8 minutes or until fish flakes easily with fork. Serves 4. *North Star, Delaware*

Chipper Fish

2 pounds sole or orange roughy
½ cup Caesar salad dressing
1 cup crushed potato chips
½ cup shredded cheddar cheese

- Preheat oven to 375°.

- Dip fish in dressing. Place in sprayed baking dish.

- Combine chips and cheese in bowl; sprinkle over fish.

- Bake for about 20 to 25 minutes. Serves 6. *Pascoag, Rhode Island*

Roughy Florentine

6 tablespoons butter, divided
2 (10 ounce) boxes frozen spinach, thawed, drained
⅛ teaspoon ground nutmeg
2 pounds orange roughy fillets
⅓ cup minced onion
1 packet cream of spinach soup mix
1 pint half-and half-cream
2 cups shredded Swiss cheese

• Preheat oven to 350°.

• Squeeze spinach between paper towels to completely remove excess moisture. Heat 3 tablespoons butter in large skillet and cook spinach for about 2 minutes. Season with nutmeg and ½ teaspoon each of salt and pepper.

• Spoon spinach into sprayed 9 x 13-inch baking dish and spread spinach over bottom of dish.

• Lay orange roughy over spinach.

• Heat remaining butter in saucepan and saute onion. Add soup mix, half-and-half cream and cheese and mix well. Heat just until cheese melts.

• Pour sauce over fillets and spinach.

• Cover and bake for 20 to 25 minutes or until fillets flake easily and sauce is bubbly. Serves 6 to 8. *Boonton, New Jersey*

Red Fish Barbecue

2 pounds red fish fillets
1 (8 ounce) bottle Italian dressing
1 (12 ounce) can beer
Several dashes hot sauce

• Place fish in glass baking dish. Pour Italian dressing, beer and hot sauce over fish.

• Cover and marinate in refrigerator for at least 2 hours.

• When ready to cook, drain fish and place in microwave-safe container. Discard marinade.

• Microwave fish for about 4 to 5 minutes per pound. Serves 4 to 6. *Jonesboro, Louisiana*

Home-Fried Fish

1½ pounds haddock, sole or cod
1 egg, beaten
2 tablespoons milk
2 cups corn flake crumbs
Oil

- Cut fish into serving-size pieces.

- Combine egg and milk in bowl. Dip fish in egg mixture and coat with crushed corn flakes on both sides.

- Fry in thin layer of oil in skillet until brown on both sides and fish is cooked. Serves 4. *Connell, Washington*

Fish and Chips

1 cup mayonnaise
2 tablespoons lime juice
3 - 4 fish fillets, rinsed, dried
1½ cups crushed corn chips
1 lime

- Preheat oven to 425°.

- Mix mayonnaise and 2 tablespoons lime juice in bowl. Spread on both sides of fish fillets.

- Place crushed corn chips on wax paper and dredge both sides of fish in chips. Shake off excess chips.

- Place fillets on foil-lined baking sheet and bake for 15 minutes or until fish flakes. Serve with lime wedges. Serves 4. *Foley, Alabama*

Sunday Best Fried Fish

1 (16 ounce) package frozen, cooked, batter-dipped fried fish
1 cup prepared spaghetti sauce
2 teaspoons Italian seasoning
1 cup shredded mozzarella cheese

- Heat fish according to package directions. While fish is heating, combine spaghetti sauce and Italian seasoning in bowl.

- When fish heats thoroughly, place each piece on serving plate and spoon spaghetti mixture over fish. Sprinkle cheese on top and serve. Serves 4 to 6. *Bedford, Pennsylvania*

Cod au Gratin 🍁

Newfoundland, Canada, is an isolated island settled by fishermen from Britain. They had to fight fishermen from France, Spain and even pirate ships to keep control of the valuable fishing grounds. There was an abundance of salmon, capelin and halibut, but, to Newfoundlanders, fish meant cod. It was fried, baked, stuffed and served many ways because cod was "king".

1½ pounds cod fillets
¼ cup (½ stick) butter
1 onion, chopped
½ red bell pepper, chopped
5 tablespoons flour
2½ cups milk
1 tablespoon lemon juice
1 teaspoon celery salt
1 cup shredded cheddar cheese

- Preheat oven to 350°.

- Place serving size pieces of cod in sprayed 9 x 13-inch baking dish.

- Melt butter in skillet and saute onion and bell pepper until tender. Stir in flour and mix well.

- Slowly stir in milk, lemon juice, celery salt and a little pepper on medium heat. Cook stirring constantly until mixture is smooth and thickened.

- Pour sauce over pieces of cod in baking dish and sprinkle with cheese.

- Bake for 35 to 40 minutes or until fish is thoroughly cooked and sauce is light brown. Serves 6. *Marystown, Newfoundland, Canada*

Golden Catfish Fillets

3 eggs
¾ cup flour
¾ cup cornmeal
1 teaspoon garlic powder
6 - 8 (4 - 8 ounce) catfish fillets
Oil

- Beat eggs in shallow bowl until foamy.

- In separate shallow bowl, combine flour, cornmeal, garlic powder and a little salt.

- Dip fillets in eggs and coat with flour-cornmeal mixture.

- Heat ¼-inch oil in large skillet and fry fish over medium-high heat for about 4 minutes on each side or until fish flakes easily with fork. Serves 6 to 8. *Fultondale, Alabama*

No-Panic Crab Casserole

2 (6 ounce) cans crabmeat, drained, flaked
1 cup half-and-half cream
1½ cups mayonnaise
6 hard-boiled eggs, finely chopped
1 cup seasoned breadcrumbs, divided
1 tablespoon dried parsley flakes
½ teaspoon dried basil
1 (8 ounce) can sliced water chestnuts, drained
2 tablespoons butter, melted

- Preheat oven to 350°.

- Combine crabmeat, half-and-half cream, mayonnaise, hard-boiled eggs, half seasoned breadcrumbs, parsley, basil, water chestnuts and a little salt and pepper in bowl and mix well. Pour into sprayed 2-quart baking dish.

- In separate bowl, combine remaining breadcrumbs and butter and sprinkle over top of casserole.

- Bake for 40 minutes. Serves 4 to 6. *Crisfield, Maryland*

Crab-Stuffed Baked Potatoes

*If you have been looking for a baked potato
that is truly a meal in itself, this is it!*

4 large baking potatoes
½ cup (1 stick) butter
½ cup whipping cream
1 bunch fresh green onions, chopped
2 (6 ounce) cans crabmeat, drained, flaked
¾ cup shredded cheddar cheese
2 tablespoons fresh minced parsley

- Preheat oven to 375°.

- Bake potatoes for 1 hour or until well done. Halve each potato lengthwise and scoop out flesh but leave skins intact.

- Mash potatoes with butter in large bowl. Add whipping cream, green onions, ¾ teaspoon salt and ½ teaspoon pepper. Stir in crabmeat.

- Fill reserved potato skins with potato mixture. Sprinkle with cheese.

- Reduce heat to 350° and bake for about 15 minutes.

- To serve, sprinkle fresh parsley over cheese. Serves 4. *Collinsville, Virginia*

Crab Mornay

2 (6 ounce) cans crabmeat, drained, flaked
1 cup cream of mushroom soup
½ cup shredded Swiss cheese
½ cup seasoned breadcrumbs

- Preheat oven to 350°.

- Combine crabmeat, soup and cheese in bowl.

- Pour into sprayed 1½-quart baking dish and sprinkle with breadcrumbs.

- Bake for 30 minutes or until soup bubbles and breadcrumbs are light brown. Serves 4. *Country Homes, Washington*

Skillet Shrimp Scampi

2 teaspoons olive oil
2 pounds shrimp, peeled, veined
⅔ cup herb-garlic marinade with lemon juice
¼ cup finely chopped green onion with tops
Rice or pasta, cooked

- Heat oil in large non-stick skillet. Add shrimp and marinade.

- Cook, stirring often, until shrimp turns pink. Stir in green onions. Serve over rice or your favorite pasta. Serves 6. *Comanche, Texas*

Shrimp Newburg

1 (10 ounce) can cream of shrimp soup
1 teaspoon seafood seasoning
1 (1 pound) package frozen cooked salad shrimp, thawed
Rice, cooked

- Combine soup, ¼ cup water and seafood seasoning in saucepan and bring to a boil.

- Reduce heat and stir in shrimp. Heat thoroughly. Serve over rice. Serves 4. *Bordentown, New Jersey*

Shrimp and Chicken Curry

2 (10 ounce) cans cream of chicken soup
⅓ cup milk
1½ teaspoons curry powder
1 (12 ounce) can chicken breast, drained
2 (6 ounce) cans shrimp, drained
Rice, cooked

- Heat soup, milk and curry powder in saucepan. Stir in chicken pieces and shrimp. Heat, stirring constantly, until mixture heats thoroughly.

- Serve over rice. Serves 6. *Kaplan, Maine*

Shrimp Delight

1½ pounds raw shrimp
Shrimp boil
1 onion, chopped
1 red bell pepper, chopped
1 green bell pepper, chopped
1 teaspoon minced garlic
2 tablespoons butter
1 (10 ounce) can cream of shrimp soup
1 (10 ounce) can cream of celery soup
2 cups cooked rice
1 teaspoon Creole seasoning
1 cup potato chips, crushed

- Preheat oven to 350°.

- Cook shrimp in shrimp boil according to package directions. Cool, peel and vein. Saute onion, bell peppers and garlic in large skillet with butter.

- Combine shrimp, onion-pepper mixture, soups, rice, ¾ teaspoon pepper and Creole seasoning in large bowl and mix well.

- Spoon into sprayed baking dish and sprinkle with potato chips. Bake for 30 minutes. Serves 6. *Cypress Gardens, Florida*

Creamed Shrimp over Rice

3 (10 ounce) cans cream of shrimp soup
1 (8 ounce) carton sour cream
1½ teaspoons curry powder
1 (12 ounce) package frozen salad shrimp, thawed
1 (7 ounce) box boil-in-bag rice

- Combine soup, sour cream, curry powder, shrimp and ½ cup water in double boiler. Heat while stirring constantly.

- Cook both bags of rice according to package directions and place on serving platter. Spoon shrimp mixture over rice. Serves 4 to 6. *Fredonia, Kansas*

Shrimp and Rice Casserole

2 cups instant rice
1½ pounds frozen cooked shrimp
1 (10 ounce) carton alfredo sauce
1 (4 ounce) can chopped pimento, drained
4 green onions with tops, chopped
1 (8 ounce) package shredded cheddar cheese, divided

- Cook rice according to package directions and place in sprayed 9 x 13-inch baking dish.

- Thaw shrimp in colander under cold running water, drain well and remove tails. Set aside.

- Heat alfredo sauce, pimento and green onions in saucepan over medium heat. Stir in shrimp and spoon mixture over rice. Sprinkle with half cheese and bake for about 15 minutes.

- Remove from oven, sprinkle remaining cheese on top and bake for 5 minutes. Serves 6 to 8. *Smyrna, Delaware*

TIP: *Thawing shrimp under running water is better than thawing in refrigerator.*

Beer Batter Shrimp

1 (12 ounce) can beer
1 cup flour
2 teaspoons garlic powder
1 pound shrimp, peeled, veined
Oil

- Make batter by mixing beer, flour and garlic powder in bowl and stir to creamy consistency.

- Dip shrimp into batter to cover and deep-fry in hot oil. Serves 4. *Leesville, Louisiana*

Salmon Patties

1 (15 ounce) can pink salmon with liquid
1 egg
½ cup cracker crumbs
1 teaspoon baking powder
Oil

- Drain liquid from salmon and set aside. Remove bones and skin.

- Stir in egg and cracker crumbs with salmon in bowl.

- In separate bowl, add baking powder to ¼ cup salmon juice. Mixture will foam. After foaming stops, add to salmon mixture.

- Drop spoonfuls of mixture into hot oil in skillet. Brown lightly on both sides. Serve hot. Serves 4. *Duvall, Washington*

Ginger Salmon Steaks

¾ cup teriyaki marinade and sauce
3 tablespoons packed brown sugar
1 teaspoon freshly peeled, grated ginger root
4 salmon steaks

- Combine teriyaki marinade, brown sugar and grated ginger and place in resealable plastic bag. Set aside ¼ cup of this mixture for later use as sauce.

- Place steaks in resealable plastic bag, pressing air out of bag. Turn bag over several times, coating well. Marinate for 30 minutes. Discard used marinade.

- Grill salmon 5 inches from heat for 5 minutes on each side, brushing occasionally with set aside sauce. Serves 4. *Eagle Point, Oregon*

Broiled Salmon Steaks

4 (1 inch) thick salmon steaks
Garlic salt
Worcestershire sauce
¼ - ½ cup (½ - 1 stick) butter, melted

- Place salmon steaks on baking sheet and sprinkle both sides with garlic salt. Splash Worcestershire sauce and half butter on top of each steak and broil for 2 to 3 minutes.

- Remove from oven and turn each steak. Splash Worcestershire sauce and remaining butter on tops and broil for additional 2 to 3 minutes. (Do not overcook. Fish should flake, but should not be dry inside.)

- Top with a little melted butter just before serving. Serves 4. *Ketchikan, Alaska*

Salmon Casserole

6 ounces dried egg noodles
1 (10 ounce) can cream of celery soup
1 (5 ounce) can evaporated milk
1 tablespoon lemon juice
½ onion, chopped
1 (15 ounce) can salmon, skin and bones removed
1 cup shredded cheddar cheese
1 (8 ounce) can small green peas, drained
1 teaspoon Creole seasoning
1 cup cheese crackers, crushed
2 tablespoons butter, melted

- Preheat oven to 350°.

- Cook noodles according to package directions and drain.

- Add soup, evaporated milk, lemon juice, onion, salmon, cheese, peas, Creole seasoning and 1 teaspoon salt in bowl. Spoon into sprayed 7 x 11-inch baking dish. Cover and bake for 25 minutes.

- Combine cheese crackers and melted butter in bowl and sprinkle over casserole and bake uncovered for 10 minutes or until crumbs are light brown. Serves 4 to 6. *Orofino, Idaho*

Baked Oysters

1 cup canned oysters, drained, rinsed
2 cups cracker crumbs
¼ cup (½ stick) butter, melted
½ cup milk

- Preheat oven to 350°.

- Make alternate layers of oysters, cracker crumbs and butter in 7 x 11-inch baking dish.

- Pour warmed milk over layers and add lots of salt and pepper.

- Bake for about 35 minutes. Serves 4 to 6. *Dudley, Massachusetts*

Tuna-in-the-Straw

1 (8 ounce) package egg noodles
2 (10 ounce) cans cream of chicken soup
1 (8 ounce) carton sour cream
1 teaspoon Creole seasoning
½ cup milk
2 (6 ounce) cans white meat tuna, drained
1 cup shredded Velveeta® cheese
1 (10 ounce) box green peas, thawed
1 (2 ounce) jar diced pimento
1 (2 ounce) can shoe-string potatoes

- Preheat oven to 350°.

- Cook noodles according to package directions and drain.

- Combine soup, sour cream, Creole seasoning and milk in large bowl and mix well.

- Add noodles, tuna, cheese, peas and pimento.

- Pour into sprayed 9 x 13-inch baking dish. Sprinkle top with shoe-string potatoes.

- Bake for about 35 minutes or until shoe-string potatoes are light brown. Serves 6 to 8. *Kiln, Mississippi*

Tuna-Asparagus Pot Pie

1 (8 ounce) package crescent rolls, divided
1 (6 ounce) can solid white tuna in water, drained, flaked
1 (15 ounce) can cut asparagus, drained
1 cup shredded cheddar cheese

- Preheat oven to 375°.

- Form 7-inch square using 4 crescent rolls. Pinch edges together to seal.

- Place in sprayed 8 x 8-inch square baking pan. Spread tuna, then asparagus, followed by shredded cheese.

- Form remaining 4 crescent rolls into a square. Place on top of cheese. Bake for about 20 minutes or until top is golden brown and cheese bubbles. Serves 4. *Falls City, Nebraska*

Tuna-Tomato Bowl

2 tablespoons olive oil
1 teaspoon minced garlic
¼ teaspoon cayenne pepper
2 teaspoons dried basil
1 (15 ounce) can stewed tomatoes
1 (12 ounce) can water-packed tuna, drained
¾ cup pitted green olives, sliced
¼ cup drained capers
1 cup pasta, cooked

- Heat olive oil in saucepan and add garlic, cayenne pepper and basil; cook over low heat for 2 minutes. Add tomatoes and bring to a boil, reduce heat and simmer for 20 minutes.

- Combine tuna, olives, capers, pasta and a little salt in bowl. Stir in oil-tomato sauce and toss. Serve immediately. Serves 4 to 6. *Tonopah, Nevada*

Tuna-Pasta Casserole

1 (8 ounce) package elbow macaroni
1 (8 ounce) package shredded Velveeta® cheese
1 (12 ounce) can tuna, drained
1 (10 ounce) can cream of celery soup
1 cup milk

- Preheat oven to 350°.

- Cook macaroni according to package directions. Drain and stir in cheese until cheese melts.

- Stir in tuna, celery soup and milk and spoon into sprayed 7 x 11-inch baking dish. Cover and bake for 35 minutes or until bubbly. Serves 6.
  Jaffrey, New Hampshire

Tuna-Stuffed Tomatoes

4 large tomatoes
1 (12 ounce) cans white meat tuna, drained
2 cups chopped celery
½ cup chopped cashews
1 small zucchini with peel, chopped
½ - ⅔ cup mayonnaise

- Cut thin slice off top of each tomato, scoop out flesh and discard. Turn tomatoes over on paper towels to drain.

- Combine tuna, celery, cashews, zucchini and a little salt and pepper in bowl and mix well. Add ½ cup mayonnaise and blend. Add more mayonnaise if needed.

- Spoon mixture into hollowed-out tomatoes and refrigerate. Serves 4.
  Croswell, Michigan

★ ★ ★

Special Desserts

Everyone loves dessert! These 25 recipes
are full of all kinds of sweet things that
will have everyone coming back for more!

1001
Community
Recipes

Special Desserts Contents

Divine Strawberries

This is wonderful served over pound cake or just served in sherbet glasses.

1 quart fresh strawberries
1 (20 ounce) can pineapple chunks, well drained
2 bananas, sliced
2 (18 ounce) cartons strawberry glaze

• Cut strawberries in half (or in quarters if strawberries are very large) in bowl. Add pineapple chunks and bananas.

• Fold in strawberry glaze and refrigerate. Serves 12. *Brockport, New York*

Apple Crescents

1 (8 ounce) can refrigerated crescent rolls
2 Granny Smith apples, peeled, quartered
1 cup orange juice
1¼ cups sugar
½ cup (1 stick) butter
1 teaspoon ground cinnamon

• Preheat oven to 350°.

• Unroll crescent rolls and separate. Wrap each apple quarter with crescent roll. Place each apple crescent in sprayed 9 x 13-inch baking dish.

• Combine orange juice, sugar, butter and cinnamon in saucepan and bring to a boil.

• Pour over crescents and bake for 30 minutes or until golden and bubbly. Serves 8. *Navajo, New Mexico*

Caramel-Apple Delight

3 (2 ounce) Snickers® candy bars, frozen
2 Granny Smith apples, chopped
1 (12 ounce) carton whipped topping, thawed
1 (3 ounce) package instant vanilla pudding

• Smash frozen candy bars in wrappers with hammer.

• Mix all ingredients and refrigerate. Serves 8. *Carroll, Iowa*

TIP: Place in a pretty crystal bowl or serve in individual sherbet glasses.

Blueberry-Angel Dessert

1 (8 ounce) package cream cheese, softened
1 cup powdered sugar
1 (8 ounce) carton whipped topping, thawed
1 (14 ounce) prepared bakery angel food cake
2 (20 ounce) cans blueberry pie filling

- Beat cream cheese and powdered sugar in large bowl and fold in whipped topping.

- Tear cake into small 1 or 2-inch cubes and fold into cream cheese mixture.

- Spread mixture evenly in 9 x 13-inch dish and top with pie filling.

- Cover and refrigerate for at least 3 hours before cutting into squares to serve. Serves 15. *Kittery, Maine*

Caramel-Cinnamon Dessert

1 (5 ounce) package French vanilla instant pudding
3 cups milk
1 (8 ounce) carton whipped topping, thawed
1 (14 ounce) box cinnamon graham crackers
1 (16 ounce) can caramel frosting

- Combine pudding and milk in bowl and mix well. Fold in whipped topping.

- Line bottom of 9 x 13-inch glass dish with whole graham crackers.

- Put half pudding mixture over crackers and top with second layer of crackers. Spread remaining pudding over top. Top with remaining crackers (2 or 3 crackers should be left in box).

- Add caramel frosting over last layer of graham crackers. Refrigerate. Serves 15 to 18. *Crestview Hills, Kentucky*

TIP: Make this a day ahead of time so the pudding can soak into crackers.

Cherry Trifle

1 (12 ounce) pound cake
⅓ cup amaretto liqueur
2 (20 ounce) cans cherry pie filling
4 cups vanilla pudding
1 (8 ounce) carton whipped topping, thawed

- Cut cake into 1-inch slices. Line bottom of 3-quart trifle bowl with one-fourth cake and brush with amaretto.

- Top with one-fourth pie filling followed by one-fourth pudding. Repeat layers 3 times. Top with whipped topping. Refrigerate for several hours. Serves 6 to 10. *Bronxville, New York*

TIP: A trifle bowl is a straight-sided, clear glass bowl that is sometimes footed. Use any clear glass bowl for a beautiful presentation.

Apricot Pudding

1 (3.4 ounce) package vanilla pudding (not instant)
1 (15 ounce) can apricots, halved with juice
1 (11 ounce) can mandarin oranges, drained
1 (8 ounce) carton whipped topping, thawed

- Cook pudding with 1¼ cups apricot juice (add water to make 1¼ cups) in saucepan. Cool.

- Add drained oranges and halved apricots. Refrigerate until mixture begins to thicken.

- Fold in whipped topping. Spoon into 6 individual sherbet dishes. Serves 6. *Brentwood, Ohio*

Candy Store Pudding

A special family dessert!

1 cup cold milk
1 (3.4 ounce) package instant chocolate pudding mix
1 (8 ounce) carton whipped topping, thawed
1 cup miniature marshmallows
½ cup chopped salted peanuts

- Whisk milk and pudding mix in bowl for 2 minutes. Fold in whipped topping, marshmallows and peanuts.

- Spoon into 6 individual dessert dishes. Place plastic wrap over tops and refrigerate. Serves 6. *Cannon Falls, Minnesota*

Blueberry Fluff

1 (20 ounce) can blueberry pie filling
1 (20 ounce) can crushed pineapple, drained
1 (14 ounce) can sweetened condensed milk
1 (8 ounce) carton whipped topping, thawed

- Mix pie filling, pineapple and sweetened condensed milk in bowl. Fold in whipped topping. (This dessert is even better if you add ¾ cup chopped pecans.)

- Combine all ingredients and pour into parfait 8 glasses. Refrigerate. Serves 8. *Fairburn, Georgia*

Chocolate Bread Pudding

1 (3 ounce) package cook-and-serve vanilla pudding
1 (3 ounce) package cook-and-serve chocolate pudding
1 quart milk
4 (4 ounce) croissants
Powdered sugar

- Preheat oven to 325°.

- Combine vanilla and chocolate pudding mixes with milk in large bowl, whisking for 2 minutes or until they blend well.

- Cut croissants into 1-inch pieces and place in sprayed 3-quart baking dish. Spoon pudding mixture over croissant pieces and push pieces into liquid.

- Bake for 50 minutes or until bubbly around edges. Sprinkle powdered sugar over top of bread pudding. Cool for 10 to 15 minutes before serving. Serves 6 to 10. *Edgewood, Kentucky*

Chocolate-Coconut Mist

2 (14 ounce) packages flaked coconut
2 tablespoons butter, melted
1⅓ cups semi-sweet chocolate chips, melted
3 quarts mint chocolate chip ice cream

- Toss coconut, butter and chocolate in bowl until mixture blends well.

- Cover baking sheet with wax paper, shape ⅓ cupfuls of mixture into 2½-inch nests. Refrigerate until firm.

- Just before serving top each nest with ½ cup ice cream. Serves 10 to 12. *Lockport, Louisiana*

Cookies and Cream

25 chocolate sandwich cookies, crushed
½ gallon vanilla ice cream, softened
1 (5 ounce) can chocolate syrup
1 (12 ounce) carton whipped topping, thawed

- Press crushed cookies in 9 x 13-inch baking dish. Spread ice cream over cookies.

- Pour syrup over ice cream and top with whipped topping. Freeze overnight. Slice into squares to serve. Serves 15. *Dade City, Florida*

Fun Fruit Fajitas

1 (20 ounce) can cherry pie filling
8 large flour tortillas
1½ cups sugar
¾ cup (1½ sticks) butter
1 teaspoon almond flavoring

- Divide pie filling equally on tortillas, roll and place in 9 x 13-inch baking dish.

- Mix sugar and butter in saucepan with 2 cups water and bring to a boil. Add almond flavoring and pour sugar mixture over flour tortillas. Place in refrigerator and soak for 1 to 24 hours.

- When ready to bake, preheat oven to 350°.

- Bake for 20 minutes or until brown and bubbly. Serve hot or at room temperature. Serves 10 to 12. *Combes, Texas*

TIP: *Use any flavor of pie filling you like.*

Honey-Rice Pudding Parfaits

12 cinnamon graham crackers, crushed
1 (22 ounce) carton refrigerated rice pudding
½ cup honey
Fresh strawberries (or raspberries)

- Spoon about 2 heaping tablespoons crushed crackers in bottom of 5 sherbet or parfait glasses.

- Mix rice pudding and honey in bowl and divide evenly into sherbet glasses. Sprinkle remaining crushed graham crackers over top of pudding and place 4 or 5 strawberries on top. Refrigerate. Serves 5. *Davis, Oklahoma*

Ice Cream Dessert

19 ice cream sandwiches
1 (12 ounce) carton whipped topping, thawed
1 (12 ounce) jar hot fudge ice cream topping
1 cup salted peanuts

- Cut 1 ice cream sandwich in half. Place 1 whole and one-half sandwich along short side of 9 x 13-inch pan. Arrange 8 sandwiches in opposite direction in pan.

- Spread with half whipped topping. Spoon teaspoonfuls of fudge topping onto whipped topping. Sprinkle with half peanuts.

- Repeat layers with remaining ice cream sandwiches, whipped topping and peanuts (pan will be full). Cover and freeze. Serves 12 to 15. *Fairview, Oregon*

TIP: To serve, take out of freezer 20 minutes before serving.

Kahlua Mousse

Light but rich and absolutely delicious

1 (12 ounce) carton whipped topping, thawed
2 teaspoons dry instant coffee
5 teaspoons cocoa
5 tablespoons sugar
½ cup Kahlua® liqueur

- Combine whipped topping, coffee, cocoa and sugar in large bowl and blend well.

- Fold in Kahlua®. Spoon into 4 sherbet dessert glasses.

- Place plastic wrap over dessert glasses and refrigerate until ready to serve. Serves 4. *Avon, Pennsylvania*

Macaroon Delight

12 soft coconut macaroons
1 (8 ounce) carton whipping cream, whipped
3 (1 pint) cartons sherbet: 1 each, orange, lime, raspberry,
    softened

- Preheat oven to 300°.

- Warm macaroons in oven for 10 minutes, break into pieces and cool.

- Spoon macaroons into whipped cream.

- Completely line 9 x 5-inch loaf pan with foil. Spread orange sherbet in
  loaf pan. Spread half whipped cream mixture, then lime sherbet and
  remaining whipped cream mixture. Raspberry sherbet goes on top.

- Freeze overnight. To serve, lift out of pan with foil, remove foil and
  slice. Serves 8 to 10. *Burton, South Carolina*

Mango Cream

2 soft mangoes
½ gallon vanilla ice cream, softened
1 (6 ounce) can frozen lemonade concentrate, thawed
1 (8 ounce) carton whipped topping, thawed

- Peel mangoes, cut slices around seeds and cut into small chunks.

- Mix ice cream, lemonade and whipped topping in large bowl. Fold in
  mango chunks. Quickly spoon mixture into parfait or sherbet glasses
  and cover with plastic wrap. Freeze. Serves 8. *Carmel, California*

Orange-Cream Dessert

2 cups crushed chocolate sandwich cookies (about 20)
⅓ cup (⅔ stick) butter, melted
1 (6 ounce) package orange gelatin
½ gallon vanilla ice cream, softened

- Combine cookie crumbs and butter in bowl and set aside ¼ cup crumb
  mixture for topping. Press remaining crumb mixture into sprayed 9 x
  13-inch dish.

- Dissolve gelatin in 1½ cups boiling water in large bowl, cover and
  refrigerate for 30 minutes.

- Stir in ice cream until smooth. Work fast. Pour over crust and sprinkle
  with reserved crumb mixture. Freeze. Remove from freezer 10 or 15
  minutes before serving. Serves 12 to 15. *Glenwood Springs, Colorado*

Oreo Sundae

A kids' favorite!

½ cup (1 stick) butter
1 (19 ounce) package chocolate sandwich cookies, crushed
½ gallon vanilla ice cream, softened
2 (12 ounce) jars fudge ice cream topping
1 (12 ounce) carton whipped topping, thawed

- Melt butter in 9 x 13-inch pan. Reserve about ½ cup crushed cookies for top and mix remaining with butter to form crust. Press crumbs into pan.

- Spread softened ice cream over crust (work fast) and add fudge sauce on top.

- Top with whipped topping and sprinkle with remaining crumbs. Freeze. Serves 12 to 15. *Farmington, Connecticut*

Twinkie Dessert

1 (10 count) box twinkies
4 bananas, sliced
1 (5 ounce) package instant vanilla pudding mix
2 cups milk
1 (20 ounce) can crushed pineapple, drained
1 (8 ounce) carton whipped topping, thawed

- Slice twinkies in half lengthwise and place in sprayed 9 x 13-inch pan cream-side up. Layer sliced bananas over twinkies.

- Prepare pudding according to package directions with milk. Pour pudding over bananas and layer pineapple over pudding.

- Top with whipped topping and refrigerate. Cut into squares to serve. Serves 12 to 15. *Geneva, Alabama*

Winter Wonder Dessert

28 chocolate cream-filled chocolate cookies, divided
2¾ cups milk
3 (3.4 ounce) packages instant pistachio pudding
1 (8 ounce) carton whipped topping, thawed

• Crush 28 cookies and set aside ⅔ cup. Spread crushed cookies in 9 x 13-inch dish.

• Combine milk and pistachio pudding in bowl. Mix for about 2 minutes or until it thickens. Pour over crushed cookies.

• Spread whipped topping over pistachio pudding.

• Sprinkle remaining cookies over whipped topping and refrigerate overnight before serving. Serves 10 to 12. *Danville, Arkansas*

Pavlova

3 large egg whites
1 cup sugar
1 teaspoon vanilla
2 teaspoons white vinegar
3 tablespoons cornstarch
Whipped cream
Fresh fruit

• Preheat oven to 300°.

• Beat egg whites in bowl until stiff and add 3 tablespoons cold water. Beat again and add sugar very gradually while beating. Continue beating slowly and add vanilla, vinegar and cornstarch.

• Draw 9-inch circle and mound mixture within circle on parchment-covered cookie sheet.

• Bake for 45 minutes. Leave in oven to cool.

• To serve, peel paper from bottom while sliding Pavlova onto serving plate. Cover with whipped cream and top with assortment of fresh fruit such as kiwi, strawberries, blueberries, etc. Serves 8 to 10. *Glastonbury, Connecticut*

Mother's Boiled Custard

½ cup sugar
4 eggs, slightly beaten
1 gallon milk
2 teaspoons vanilla

- Combine sugar, dash of salt and eggs in bowl and mix well.

- Scald milk in double boiler and add a little into egg mixture. Pour egg-milk mixture into double boiler with remaining milk and cook. Stir constantly until mixture is thick enough to coat spoon. Remove from heat and add vanilla.

- Refrigerate until ready to serve. Serves 8 to 10. *Calhoun Falls, South Carolina*

TIP: Serve custard in crystal cups with dollop of whipped topping over top.

Rhubarb Fool 🍁

6 - 8 cups chopped rhubarb
1½ cups sugar
2 (8 ounce) cartons whipping cream
1 teaspoon vanilla

- Place chopped rhubarb in large saucepan and add 1 cup water. Bring to a boil, reduce heat to medium and cook until mixture is thick, soft and mushy. Stir in sugar and refrigerate.

- Whip cream in bowl until thick, add vanilla and fold into stewed rhubarb and return to refrigerator. Serve in individual sherbet glasses. Serves 8. *Hay River, Northwest Territories, Canada*

TIP: In Canadian cookery, "fools" are essentially any fruit or berries stewed with sugar with heavy cream added.

★ ★ ★

Cakes

Cakes are the finishing touch for dinner
or the centerpiece of a special occasion –
and there are 30 plus 12 frostings!

**1001
Community
Recipes**

Cakes Contents

Coconut Cupcakes

2 cups flaked coconut
½ cup sweetened condensed milk
1 (18 ounce) box yellow cake mix
⅓ cup oil
3 eggs
1 (16 ounce) can vanilla frosting
1 cup flaked coconut, toasted

- Preheat oven to 375°.

- Place paper baking cups in 24 regular-size muffin cups. Combine coconut and sweetened condensed milk in medium bowl and set aside.

- In separate bowl, beat cake mix, 1¼ cups water, oil and eggs on low speed for 30 seconds. Beat for 2 minutes on medium speed. Divide batter evenly among muffin cups and top each cupcake with 1 tablespoon coconut mixture.

- Bake for 18 to 22 minutes or until top springs back when lightly touched. Cool completely. Spread frosting on each cupcake and dip tops in toasted coconut. Serves 20 to 24. *Caryville, Tennessee*

TIP: Toast coconut on baking sheet at 325° for about 5 minutes.

Pecan Cake

1 (18 ounce) box butter-pecan cake mix
½ cup (1 stick) butter, melted
1 egg
1 cup chopped pecans

- Preheat oven to 325°.

- Combine cake mix, ¾ cup water, butter and egg in bowl and mix well. Stir in pecans. Pour into 9 x 13-inch baking dish.

Topping:

1 (8 ounce) package cream cheese, softened
2 eggs
1 (1 pound) box powdered sugar

- Beat cream cheese, eggs and powdered sugar in bowl. Pour over cake mixture.

- Bake for 40 minutes. Cake is done when toothpick inserted in center comes out clean. Serves 12 to 14. *Lutcher, Louisiana*

Oreo Cake

1 (18 ounce) box white cake mix
⅓ cup oil
4 egg whites
1¼ cups coarsely chopped Oreo® cookies

- Preheat oven to 350°.

- Combine cake mix, oil, 1¼ cups water and egg whites in bowl. Blend on low speed until moist. Beat for 2 minutes at high speed.

- Gently fold in coarsely chopped cookies. Pour batter into 2 sprayed, floured 8-inch round cake pans.

- Bake for 25 to 30 minutes or until toothpick inserted in center comes out clean.

- Cool for 15 minutes and remove from pan. Cool completely and frost.

Frosting:

4¼ cups powdered sugar
1 cup (2 sticks) butter, softened
1 cup shortening (not butter-flavored)
1 teaspoon almond flavoring
Oreo® cookies, crushed, for topping

- Combine all ingredients in bowl and beat until creamy.

- Frost first layer of cake and place second layer on top and frost top and sides.

- Sprinkle crushed cookies on top. Serves 18. *Cloverdale, Indiana*

Miracle Cake

1 (18 ounce) box lemon cake mix
3 eggs
⅓ cup oil
1 (20 ounce) can crushed pineapple with juice

- Preheat oven to 350°.

- Combine all ingredients in bowl. Blend on low speed and beat on medium for 2 minutes.

- Pour batter into sprayed, floured 9 x 13-inch baking dish.

- Bake for 30 to 35 minutes or until toothpick inserted in center comes out clean.

Topping:

1 (14 ounce) can sweetened condensed milk
¼ cup lemon juice
1 (8 ounce) carton whipped topping, thawed

- Blend all ingredients in bowl and mix well. Spread over cake. Refrigerate. Serves 14 to 16. *Fair Oaks, Georgia*

Lemon-Poppy Seed Cake

1 (18 ounce) box lemon pudding cake mix
1 (8 ounce) carton sour cream
3 eggs
⅓ cup oil
2 tablespoons poppy seeds
Powdered sugar for topping

- Preheat oven to 350°.

- Combine cake mix, sour cream, eggs, oil and ¼ cup water in bowl and beat on medium speed until it mixes well.

- Stir in poppy seeds and mix until seeds are evenly distributed.

- Pour batter into sprayed, floured bundt pan and bake for 45 minutes or until toothpick inserted in center comes out clean.

- Dust with powdered sugar or use part of 1 (16 ounce) can vanilla frosting. Serves 16. *Payette, Idaho*

Lemon-Pineapple Cake

1 (18 ounce) box lemon cake mix
1 (20 ounce) can crushed pineapple with juice
3 eggs
⅓ cup oil

- Preheat oven to 350°.

- Combine all ingredients in bowl. Beat on low speed to moisten and beat on medium for 2 minutes.

- Pour batter into sprayed, floured 9 x 13-inch baking pan.

- Bake for 30 minutes. Cake is done when toothpick inserted in center comes out clean.

- While cake is baking, start topping for cake. Cool for about 15 minutes.

Topping:

1 (14 ounce) can sweetened condensed milk
1 cup sour cream
¼ cup lemon juice

- Combine all ingredients in medium bowl. Stir well to blend.

- Pour over warm cake. Refrigerate. Serves 12 to 14. *Desoto Lakes, Florida*

Lemon Cake

This is an easy cake to make early in the day. Just don't freeze it.

Cake:

1 (18 ounce) box yellow cake mix
4 eggs
1 (3 ounce) package lemon gelatin
¾ cup oil

- Preheat oven to 350°.

- Mix cake ingredients as listed with ¾ cup water in bowl and beat until fluffy. Pour into sprayed, floured 9 x 13-inch pan. Bake for 30 to 35 minutes.

- Remove cake from oven and jab with fork at 1-inch intervals to bottom.

Glaze:

2 cups powdered sugar
1 teaspoon grated lemon peel
Juice of 2 lemons
1 (7 ounce) package flaked coconut

- Combine powdered sugar, grated lemon peel and lemon juice in bowl.

- Spoon glaze mixture over warm cake, sprinkle with coconut and serve warm. Serves 12 to 14. *Coal Valley, Illinois*

Easy Breezy Favorite Cake

1 (18 ounce) box butter-pecan cake mix
½ cup (1 stick) butter, softened
3 eggs
1 cup almond-toffee bits
1 cup chopped pecans
Powdered sugar

- Preheat oven to 350°.

- Prepare cake mix according to package directions using butter, egg and 1¼ cups water in bowl. Fold in almond-toffee bits and pecans.

- Pour into sprayed, floured bundt cake pan. Bake for 45 minutes or until toothpick inserted in center comes out clean.

- Allow cake to cool for 15 minutes and remove from pan. Dust with sifted powdered sugar. Serves 20. *Hyde Park, Utah*

Holiday Red Velvet Cake

1 (18 ounce) box German chocolate cake mix
1 (1 ounce) bottle red food coloring
⅓ cup oil
3 eggs, slightly beaten
1 (16 ounce) can white frosting
Small red decorative candies and sprinkles

- Preheat oven to 350°.

- Before you measure water for cake mix, place red food coloring in cup first, then add enough water to make 1⅓ cups.

- Prepare cake mix according to package directions with water, oil and eggs in bowl. Pour into 2 sprayed, floured 8 or 9-inch pans. Bake for 25 to 30 minutes. Cake is done when toothpick inserted in center comes out clean.

- Frost each layer with white frosting and decorate top layer with tiny red candies. Serves 20. *Littleton, New Hampshire*

TIP: *Decorative candies are near the cake mixes.*

Hawaiian Dream Cake

1 (18 ounce) box yellow cake mix
4 eggs
¾ cup oil
½ (20 ounce) can crushed pineapple with ½ juice

- Preheat oven to 350°.

- Beat all ingredients in bowl for 4 minutes. Pour into sprayed, floured 9 x 13-inch baking pan. Bake for 30 to 35 minutes or until toothpick inserted in center comes out clean.

Frosting:

½ (20 ounce) can crushed pineapple with ½ juice
½ cup (1 stick) butter
1 (16 ounce) box powdered sugar
1 (7 ounce) can flaked coconut

- Heat pineapple and butter in saucepan and boil for 1½ minutes.

- Add powdered sugar and coconut.

- Punch holes in cake with knife. Pour hot icing over warm cake. Serves 12 to 14. *Campbell, Ohio*

Golden Rum Cake

1 (18 ounce) box yellow cake mix with pudding
3 eggs
⅓ cup oil
¼ cup plus 1 tablespoon rum, divided
1 cup chopped pecans
1 (16 ounce) can caramel frosting

- Preheat oven to 325°.

- Mix cake mix, eggs, 1¼ cups water and ¼ cup rum in bowl and blend well. Stir in pecans and pour into sprayed, floured 10-inch tube pan. Bake for 1 hour or until toothpick inserted in center comes out clean.

- Mix caramel frosting with 1 tablespoon rum. Spread over cool cake. Serves 20. *Rugby, North Dakota*

Fluffy Orange Cake

1 (18 ounce) box orange cake mix
4 eggs
⅔ cup oil

- Preheat oven to 350°.

- Combine all ingredients with ½ cup water in bowl.

- Beat on low speed to blend and beat on medium speed for 2 minutes. Pour into sprayed, floured 9 x 13-inch baking pan.

- Bake for 30 minutes or until toothpick inserted in center comes out clean. Cool.

Topping:

1 (14 ounce) can sweetened condensed milk
⅓ cup lemon juice
1 (8 ounce) carton whipped topping, thawed
2 (11 ounce) cans mandarin oranges, drained, halved, chilled

- Blend sweetened condensed milk and lemon juice in large bowl and mix well.

- Fold in whipped topping until they blend well. Fold in oranges.

- Pour mixture over cooled cake. Cover and refrigerate. Serves 12 to 14. *Gunnison, Colorado*

Easy Applesauce-Spice Cake

1 (18 ounce) box spice cake mix
3 eggs
1¼ cups applesauce
⅓ cup oil
1 cup chopped walnuts

- Preheat oven to 350°.

- Beat cake mix, eggs, applesauce and oil in bowl on medium speed for 2 minutes. Stir in walnuts.

- Pour into sprayed, floured 9 x 13-inch baking pan.

- Bake for 40 minutes. Cake is done when toothpick inserted in center comes out clean. Cool completely.

Frosting:

1 (16 ounce) can vanilla frosting
½ teaspoon ground cinnamon

- Combine frosting and cinnamon and spread over cake. Serves 12 to 14. *Chilton, Wisconsin*

Delightful Pear Cake

1 (15 ounce) can pears with juice
1 (18 ounce) box white cake mix
2 egg whites
1 egg
Powdered sugar

- Preheat oven to 350°.

- Drain pears, save juice and chop pears.

- Place pears and juice in bowl and add cake mix, egg whites and egg. Beat on low speed for 30 seconds. Beat on high for 4 minutes.

- Pour batter into sprayed, floured 1-inch bundt pan.

- Bake for 50 to 55 minutes. Cook until toothpick inserted in center comes out clean. Cool in pan for 10 minutes.

- Remove cake and dust with sifted powdered sugar. Serves 18 to 20. *Florence, Oregon*

Chocolate-Cherry Cake

1 (18 ounce) box milk chocolate cake mix
1 (20 ounce) can cherry pie filling
3 eggs

- Preheat oven to 350°.

- Combine all ingredients in bowl and mix with spoon. Pour into sprayed, floured 9 x 13-inch baking dish.

- Bake for 35 to 40 minutes. Cake is done when toothpick inserted in center comes out clean.

Frosting:

5 tablespoons butter
1¼ cups sugar
½ cup milk
1 (6 ounce) package chocolate chips

- Just before cake is done, combine butter, sugar and milk in medium saucepan.

- Boil for 1 minute, stirring constantly. Add chocolate chips and stir until chips melt. Pour over hot cake. Serves 12 to 14. *Circle Pines, Minnesota*

White Chocolate-Almond Cake

1 (18 ounce) box white cake mix
4 egg whites
¼ cup oil
1 teaspoon almond extract
1 cup slivered almonds, chopped
6 (1 ounce) squares white chocolate, melted
1 (16 ounce) can caramel frosting

- Preheat oven to 350°.

- Combine cake mix, egg whites, oil, almond extract and 1½ cups water in bowl; beat until mixture blends well.

- Stir in almonds and melted white chocolate and pour into 2 sprayed, floured 9-inch round cake pans. Bake for 30 to 35 minutes or until toothpick inserted in center comes out clean.

- Spread one layer with frosting. Place second layer on top of first layer and frost top and sides. Serves 20. *Three Rivers, Massachusetts*

Chocolate Pudding Cake

1 (18 ounce) box milk chocolate cake mix
1¼ cups milk
⅓ cup oil
3 eggs

- Preheat oven to 350°.

- Combine all ingredients in bowl and beat well.

- Pour into sprayed 9 x 13-inch baking pan.

- Bake for 35 minutes or until toothpick inserted in center comes out clean.

Topping:

1 (14 ounce) can sweetened condensed milk
¾ (16 ounce) can chocolate syrup
1 (8 ounce) carton whipped topping, thawed
⅓ cup chopped pecans

- Mix sweetened condensed milk and chocolate syrup in small bowl.

- Pour over cake and let soak into cake. Refrigerate for several hours.

- Spread whipped topping over top of cake and sprinkle pecans on top. Refrigerate. Serves 12 to 14. *West Wendover, Nevada*

Special Cherry Dump Cake

1 (20 ounce) can crushed pineapple with juice
1 (20 ounce) can cherry pie filling
1 (18 ounce) box yellow cake mix
¾ cup (1½ sticks) butter, melted
¾ cup flaked coconut
1 cup chopped pecans

- Preheat oven to 350°.

- Spoon pineapple evenly over bottom of 9 x 13-inch baking pan; cover evenly with pie filling.

- Sprinkle cake mix evenly over filling and drizzle with melted butter; do not stir. Sprinkle coconut and pecans evenly over cake mix.

- Bake for 55 minutes to 1 hour or until top browns. Serves 15 to 18. *Gladstone, Michigan*

Caramel-Coconut Cake

1 (18 ounce) box white cake mix with pudding
3 large eggs
⅓ cup oil
2 cups flaked coconut, divided

- Preheat oven to 350°.

- Combine cake mix, eggs, oil and 1¼ cups water in bowl and beat on low speed for 1 minute; then beat on high speed for 2 minutes.

- Stir in ¾ cup coconut and pour into sprayed, floured 9 x 13-inch baking pan.

- Bake for 30 minutes or until toothpick inserted in center comes out clean.

Topping:

½ cup (1 stick) butter
⅔ cup caramel ice cream topping
¼ cup milk
1 cup chopped pecans
1 (6 ounce) package butterscotch chips

- Before cake is done, melt butter in saucepan over medium heat and stir in caramel topping and milk. Boil for 5 to 6 minutes or until thick and it reaches spreading consistency; stir constantly.

- Stir in pecans and remaining coconut and spread over cake immediately after it comes out of oven.

- Sprinkle butterscotch chips over top and cool completely before cutting into squares. Serves 12 to 14. *Freeland, Michigan*

White Cake with Special Topping

1 (18 ounce) box white cake mix
1 cup graham cracker crumbs
⅓ cup oil
3 eggs
½ cup chopped pecans
1 (16 ounce) jar chocolate ice cream topping, divided
1 (7 ounce) jar marshmallow creme

- Preheat oven to 350°.

- Beat cake mix, cracker crumbs, 1¼ cups water, oil and eggs in bowl on medium speed for 2 minutes.

- Stir in chopped pecans and pour into sprayed, floured 9 x 13-inch baking pan. Reserve ¼ cup chocolate topping and drop generous tablespoonfuls of remaining topping randomly in 12 to 14 mounds onto batter in pan. Bake for 40 to 45 minutes. Cool for 15 minutes.

- Spoon teaspoonfuls of marshmallow creme onto warm cake and carefully spread with knife dipped in hot water. Drop small dollops of reserved chocolate topping randomly over marshmallow creme. Swirl topping through marshmallow creme with knife for marbled design. Cool for 2 hours before cutting.

- To cut cake easily, use serrated knife and dip in hot water before cutting each piece to keep frosting from sticking. Serves 20.
  Chatham, New Jersey

Pineapple Cake

2 eggs, beaten
2 cups sugar
1 (20 ounce) can crushed pineapple with juice
2 cups flour
2 teaspoons baking soda
1 teaspoon vanilla
1 cup chopped pecans
1 (16 ounce) can cream cheese frosting

- Preheat oven to 350°.

- Combine beaten eggs, sugar and pineapple in large bowl. Stir in flour, baking soda, vanilla and pecans.

- Pour into sprayed, floured 9 x 13-inch baking pan and bake for 35 to 40 minutes. After cake cools completely, spread frosting over cake. Serves 12 to 14. *Edenton, North Carolina*

Easy Pineapple Cake

Cake:

2 cups sugar
2 cups flour
1 (20 ounce) can crushed pineapple with juice
1 teaspoon baking soda

- Preheat oven to 350°.

- Combine all cake ingredients in bowl and mix with spoon. Pour into sprayed, floured 9 x 13-inch baking pan.

- Bake for 30 to 35 minutes.

Topping:

1 (8 ounce) package cream cheese, softened
½ cup (1 stick) butter, melted
1 cup powdered sugar
1 cup chopped pecans

- Just before cake is done, beat cream cheese, butter and powdered sugar in bowl.

- Add chopped pecans and pour over HOT cake. Serves 12 to 14.
  Delmar, New York

Vanilla Wafer Cake

1 cup (2 sticks) butter, softened
2¼ cups sugar
6 eggs, slightly beaten
1 (12 ounce) package vanilla wafer cookies
½ cup milk
1 cup flaked coconut
1 cup chopped pecans
1 (16 ounce) can coconut-pecan frosting

- Preheat oven to 325°.

- Cream butter and sugar in bowl. Add eggs 1 at a time and beat after each addition.

- Crush wafers with rolling pin into fine crumbs. Stir crumbs and milk alternately into egg-sugar mixture. Fold in coconut and pecans and pour into sprayed, floured tube pan.

- Bake for 1 hour 30 minutes. Cool in pan for about 15 minutes. Remove cake from pan and cool completely. Frost cake with coconut-pecan frosting. Serves 20. *Delta, Ohio*

Butterscotch Finale

1 (16 ounce) carton whipping cream
¾ cup butterscotch ice cream topping
1 (9 inch) angel food cake
¾ pound toffee bars, crushed, divided

- Whip cream in bowl until it begins to thicken. Slowly add topping and continue beating until mixture is thick.
- Slice cake into 3 equal horizontal layers.
- With bottom layer on cake plate, spread with 1½ cups whipped cream mixture. Sprinkle with one-fourth crushed toffee. Repeat layers and frost top as well as sides of cake.
- Sprinkle toffee over top and sides of cake. Refrigerate for at least 8 hours before serving. Serves 12. *White River Junction, Vermont*

O'Shaughnessy's Special

1 (10 ounce) pound cake loaf
1 (15 ounce) can crushed pineapple with juice
1 (3.4 ounce) box pistachio pudding mix
1 (8 ounce) carton whipped topping, thawed

- Slice cake horizontally and make 3 layers.
- Combine pineapple and pudding in bowl and beat until mixture begins to thicken. Fold in whipped topping and blend well. (Add a few drops of green food coloring if you would like the cake to be a brighter green.)
- Spread on each layer and on top. Refrigerate. Serves 12 to 14. *Eden, New York*

Coconut-Angel Cake

1 (14 ounce/10 inch) round angel food cake
1 (20 ounce) can coconut pie filling
1 (12 ounce) carton whipped topping, thawed
3 tablespoons flaked coconut

- Cut angel food cake horizontally to make 3 layers.
- Combine coconut pie filling and whipped topping in bowl. Spread one-third mixture on first layer. Top with second layer. Spread one-third mixture on second layer and top with third layer. Spread remaining whipped topping mixture on top of cake.
- Sprinkle coconut on top. Refrigerate. Serves 16. *Creston, Iowa*

Chiffon Torte

1 round bakery orange chiffon cake
1 (20 ounce) can crushed pineapple with juice
1 (5 ounce) package vanilla instant pudding
1 (8 ounce) carton whipped topping, thawed

- Slice cake horizontally to make 3 layers.

- Combine pineapple and pudding in bowl and beat with spoon until mixture begins to thicken. Fold in whipped topping. Spread on each layer and cover top of cake. Refrigerate overnight. Serves 16. *Girard, Kansas*

TIP: Toasted almonds may be sprinkled on top of cake, if you like.

Pound Cake Deluxe

1 (10 inch) round bakery pound cake
1 (20 ounce) can crushed pineapple with juice
1 (5 ounce) package coconut instant pudding mix
1 (8 ounce) carton whipped topping, thawed
Coconut

- Slice cake horizontally to make 3 layers.

- Mix pineapple, pudding and whipped topping in bowl and blend well. Spread on each layer and top of cake. Coconut may be sprinkled on top layer. Refrigerate. Serves 12 to 14. *Greenfield, Tennessee*

Quick Summer Cake

1 (16 ounce) frozen loaf pound cake
1 (8 ounce) carton whipping cream
1 (20 ounce) can coconut pie filling
2 kiwifruit, peeled, halved, sliced

- Split cake into 3 horizontal layers and place bottom layer on serving platter.

- Beat whipping cream in bowl until thick and fold in coconut pie filling. Mix until they blend well. Spread one-third mixture over bottom cake layer.

- Place second layer on top and spread half remaining cream mixture on top. Top with third layer and spread remaining cream mixture on top.

- Garnish with slices of kiwifruit over top of cake. Refrigerate. Serves 8 to 10. *Hazard, Kentucky*

Strawberry Delight

1 (6 ounce) package strawberry gelatin
2 (10 ounce) packages frozen strawberries with juice
1 (8 ounce) carton whipped topping, thawed
1 (12 ounce) prepared angel food cake

- Dissolve strawberry gelatin in 1 cup boiling water in bowl and mix well. Add strawberries.

- Refrigerate until partially set and fold in whipped topping.

- Break angel food cake into large bite-size pieces and layer cake and gelatin mixture half at a time in 9 x 13-inch shallow dish. Refrigerate.

- Cut in squares to serve. Serves 12 to 14. *Forest Heights, Maryland*

★ ★ ★

Pies &
Cobblers

Among the best-loved desserts are pies,
crunches and cobblers. Your family and
friends will enjoy these 38 recipes!

1001
Community
Recipes

Pies & Cobblers Contents

Pecan Pie Favorite

2 tablespoons flour
3 tablespoons butter, melted
3 eggs, beaten
⅔ cup sugar
1 cup corn syrup
1 teaspoon vanilla
1 cup chopped pecans
1 (9 inch) frozen piecrust, thawed

• Preheat oven to 350°.

• Combine flour, butter, eggs, sugar, corn syrup and vanilla in bowl and mix well. Place pecans in piecrust and pour egg mixture over pecans.

• Bake for 10 minutes, reduce heat to 275° and bake for 50 to 55 minutes or until center of pie is fairly firm. Serves 6 to 8. *Grovetown, Georgia*

Fudgy Brownie Pie

1 (9 inch) frozen piecrust, thawed
1 (6 ounce) package semi-sweet chocolate chips
¼ cup (½ stick) butter
1 (14 ounce) can sweetened condensed milk
½ cup biscuit mix
2 eggs, slightly beaten
1 teaspoon vanilla
1 cup chopped pecans

• Preheat oven to 375°.

• Bake piecrust for 10 minutes and remove from oven. Reduce heat to 325°.

• Melt chips in butter in saucepan over low heat and pour into bowl. Add sweetened condensed milk, biscuit mix, eggs and vanilla. Beat until they mix well, add pecans and pour into piecrust.

• Cover crust edges with strips of foil to prevent excessive browning. Bake for 40 minutes or until center is firm. Allow several hours to cool. Serves 6 to 8. *Santa Rosa, New Mexico*

Cinnamon-Almond-Pecan Pie

This is a little different from the traditional
pecan pie and it is a good one!

⅔ cup sugar
1 tablespoon flour
2½ teaspoons ground cinnamon
4 eggs, lightly beaten
1 cup light corn syrup
2 tablespoons butter, melted
1 tablespoon vanilla
1½ teaspoons almond extract
1 cup coarsely chopped pecans
½ cup slivered almonds
1 (9 inch) frozen piecrust, thawed

- Preheat oven to 400°.

- Combine sugar and flour in large bowl. Add cinnamon, eggs, corn syrup, butter, vanilla and almond extract and mix well.

- Stir in pecans and almonds. Pour filling into piecrust. Cover crust edges with strips of foil to prevent excessive browning.

- Bake for 10 minutes, reduce heat to 325° and bake for 40 to 45 minutes more or until center of pie is firm.

- Cool completely before serving. Serves 6 to 8. *Many, Louisiana*

Creamy Pecan Pie

1½ cups light corn syrup
1 (3 ounce) package instant vanilla pudding
3 eggs
2½ tablespoons butter, melted
2 cups pecan halves
1 (9 inch) frozen deep-dish piecrust, thawed

- Preheat oven to 325°.

- Combine corn syrup, pudding, eggs and butter in bowl, mix well and stir in pecans.

- Pour into deep-dish piecrust. Cover piecrust edges with strips of foil to prevent excessive browning.

- Bake for 35 to 40 minutes or until center of pie is firm. Serves 6 to 8. *Kingston, Tennessee*

Easy Chocolate Pie

1 (8 ounce) milk chocolate candy bar
1 (16 ounce) carton whipped topping, thawed, divided
¾ cup chopped pecans
1 (9 inch) frozen piecrust, baked

- Break candy into small pieces in saucepan and melt over low heat. Remove and cool for several minutes.

- Fold in two-thirds whipped topping and mix well. Stir in chopped pecans and pour into piecrust.

- Spread remaining whipped topping over top of pie. Refrigerate for at least 8 hours. Serves 6 to 8. *Wahpeton, North Dakota*

Cool Chocolate Pie

22 large marshmallows
2 (7 ounce) milk chocolate-almond candy bars
1 (8 ounce) carton whipped topping, thawed
½ cup chopped pecans
1 (6 ounce) ready graham cracker piecrust

- Melt marshmallows and chocolate bars in double boiler. Cool partially and fold in whipped topping and pecans.

- Pour into piecrust. Refrigerate for several hours before serving. Serves 6 to 8. *Pine Ridge, South Dakota*

Chocolate-Amaretto Pie

2 (7 ounce) milk chocolate-almond candy bars
⅓ cup amaretto liqueur
2 (8 ounce) cartons whipping cream, whipped
1 (6 ounce) ready shortbread piecrust

- Melt chocolate in double boiler on low heat. Remove from heat and pour in amaretto.

- Stir chocolate and amaretto for about 10 or 15 minutes until mixture reaches room temperature. Fold in whipped cream.

- Pour into piecrust. Refrigerate for several hours before serving. Serves 6 to 8. *Braddock, Pennsylvania*

Chocolate-Pecan Chess Pie

This pie is absolutely ultra-decadent and delicious. It is so rich you can even cut pieces a little smaller than usual.

1 (9 inch) frozen piecrust, thawed
1⅓ cups sugar
1 tablespoon cornmeal
4 eggs, beaten
⅓ cup half-and-half cream
¼ cup (½ stick) butter, melted
1 teaspoon vanilla
⅔ cup chopped pecans
½ cup miniature semi-sweet chocolate chips

- Preheat oven to 425°.

- Roll out piecrust according to package directions and place in 9-inch pie pan. Trim pastry ½-inch beyond edge of pie pan and fold over extra pastry. Flute edge high around pie pan. Bake for 8 minutes. Reduce heat to 325°.

- Combine sugar and cornmeal in bowl. Stir in eggs, mix well and gradually stir in half-and-half cream, butter and vanilla. Add pecans.

- Sprinkle chocolate chips over piecrust and carefully pour filling over chocolate chips.

- Cover crust edges with strips of foil to prevent excessive browning.

- Bake for 40 to 45 minutes or until center appears set. Cool; refrigerate pie. Serves 6 to 8. *Hominy, Oklahoma*

Chocolate-Coconut Pie

1½ cups flaked coconut
1½ cups chopped pecans
1 (12 ounce) package chocolate chips
1 (6 ounce) ready graham cracker piecrust
1 (14 ounce) can sweetened condensed milk

- Preheat oven to 350°.

- Combine coconut, pecans and chocolate chips in bowl. Sprinkle mixture over piecrust.

- Pour sweetened condensed milk evenly over coconut mixture.

- Bake for 25 to 30 minutes. Cool before serving. Serves 6 to 8. *Cheraw, South Carolina*

Chocolate-Caramel Pie

½ cup chopped pecans
1 (6 ounce) ready chocolate-crumb piecrust
18 caramels
¼ cup evaporated milk
1 (8 ounce) package semi-sweet chocolate chips
1 (8 ounce) carton whipping cream
3 tablespoons butter

- Sprinkle pecans over piecrust. Melt caramels and evaporated milk in heavy saucepan over low heat and stir often until mixture is smooth. Pour caramel mixture over pecans.

- Heat chocolate chips, cream and butter in heavy saucepan and stir until mixture is smooth. Pour over caramel layer and refrigerate for at least 4 hours before serving. Serves 6 to 8. *Peacedale, Rhode Island*

Five-Citrus Cream Pie

1 (4 ounce) can sweetened condensed milk
1 (6 ounce) can frozen five-citrus concentrate, partially thawed
1 (8 ounce) carton frozen whipped topping, thawed
1 (6 ounce) ready graham cracker piecrust

- Stir sweetened condensed milk and five-citrus concentrate in bowl until they blend well.

- Fold in whipped topping.

- Spoon mixture into piecrust. Refrigerate for 6 to 8 hours. Serves 6 to 8. *Highpoint, Florida*

Grasshopper Pie

22 large marshmallows
⅓ cup creme de menthe liqueur
1 (12 ounce) carton whipping cream, whipped
1 (6 ounce) ready chocolate piecrust

- Melt marshmallows with creme de menthe in large saucepan over low heat and cool.

- Fold whipped cream into marshmallow mixture.

- Pour filling into piecrust and freeze until ready to serve. Serves 6. *Ferry Farms, Virginia*

Holiday Pie

1 (8 ounce) package cream cheese, softened
1 (14 ounce) can sweetened condensed milk
1 (3.4 ounce) box instant vanilla pudding mix
1½ cups whipped topping, thawed
1 (6 ounce) ready graham cracker piecrust
Holiday candies

- Beat cream cheese in bowl until smooth. Gradually add sweetened condensed milk and beat until smooth. Add ¾ cup water and pudding mix and beat until smooth. Fold in whipped topping.

- Pour into piecrust. Top with crumbled holiday candies. Refrigerate. Serves 6 to 8. *Walpole, Massachusetts*

Limeade Pie

1 (6 ounce) can frozen limeade concentrate, thawed
1 (16 ounce) carton low-fat frozen yogurt, softened
1 (8 ounce) carton whipped topping, thawed
1 (6 ounce) ready graham cracker piecrust

- Combine limeade concentrate and yogurt in large bowl and mix well. Fold in whipped topping. Pour into piecrust. Freeze for at least 4 hours or overnight. Serves 6 to 8. *High Ridge, Missouri*

Luscious Strawberry Pie

1 (24 ounce) package frozen, sweetened strawberries, thawed
¼ cup cornstarch
1 (6 ounce) ready shortbread piecrust
1½ cups whipping cream
⅓ cup powdered sugar

- Combine strawberries, ¼ cup water and cornstarch in saucepan. Stir constantly over medium heat until mixture boils. Continue cooking and stir until mixture is thick. Remove from heat, cool for 20 minutes and spoon into piecrust. Refrigerate for 2 to 4 hours.

- Beat cream and powdered sugar in bowl until stiff peaks form. Spread over strawberry mixture. Refrigerate. Serves 6 to 8.
  Macon, Mississippi

Magic Cherry Pie

2 (6 ounce) cartons cherry yogurt
1 (3 ounce) package cherry gelatin
1 (8 ounce) carton whipped topping, thawed
1 (6 ounce) ready shortbread piecrust

- Combine yogurt and gelatin in bowl and mix well.

- Fold in whipped topping and spoon into piecrust.

- Freeze. Take out of freezer 20 minutes before slicing. Serves 6 to 8.
  Grandview, Washington

TIP: You could also place a dab of cherry pie filling on top of pie to make it even better.

Melt-in-Your-Mouth Cranberry Pie

2 cups fresh or frozen cranberries
1½ cups sugar, divided
½ cup chopped walnuts or pecans
2 eggs
1 cup flour
¼ cup shortening, melted
½ cup (1 stick) butter, melted

- Preheat oven to 325°.

- Spread cranberries in sprayed 10-inch deep-dish pie pan. Sprinkle with ½ cup sugar and nuts.

- Beat eggs well in bowl, add remaining sugar gradually and beat thoroughly. Add flour, shortening and butter to sugar mixture and mix well.

- Pour over top of cranberries and bake for 1 hour or until crust is golden brown. Serves 8. *Dunbar, West Virginia*

Million Dollar Pie

24 round, buttery crackers, crumbled
1 cup chopped pecans
4 egg whites (absolutely no yolks at all)
1 cup sugar

- Preheat oven to 350°.

- Mix cracker crumbs with pecans in bowl.

- In separate bowl, beat egg whites until stiff and slowly add sugar while still mixing.

- Gently fold crumbs and pecan mixture into egg whites.

- Pour into pie pan and bake for 20 minutes. Refrigerate. Top with a dip of chocolate ice cream, if desired. Serves 6 to 8.
  Darlington, Wisconsin

Peach-Apricot Pie

1 (15 ounce) can sliced peaches, drained
1 (15 ounce) can apricots, drained
1 cup sugar
3 tablespoons flour
2 (9 inch) frozen piecrusts, thawed
2 tablespoons butter

- Preheat oven to 400°.

- Combine peaches, apricots, sugar and flour in bowl and mix well. Place fruit in 1 piecrust. Place second piecrust over fruit and pinch edges of crusts together.

- Make several slits in top piecrust and dot with chunks of butter. Bake for 45 minutes or until top crust is light brown. Serves 6 to 8.
  Jackson, Wyoming

Mock Cherry Pie 🍁

Early settlers braved the cold winters in Manitoba, Canada, and made a fortune from beaver pelts. They moved the pelts by canoes over tortuous inland water routes to trading posts to trade for dried beans, peas, salt pork, wild rice and buffalo meat. By 1885, there was an influx of settlers from all over the world wanting farmlands in the great open prairies. Crops and gardens were planted and berries of all kinds were plentiful; eventually they secured a new food supply.

1 (15 ounce) package frozen piecrust (2 crusts), thawed
2 cups fresh cranberries
1 cup golden raisins
1 cup sugar
2 tablespoons flour
1 teaspoon vanilla
2 tablespoons butter
1 - 2 tablespoons milk
Extra sugar for topping
1 (8 ounce) carton whipping cream, whipped

- Preheat oven to 375°.

- Place 1 piecrust in 9-inch pie pan. Combine cranberries, raisins, sugar and flour in large saucepan. Stir in 1 cup water and bring to a boil. Reduce heat to medium and cook stirring constantly for about 5 to 6 minutes or until mixture thickens. Stir in vanilla and butter and mix well.

- Pour mixture into pie pan. Place second piecrust over top of cranberry mixture and crimp edges together. Brush top lightly with milk and sprinkle extra sugar on top.

- Bake for 40 to 45 minutes or until top is light brown. Serve warm or chilled and topped with whipped cream. Serves 6. *Steinbach, Manitoba, Canada*

TIP: *Cranberries were so plentiful, housewives learned many new ways of cooking their delicious and best-loved pies – like the Mock Cherry!*

Pineapple-Coconut Pie

1½ cups sugar
3 tablespoons flour
3 eggs, well beaten
2 tablespoons lemon juice
1 teaspoon vanilla
1 cup flaked coconut
1 (8 ounce) can crushed pineapple, drained
⅓ cup (⅔ stick) butter, melted
1 (9 inch) frozen piecrust, thawed

• Preheat oven to 350°.

• Combine sugar and flour in bowl, stir in eggs, lemon juice and vanilla and mix well. Stir in coconut, pineapple and butter and pour into piecrust.

• Cover crust edges with strips of foil to prevent excessive browning. Bake for 1 hour or until pie is firm in middle. Cool before serving. Serves 6 to 8. *Lindon, Utah*

Pineapple-Fluff Pie

1 (20 ounce) can crushed pineapple with juice
1 (3.4 ounce) package instant lemon pudding mix
1 (8 ounce) carton whipped topping, thawed
1 (6 ounce) ready graham cracker piecrust

• Combine pineapple and pudding mix in bowl and beat until it thickens. Fold in whipped topping and spoon into piecrust.

• Refrigerate for several hours before serving. Serves 6 to 8. *Springfield, Vermont*

Pink Lemonade Pie

1 (6 ounce) can frozen pink lemonade concentrate, thawed
1 (14 ounce) can sweetened condensed milk
1 (12 ounce) carton whipped topping, thawed
1 (6 ounce) ready graham cracker piecrust

• Combine lemonade concentrate and sweetened condensed milk in large bowl and mix well.

• Fold in whipped topping and pour into piecrust. Refrigerate for several hours. Serves 6 to 8. *Great Falls, Virginia*

Strawberry Pie

1 (6 ounce) box strawberry gelatin
2 (10 ounce) packages frozen strawberries, thawed, divided
1 (8 ounce) carton whipped topping, thawed
1 (6 ounce) ready graham cracker piecrust

- Combine gelatin and ¾ cup boiling water in bowl and mix well until gelatin dissolves. Cool gelatin in refrigerator until it begins to thicken. (Watch closely.)

- Drain 1 package strawberries and stir into gelatin. Fold in whipped topping and remaining strawberries. Spoon into piecrust.

- Refrigerate for several hours before serving. Serves 6 to 8. *Maltby, Washington*

Sunny Lime Pie

2 (6 ounce) cartons key lime pie yogurt
1 (3 ounce) package lime gelatin
1 (8 ounce) carton whipped topping, thawed
1 (6 ounce) ready graham cracker piecrust

- Combine yogurt and gelatin in bowl and mix well.

- Fold in whipped topping, spread in piecrust and freeze.

- Take out of freezer 20 minutes before slicing. Serves 6 to 8. *Fort Meade, Florida*

Thanksgiving Pie

1 (15 ounce) can pumpkin
1 cup sugar
2 eggs, beaten
1½ teaspoons pumpkin pie spice
1 (12 ounce) can evaporated milk
1 (9 inch) piecrust

- Preheat oven to 425°.

- Combine pumpkin, sugar, eggs, pumpkin pie spice, evaporated milk and a pinch of salt in bowl and mix well. Pour into piecrust and bake for 15 minutes.

- Lower oven heat to 325° and continue baking for an additional 50 minutes or until knife inserted in center comes out clean. Serves 6 to 8. *Lincoln, Maine*

Deep Dish Apple Pie 🍁

2 (16 ounce) packages frozen sliced apples, thawed
1 (16 ounce) box light brown sugar
⅓ cup flour
2 teaspoons ground cinnamon
½ teaspoon ground nutmeg
A pinch of ground cloves
¼ cup (½ stick) butter, melted
Refrigerated piecrust large enough to cover 10-inch deep-dish
    pie pan

• Preheat oven to 375°.

• Place apples in the bottom of 10-inch deep-dish pie pan. Combine
  brown sugar, flour and spices in bowl; sprinkle over apples and drizzle
  with melted butter.

• Roll pastry to round size and cover apples. Seal edges and cut several
  slits for vents.

• Bake for 50 to 55 minutes or until crust is light brown. Serves 8 to 10.
  Medicine Hat, Alberta, Canada

Creamy Pumpkin Pie

1 (6 serving) instant vanilla pudding mix
½ cup milk
½ cup sugar
1 teaspoon pumpkin pie spice
1 cup canned pumpkin
1 (8 ounce) carton whipped topping, thawed
1 (6 ounce) ready graham cracker piecrust

• Combine instant pudding, milk, sugar and pumpkin pie spice in large
  bowl; beat or whisk for 1 minute (mixture will be very thick). Stir in
  pumpkin, fold in whipped topping and blend well.

• Spoon into piecrust and spread evenly over crust. Refrigerate
  for at least 3 hours before slicing to serve. Serves 6 to 8.
  Marksville, Louisiana

*TIP: Make 1 teaspoon pumpkin pie spice by combining ½ teaspoon
    ground cinnamon, ¼ teaspoon ground ginger, ⅛ teaspoon ground
    allspice and ⅛ teaspoon ground nutmeg.*

Easy Pumpkin Pie

2 eggs
1 (30 ounce) can pumpkin pie mix
1 (5 ounce) can evaporated milk
1 (9 inch) deep-dish piecrust

- Preheat oven to 400°.

- Beat eggs lightly in large bowl. Stir in pumpkin pie mix and evaporated milk. Pour into piecrust.

- Cover crust edges with strips of foil to prevent excessive browning.

- Bake for 15 minutes. Reduce temperature to 325° and bake for 40 more minutes or until knife inserted in center comes out clean. Cool. Serves 6 to 8. *Elkins, West Virginia*

Beloved Traditional Pie ❁

1 (15 ounce) package frozen piecrusts (2 crusts), thawed
3 cups packed light brown sugar, divided
1 cup milk, divided
½ cup (1 stick) butter, sliced
1 (8 ounce) carton whipping cream, whipped

- Preheat at 400°.

- Place piecrusts in 2 (9 inch) pie pans. Sprinkle half brown sugar in each piecrust; do not pack. Slowly pour half milk into each pie and dot with butter slices.

- Bake for 10 minutes; reduce heat to 375° and bake for an additional 20 minutes or until crust is baked. Remove from oven and cool. Filling thickens upon cooling. Place a dollop of whipped cream on each piece of pie. Serves 12. *Beauharnois, Quebec, Canada*

Holiday Fruit Cobbler

Crust:

1¾ cups biscuit mix
¾ cup sugar
1 teaspoon ground cinnamon
¼ cup (½ stick) butter, softened
1 cup evaporated milk

Fruit:

1 (20 ounce) can apple pie filling
1 cup Craisins®
½ cup chopped pecans

- Preheat oven to 350°.

- Combine biscuit mix, sugar and cinnamon in bowl. Cut butter into mixture until crumbly. Stir in evaporated milk and mix well.

- Pour into sprayed, floured 9 x 13-inch baking pan.

- Combine apple pie filling and Craisins® in bowl, mix well and spread evenly over batter.

- Sprinkle pecans over fruit and pour ¾ cup hot water over top. Bake for 45 minutes. Serves 10 to 12. *New Milford, Connecticut*

Blueberry Bounce

1½ cups quick-cooking oats
2 cups packed brown sugar
1 (20 ounce) can blueberry pie filling
1 (18 ounce) box yellow cake mix
¾ cup chopped pecans
½ cup (1 stick) butter, melted

- Preheat oven to 350°.

- Combine oats and brown sugar in medium bowl and sprinkle half in sprayed 9 x 13-inch glass baking dish.

- Spoon blueberry pie filling over oat-sugar mixture and spread evenly. Crumble cake mix over filling and spread evenly.

- Combine pecans with remaining oat mixture and sprinkle over cake mix.

- Drizzle butter evenly over top and bake for 35 to 40 minutes or until brown sugar looks like caramel. Serves 20. *Madison, Maine*

Express Fruit Cobbler

*Use any kind of fruit pie filling to create this
fast, last-minute cobbler for a great dessert.*

2 (20 ounce) cans blueberry pie filling
½ cup (1 stick) butter, softened
1 (18 ounce) box white cake mix
1 egg

- Preheat oven to 350°.

- Spread pie filling to cover bottom of 9 x 13-inch baking pan.

- Cream butter in large bowl to smooth texture. Add dry cake mix and egg and blend well. (Mixture will be very stiff.)

- Spoon mixture over pie filling.

- Bake for 40 minutes or until golden brown. Serves 10 to 12. *Grand Bay, Alabama*

Blueberry Cobbler 🍁

1 cup sugar
½ cup shortening
1 egg, beaten
2 cups flour
½ teaspoon baking powder
½ cup milk
1 (16 ounce) package frozen blueberries, thawed

- Preheat oven to 350°.

- Combine sugar and shortening in bowl and beat until creamy. Stir in egg; add flour, baking powder and ½ teaspoon salt alternately with milk and mix well. Fold in blueberries and spoon into sprayed 7 x 11-inch baking pan.

Topping:

⅔ cup sugar
½ cup flour
½ teaspoon ground cinnamon
¼ cup (½ stick) butter, softened

- Combine sugar, flour and cinnamon in bowl. Mix in butter with fork until mixture is crumbly. Sprinkle over blueberry mixture and bake for 50 minutes. Serves 8. New Glasgow, *Nova Scotia, Canada*

Cherry Cobbler

2 (20 ounce) cans cherry pie filling
1 (18 ounce) box white cake mix
¾ cup (1½ sticks) butter, melted
1 (4 ounce) package almonds, slivered
Whipped topping, thawed

- Preheat oven to 350°.

- Spread pie filling in sprayed 9 x 13-inch baking pan.

- Sprinkle cake mix over cherries. Drizzle with melted butter over top. Sprinkle almonds over top.

- Bake for 45 minutes. Top with whipped topping to serve. Serves 10 to 12. *Parker, Arizona*

Apple Crumble

1 (20 ounce) can apple pie filling
½ cup packed brown sugar
½ teaspoon ground cinnamon
½ teaspoon ground ginger

- Preheat oven to 350°.

- Combine apple pie filling, brown sugar, cinnamon and ginger in bowl. Spoon into sprayed 9-inch square baking dish.

Topping:

1 cup flour
¾ cup packed brown sugar
¼ teaspoon ground cinnamon
½ cup (1 stick) butter
⅓ cup slivered almonds

- Combine flour, brown sugar and cinnamon in bowl.

- Cut in butter until mixture resembles coarse crumbs. Add almonds and sprinkle over apple mixture.

- Bake for 35 to 40 minutes or until filling is bubbly and topping is golden brown. Serves 6 to 8. *Earle, Arkansas*

Peach Crunch

2 (20 ounce) cans peach pie filling
1 (18 ounce) box white cake mix
1 cup slivered almonds
½ cup (1 stick) butter

- Preheat oven to 350°.

- Spread pie filling evenly in sprayed, floured 9 x 13-inch baking pan.

- Sprinkle cake mix evenly over pie filling and smooth over top. Sprinkle almonds evenly over cake mix.

- Slice butter into ⅛-inch slices and place over entire surface.

- Bake for 40 to 45 minutes or until top is brown. Serves 10 to 12. *Garden Acres, California*

Fruit Crispy

6 cups peeled, sliced apples
3 tablespoons lemon juice
½ cup flour
⅓ cup old-fashioned oats
⅓ cup packed brown sugar
1 teaspoon ground cinnamon
¼ cup (½ stick) butter
⅓ cup chopped pecans

- Preheat oven to 425°.

- Toss apple slices with lemon juice in bowl and place in sprayed 7 x 11-inch baking dish.

- Combine flour, oats, brown sugar, cinnamon and a pinch of salt in bowl.

- Cut butter in with pastry blender and stir in pecans.

- Spoon mixture over apples and bake for 25 to 30 minutes until fruit bubbles and topping begins to brown. Serves 4 to 6.
  Johnstown, Colorado

★ ★ ★

Cookies
& Bars

Cookies, bars, brownies and squares are
super for quick treats anytime – platefuls
are great for entertaining! Choose from 46!

1001
Community
Recipes

Cookies & Bars Contents

Butter Cookie Special

1 (18 ounce) box butter cake mix
1 (3.4 ounce) package butterscotch instant pudding mix
1 cup oil
1 egg, beaten
1¼ cups chopped pecans

- Preheat oven to 350°.

- Combine cake mix, pudding mix, oil and egg in bowl and mix with spoon. Beat thoroughly.

- Stir in pecans. Drop teaspoonfuls of cookie dough onto cookie sheet about 2 inches apart.

- Bake for about 8 minutes. Do not overcook. Yields 4 dozen cookies. East *Rutherford, New Jersey*

Butter Cookies

1 pound butter (4 sticks)
¾ cup packed brown sugar
¾ cup sugar
4½ cups flour

- Preheat oven to 350°.

- Cream butter, brown sugar and sugar in bowl; slowly add flour and mix well. (Batter will be very thick.)

- Roll into small balls and place onto cookie sheet.

- Bake for about 15 minutes until only slightly brown. Do not over-bake. Yields 6 dozen cookies. *Hurricane, West Virginia*

Butterscotch Cookies

1 (12 ounce) and 1 (6 ounce) package butterscotch chips
2¼ cups chow mein noodles
½ cup chopped walnuts
¼ cup flaked coconut

- Melt butterscotch chips in double boiler. Add noodles, walnuts and coconut.

- Drop tablespoonfuls of mixture onto wax paper. Yields 3 dozen cookies. *Girard, Indiana*

Butterfinger Cookies

½ cup (1 stick) butter, softened
¾ cup sugar
¾ cup packed brown sugar
2 egg whites
1½ teaspoons vanilla
1 cup flour
½ teaspoon baking soda
1¼ cups crunchy peanut butter
6 mini Butterfinger® candy bars

- Preheat oven to 350°.

- Combine butter, sugar and brown sugar in large bowl. Add egg whites and mix well.

- Stir in vanilla, flour, baking soda, pinch of salt and peanut butter and mix gently. Chop candy bars into coarse chunks and stir into cookie mixture.

- Drop tablespoonfuls of dough onto sprayed cookie sheet and bake for 16 minutes or until edges are golden brown. (Watch closely because you may need to rotate cookie sheet for cookies to bake evenly.) Yields 3 dozen cookies. *Northford, Connecticut*

Chinese Cookies

1 (6 ounce) package chocolate chips
1 (6 ounce) package butterscotch chips
1 cup salted peanuts
1 (3 ounce) can chow mein noodles

- Melt chocolate and butterscotch chips in large saucepan. Add peanuts and noodles and mix well.

- Drop teaspoonfuls of mixture onto wax paper. Refrigerate just to harden. Yields 2 dozen cookies. *Forestville, California*

Christmas Cookies

1 cup (2 sticks) butter, softened
¾ cup sugar
1 cup packed brown sugar
1 teaspoon vanilla
2 eggs
2½ cups flour
1 teaspoon baking soda
1 (12 ounce) package white chocolate chips
1 cup chopped pecans
1 (3.5 ounce) can flaked coconut
20 red candied cherries, chopped
20 green candied cherries, chopped

- Preheat oven to 350°.

- Cream butter, sugar, brown sugar, vanilla and eggs in bowl and beat well.

- Add flour, baking soda and ½ teaspoon salt and mix well. Stir in chocolate chips, pecans, coconut and cherries.

- Drop teaspoonfuls of dough onto cookie sheet. (Dough will be very stiff.)

- Bake for 8 to 10 minutes. Cool before storing. Yields 5 dozen cookies.
  Pittsfield, Maine

Double Chocolate Cookies

6 egg whites
3 cups powdered sugar
¼ cup cocoa
3½ cups finely chopped pecans

- Preheat oven to 325°.

- Beat egg whites in bowl until light and frothy. Fold powdered sugar and cocoa into egg whites and beat lightly. Fold in pecans.

- Drop teaspoonfuls of mixture onto lightly sprayed, floured cookie sheet. Bake for about 20 minutes. Do not over-bake and cool completely before removing from cookie sheet. Yields 3 dozen cookies.
  Fort Wright, Kentucky

Decadent Oatmeal Cookies

1 cup (2 sticks) butter, softened
1 cup packed brown sugar
⅔ cup sugar
1½ teaspoons baking soda
2 eggs
1 teaspoon vanilla
2¼ cups flour
2 cups old-fashioned oats
1 cup coarsely chopped cashews
1 cup white chocolate chips
⅔ cup butterscotch chips

- Preheat oven to 375°.

- Combine and beat butter, brown sugar, sugar, baking soda and ½ teaspoon salt in bowl. Beat in eggs and vanilla until they blend well.

- Beat in as much flour as possible. Stir in with spoon any remaining flour, oats, cashews, white chocolate chips and butterscotch chips.

- Drop rounded teaspoonfuls of dough 2 inches apart onto cookie sheet.

- Bake for 8 to 10 minutes or until edges are golden. Cool on wire rack. Yields 5 dozen cookies. *Louisburg, Kansas*

Peanut Butter Cookies

1 cup sugar
¾ cup light corn syrup
1 (16 ounce) jar crunchy peanut butter
4½ cups chow mein noodles

- Bring sugar and corn syrup in saucepan over medium heat to a boil and stir in peanut butter.

- Remove from heat and stir in noodles.

- Drop spoonfuls of mixture onto wax paper and cool. Yields 3 dozen cookies. *Hartsville, South Carolina*

Seven-Layer Cookies

½ cup (1 stick) butter
1 cup crushed graham crackers
1 (6 ounce) package semi-sweet chocolate chips
1 (6 ounce) package butterscotch chips
1 (3.5 ounce) can flaked coconut
1 (14 ounce) can sweetened condensed milk
1 cup chopped pecans

- Preheat oven to 350°.

- Melt butter in 9 x 13-inch baking pan. Sprinkle remaining ingredients in order listed on top of butter.

- Do not stir or mix. Bake for 30 minutes and cool before cutting. Yields 15 squares. *Iowa Falls, Iowa*

Speedy Chocolate Cookies

1½ cups sugar
½ cup (1 stick) butter
½ cup milk
½ cup cocoa
1 teaspoon vanilla
3½ cups old-fashioned oats
½ cup flaked coconut
¾ cup chopped pecans

- Combine sugar, butter, milk and cocoa in saucepan over medium heat. Cook, stirring constantly, until mixture begins to boil. Remove from heat and stir in vanilla, oats, coconut and pecans.

- Work quickly and drop tablespoonfuls of mixture onto sprayed wax paper.

- Let stand at room temperature to cool before storing in airtight containers. Yields 3 dozen cookies. *Etna, Pennsylvania*

Vanishing Butter Cookies

1 (18 ounce) box butter cake mix
1 (3.4 ounce) package butterscotch instant pudding mix
1 cup oil
1 egg, beaten
1¼ cups chopped pecans

- Preheat oven to 350°.

- Mix cake and pudding mixes in bowl with spoon and stir in oil. Add egg, mix thoroughly and stir in pecans.

- Place teaspoonfuls of dough onto cookie sheet about 2 inches apart.

- Bake for 8 or 9 minutes. Do not overcook. Yields 4 dozen cookies.
  Irvine, Kentucky

Toffee Bars

1½ cups (3 sticks) butter, softened
2 cups packed light brown sugar
2 teaspoons vanilla
3 cups flour
1 (8 ounce) package chocolate chips
¾ cup chopped chocolate-covered English toffee candy

- Preheat oven to 350°.

- Combine butter, brown sugar and vanilla in bowl and beat on medium speed for 3 minutes. Add flour, mix until they blend completely and stir in chocolate chips.

- Place dough on sprayed 9 x 13-inch baking pan and bake for 30 minutes or until light brown.

- While bars are still hot, scatter chopped candy over top. Cool and cut into bars. Yields 15 bars. *Gretna, Nebraska*

Pineapple-Coconut Bars

1 (18 ounce) roll refrigerated sugar cookie dough
1 cup chopped pecans
½ cup butterscotch chips
½ cup coarsely chopped candied pineapple
½ cup Craisins®
½ cup flaked coconut

- Preheat oven to 325°.

- Stir cookie dough in bowl with wooden spoon until softened. Stir in pecans, butterscotch chips, pineapple and Craisins® and pat dough evenly in sprayed 9 x 13-inch baking pan. Sprinkle coconut over top and press lightly.

- Bake for 20 minutes or until toothpick inserted in center comes out clean. Cool completely and cut into bars. Yields 24 bars. *Lockwood, Montana*

Pineapple-Crumb Bars

1 (18 ounce) box yellow cake mix
½ cup (1 stick) butter, softened, divided
1½ cups old-fashioned oats, divided
1 large egg
1 (20 ounce) can pineapple pie filling
⅓ cup packed brown sugar

- Preheat oven to 350°.

- Beat cake mix, 5 tablespoons butter and 1 cup oats in bowl. Mix until crumbly and set aside 1 cup for topping.

- Combine egg with remaining mixture and stir well. Press into sprayed, floured 9 x 13-inch baking pan. Spread pineapple pie filling evenly over crust.

- In same bowl, combine remaining crumb mixture, remaining oats, remaining butter and brown sugar and blend well. Sprinkle over pineapple filling and bake for 35 minutes or until light brown on top. Yields 15 bars. *Gray Summit, Missouri*

Rainbow Bars

2 large eggs, beaten
1¼ cups sugar
¾ cup (1½ sticks) butter
1 teaspoon vanilla
2½ cups miniature colored marshmallows
32 graham crackers, crushed
½ cup flaked coconut
½ cup M&M's®

- Combine eggs, sugar and butter in heavy saucepan over medium heat and cook, stirring constantly, until mixture thickens. Remove from heat and cool.

- Stir in vanilla, marshmallows, crackers, coconut and M&M's®. Press into sprayed 9 x 13-inch baking pan.

- When cool, cut into bars and refrigerate. Yields 15 bars. *Newport, New Hampshire*

Peanut Butter-Toffee Bars

1 (18 ounce) box yellow cake mix
1 cup crunchy peanut butter
2 eggs
1 (8 ounce) package milk chocolate-toffee bits
½ cup chopped peanuts
1 (12 ounce) package milk chocolate chips

- Preheat oven to 350°.

- Combine cake mix, peanut butter, ½ cup water and eggs in large bowl and mix with spoon.

- Stir in toffee bits and peanuts and spread evenly in sprayed, floured 10 x 15-inch baking pan.

- Bake for 25 minutes; then immediately sprinkle chocolate chips over top. Let stand for about 5 minutes or until chips melt. With back of spoon spread chocolate evenly.

- Cool completely before cutting into bars. Yields 24 bars. *Oakdale, Louisiana*

Rocky Road Bars

1 (12 ounce) package semi-sweet chocolate chips
1 (14 ounce) can sweetened condensed milk
2 tablespoons butter
2 cups dry-roasted peanuts
1 (10 ounce) package miniature marshmallows

- Place chocolate chips, sweetened condensed milk and butter in double boiler, heat until chocolate and butter melt and stir constantly.

- Remove from heat and stir in peanuts and marshmallows.

- Spread mixture quickly on wax paper-lined 9 x 13-inch pan.

- Refrigerate for at least 2 hours before cutting into bars. Yields 15 bars. *Garwood, New Jersey*

Peanut Brittle Bars

2¼ cups flour
⅔ cup packed brown sugar
¾ cup (1½ sticks) butter, softened
1 (16 ounce) jar cocktail peanuts
1 (6 ounce) package milk chocolate chips
1 (12 ounce) jar caramel ice cream topping
3 tablespoons flour

- Preheat oven to 350°.

- Line 10 x 15-inch baking pan with foil. Spray foil and set aside.

- Combine flour and brown sugar in bowl. Use pastry blender to cut in butter until mixture is crumbly. Press mixture onto bottom of pan and bake for 12 minutes.

- Sprinkle peanuts and milk chocolate chips over warm crust. Stir caramel topping and 3 tablespoons flour in small bowl and drizzle over top.

- Return to oven for 13 to 15 minutes more or until caramel bubbles. Cool. Carefully lift foil and gently peel foil away from edges. Cut into bars. Yields 15 bars. *Patterson, Louisiana*

Honey-Nut Bars

⅓ cup (⅔ stick) butter
¼ cup cocoa
1 (10 ounce) package miniature marshmallows
6 cups honey-nut clusters cereal

- Melt butter in large saucepan and stir in cocoa and marshmallows. Cook over low heat, stirring constantly until marshmallows melt and mixture is smooth.

- Remove from heat and stir in honey-nut clusters.

- Pour into sprayed 7 x 11-inch pan. With spatula, smooth mixture in pan. Cool completely and cut into bars. Yields 12 bars. *Golden Beach, Maryland*

Lemon Bars

You just can't have a bake sale without several pans of lemon bars. Everyone loves lemon bars.

1 cup (2 sticks) butter
2 cups flour
½ cup powdered sugar

- Preheat oven to 350°.

- Melt butter in 9 x 13-inch baking pan in oven. Add flour and powdered sugar to mixture, stir and mix well.

- Press down evenly and firmly and bake for 15 minutes.

Topping:

2 cups sugar
6 tablespoons flour
6 tablespoons lemon juice
½ teaspoon finely grated lemon peel
4 eggs, lightly beaten
Powdered sugar

- Combine sugar and flour in bowl. Add lemon juice, lemon peel and eggs and mix. Pour over crust.

- Bake for 20 minutes more. Cool and dust with powdered sugar. To serve, cut into bars. Yields 18 bars. *Jasonville, Indiana*

Gooey Good Turtle Bars

½ cup (1 stick) butter, melted
2 cups vanilla wafer crumbs
1 (12 ounce) semi-sweet chocolate chips
1 cup pecan pieces
1 (12 ounce) jar caramel ice cream topping

- Preheat oven to 350°.

- Combine butter and wafer crumbs in 9 x 13-inch baking pan and press into bottom of pan. Sprinkle with chocolate chips and pecans.

- Remove lid from caramel topping, microwave on HIGH for 30 seconds or until hot and drizzle over pecans.

- Bake for about 15 minutes or until chocolate chips melt.

- Cool in pan and refrigerate for at least 30 minutes before cutting into bars. Yields 15 bars. *Greenbrier, Arkansas*

TIP: Watch bars closely so chips melt, but crumbs do not burn.

Double Delicious Bars

½ cup (1 stick) butter
1½ cups graham cracker crumbs
1 (14 ounce) can sweetened condensed milk
1 (12 ounce) package semi-sweet chocolate chips
1 cup peanut butter chips

- Preheat oven to 325°.

- Melt butter in 9 x 13-inch baking pan in oven. Sprinkle crumbs evenly over butter and pour sweetened condensed milk evenly over crumbs.

- Top with chocolate chips and peanut butter chips and press down firmly. Bake for 25 to 30 minutes or until light brown. Cool and cut into bars. Yields 15 bars. *Lexington, Virginia*

Coconut-Brownie Bars

2 (18 ounce) packages refrigerated chocolate chip cookie dough
2 eggs, slightly beaten
⅓ cup oil
1 (18 ounce) box brownie mix
1 cup chopped walnuts
1 cup flaked coconut
1 (16 ounce) can coconut-pecan frosting

- Preheat oven to 350°.

- Press cookie dough into sprayed 10 x 15-inch jellyroll pan. Combine eggs, oil, brownie mix and ¼ cup water in large bowl and mix until they blend well. Spoon brownie mixture over cookie dough. Sprinkle with walnuts and coconut.

- Bake for 55 minutes. Cool and place thin layer of frosting over top. Yields 24 bars. *Rogersville, Tennessee*

Creamy-Crunchy Chocolate Bars

¾ cup whipping cream
1 (12 ounce) package milk chocolate chips
4 cups miniature marshmallows
1 (7.5 ounce) package chocolate-covered graham crackers
¾ cup chopped pecans
2 (1.5 ounce) bars milk chocolate bars

- Place whipping cream in large saucepan and heat over medium-low heat. Add chocolate chips and stir until chips melt. Remove from heat, add marshmallows and stir to coat.

- Break up graham crackers into bite-size pieces (not crushed), add pecans and gently stir into cream-marshmallow mixture. Spread into 9-inch foil-lined square pan. Place a bite-size piece of chocolate, vertically, on top of each bar.

- Refrigerate for at least 3 hours or until firm. Cut into bars. Yields 12 bars. *Marble Falls, Texas*

Date Bars 🍁

3 cups pitted, chopped dates
2 teaspoons vanilla
2¼ cups flour
2½ teaspoons baking powder
1 (16 ounce) box brown sugar
3¾ cups old-fashioned oats
1½ cups (3 sticks) butter, softened
1 cup chopped walnuts, optional

- Preheat oven to 350°.

- Cover dates with 3 cups water in saucepan and cook until thick and mushy, stirring often. Add a little more water if dates become too dry. Remove from heat and add vanilla. Set aside.

- Combine flour, baking powder, brown sugar, oats and ½ teaspoon salt in bowl. Mix butter into flour mixture with fork until mixture resembles coarse crumbs. Stir in walnuts, if adding.

- Spoon half flour mixture into sprayed 9 x 13-inch baking pan and pat down with back of large spoon. Spread date filling over top; then sprinkle remaining crumb mixture over date filling.

- Bake for 40 minutes or until light brown. Cool and cut into bars to serve. Yields 15 bars. *Prince Albert, Saskatchewan, Canada*

TIP: These bars can be served chilled or warm with a dollop of vanilla ice cream.

Date-Pecan Bars

Filling:

2 (8 ounce) boxes pitted dates, chopped
1½ cups orange juice
¼ cup sugar
¼ teaspoon ground cinnamon

Crust and Topping:

1½ cups flour
1½ cups oats
¾ cup packed brown sugar
1½ cups finely chopped pecans
1¼ cups (2½ sticks) cold butter, cut up

- Preheat oven to 350°.

- Combine dates, orange juice, sugar and cinnamon in saucepan and bring to boiling; reduce heat and simmer, stirring several times, for 15 minutes until mixture thickens.

- Place flour, oats, brown sugar and pecans in bowl; cut in butter until mixture is crumbly. Set aside 2½ cups mixture.

- Press remaining crumbs over bottom of sprayed 9 x 13-inch baking pan.

- Spoon filling over crust and spread up to ¼ inch from edge. Sprinkle set aside crust mixture over top and bake for 35 minutes. Cool and cut into bars. Yields 15 bars. *Oxford, Michigan*

Chocolate-Cherry Bars

1 (18 ounce) box devils food cake mix
1 (20 ounce) can cherry pie filling
2 eggs
1 cup milk chocolate chips

- Preheat oven to 350°.

- Mix all ingredients in large bowl with spoon and blend well. Pour batter into sprayed, floured 9 x 13-inch baking dish.

- Bake for 25 to 30 minutes or until toothpick inserted in center comes out clean. Cool and frost.

Frosting:

3 (1 ounce) squares semi-sweet chocolate, melted
1 (3 ounce) package cream cheese, softened
½ teaspoon vanilla
1½ cups powdered sugar

- Beat chocolate, cream cheese and vanilla in medium bowl until smooth. Gradually beat in powdered sugar.

- Spread over chocolate-cherry bars. Yields 15 bars. *Magee, Mississippi*

Chocolate Ribbon Bars

½ cup (1 stick) butter, melted
1 (18 ounce) box yellow cake mix
1 (5 ounce) can evaporated milk
1 cup chopped pecans
1 cup caramel ice cream topping
1½ cups chocolate chips

- Preheat oven to 350°.

- Combine butter, cake mix and evaporated milk in bowl and stir in pecans. Spoon half batter into sprayed, floured 9 x 13-inch baking pan and bake for about 12 minutes.

- Remove pan from oven, drizzle caramel topping over cake mixture and sprinkle chocolate chips evenly over batter.

- Drop spoonfuls of remaining batter on top and return to oven for an additional 25 minutes or until slightly golden. Yields 15 bars.
  Helena, Georgia

Caramel-Chocolate Chip Bars

1 (18 ounce) box caramel cake mix
2 eggs
⅔ cup firmly packed light brown sugar
¼ cup (½ stick) butter, softened
1 cup semi-sweet chocolate chips
1 (16 ounce) can caramel frosting

- Preheat oven to 350°.

- Combine cake mix, eggs, ¼ cup water, brown sugar and butter in large bowl. Stir until it blends thoroughly. (Mixture will be thick.) Stir in chocolate chips.

- Spread in sprayed, floured 9 x 13-inch baking pan.

- Bake for about 25 to 30 minutes or until toothpick inserted in center comes out clean. Cool.

- Frost and cut into bars. Yields 15 bars. *Rupert, Idaho*

Chocolate Fudge Brownies

4 (1 ounce) squares unsweetened chocolate
1 cup (2 sticks) butter, softened
2 cups sugar
4 large eggs
1 cup flour
1 teaspoon vanilla
1 cup semi-sweet chocolate chips
⅔ cup chopped pecans

- Preheat oven to 350°.

- Microwave chocolate squares in microwave-safe bowl on MEDIUM for 90 seconds. Stir at 30-second intervals until chocolate melts and is smooth.

- Beat butter and sugar in bowl at medium speed until light and fluffy. Add eggs 1 at a time and beat after each addition. Add melted chocolate and beat well. Add flour and beat on low speed. Stir in vanilla, chocolate chips and pecans.

- Spread batter into sprayed, floured 9 x 13-inch baking pan. Bake for 35 to 40 minutes or until center is set. Cool completely on wire rack and cut into squares. Yields 15 squares. *Dwight, Illinois*

TIP: *To easily remove and cut brownies, line pan with sprayed, floured heavy-duty foil and allow several inches to extend over sides. After baking and cooling, lift block of brownies from the pan using foil. Pull foil sides down and cut into squares.*

Snicker Brownies

1 (18 ounce) box German chocolate cake mix
¾ cup (1½ sticks) butter, melted
½ cup evaporated milk
4 (3 ounce) Snickers® candy bars

- Preheat oven to 350°.

- Combine cake mix, butter and evaporated milk in large bowl. Beat on low speed until mixture blends well.

- Place half batter into sprayed, floured 9 x 13-inch baking pan. Bake for 10 minutes.

- Remove from oven. Cut candy bars in ⅛-inch slices and place evenly over brownies. Drop remaining half of batter by spoonfuls over candy bars and spread as evenly as possible.

- Bake for additional 20 minutes. When cool, cut into bars. Yields 15 bars. *Missouri Valley, Iowa*

Cashew Brownies

1 (19.5 ounce) box fudge brownie mix
¼ cup oil
1 egg, slightly beaten
1 cup milk chocolate chips
1 (16 ounce) can cream cheese frosting
1 cup salted, coarsely chopped cashews

- Preheat oven to 350°.

- Combine brownie mix, ⅓ cup water, oil and egg in large bowl and mix well. Stir in chocolate chips and pour into sprayed, floured 9 x 13-inch baking pan.

- Bake for about 25 minutes or until toothpick inserted in center comes out clean. Cool on wire rack.

- Spread frosting over brownies and sprinkle chopped cashews on top.

- Cut brownies in squares. Yields 15 squares. *Sunset, Louisiana*

Easy Blonde Brownies

This is another one of those recipes that seems too easy to be a recipe – and you already have everything right in the pantry. These brownies are so good and chewy.

1 (16 ounce) box light brown sugar
4 eggs
2 cups biscuit mix
2 cups chopped pecans

• Preheat oven to 350°.

• Beat brown sugar, eggs and biscuit mix in bowl. Stir in pecans and pour into sprayed 9 x 13-inch baking pan.

• Bake for 35 minutes. Cool and cut into squares. Yields 15 squares.
Newcastle, Wyoming

Cheesecake Squares

1 (8 ounce) carton sour cream
1 (8 ounce) package cream cheese, softened
1 (3.4 ounce) package instant French vanilla pudding
⅓ cup milk
1 (8 ounce) carton whipped topping, thawed
1 (20 ounce) can pineapple pie filling

• Beat sour cream and cream cheese in bowl until creamy. Stir in pudding and milk and mix well. Fold in whipped topping and spoon into 9 x 13-inch dish. Refrigerate for about 15 minutes.

• Spoon pineapple pie filling over top using back of large spoon to spread filling evenly.

• Refrigerate for at least 3 hours before cutting into squares. Yields 15 squares. *Denmark, Wisconsin*

Mint-Chocolate Squares

2 cups crushed chocolate sandwich cookies
1¼ cups chopped walnuts
1 cup flaked coconut
1½ cups mint-flavored chocolate chips
1 teaspoon vanilla
1 (14 ounce) can sweetened condensed milk

- Preheat oven to 350°.

- Spread chocolate cookie crumbs evenly in sprayed 9 x 13-inch baking pan. Spread evenly with walnuts, coconut and mint-chocolate chips.

- Combine vanilla and sweetened condensed milk in bowl and drizzle evenly over layers. Bake for 20 to 25 minutes. Cool in pan and cut into squares. Yields 15 squares. *Perry, Utah*

Pecan Squares

2 cups flour
¾ cup powdered sugar
1¼ cups (2½ sticks) plus 2 tablespoons butter, softened, divided
½ cup packed brown sugar
½ cup corn syrup
3 tablespoons whipping cream
3 cups coarsely chopped pecans

- Preheat oven to 350°.

- Sift flour and powdered sugar into bowl. Cut in ¾ cup (1½ sticks) butter with pastry blender until mixture resembles coarse meal.

- Pat mixture on bottom and 1½ inches up sides of sprayed 9 x 13-inch baking pan. Bake for 20 minutes or until edges are light brown. Cool.

- Bring brown sugar, corn syrup, ½ cup (1 stick) plus 2 tablespoons butter and whipping cream to a rolling boil in saucepan over medium-high heat. Stir in pecans and pour over baked crust.

- Bake for 25 to 30 minutes or until golden. Cool completely before slicing into squares. Yields 15 squares. *Hayfield, Vermont*

Holiday Fruit Balls

1½ pounds candied cherries
½ pound candied pineapple
1 (8 ounce) box pitted chopped dates
1 (7 ounce) can flaked coconut
4 cups chopped pecans
1 (14 ounce) can sweetened condensed milk

- Preheat oven to 350°.

- Chop cherries, pineapple and dates in bowl and mix well with spoon.

- Add coconut and pecans, pour sweetened condensed milk over mixture and mix well.

- Put teaspoonfuls of mixture in miniature paper cups and place on cookie sheet.

- Bake for 20 to 25 minutes and store in covered container. Yields 150 to 200 fruit balls. *McLean, Virginia*

TIP: *These will keep in refrigerator for months if you can keep the family from eating them! My friend says it is not Christmas unless she makes these!*

No-Cook Lemon Balls

2 cups graham cracker crumbs, divided
1 (6 ounce) can frozen lemonade concentrate, thawed
½ cup (1 stick) butter, softened
1 (16 ounce) box powdered sugar, sifted

- Combine 1½ cups cookie crumbs, lemonade concentrate, butter and powdered sugar in bowl. Shape into small balls.

- Roll in reserved cookie crumbs and put on wax paper.

- Refrigerate for 3 to 4 hours in sealed container or freeze to serve later. Yields 3 dozen balls. *Lindsay, Oklahoma*

TIP: *It's okay to use almond or pecan shortbread cookie crumbs, too.*

Peanut Butter Balls

¾ cup light corn syrup
2½ cups crunchy peanut butter
2¼ cups graham cracker crumbs
1¼ cups powdered sugar

- Combine corn syrup, peanut butter, cracker crumbs and powdered sugar in bowl and mix until smooth.

- Shape 1-inch balls and place on wax paper lined baking sheet. Refrigerate for about 30 minutes. Yields 3 dozen balls. *Myrtle Point, Oregon*

TIP: If you would like to make this for a kids' party, pour some chocolate ice cream topping in shallow bowl and let the kids dip their peanut butter balls in chocolate. (Of course, get the paper towels ready.)

Snappy Oats

3 cups quick-cooking oats
1 cup chocolate chips
½ cup flaked coconut
½ cup chopped pecans
2 cups sugar
¾ cup (1½ sticks) butter
½ cup evaporated milk

- Combine oats, chocolate chips, coconut and pecans in large bowl.

- Boil sugar, butter and evaporated milk in saucepan for 1 to 2 minutes and stir constantly.

- Pour hot mixture over oat-chocolate mixture in bowl and stir until chocolate chips melt.
  Drop teaspoonfuls of mixture onto wax paper. Cool at room temperature and store in covered container. Yields 3½ dozen. *Burnham, Pennsylvania*

TIP: Use white chocolate chips and ¾ cup sliced candied cherries for a colorful variation.

Pecan Tassies

Crust:

½ cup (1 stick) butter, softened
2 (3 ounce) packages cream cheese, softened
2 cups flour

- Preheat oven to 350°.

- Beat butter and cream cheese in bowl until smooth. Stir in flour until they blend well. Refrigerate for at least 30 to 45 minutes.

- Divide dough into 24 equal pieces, flatten each into 3-inch round and fit into 24 mini muffin cups. Let dough extend slightly above each cup.

Filling:

3 eggs, slightly beaten
¼ cup (½ stick) butter, melted
2 cups packed brown sugar
1 cup chopped pecans

- Combine all filling ingredients in bowl and spoon about 1 tablespoon into each cup. Bake for 20 minutes or until crust is light brown and filling is set. Yields 24. *Landrum, South Carolina*

Pecan Puffs

2 egg whites
¾ cup packed light brown sugar
1 teaspoon vanilla
1 cup chopped pecans

- Preheat oven to 250° (120° C).

- Beat egg whites in bowl until foamy. Gradually add (¼ cup at a time) brown sugar and vanilla. Continue beating until stiff peaks form (about 3 or 4 minutes). Fold in pecans.

- Line cookie sheet with foil. Drop teaspoonfuls of mixture onto foil.

- Bake for 45 minutes. Yields 2 dozen. *Sisseton, South Dakota*

Peanut Butter Crunchies

1 cup sugar
½ cup white corn syrup
2 cups peanut butter
4 cups rice crispy cereal

• Mix sugar and syrup in saucepan and bring to a rolling boil. Remove from stove and stir in peanut butter. Add cereal and mix well.

• Drop teaspoonfuls of mixture onto wax paper. Place in refrigerator for a few minutes to set. Yields 24. *Trenton, Tennessee*

Morning Meringues

¾ cup sugar
2 egg whites, beaten stiff
1 cup nuts
1 cup chocolate chips

• Preheat oven to 350°.

• Add sugar to stiffly beaten egg whites in bowl. Add in nuts and chocolate chips.

• Line cookie sheet with foil. Drop teaspoonfuls of mixture and press down.

• Bake for 10 minutes. Turn oven off. Let cookies sit in oven for 8 to 10 hours. Yields 2 dozen cookies. *Raymond, Washington*

Marshmallow Treats

¼ cup (½ stick) butter
4 cups miniature marshmallows
½ cup chunky peanut butter
5 cups rice crispy cereal

• Melt butter in saucepan and add marshmallows. Stir until they melt and add peanut butter. Remove from heat. Add cereal and stir well.

• Press mixture into 9 x 13-inch pan. Cut in squares when cool. Yields 15 squares. *Jefferson, Texas*

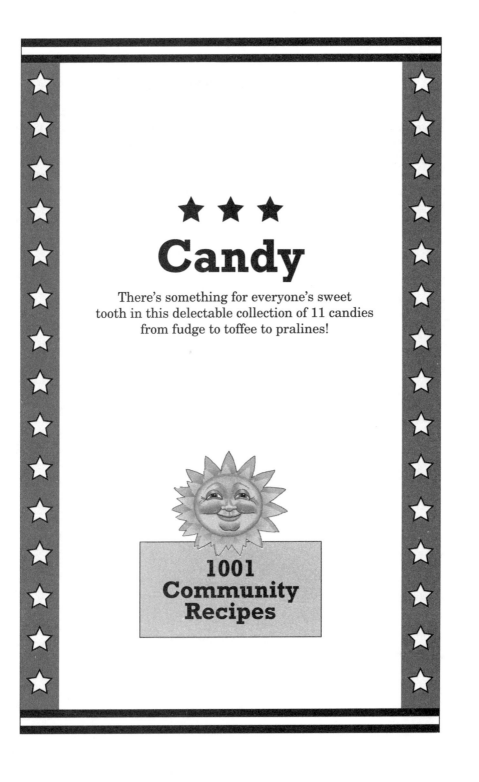

★ ★ ★

Candy

There's something for everyone's sweet
tooth in this delectable collection of 11 candies
from fudge to toffee to pralines!

1001 Community Recipes

Candy Contents

Cracker Candy Bites

2¾ cups round buttery crackers, crushed
¾ cup (1½ sticks) butter
2 cups packed brown sugar
1 (12 ounce) package milk chocolate chips

• Preheat oven to 350°.

• Place crackers in sprayed 9 x 13-inch baking dish.

• Combine butter and brown sugar in saucepan and bring to a boil. Boil for 3 minutes, stirring constantly. Pour over crackers.

• Bake for 5 minutes and turn oven off. Sprinkle chocolate chips over cracker mixture. Return to oven and let stand for about 5 minutes or until chocolate melts.

• Remove from oven and spread chocolate evenly over cracker mixture. Cool and break into pieces. Yields 15 pieces. *Flanders, New York*

Creamy Peanut Butter Fudge

3 cups sugar
¾ cup (1½ sticks) butter
⅔ cup evaporated milk
1 (10 ounce) package peanut butter-flavored chips
1 (7 ounce) jar marshmallow creme
1 teaspoon vanilla

• Combine sugar, butter and evaporated milk in large saucepan. Bring to a boil over medium heat and stir constantly. Cover and cook for 3 minutes without stirring. Uncover and boil for 5 minutes (do not stir).

• Remove from heat, add peanut butter chips and stir until they melt. Stir in marshmallow creme and vanilla.

• Pour into sprayed 9 x 13-inch pan. Place in freezer for 10 minutes. Cut into squares. Yields 15 squares. *Raton, New Mexico*

Dream Candy

2 (8 ounce) cartons whipping cream
3 cups sugar
1 cup light corn syrup
1 cup chopped pecans

- Combine whipping cream, sugar and corn syrup in saucepan. Cook to soft-boil stage.

- Stir and beat until candy cools but is still warm.

- Add pecans and pour into sprayed 9-inch square pan. Yields 15 squares. *Granite Falls, North Carolina*

Microwave Fudge

3 cups semi-sweet chocolate chips
1 (14 ounce) can sweetened condensed milk
¼ cup (½ stick) butter, cut into pieces
1 cup chopped walnuts

- Combine chocolate chips, sweetened condensed milk and butter in 2-quart glass bowl.

- Microwave on MEDIUM for 4 to 5 minutes, stirring at 1½-minute intervals.

- Stir in walnuts and pour into sprayed 8-inch square dish. Refrigerate for 2 hours. Cut into squares. Yields 15 squares. *Lake Orion, Michigan*

Peanut Butter Fudge

1 (12 ounce) jar chunky peanut butter
1 (12 ounce) package milk chocolate chips
1 (14 ounce) can sweetened condensed milk
1 cup chopped pecans

- Combine peanut butter, chocolate chips and sweetened condensed milk in saucepan. Heat on low, stirring constantly, until chocolate melts.

- Add pecans and mix well. Pour into sprayed 9 x 9-inch dish. Cut into squares. Yields 15 squares. *Pine Beach, New Jersey*

Pecan Toffee

This delightful candy is very easy to make.

1 cup (2 sticks) butter
1 cup firmly packed brown sugar
1 cup coarsely chopped pecans
2 (3.5 ounce) milk chocolate bars

- Place butter in saucepan and melt over medium-high heat. Stir in brown sugar and bring to a boil.

- Boil sugar mixture for 12 minutes, stirring constantly. Occasionally wash down sides of pan with wet pastry brush.

- Remove pan from heat and quickly stir in pecans. Pour mixture into sprayed 9 x 13-inch baking pan and use buttered spatula to spread evenly.

- Place chocolate bars on top of toffee; when chocolate melts, spread chocolate evenly over surface. Cool and cut into pieces. Yields 15 pieces. *Dilworth, Minnesota*

Pecan Topped Toffee

1 cup (2 sticks) butter
1¼ cups packed brown sugar
6 (1.5 ounce) milk chocolate bars
⅔ cup finely chopped pecans

- Combine butter and brown sugar in saucepan. Cook on medium-high heat, stirring constantly until mixture reaches 300° on candy thermometer. Pour immediately into sprayed 9-inch baking pan.

- Lay chocolate bars evenly over hot candy. When candy is soft, spread into smooth layer.

- Sprinkle pecans over chocolate and press lightly with back of spoon. Refrigerate for about 1 hour.

- Invert candy onto wax paper and break into small irregular pieces. Yields 1 quart. *Kearney, Missouri*

Red Peanut Patties

3 cups sugar
1 cup light corn syrup
1 pound raw Spanish peanuts
6 drops red food coloring
¼ cup (½ stick) butter

- Combine sugar, 1 cup water and corn syrup in heavy saucepan, bring to a boil and stir constantly. Add peanuts and coloring and cook until hard-ball stage 250° on candy thermometer.

- Remove from heat, add butter and a pinch of salt and beat until mixture thickens.

- Pour just enough to make ½-inch thick patty in sprayed muffin cups. Allow to cool completely. Yields 12 patties. *Lineville, Alabama*

Santa's Favorite Fudge

4½ cups sugar
1 (12 ounce) can evaporated milk
1 cup (2 sticks) butter
3 (6 ounce) packages chocolate chips
1 tablespoon vanilla
1½ cups chopped pecans

- Combine sugar and evaporated milk in saucepan and bring to a rolling boil (boiling that cannot be stirred down). Boil for exactly 6 minutes, stirring constantly.

- Remove from heat, add butter and chocolate chips and stir until they melt. Add vanilla and pecans and stir well.

- Pour into sprayed 9 x 13-inch dish and let stand for 6 hours to overnight before cutting.

- Store in airtight container. Yields 15 to 18 pieces. *Grove City, Delaware*

White Chocolate Fudge

This is a little different slant to fudge – really creamy and really good!

1 (8 ounce) package cream cheese, softened
4 cups powdered sugar
1½ teaspoons vanilla
12 ounces almond bark, melted
¾ cup chopped pecans

- Beat cream cheese in bowl at medium speed until smooth. Gradually add powdered sugar and vanilla and beat well.

- Stir in melted almond bark and pecans. Spread into sprayed 8-inch square pan.

- Refrigerate until firm. Cut into squares. Yields 15 squares.
  Inwood, Florida

Yummy Pralines

½ cup (1 stick) butter
1 (16 ounce) box light brown sugar
1 (8 ounce) carton whipping cream
2½ cups pecan halves

- Combine butter, brown sugar and whipping cream in heavy saucepan.

- Cook until temperature comes to soft-ball stage (235°) for about 20 minutes, stirring constantly. Remove from heat and set aside for 5 minutes.

- Fold in pecans and stir until ingredients are glassy. (This will take several minutes of stirring.)

- Drop mixture with large spoon onto wax paper. Remove after pralines after they have cooled. Yields 16 to 20 pralines. *Oak Grove, Louisiana*

Index

A

Cookbooks Published by Cookbook Resources, LLC
Bringing Family and Friends to the Table

Easy Diabetic Recipes

*The Best of Cooking
with 3 Ingredients*

*The Ultimate Cooking
with 4 Ingredients*

Easy Cooking with 5 Ingredients

Gourmet Cooking with 5 Ingredients

*4-Ingredient Recipes
for 30-Minute Meals*

Essential 3-4-5 Ingredient Recipes

The Best 1001 Short, Easy Recipes

1001 Fast Easy Recipes

1001 Community Recipes

Busy Woman's Quick & Easy Recipes

Busy Woman's Slow Cooker Recipes

Easy Slow Cooker Cookbook

Easy One-Dish Meals

Easy Potluck Recipes

Easy Casseroles

Easy Desserts

Sunday Night Suppers

Easy Church Suppers

365 Easy Meals

365 Easy Soups and Stews

365 Easy Vegetarian Recipes

365 Easy Chicken Recipes

365 Easy Soup Recipes

365 Easy One-Dish Recipes

365 Easy Pasta Recipes

365 Easy Slow Cooker Recipes

365 Easy Casserole Recipes

Quick Fixes with Cake Mixes

*Kitchen Keepsakes/
More Kitchen Keepsakes*

Gifts for the Cookie Jar

All New Gifts for the Cookie Jar

Muffins In A Jar

The Big Bake Sale Cookbook

Classic Tex-Mex and Texas Cooking

Classic Southwest Cooking

Miss Sadie's Southern Cooking

Texas Longhorn Cookbook

Cookbook 25 Years

A Little Taste of Texas

A Little Taste of Texas II

*Trophy Hunters'
Wild Game Cookbook*

Recipe Keeper

*Leaving Home Cookbook
and Survival Guide*

Classic Pennsylvania Dutch Cooking

Healthy Cooking with 4 Ingredients

Simple Old-Fashioned Baking

www.cookbookresources.com

**cookbook
resources** ® LLC

Your Ultimate Source for Easy Cookbooks